Martin F. Tupper

Proverbial Philosophy

in four series

Martin F. Tupper

Proverbial Philosophy
in four series

ISBN/EAN: 9783337237554

Printed in Europe, USA, Canada, Australia, Japan

Cover: Foto ©Thomas Meinert / pixelio.de

More available books at **www.hansebooks.com**

TUPPER'S

PROVERBIAL PHILOSOPHY,

COMPLETE.

COMPLETE EDITION.

PROVERBIAL PHILOSOPHY.

IN FOUR SERIES.

By MARTIN F. TUPPER

D.C.L., F.R.S.

LONDON:

WARD, LOCK, & CO., WARWICK HOUSE,

Dorset Buildings, Salisbury Square, E.C.

NOTICE.

THE reader who may wish to see how this book had beginning, continuation, and as now conclusion, is referred to the second Essay in the last series,—"Of this book's story." Concerning its merits or demerits, perhaps these have been sufficiently discussed both by friends and by foes; the author having now for some five and thirty years run the gauntlet of praise and censure with (he trusts) appropriate equanimity. The book then may by this time be allowed to speak for itself. As for the author, he would willingly have been left unnoticed by way both of portraiture and of memoir, but as the publisher desires the twain, because the public is supposed to require them, there is nothing for it but humble acquiescence: so, a recent likeness is affixed from a photograph; while the following sketch (originally published in the volume, "Representative Men") probably is enough by way of biography.—T.

BIOGRAPHICAL SKETCH,

BY THE EDITOR OF "REPRESENTATIVE MEN."

"MR. MARTIN FARQUHAR TUPPER, widely known as the author of 'Proverbial Philosophy,' was born July 17, 1810, at No. 20 Devonshire Place, in the parish of Marylebone. He is the eldest son of a medical man, highly esteemed in his day, the late Martin Tupper, Esq., F.R.S.; to whom a baronetcy was twice offered,—in the first instance by the Earl of Liverpool, in the second, under the administration of the Duke of Wellington. This honour was proffered to Mr. Tupper, not alone as a mark of distinction to himself, but also to his elder brother Peter, who had, during the Peninsular War, evinced great diplomatic ability, and to whom the title had been first presented, but by whom it had been declined, on account of his having no son.

"The family of Tupper (spelt Töpper in Germany, and Toupard in France and the Low Countries) is of ancient and honourable standing, and was originally German. During the Persecution of the Lutheran Protestants by the Emperor Charles V., about the year 1548, the Töppers were exiled from Hesse Cassel; and Heinrich Töpper, the immediate ancestor of the 'Proverbial Philosopher,' settled, in 1551, in Guernsey, where he purchased an estate, and where his descendants still rank as among the 'first families' of the island. Rodolph Töpper, of German celebrity as an author, is of the same staunch stock.

"Those learned in heraldry tell us that the ancient armorial bearings of this family include the 'Three Escallops Gules,' dating from the Crusades.

"During the reign of William and Mary an ancestor of Martin Farquhar Tupper received from the sovereign a gold medal and chain, with the privilege descending to his heirs of wearing them before the king, and of bearing them on a canton in his coat of arms. John Tupper received this mark of distinction in recognition of an act of important service, rendered to the Crown at the risk of danger to life and limb. Recognizing the helpless condition of the French fleet, John Tupper conveyed intelligence of it to Admiral Russell, which led to the action and victory of La Hogue. This fact is slightly referred to by Macaulay in his 'History of England;' but no mention is made of John Tupper, on his way to the British admiral, passing in an open boat through the midst of the French fleet, as it lay enveloped in dense fog : he is alluded to only as 'a gentleman of Guernsey.'

"A branch of the Tupper family sailed with the 'Pilgrim Fathers' to the United States, where many of its descendants are still to be found. A Major John Tupper, an ancestor of the subject of this memoir, commanded the Marines at Bunker's Hill, after the death of Pitcairn, and gained for the corps their crown and laurel, as recorded at the Horse Guards. It is related that 'by a strange coincidence there was in Washington's army another Major **Tupper** (originally of the same expatriated stock), and it is known to the family that when the cousins met in opposite ranks, some courtesies generously proffered by the "rebel" were indignantly refused by the royalist.'

"The future popular author received his early education at the Charterhouse, during the period when the Rev. Dr. Russell filled the important post of Head-Master. In due course of time he was transferred to Christ Church, Oxford, where he took his degree of B.A. in 1832, of M.A. in 1835, and of D.C.L. in 1847. At Christ Church, as a member of the Aristotle class, he was a fellow-student of many distinguished men,—as the late Duke of Newcastle, the late Marquis of Dalhousie, the late Earl of Elgin, the Right Hon. W. E. Gladstone, and Professors Jelf, Hill, Doyle, and Vaughan.

"Having taken his degree of M.A., as we have already seen, Martin Tupper became a student at Lincoln's Inn, and was called to the Bar in the Michaelmas Term, 1835. He has, however, never practised as a barrister. About the same period commenced Mr. Tupper's literary career. He appears to have contributed to the periodicals of the day, but his first important essay in literature was a small volume entitled 'Sacra Poesis.'

"In 1837 appeared the first series of 'Proverbial Philosophy,' composed in a lawyer's chambers in Old Square, Lincoln's Inn, during part of the year previous. This work, which has spread its author's name far and wide, met at first with but moderate success in England, while in America it was almost a failure. Within thirty years, however, it has passed through forty large editions in England, while nearly a million of copies have been sold in America. The annual sale of some 5000 copies still witnesses to its almost unexampled popularity.

"In 1835 Mr. Tupper was united in marriage with Isabella, only daughter of A. W. Devis, Esq., by whom he has four sons and three daughters.

"In 1845 Mr. Tupper was elected a Fellow of the Royal Society. He has received the gold medal for science and literature from the King of Prussia; he has likewise been honoured by marks of distinction from other potentates: and he is a D.C.L. of Oxford.

"Mr. Tupper resides near Guildford, in the parish of Albury, upon his own property, inherited from his mother, a direct descendant of Colonel Marris, who, in 1648, gallantly held Pomfret Castle for **Charles I.** against General Lambert.

"In 1839 Mr. Tupper published 'A Modern Pyramid to commemorate a Septuagint of Worthies,' being sonnets and essays on seventy famous men and women; in 1841, 'An Author's Mind,' containing skeletons of thirty unpublished books; in 1844, 'The Crock of Gold,' 'The Twins,' and 'Heart,' tales illustrative of social vices, and which passed through numerous editions; in 1847, 'Probabilities, an Aid to Faith,' giving a new view of Christian evidences; 'A Thousand Lines,' 'Hactenus,' 'Geraldine,' 'Lyrics,' 'Ballads for the Times,' 'Things to Come,' 'A Dirge for Wellington,' 'Church Ballads,' 'White Slavery Ballads,' 'American Ballads,' 'Rifle Ballads,' 'King Alfred,' a patriotic play; 'King Alfred's Poems,' translated from the Anglo-Saxon into corresponding English metres. In 1856, 'Paterfamilias's Diary of Everybody's Tour,' 'The Rides and Reveries of Æsop Smith,' and 'Stephan Langton,' a biographical novel, which seeks, with much graphic painting, to delineate Old England in the time of King John. He has also published 'Cithara, a collection of Lyrics;' 'Three Hundred Sonnets,' 'A Prophetic Ode;' and a multitude of fugitive pieces, both verse and prose, which have been scattered through newspapers and magazines. His most recent productions have been 'Raleigh,' a play; 'A Creed, &c;' 'The Antiritualistic Directorium,' a satire; and 'The Third Series of Proverbial Philosophy;' the whole work to be concluded by a fourth series, now understood to be in preparation. There are several translations of the two first series, as French, German, Swedish, &c.

"The writings of Mr. Tupper, bearing the impress of an impulsive enthusiastic nature, are, it is asserted, poured forth with exceeding ease and rapidity, and partake much of the character of improvisation. That Mr. Tupper's sympathy is readily excited by the interests of the day, is not alone evinced in his numerous writings, both in prose and verse, but also by the acts of his life, as for instance the encouragement given by him to Liberian colonization, his bestowal of a gold medal for the encouragement of African literature, his active exertions in the Rifle Corps movement, and in the promotion of international kindliness between England and America.

"A notice of the life and labours of Mr. Tupper would scarcely be complete without some reference to the disfavour with which he has been almost universally treated by the writers of the public press, to a degree indeed which almost amounts to persecution. Whether Mr. Tupper's works appeal invariably to the highest order of intellect, it is unnecessary to inquire; but assuredly some respect is due to a writer who, in an age remarkable for intellectul activity amongst all classes, has appealed so successfully to the public mind, has provided it with innocent and elevating *pabulum*, and has enjoyed so wide-spread—and on that account it may be inferred—deserved popularity, a popularity for which the author may at all events claim to be but little indebted to contemporary criticism."

CONTENTS.

FIRST SERIES.

	PAGE
Prefatory	1
The Words of Wisdom	2
Of Truth in Things False	4
Of Anticipation	7
Of Hidden Uses	9
Of Compensation	13
Of Indirect Influences	17
Of Memory	21
The Dream of Ambition	24
Of Subjection	26
Of Rest	35
Of Humility	37
Of Pride	41
Of Experience	42
Of Estimating Character	44
Of Hatred and Anger	52
Of Good in Things Evil	53
Of Prayer	58
The Lord's Prayer	61
Of Discretion	63
Of Trifles	65
Of Recreation	68
The Train of Religion	71

	PAGE
OF A TRINITY	73
OF THINKING	76
OF SPEAKING	81
OF READING	85
OF WRITING	87
OF WEALTH	89
OF INVENTION	94
OF RIDICULE	96
OF COMMENDATION	98
OF SELF-ACQUAINTANCE	102
OF CRUELTY TO ANIMALS	108
OF FRIENDSHIP	110
OF LOVE	114
OF MARRIAGE	116
OF EDUCATION	120
OF TOLERANCE	129
OF SORROW	132
OF JOY	133

SECOND SERIES.

INTRODUCTORY	136
OF CHEERFULNESS	138
OF YESTERDAY	142
OF TO-DAY	145
OF TO-MORROW	148
OF AUTHORSHIP	150
OF MYSTERY	156
OF GIFTS	163
OF BEAUTY	167
OF FAME	179
OF FLATTERY	186
OF NEGLECT	193
OF CONTENTMENT	200
OF LIFE	204
OF DEATH	209
OF IMMORTALITY	215
OF IDEAS	231
OF NAMES	234
OF THINGS	238

Of Faith	240
Of Honesty	247
Of Society	252
Of Solitude	259
The End	262

THIRD SERIES.

Preamble	267
Of Innocence and Guilt	270
Of this World's Age	274
Of Circumstance	277
Of the Starry Heavens	280
Of Probabilities	286
Of Scripture and Science	289
Of Silence	292
Of Spiritual Presences	295
Of Time	301
Of Little Providences	304
Of Success	307
Of the Smaller Morals	309
Of Rhyme and Rhythm	312
Of Zoilism	314
Of Creeds	320
Of the Future of Animals	323
Of Happiness Together or Alone	331
A National Hymn for Harvest	335
A National Dirge in Trouble	337
A National Psalm of Victory	339
The Seven Sayings	341
Final	345

FOURTH AND FINAL SERIES.

Opening	347
Of this Book's Story	349
Of the Bible	355
Of Home	361
Of Social Pride	367

	PAGE
Of Change and Travel	372
Of Livelihoods	376
Of Fourfold Differences	381
Of Curious Questions	387
Of Man's Date upon Earth	395
Of Sleep	401
Of Delay	403
Of Great and Small	405
Of Selfishness	408
Of Slander	411
Of Real and Ideal	415
Of Habit	418
Of Economy	419
Of Industry and Idleness	420
Of Representation	423
Of Life's Work	425
Of Life's Lessons	430
Of Life's End	438
The Consummation	441

PROVERBIAL PHILOSOPHY.

FIRST SERIES.

PREFATORY.

THOUGHTS, that have tarried in my mind, and peopled its inner chambers,
The sober children of reason, or desultory train of fancy;
Clear-running wine of conviction, with the scum and the lees of speculation;
Corn from the sheaves of science, with stubble from mine own garner:
Searchings after Truth, that have tracked her secret lodes,
And come up again to the surface-world, with a knowledge grounded deeper;
Arguments of high scope, that have soared to the keystone of heaven,
And thence have swooped to their certain mark, as the falcon to its quarry;
The fruits I have gathered of prudence, the ripened harvest of my musings,
These commend I unto thee, O docile scholar of Wisdom,
These I give to thy gentle heart, thou lover of the right.

What, though a guilty man renew that hallowed theme,
And strike with feebler hand the harp of Sirach's son?
What, though a youthful tongue take up that ancient parable,
And utter faintly forth dark sayings as of old?

Sweet is the virgin honey, though the wild bee have stored it in a
  reed,
And bright the jewelled band, that circleth an Ethiop's arm;
Pure are the grains of gold in the turbid stream of Ganges,
And fair the living flowers, that spring from the dull cold sod.
Wherefore, thou gentle student, bend thine ear to my speech,
For I also am as thou art; our hearts can commune together:
To meanest matters will I stoop, for mean is the lot of mortal;
I will rise to noblest themes, for the soul hath an heritage of glory:
The passions of puny man; the majestic characters of God;
The feverish shadows of time, and the mighty substance of
  eternity.

Commend thy mind unto candour, and grudge not as though thou
  hadst a teacher,
Nor scorn angelic Truth for the sake of her evil herald;
Heed not him, but hear his words, and care not whence they
  come;
The viewless winds might whisper them, the billows roar them
  forth,
The mean unconscious sedge sigh them in the ear of evening,
Or the mind of pride conceive, and the mouth of folly speak them.
Lo now, I stand not forth laying hold on spear and buckler,
I come a man of peace, to comfort, not to combat;
With soft persuasive speech to charm thy patient ear,
Giving the hand of fellowship, acknowledging the heart of sym-
  pathy:
Let us walk together as friends in the shaded paths of meditation,
Nor Judgment set his seal until he hath poised his balance;
That the chastenings of mild reproof may meet unwitting error,
And Charity not be a stranger at the board that is spread for
  brothers.

THE WORDS OF WISDOM.

FEW and precious are the words which the lips of Wisdom utter:
To what shall their rarity be likened? What price shall count
  their worth?
Perfect and much to be desired, and giving joy with riches,
No lovely thing on earth can picture all their beauty.

They be chance pearls, flung among the rocks by the sullen waters
 of Oblivion,
Which Diligence loveth to gather, and hang around the neck of
 Memory;
They be white-winged seeds of happiness, wafted from the islands
 of the blessed,
Which Thought carefully tendeth, in the kindly garden of the
 heart;
They be sproutings of an harvest for eternity, bursting through the
 tilth of time,
Green promise of the golden wheat, that yieldeth angels' food;
They be drops of the crystal dew, which the wings of seraphs
 scatter,
When on some brighter sabbath, their plumes quiver most with
 delight:
Such, and so precious, are the words which the lips of Wisdom
 utter.

Yet more, for the half is not said, of their might, and dignity, and
 value;
For life-giving be they and glorious, redolent of sanctity and
 heaven:
As the fumes of hallowed incense, that veil the throne of the Most
 High;
As the beaded bubbles that sparkle on the rim of the cup of im-
 mortality;
As wreaths of the rainbow spray, from the pure cataracts of truth:
Such, and so precious, are the words which the lips of Wisdom
 utter.

Yet once again, loving student, suffer the praises of thy teacher:
For verily the sun of the mind, and the life of the heart is
 Wisdom:
She is pure and full of light, crowning grey hairs with lustre,
And kindling the eye of youth with a fire not its own:
And her words, whereunto canst thou liken them? for earth can-
 not show their peers:
They be grains of the diamond sand, the radiant floor of heaven,
Rising in sunny dust behind the chariot of God;
They be flashes of the day-spring from on high, shed from the
 windows of the skies;

They be streams of living waters, fresh from the fountain of Intelligence:
Such, and so precious, are the words which the lips of Wisdom utter.

For these shall guide thee well, and guard thee on thy way;
And, wanting all beside, with these shalt thou be rich:
Though all around be woe, these shall make thee happy;
Though all within be pain, these shall bring thee health;
Thy good shall grow into ripeness, thine evil wither and decay,
And Wisdom's words shall sweetly charm thy doubtful into virtues:
Meanness shall then be frugal care; where shame was, thou art modest;
Cowardice riseth into caution, rashness is sobered into courage;
The wrathful spirit, rendering a reason, standeth justified in anger;
The idle hand hath fair excuse, propping the thoughtful forehead.
Life shall have no labyrinth but thy steps can track it,
For thou hast a silken clue, to lead thee through the darkness:
The rampant Minotaur of ignorance shall perish at thy coming,
And thine enfranchised fellows hail thy white victorious sails.
Wherefore, friend and scholar, hear the words of Wisdom;
Whether she speaketh to thy soul in the full chords of revelation;
In the teaching earth, or air, or sea; in the still melodies of thought;
Or, haply, in the humbler strains that would detain thee here.

OF TRUTH IN THINGS FALSE.

ERROR is a hardy plant; it flourisheth in every soil;
In the heart of the wise and good, alike with the wicked and foolish.
For there is no error so crooked, but it hath in it some lines of truth:
Nor is any poison so deadly, that it serveth not some wholesome use:
And the just man, enamoured of the right, is blinded by the speciousness of wrong;
And the prudent, perceiving an advantage, is content to overlook the harm.

On all things created remaineth the half-effaced signature of God,
Somewhat of fair and good, though blotted by the finger of corruption:
And if error cometh in like a flood, it mixeth with streams of truth;
And the Adversary loveth to have it so, for thereby many are decoyed.
Providence is dark in its permissions; yet one day, when all is known,
The universe of reason shall acknowledge how just and good were they;
For the wise man leaneth on his wisdom, and the righteous trusteth to his righteousness,
And those, who thirst for independence, are suffered to drink of disappointment.
Wherefore?—to prove and humble them: and to teach the idolators of Truth,
That it is but the ladder unto Him, on whom only they should trust.

There is truth in the wildest scheme that imaginative heat hath engendered,
And a man may gather somewhat from the crudest theories of fancy:
The alchymist laboureth in folly, but catcheth chance gleams of wisdom,
And findeth out many inventions, though his crucible breed not gold;
The sinner, toying with witchcraft, thinketh to delude his fellows,
But there be very spirits of evil, and what if they come at his bidding?
He is a bold bad man who dareth to tamper with the dead;
For their whereabout lieth in a mystery—that vestibule leading to Eternity,
The waiting-room for unclad ghosts, before the presence-chamber of their King.
Mind may act upon mind, though bodies be far divided;
For the life is in the blood, but souls communicate unseen:
And the heat of an excited intellect, radiating to its fellows,
Doth kindle dry leaves afar off, while the green wood around it is unwarmed.

The dog may have a spirit, as well as his brutal master;
A spirit to live in happiness: for why should he be robbed of his
 existence?
Hath he not a conscience of evil, a glimmer of moral sense,
Love and hatred, courage and fear, and visible shame and pride?
There may be a future rest for the patient victims of the cruel;
And a season allotted for their bliss, to compensate for unjust
 suffering.
Spurn not at seeming error, but dig below its surface for the truth;
And beware of seeming truths, that grow on the roots of error;
For comely are the apples that spring from the Dead Sea's cursed
 shore,
But within are they dust and ashes, and the hand that plucked
 them shall rue it.

A frequent similar effect argueth a constant cause:
Yet who hath counted the links that bind an omen to its issue?
Who hath expounded the law that rendereth calamities gregarious,
Pressing down with yet more woes the heavy-laden mourner?
Who knoweth wherefore a monsoon should swell the sails of the
 prosperous,
Blithely speeding on their course the children of good luck?
Who hath companied a vision from the horn or ivory gate?
Or met another's mind in his, and explained its presence?
There is a secret somewhat in antipathies; and love is more than
 fancy;
Yea, and a palpable notice warneth of an instant danger;
For the soul hath its feelers, cobwebs floating on the wind,
That catch events in their approach with sure and apt presenti-
 ment,
So that some halo of attraction heraldeth a coming friend,
Investing in his likeness the stranger that passed on before;
And while the word is in thy mouth, behold thy word fulfilled,
And he of whom we spake can answer for himself.
O man, little hast thou learnt of truth in things most true,
How therefore shall thy blindness wot of truth in things most
 false?
Thou hast not yet perceived the causes of life or motion,
How then canst thou define the subtle sympathies of mind?
For the spirit, sharpest and strongest when disease hath rent the
 body,

Hath welcomed kindred spirits in nightly visitations,
Or learnt from restless ghosts dark secrets of the living,
And helped slow justice to her prey by the dreadful teaching of a dream.

Verily, there is nothing so true, that the damps of error have not warped it;
Verily, there is nothing so false, that a sparkle of truth is not in it.
For the enemy, the father of lies, the giant Upas of creation,
Whose deadly shade hath blasted this once green garden of the Lord,
Can but pervert the good, but may not create the evil!
He destroyeth, but cannot build; for he is not antagonist deity:
Mighty is his stolen power, yet is he a creature and a subject;
Not a maker of abstract wrong, but a spoiler of concrete right:
The fiend hath not a royal crown; he is but a prowling robber,
Suffered, for some mysterious end, to haunt the King's highway;
And the keen sword he beareth, once was a simple ploughshare;
Yea, and his panoply of error is but a distortion of the truth:
The sickle that once reaped righteousness, beaten from its useful curve,
With axe, and spike, and bar, headeth the marauder's halbert.
Seek not further, O man, to solve the dark riddle of sin;
Suffice it, that thine own bad heart is to thee thine origin of evil.

OF ANTICIPATION.

THOU hast seen many sorrows, travel-stained pilgrim of the world,
But that which hath vexed thee most hath been the looking for evil;
And though calamities have crossed thee, and misery been heaped on thy head,
Yet ills, that never happened, have chiefly made thee wretched.
The sting of pain and the edge of pleasure are blunted by long expectation,
For the gall and the balm alike are diluted in the waters of patience:
And often thou sippest sweetness, ere the cup is dashed from thy lip;
Or drainest the gall of fear, while evil is passing by thy dwelling.

OF ANTICIPATION.

A man too careful of danger liveth in continual torment,
But a cheerful expecter of the best hath a fountain of joy within him:
Yea, though the breath of disappointment should chill the sanguine heart,
Speedily gloweth it again, warmed by the live embers of hope;
Though the black and heavy surge close above the head for a moment,
Yet the happy buoyancy of Confidence riseth superior to Despair.
Verily, evils may be courted, may be wooed and won by distrust:
For the wise Physician of our weal loveth not an unbelieving spirit;
And to those giveth He good, who rely on His hand for good;
And those leaveth He to evil, who fear, but trust Him not.
Ask for good, and hope it; for the ocean of good is fathomless;
Ask for good, and have it; for thy Friend would see thee happy;
But to the timid heart, to the child of unbelief and dread,
That leaneth on his own weak staff, and trusteth the sight of his eyes,
The evil he feared shall come, for the soil is ready for the seed,
And suspicion hath coldly put aside the hand that was ready to help him.
Therefore look up, sad spirit; be strong, thou coward heart,
Or fear will make thee wretched, though evil follow not behind:
Cease to anticipate misfortune; there are still many chances of escape;
But if it come, be courageous: face it, and conquer thy calamity.
There is not an enemy so stout, as to storm and take the fortress of the mind,
Unless its infirmity turn traitor, and Fear unbar the gates.
The valiant standeth as a rock, and the billows break upon him;
The timorous is a skiff unmoored, tost and mocked at by a ripple:
The valiant holdeth fast to good, till evil wrench it from him;
The timorous casteth it aside, to meet the worst half way:
Yet oftentimes is evil but a braggart, that provoketh and will not fight;
Or the feint of a subtle fencer, who measureth his thrust elsewhere:
Or perchance a blessing in a masque, sent to try thy trust,
The precious smiting of a friend, whose frowns are all in love:

Often the storm threateneth, but is driven to other climes,
And the weak hath quailed in fear, while the firm hath been glad
    in his confidence.

OF HIDDEN USES.

The sea-wort floating on the waves, or rolled up high along the
    shore,
Ye counted useless and vile, heaping on it names of contempt :
Yet hath it gloriously triumphed, and man been humbled in his
    ignorance,
For health is in the freshness of its savour, and it cumbereth the
    beach with wealth ;
Comforting the tossings of pain with its violet tinctured essence,
And by its humbler ashes enriching many proud.
Be this, then, a lesson to thy soul, that thou reckon nothing
    worthless,
Because thou heedest not its use, nor knowest the virtues thereof.
And herein, as thou walkest by the sea, shall weeds be a type and
    an earnest
Of the stored and uncounted riches lying hid in all creatures of
    God :
There be flowers making glad the desert, and roots fattening the
    soil,
And jewels in the secret deep, scattered among groves of coral,
And comforts to crown all wishes, and aids unto every need,
Influences yet unthought, and virtues, and many inventions,
And uses above and around, which man hath not yet regarded.
Not long to charm away disease hath the crocus yielded up its
    bulb,
Nor the willow lent its bark, nor the nightshade its vanquished
    poison ;
Not long hath the twisted leaf, the fragrant gift of China,
Nor that nutritious root, the boon of far Peru,
Nor the many-coloured dahlia, nor the gorgeous flaunting cactus,
Nor the multitude of fruits and flowers ministered to life and
    luxury :
Even so, there be virtues yet unknown in the wasted foliage of the
    elm,
In the sun-dried harebell of the downs, and the hyacinth drinking
    in the meadow,

In the sycamore's winged fruit, and the facet-cut cones of the
    cedar;
And the pansy and bright **geranium live** not alone for beauty,
Nor the **waxen** flower of **the arbute, though** it dieth in a day,
Nor the **sculptured** crest of the fir, **unseen but by** the **stars**;
And **the** meanest weed of the garden serveth unto many **uses,**
The **salt** tamarisk, and juicy flag, the freckled orchis, and the
    daisy.
The world may laugh at famine, when forest-trees yield bread,
When acorns give out fragrant drink, and the sap of the linden is
    as fatness:
For every green herb, from the lotus to the darnel,
Is rich with delicate aids to help incurious man.

Still, **Mind** is up and stirring, and **pryeth** in the corners of con-
    trivance,
Often from the dark recesses picking out bright seeds of truth:
Knowledge hath clipped the lightning's wings, and mewed it up
    for a purpose,
Training **to some** domestic task the **fiery bird of heaven**;
Tamed is the spirit of the storm, to slave in all peaceful arts,
To **walk** with **husbandry and science**; to stand in the **vanguard**
    against death:
And the **chemist balanceth his** elements with **more than** magic
    skill,
Commanding stones that they be bread, and **draining sweetness**
    out of wormwood.
Yet man, heedless of a God, counteth up vain reckonings,
Fearing to be jostled and starved out, by the too prolific increase
    of his kind;
And **asketh, in** unbelieving dread, for how few years to come
Will the black cellars of the world yield unto him fuel for his
    winter.
Might not the wide waste sea be pent within narrower bounds?
Might not **the arm of** diligence make the tangled wilderness a
    garden?
And for aught **thou canst tell, there may be** a thousand methods
Of comforting thy limbs in warmth, though thou kindle not a
    spark.
Fear not, son of man, for thyself nor thy seed :—with a multitude
    is plenty;

God's blessing giveth increase, and with it larger than enough.

Search out the wisdom of nature, there is depth in all her doings;
She seemeth prodigal of power, yet her rules are the maxims of frugality:
The plant refresheth the air, and the earth filtereth the water,
And dews are sucked into the cloud, dropping fatness on the world:
She hath, on a mighty scale, a general use for all things;
Yet hath she specially for each its microscopic purpose:
There is use in the prisoned air, that swelleth the pods of the laburnum;
Design in the venomed thorns, that sentinel the leaves of the nettle;
A final cause for the aromatic gum, that congealeth the moss around a rose:
A reason for each blade of grass, that reareth its small spire.
How knoweth discontented man what a train of ills might follow,
If the lowest menial of nature knew not her secret office,
If the thistle never sprang up to mock the loose husbandry of indolence,
Or the pestilence never swept away an unknown curse from among men?
Would ye crush the buzzing myriads that float on the breath of evening?
Would ye trample the creatures of God that people the rotting fruit?
Would ye suffer no mildew forest to stain the unhealthy wall,
Nor a noisome savour to exhale from the pool that breedeth disease?
Pain is useful unto man, for it teacheth him to guard his life,
And the fetid vapours of the fen warn him to fly from danger:
And the meditative mind, looking on, winneth good food for its hunger,
Seeing the wholesome root bring forth a poisonous berry;
For otherwhile falleth it out that truth, driven to extremities,
Yieldeth bitter folly as the spoilt fruit of wisdom.
O, blinded is thine eye, if it see not just aptitude in all things:
O, frozen is thy heart, if it glow not with gratitude for all things:

In the perfect circle of creation not an atom could be spared,
From earth's magnetic zone to the bindweed round a hawthorn.

The sage, and the beetle at his feet, hath each a ministration to perform:
The briar and the palm have the wages of life, rendering secret service.
Neither is it thus alone with the definite existences of matter;
But motion and sound, circumstance and quality, yea, all things have their office.
The zephyr playing with an aspen-leaf,—the earthquake that rendeth a continent;
The moon-beam silvering a ruined arch,—the desert-wave dashing up a pyramid;
The thunder of jarring icebergs,—the stops of a shepherd's pipe;
The howl of the tiger in the glen,—and the wood-dove calling to her mate;
The vulture's cruel rage,—the grace of the stately swan;
The fierceness looking from the lynx's eye, and the dull stupor of the sloth:
To these, and to all, is there added each its USE, though man considereth it lightly:
For Power hath ordained nothing which Economy saw not needful.

All things being are in concord with the ubiquity of God,
Neither is there one thing overmuch, nor freed from honourable servitude.
Were there not a need-be of wisdom, nothing would be as it is,
For essence without necessity argueth a moral weakness.
We look through a glass darkly, we catch but glimpses of truth;
But, doubtless, the sailing of a cloud hath Providence to its pilot,
Doubtless, the root of an oak is gnarled for a special purpose,
The foreknown station of a rush is as fixed as the station of a king,
And chaff from the hand of the winnower, steered as the stars in their courses.
Man liveth only in himself, but the Lord liveth in all things;
And his pervading unity quickeneth the whole creation.
Man doeth one thing at once, nor can he think two thoughts together;

But God compasseth all things, mantling the globe like air :
And we render homage to his wisdom, seeing use in all his creatures,
For, perchance, the universe would die, were not all things as they are.

OF COMPENSATION.

EQUAL is the government of heaven in allotting pleasures among men,
And just the everlasting law, that hath wedded happiness to virtue :
For verily on all things else broodeth disappointment with care,
That childish man may be taught the shallowness of earthly enjoyment.
Wherefore, ye that have enough, envy ye the rich man his abundance?
Wherefore, daughters of affluence, covet ye the cottager's content?
Take the good with the evil, for ye all are pensioners of God,
And none may choose or refuse the cup His wisdom mixeth
The poor man rejoiceth at his toil, and his daily meat is sweet to him :
Content with present good, he looketh not for evil to the future :
The rich man languisheth with sloth, and findeth pleasure in nothing,
He locketh up care with his gold, and feareth the fickleness of fortune.
Can a cup contain within itself the measure of a bucket?
Or the straitened appetites of man drink more than their fill of luxury?
There is a limit to enjoyment, though the sources of wealth be boundless :
And the choicest pleasures of life lie within the ring of moderation.

Also, though penury and pain be real and bitter evils,
I would reason with the poor afflicted, for he is not so wretched as he seemeth.
What right hath an offender to complain, though others escape punishment,
If the stripes of earned misfortune overtake him in his sin?

Wherefore not endure with resignation the evils thou canst not avert?

For the coward pain will flee, if thou meet him as a man:

Consider, whatever be thy fate, that it might and ought to have been worse,

And that it lieth in thy hand to gather even blessing from afflictions:

Bethink thee, wherefore were they sent? and hath not use blunted their keenness?

Need hope, and patience, and courage, be strangers to the meanest hovel?

Thou art in an evil case, it were cruel to deny to thee compassion,

But there is not unmitigated ill in the sharpest of this world's sorrows:

I touch not the sore of thy guilt; but of human griefs I counsel thee,

Cast off the weakness of regret, and gird thee to redeem thy loss:

Thou hast gained, in the furnace of affliction, self knowledge, patience, and humility,

And these be as precious ore, that waiteth the skill of the coiner:

Despise not the blessings of adversity, nor the gain thou hast earned so hardly,

And now thou hast drained the bitter, take heed that thou lose not the sweet.

Power is seldom innocent, and envy is the yoke-fellow of eminence;

And the rust of the miser's riches wasteth his soul as a canker.

The poor man counteth not the cost at which such wealth hath been purchased;

He would be on the mountain's top, without the toil and travail of the climbing.

But equity demandeth recompense: for high-place, calumny and care;

For state, comfortless splendour eating out the heart of home;

For warrior fame, dangers and death; for a name among the learned, a spirit overstrained;

For honour of all kinds, the goad of ambition; on every acquirement, the tax of anxiety.

He that would change with another, must take the cup as it is mixed:

Poverty, with largeness of heart; or a full purse, with a sordid spirit;
Wisdom, in an ailing body; or a common mind, with health·
Godliness, with man's scorn; or the welcome of the mighty, with guilt:
Beauty, with a fickle heart; or plainness of face, with affection.
For so hath Providence determined, that a man shall not easily discover
Unmingled good or evil, to quicken his envy or abhorrence.
A bold man or a fool must he be, who would change his lot with another;
It were a fearful bargain, and mercy hath lovingly refused it:
For we know the worst of ourselves, but the secrets of another we see not,
And better is certain bad, than the doubt and dread of worse.

Just, and strong, and opportune is the moral rule of God;
Ripe in its times, firm in its judgments, equal in the measure of its gifts:
Yet men, scanning the surface, count the wicked happy,
Nor heed the compensating peace, which gladdeneth the good in his afflictions.
They see not the frightful dreams that crowd a bad man's pillow,
Like wreathed adders crawling round his midnight conscience;
They hear not the terrible suggestions, that knock at the portal of his will,
Provoking to wipe away from life the one weak witness of the deed;
They know not the torturing suspicions that sting his panting breast,
When the clear eye of penetration quietly readeth off the truth.
Likewise of the good what know they? the memories bringing pleasure,
Shrined in the heart of the benevolent, and glistening from his eye;
The calm self-justifying reason that establisheth the upright in his purpose;
The warm and gushing bliss that floodeth all the thoughts of the religious.
Many a beggar at the cross way, or grey-haired shepherd on the plain,
Hath more of the end of all wealth, than hundreds who multiply the means.

Moreover, a moral compensation reacheth to the secrecy of
 thought;
For if thou wilt think evil of thy neighbour, soon shalt thou have
 him for thy foe:
And yet he may know nothing of the cause that maketh thee dis-
 tasteful to his soul,—
The cause of unkind suspicion, for which thou hast thy punish-
 ment;
And if thou think of him in charity, wishing or praying for his
 weal,
He shall not guess the secret charm that lureth his soul to love
 thee.
For just is retributive ubiquity: Samson did sin with Dalilah,
And his eyes and captive strength were forfeit to the Philistine.
Jacob robbed his brother, and sorrow was his portion to the
 grave:
David must fly before his foes, yea, though his guilt is covered:
And He, who, seeming old in youth, was marred for others' sin,
For every special crime must bear its special penalty:
By luxury, or rashness, or vice, the member that hath erred
 suffereth,—
And therefore the Sacrifice for all was pained at every pore.

Alike to the slave and his oppressor cometh night with sweet
 refreshment,
And half of the life of the most wretched is gladdened by the
 soothings of sleep:
Pain addeth zest unto pleasure, and teacheth the luxury of health;
There is a joy in sorrow, which none but a mourner can know:
Madness hath imaginary bliss, and most men have no more;
Age hath its quiet calm, and youth enjoyeth not for haste:
Daily, in the midst of its beatitude, the righteous soul is vexed;
And even the misery of guilt doth attain to the bliss of pardon.
Who, in the face of the born-blind, ever looked on other than con-
 tent?
And the deaf ear listeneth within to the silent music of the heart.
There is evil poured upon the earth from the overflowings of cor-
 ruption,—
Sickness, and poverty, and pain, and guilt, and madness, and
 sorrow;
But, as the water from a fountain riseth and sinketh to its level,

Ceaselessly toileth justice to equalize the lots of men:
For, habit and hope and ignorance, and the being but one of a multitude,
And strength of reason in the sage, and dulness of feeling in the fool,
And the light elasticity of courage, and the calm resignation of meekness,
And the stout endurance of decision, and the weak carelessness of apathy,
And helps invisible but real, and ministerings not unfelt,
Angelic aid with worldly discomfiture, bodily loss with the soul's gain,
Secret griefs, and silent joys, thorns in the flesh, and cordials for the spirit,
(—Short of the insuperable barrier dividing innocence from guilt,—)
Go far to level all things, by the gracious rule of Compensation.

OF INDIRECT INFLUENCES.

Face thy foe in the field, and perchance thou wilt meet thy master,
For the sword is chained to his wrist, and his armour buckled for the battle;
But find him when he looketh not for thee, aim between the joints of his harness,
And the crest of his pride will be humbled, his cruelty will bite the dust.
Beard not a lion in his den, but fashion the secret pitfall,
So shalt thou conquer the strong, thyself triumphing in weakness.
The hurricane rageth fiercely, and the promontory standeth in its might,
Breasting the artillery of heaven, as darts glance from the crocodile:
But the small continual creeping of the silent footsteps of the sea
Mineth the wall of adamant, and stealthily compasseth its ruin.
The weakness of accident is strong, where the strength of design is weak:
And a casual analogy convinceth, when a mind beareth not argument.

B

Will not a man listen? be silent; and prove thy maxim by
    example:
Never fear, thou losest not thy hold, though thy mouth doth not
    render a reason.
Contend not in wisdom with a fool, for thy sense maketh much of
    his conceit;
And some errors never would have thriven, had it not been for
    learned refutation:
Yea, much evil hath been caused by an honest wrestler for truth,
And much of unconscious good, by the man that hated wisdom:
For the intellect judgeth closely, and if thou overstep thy argu-
    ment,
Or seem not consistent with thyself, or fail in thy direct purpose,
The mind that went along with thee, shall stop and return without
    thee,
And thou shalt have raised a foe, where thou mightest have
    won a friend.

Hints, shrewdly strown, mightily disturb the spirit,
Where a bare-faced accusation would be too ridiculous for ca-
    lumny:
The sly suggestion toucheth nerves, and nerves contract the fronds,
And the sensitive mimosa of affection trembleth to its root;
And friendships, the growth of half a century, those oaks that
    laugh at storms,
Have been cankered in a night by a worm, even as the prophet's
    gourd.
Hast thou loved and not known jealousy? for a sidelong look
Can please or pain thy heart more than the multitude of proofs:
Hast thou hated, and not learned that thy silent scorn
Doth deeper aggravate thy foe than loud-cursing malice?—
A wise man prevaileth in power, for he screeneth his battering
    engine,
But a fool tilteth headlong, and his adversary is aware.

Behold those broken arches, that oriel all unglazed,
That crippled line of columns bleaching in the sun,
The delicate shaft stricken midway, and the flying buttress
Idly stretching forth to hold up tufted ivy:
Thinkest thou the thousand eyes that shine with rapture on a ruin,
Would have looked with half their wonder on the perfect pile?

And wherefore not—but that light hints, suggesting unseen
    beauties,
Fill the complacent gazer with self-grown conceits?
And so, the rapid sketch winneth more praise to the painter,
Than the consummate work elaborated on his easel:
And so, the Helvetic lion caverned in the living rock
Hath more of majesty and force, than if upon a marble pedestal.

Tell me, daughter of taste, what hath charmed thine ear in
    music?
Is it the laboured theme, the curious fugue or cento,—
Nor rather the sparkles of intelligence flashing from some strange
    note,
Or the soft melody of sounds far sweeter for simplicity?
Tell me, thou son of science, what hath filled thy mind in reading?
Is it the volume of detail where all is orderly set down
And they that read may run, nor need to stop and think;
The book carefully accurate, that counteth thee no better than a
    fool,
Gorging the passive mind with annotated **notes**;—
Nor rather **the** half-suggested thoughts, the riddles thou mayst
    solve,
The fair ideas, coyly peeping like young loves out of roses,
The quaint arabesque conceptions, half cherub and half flower,
The light analogy, or deep allusion, trusted to thy learning,
The confidence implied in thy skill to unravel meaning mysteries?
For ideas are ofttimes shy of the close furniture of words,
And thought, wherein only is power, may be best conveyed by a
    suggestion:
The flash that lighteth up a valley, amid the dark midnight of a
    storm,
Coineth the mind with **that** scene sharper than **fifty summers.**

A worldly man boasteth in his pride, that there is no power but of
    money;
And he judgeth the characters of men by the differing measures of
    their means:
He stealeth all goodly names, as worth, and value, and substance,
Which be the ancient heritage of Virtue, but such an one ascribeth
    unto Wealth:
He spurneth the needy sage, whose wisdom hath enriched nations,

And the sons of poverty and learning, without whom earth were a desert :

Music, the soother of cares, the tuner of the dank discordant heart-strings,

It is nought unto such an one but sounds, whereby some earn their living :

The poem, and the picture, and the statue, to him seem idle baubles,

Which wealth condescendeth to favour, to gain him the name of patron.

But little wotteth he the might of the means his folly despiseth ;

He considereth not that these be the wires which move the puppets of the world.

A sentence hath formed a character, and a character subdued a kingdom ;

A picture hath ruined souls, or raised them to commerce with the skies :

The pen hath shaken nations, and stablished the world in peace ;

And the whole full horn of plenty been filled from the vial of science.

He regardeth man as sensual, the monarch of created matter,

And careth not aught for mind, that linketh him with spirits unseen ;

He feedeth his carcase and is glad, though his soul be faint and famished,

And the dull brute power of the body bindeth him a captive to himself.

Man liveth from hour to hour, and knoweth not what may happen ;

Influences circle him on all sides, and yet must he answer for his actions :

For the being that is master of himself, bendeth events to his will,

But a slave to selfish passion is the wavering creature of circumstance.

To this man temptation is a poison, to that man it addeth vigour ;

And each may render to himself influences good or evil.

As thou directest the power, harm or advantage will follow,

And the torrent that swept the valley, may be led to turn a mill ;

The wild electric flash, that could have kindled comets,

May by the ductile wire give ease to an ailing child.

For outward matter or event fashion not the character within,
But each man, yielding or resisting, fashioneth his mind for himself.

Some have said, What is in a name?—most potent plastic influence;
A name is a word of character, and repetition stablisheth the fact:
A word of rebuke, or of honour, tending to obscurity or fame;
And greatest is the power of a mean, when its power is least suspected.
A low name is a thorn in the side, that hindereth the footman in his running;
But a name of ancestral renown shall often put the racer to his speed.
Few men have grown unto greatness whose names are allied to ridicule,
And many would never have been profligate, but for the splendour of a name.
A wise man scorneth nothing, be it never so small or homely,
For he knoweth not the secret laws that may bind it to great effects.
The world in its boyhood was credulous, and dreaded the vengeance of the stars,
The world in its dotage is not wiser, fearing not the influence of small things:
Planets govern not the soul, nor guide the destinies of man,
But trifles, lighter than straws, are levers in the building up of character.
A man hath the tiller in his hand, and may steer against the current,
Or may glide down idly with the stream, till his vessel founder in the whirlpool.

OF MEMORY.

Where art thou, storehouse of the mind, garner of facts and fancies,—
In what strange firmament are laid the beams of thine airy chambers?
Or art thou that small cavern, the centre of the rolling brain,

Where still one sandy morsel testifieth man's original?
Or hast thou some grand globe, some common hall of intellect,
Some spacious market-place for thought, **where all do bring their wares,**
And gladly rescued from the littleness, the narrow closet of a self,
The privileged **soul hath large access, coming** in the livery of learning?
Live we as isolated worlds, perfect in substance and spirit,
Each a sphere, with a special mind, prisoned in its shell of **matter?**
Or **rather, as** converging radiations, parts of one majestic whole,
Beams of the Sun, streams from the River, branches of the mighty Tree,
Some bearing fruit, some bearing leaves, and some diseased and barren,—
Some for the feast, some for the floor, and some,—how many,—for the fire?
Memory may be but a power of coming to the treasury of Fact,
A momentary self-desertion, an absence in spirit from the now,
An actual coursing hither and thither, by the mind, slipped from its leash,
A life, as in the mystery of dreams, spent within the limits of a moment.

A brutish man knoweth not this, neither can a fool comprehend it,
But there be secrets of the memory, deep, wondrous, and fearful.
Were I at Petra, could I not declare, My soul hath been here **before me?**
Am I strange to the columned halls, the calm dead grandeur of Palmyra?
Know I not thy mount, O Carmel! Have I not voyaged on the **Danube,**
Nor seen the glare of Arctic snows,—nor the black tents of the **Tartar?**
Is **it then** a dream, **that I** remember the faces of them of old,
While wandering in the grove with Plato, and listening to Zeno in the porch?
Paul have I seen, and Pythagoras, and the Stagyrite hath spoken me friendly,
And His meek eye looked also upon me, standing with Peter in the palace.

Athens and Rome, Persepolis and Sparta, am I not a freeman of
    you all?
And chiefly can my yearning heart forget thee, O Jerusalem?—
For the strong magic of conception, mingled with the fumes of
    memory,
Giveth me a life in all past time, yea, and addeth substance to the
    future.
Be ye my judges, imaginative minds, full-fledged to soar into the
    sun,
Whose grosser natural thoughts the chemistry of wisdom hath
    sublimed,
Have ye not confessed to a feeling, a consciousness strange and
    vague,
That ye have gone this way before, and walk again your daily life,
Tracking an old routine, and on some foreign strand,
Where bodily ye have never stood, finding your own footsteps?
Hath not at times some recent friend looked out an old familiar,
Some newest circumstance or place teemed as with ancient
    memories?
A startling sudden flash lighteth up all for an instant,
And then it is quenched, as in darkness, and leaveth the cold
    spirit trembling.

Memory is not wisdom; idiots can rote volumes:
Yet what is wisdom without memory? a babe that is strangled in
    its birth,
The path of the swallow in the air, the path of the dolphin in the
    waters,
A cask running out, a bottomless chasm: such is wisdom without
    memory.
There be many wise, who cannot store their knowledge;
Yet from themselves are they satisfied, for the fountain is within:
There be many who store, but have no wisdom of their own,
Lumbering their armoury with weapons their muscles cannot lift:
There be many thieves and robbers, who glean and store
    unlawfully,
Calling in to memory's help some cunningly devised Cabala:
But to feed the mind with fatness, to fill thy granary with corn,
Nor clog with chaff and straw the threshing-floor of reason,
Reap the ideas, and house them well; but leave the words high
    stubble:

Strive to store up what was thought, despising what was said.
For the mind is a spirit, and drinketh in ideas, as flame melteth
    into flame;
But for words it must pack them as on floors, cumbrous and
    perishable merchandize.

To be pained for a minute, to fear for an hour, to hope for a
    week,—how long and weary!
But to remember fourscore years, is to look back upon a day.
An avenue seemeth to lengthen in the eyes of the wayfaring man,
But let him turn, those stationed elms crowd up within a yard;
Pace the lamp-lit streets of some sleeping city,
The multitude of cressets shall seem one, in the false picture of
    perspective;
Even so, in sweet treachery, dealeth the aged with himself,
He gazeth on the green hill-tops, while the marshes beneath are
    hidden;
And the partial telescope of memory pierceth the blank between,
To look with lingering love at the fair star of childhood.
Life is as the current spark on the miner's wheel of flints;
Whiles it spinneth there is light; stop it, all is darkness:
Life is as a morsel of frankincense burning in the hall of Eternity;
It is gone, but its odorous cloud curleth to the lofty roof:
Life is as a lump of salt, melting in the temple-laver;
It is gone,—yet its savour reacheth to the farthest atom:
Even so, for evil or for good, is life the criterion of a man,
For its memories of sanctity or sin pervade all the firmament of
    being.
There is but the flitting moment, wherein to hope or to enjoy,
But in the calendar of memory, that moment is all time.

THE DREAM OF AMBITION.

I LEFT the happy fields that smile around the village of Content,
And sought with wayward feet the torrid desert of Ambition.
Long time, parched and weary, I travelled that burning sand,
And the hooded basilisk and adder were strewed in my way for
    palms;
Black scorpions thronged me round, with sharp uplifted stings,
Seeming to mock me as I ran; (then I guessed it was a dream,—

But life is oft so like a dream, we know not where we are.)
So I toiled on, doubting in myself, up a steep gravel cliff,
Whose yellow summit shot up far into the brazen sky;
And quickly, I was wafted to the top, as upon unseen wings
Carrying me upward like a leaf: (then I thought it was a
    dream,—
Yet life is oft so like a dream, we know not where we are.)
So I stood on the mountain, and behold! before me a giant
    pyramid,
And I clomb with eager haste its high and difficult steps;
For I longed, like another Belus, to mount up, yea to heaven,
Nor sought I rest until my feet had spurned the crest of earth.

Then I sat on my granite throne under the burning sun,
And the world lay smiling beneath me, but I was wrapt in
    flames;
(And I hoped, in glimmering consciousness, that all this torture
    was a dream,—
Yet life is oft so like a dream, we know not where we are.)
And anon, as I sat scorching, the pyramid shuddered to its root,
And I felt the quarried mass leap from its sand foundations:
Awhile it tottered and tilted, as raised by invisible levers,—
(And now my reason spake with me; I knew it was a dream:
Yet I hushed that whisper into silence, for I hoped to learn of
    wisdom,
By tracking up my truant thoughts, whereunto they might lead.)
And suddenly, as rolling upon wheels, adown the cliff it rushed,
And I thought, in my hot brain, of the Muscovites' icy slope;
A thousand yards in a moment we ploughed the sandy seas,
And crushed those happy fields, and that smiling village,
And onward, as a living thing, still rushed my mighty throne,
Thundering along, and pounding, as it went, the millions in my
    way:
Before me all was life, and joy, and full-blown summer,
Behind me death and woe, the desert and simoom.
Then I wept and shrieked aloud, for pity and for fear;
But might not stop, for, comet-like, flew on the maddened mass
Over the crashing cities, and falling obelisks and towers,
And columns, razed as by a scythe, and high domes, shivered as
    an egg-shell,
And deep embattled ranks, and women, crowded in the streets,

And children, kneeling as for mercy, and all I had ever loved,
Yea, over all, mine awful throne rushed on with seeming instinct,—
And over the crackling forests, and over the rugged beach,
And on with a terrible hiss through the foaming wild Atlantic
That roared around me as I sat, but could not quench my spirit,—
Still on, through startled solitudes we shattered the pavement of the sea,
Down, down, to that central vault, the bolted doors of hell;
And these, with horrid shock, my huge throne battered in,
And on to the deepest deep, where the fierce flames were hottest,
Blazing tenfold as conquering furiously the seas that rushed in with me,—
And there I stopped: and a fearful voice shouted in mine ear,
"Behold the home of Discontent; behold the rest of Ambition!"

OF SUBJECTION.

Law hath dominion over all things, over universal mind and matter;
For there are reciprocities of right, which no creature can gainsay.
Unto each was there added by its Maker in the perfect chain of being,
Dependencies and sustentations, accidents, and qualities, and powers:
And each must fly forward in the curve, unto which it was forced from the beginning:
Each must attract and repel, or the monarchy of Order is no more.
Laws are essential emanations from the self-poised character of God,
And they radiate from that sun to the circling edges of creation.
Verily, the mighty Lawgiver hath subjected Himself unto laws,
And God is the primal grand example of free unstrained obedience;
His perfection is limited by right, and cannot trespass into wrong,
Because He hath established Himself as the fountain of only good,
And in thus much is bounded, that the evil hath He left unto another,
And that dark other hath usurped the evil which Omnipotence laid down.

Unto God there exist impossibilities: for the True One cannot
   lie,
Nor the Wise One wander from the track **which He hath** deter-
   mined **for Himself**:
For his will was purposed from eternity, strong in the love of
   order;
And that will altereth not, as the law of the Medes and Persians.
God is the origin of order, and the first exemplar of his precept;
For there **is subordination** of his Essence, self-guided unto holi-
   ness;
And there is subordination of his Persons, in due procession of
   dignity;
For the Son, **as** a son, is subject; **and** to him doth the Spirit
   minister:
But these things be mysteries to man, he cannot reach nor fathom
   them,
And ever must he speak in paradox, when labouring to expound
   his God;
For, behold, God is alone, mighty in unshackled freedom;
And with those wondrous Persons abideth eternal equality.

So **then, start ye** from the fountain, and follow the river of exist-
   ence;
For its current is **bounded** throughout **by** the banks of just **subor-**
   dination:
Thrones, and dominions, and powers, Archangels, Cherubim, and
   Seraphim,
Angels, and flaming ministers, and breathing chariots **and harps.**
For there are degrees in heaven, and varied capabilities of bliss,
And steps in the ladder of Intelligence, and ranks in approaches to
   Perfection:
Doubtless, reverence is given, as their due, to the masters in
   wisdom;
Doubtless, there are who serve; or a throne would have small
   glory.
Regard now the universe of matter, the substance of visible
   creation,
Which of old with well-observing truth, the Greek **hath surnamed**
   ORDER:
Where is there an atom out of place? or a particle **that** yieldeth
   not obedience?

Where is there a fragment that is free? or one thing the equal of
    another?—
The chain is unbroken down to man, and beyond him the links
    are perfect:
But he standeth solitary sin, a marvel of permitted chaos.

And shall this seeming error in the scale of due subordination
Be a spot of desert unreclaimed, in the midst of the vineyard of
    the Lord?
Shall his presumptuous pride snap the safe tether of connexion,
And his blind selfish folly refuse the burden of maintenance?
O man, thou art a creature; boast not thyself above the law:
Think not of thyself as free: thou art bound in the trammels of
    dependence.
What is the sum of thy duty, but obedience to righteous rule,
To the great commanding oracle, uttered by delegated organs?
Thou canst not render homage to abstract Omnipresent Power,
Save through the concrete symbol of visible ordained authority.
Those who obey not man, are oftenest found rebels against God;
And seldom is the delegate so bold, as to order what he knoweth
    to be wrong.
Yet mark me, proud gainsayer! I say not, obey unto sin,
But, where the Principal is silent, take heed thou despise not the
    Deputy:
And He that loveth order, will bless thee for thy faith,
If thou recognize his sanction in the powers that fashion human
    laws.

Thou, the vicegerent of the Lord, his high anointed image,
Towards whom a good man's loyalty floweth from the heart of his
    religion,
Thou, whose deep responsibilities are fathomed by a nation's
    prayers,
Whom wise men fear for while they love, and envy thee nothing
    but thy virtues,
From thy dizzy pinnacle of greatness, remember thou also art a
    subject,
And the throne of thine earthly glory is itself but the footstool of
    thy God.
The homage thy kingdoms yield thee, regard thou as yielded unto
    Him;

And while girt with all the majesty of state, consider thee the
    Lord's chief servant;
So shalt thou prosper, and be strong, grafted on the strength of
    Another;
So shall thy virgin heart be happy, in being humble.
And thou shalt flourish as an oak, the monarch of thine island
    forests,
Whose deep-dug roots are twisted around the stout ribs of the
    globe,
That mocketh at the fury of the storm, and rejoiceth in summer
    sunshine,
Glad in the smiles of heaven, and great in the stability of earth.

A ruler hath not power for himself, neither is his pomp for his
    pride;
But beneath the ermine of his office should he wear the rough hair-
    cloth of humility.
Nevertheless, every way obey him, so thou break not a higher
    commandment;
For Nero was an evil king, yet Paul prescribeth subjection.
If the rulers of a nation be holy, the Lord hath blessed that
    nation;
If they be lewd and impious, chastisement hath come upon that
    people:
For the bitterest scourge of a land is ungodliness in them that
    govern it,
And the guilt of the sons of Josiah drove Israel weeping into
    Babylon.
Yet be thou resolute against them, if they change the mandates of
    thy God,
If they touch the ark of his covenant, wherein all his mercies are
    enshrined:
Be resolute, but not rebellious; lest thou be of the company of
    Korah:
Set thy face against them as a flint: but be not numbered with
    Abiram.
Daniel nobly disobeyed; but not from a spirit of sedition,
And Azarias shouted from the furnace,—I will not bow down, O
    KING.
If truth must be sacrificed to unity, then faithfulness were folly;
If man must be obeyed before God, the martyrs have bled in vain:

Yet none of that blessed army reviled the rulers of the land,
They were loud and bold against the sin, but bent before the ensign of authority,
Honesty, scorning compromise, walketh most suitably with Reverence ;
Otherwise righteous daring may show but as obstinate rebellion :
Therefore, suffer not thy censure to lack the savour of courtesy,
And remember, the mortal sinneth, but the staff of his power is from God.
Man, thou hast a social spirit, and art deeply indebted to thy kind :

Therefore claim not all thy rights ; but yield, for thine own advantage.
Society is a chain of obligations, and its links must support each other ;
The branch can not but wither, that is cut from the parent vine.
Wouldst thou be a dweller in the woods, and cast away the cords that bind thee,
Seeking, in thy bitterness or pride, to be exiled from thy fellows?
Behold, the beasts shall hunt thee, weak, naked, houseless outcast,
Disease and Death shall track thee out, as bloodhounds in the wilderness :
Better to be lowliest of thy kind, in the hated company of men,
Than to live a solitary wretch, dreading and wanting all things ;
Better to be chained to thy labour, in the dusky thoroughfares of life,
Than to reign monarch of Sloth, in lonesome savage freedom.

Whence then cometh the doctrine, that all should be equal and free ?—
It is the lie that crowded hell, when Seraphs flung away subjection.
No man is his neighbour's equal, for no two minds are similar,
And accidents, alike with qualities, have every shade but sameness :
The lightest atom of difference shall destroy the nice balance of equality,
And all things from without and from within, make one man to differ from another.
We are equal and free ! was the watchword that spirited the legions of satan ;

We are equal and free! is the double lie that entrappeth to him
    conscripts from earth;
The messengers of that dark despot will pander to thy license and
    thy pride,
And draw thee from the crowd where thou art safe, to seize thee
    in the solitary desert.
Woe unto him whose heart the syren song of Liberty hath
    charmed :
Woe unto him whose mind is bewitched by her treacherous beauty;
In mad zeal flingeth he away the fetters of duty and restraint,
And yieldeth up the holocaust of self to that fair Idol of the
    Damned.
No man hath freedom in aught, save in that from which the
    wicked would be hindered,
He is free toward God and good ; but to all else a bondman.

Thou art in a middle sphere, to render and receive honour ;
If thy king commandeth, obey; and stand not in the way with
    rebels :
But if need be, lay thy hand upon thy sword, and fear not to
    smite a traitor,
For the universe acquitteth thee with honour, fighting in defence
    of thy king.
If a thief break thy dwelling, and thou take him, it were sin in
    thee to let him go ;
Yea, though he pleadeth to thy mercy, thou canst not spare him
    and be blameless;
For his guilt is not only against thee, it is not thy monies or thy
    merchandize,
But he hath done damage to the Law, which duty constraineth
    thee to sanction.
Feast not thine appetite of vengeance, remembering thou also art
    a man,
But weep for the sad compulsion, in which the chain of Providence
    hath bound thee:
Mercy is not thine to give; wilt thou steal another's privilege?
Or send abroad, among thy neighbours, a felon whom impunity
    hath hardened?
Remember the Roman father, strong in his stern integrity,
And let not thy slothful self-indulgence make thee a conniver at
    the crime.

Also, if the knife of the murderer be raised against thee or thine,
And through good providence and courage, thou slay him that would have slain thee,
Thou losest not a tittle of thy rectitude, having executed sudden justice;
Still mayst thou walk among the blessed, though thy hands be red with blood.
For thyself, thou art neither worse nor better; but thy fellows should count thee their creditor:
Thou hast manfully protected the right, and the right is stronger for thy deed.
Also, in the rescuing of innocence, fear not to smite the ravisher;
What though he die at thy hand? for a good name is better than the life;
And if Phineas had everlasting praise in the matter of Salu's son,
With how much greater honour standeth such a rescuer acquitted?
Uphold the laws of thy country, and fear not to fight in their defence;
But first be convinced in thy mind; for herein the doubter sinneth.
Above all things, look thou well around, if indeed stern duty forceth thee
To draw the sword of justice, and stain it with the slaughter of thy fellows.

She, that lieth in thy bosom, the tender wife of thy affections,
Must obey thee, and be subject, that evil drop not on thy dwelling.
The child that is used to constraint, feareth not more than he loveth;
But give thy son his way, he will hate thee and scorn thee together.
The master of a well-ordered home knoweth to be kind to his servants;
Yet he exacteth reverence, and each one feareth at his post.
There is nothing on earth so lowly, but duty giveth it importance;
No station so degrading, but it is ennobled by obedience:
Yea, break stones upon the highway, acknowledging the Lord in thy lot,
Happy shalt thou be, and honourable, more than many children of the mighty.
Thou that despisest the outward forms, beware thou lose not the inward spirit;

For they are as words unto ideas, as symbols to things unseen.
Keep then the form that is good; retain, and do reverence to
    example;
And in all things observe subordination, for that is the whole duty
    of man.

A horse knoweth his rider, be he confident or timid,
And the fierce spirit of Bucephalus stoopeth unto none but Alex-
    ander;
The tigress, roused in the jungle by the prying spaniels of the fowler,
Will quail at the eye of man, so he assert his dignity;
Nay, the very ships, those giant swans breasting the mighty waters,
Roll in the trough, or break the wave, to the pilot's fear or
    courage:
How much more shall man, discerning the Fountain of authority,
Bow to superior commands, and make his own obeyed.
And yet, in travelling the world, hast thou not often known
A gallant host led on to ruin by a feeble Xerxes?
Hast thou not often seen the wanton luxury of indolence
Sullying with its sleepy mist the tarnished crown of headship?
Alas! for a thousand fathers, whose indulgent sloth
Hath emptied the vial of confusion over a thousand homes:
Alas! for the palaces and hovels, that might have been nurseries
    for heaven,
By hot intestine broils blighted into schools for hell:
None knoweth his place, yet all refuse to serve,
None weareth the crown, yet all usurp the sceptre;
And perchance some fiercer spirit, of natural nobility of mind,
That needed but the kindness of constraint to have grown up great
    and good,
Now—the rich harvest of his heart choked by unweeded tares,—
All bold to dare and do, unchecked by wholesome fear,
A scoffer about bigotry and priestcraft, a rebel against government
    and God,
And standard-bearer of the turbulent, leading on the sons of Belial,
Such an one is king of that small state, head tyrant of the thirty,
Brandishing the torch of discord in his village-home:
And the timid Eli of the house, yon humble parish-priest,
Liveth in shame and sorrow, fearing his own handywork:
The mother, heartstricken years agone, hath dropped into an early
    grave;

The silent sisters long to leave a home they cannot **love**;
The brothers, casting off restraint, follow their wayward wills;
And the chance-guest, early departing, blesseth his kind stars,
That on his humbler home hath brooded no domestic curse!
Yet is that curse the fruit; wouldest thou the root of the evil?
A kindness—most unkind, that hath always spared the rod;
A weak and numbing indecision in the mind that should be master;
A **foolish love, pregnant of hate, that never** frowned on sin;
A **moral cowardice of heart, that** never dared command.

A kingdom is a nest of families, and a family a small kingdom;
And the government of whole or part differeth in nothing but extent.
The house, where the master ruleth, is strong in united subjection,
And the only commandment with promise, being honoured, is a blessing to that house:
But and if he yieldeth up the reins, it is weak in discordant anarchy,
And the bonds of love and union melt away, as ropes of sand.
The realm, that is ruled with vigour, lacketh neither peace nor glory,
It dreadeth not foes from without, nor the sons of riot from within:
But the meanness of temporizing fear robbeth a kingdom of its honour,
And the weakness of indulgent sloth ravageth its bowels with discord.
The best of human governments is the patriarchal rule;
The authorized supremacy of one, the prescriptive subjection of many:
Therefore, the children of the east have thriven from age to age,
Obeying, even as a god, the royal father of Cathay:
Therefore, to this our day, the Rechabite wanteth not a man,
But they stand before the Lord, forsaking not the mandate of their sire:
Therefore shall Magog among nations arise from his northern lair,
And rend, in the fury of his power, the insurgent world beneath him:
For the thunderbolt of concentrated strength can be hurled by the will of one,
While the dissipated forces of many are harmless as summer lightning.

OF REST.

In the silent watches of the night, calm night that breedeth thoughts,
When the task-weary mind disporteth in the careless play-hours of sleep,
I dreamed; and behold, a valley, green and sunny and well watered,
And thousands moving across it, thousands and tens of thousands:
And though many seemed faint and toil-worn, and stumbled often, and fell,
Yet moved they on unresting, as the ever-flowing cataract.
Then I noted adders in the grass, and pitfalls under the flowers,
And chasms yawned among the hills, and the ground was cracked and slippery:
But Hope and her brother Fear suffered not a foot to linger;
Bright phantoms of false joys beckoned alluringly forward,
While yelling grisly shapes of dread came hunting on behind:
And ceaselessly, like Lapland swarms, that miserable crowd sped along
To the mist-involved banks of a dark and sullen river.
There saw I, midway in the water, standing a giant fisher,
And he held many lines in his hand, and they called him Iron Destiny:
So I tracked those subtle chains, and each held one among the multitude:
Then I understood what hindered, that they rested not in their path:
For the fisher had sport in his fishing, and drew in his lines continually,
And the new-born babe, and the aged man, were dragged into that dark river:
And he pulled all those myriads along, and none might rest by the way,
Till many, for sheer weariness, were eager to plunge into the drowning stream.

So I knew that valley was Life, and it sloped to the waters of Death.
But far on the thither side spread out a calm and silent shore,
Where all was tranquil as a sleep, and the crowded strand was quiet:

And I saw there many I had known, but their eyes glared chillingly upon me,
As set in deepest slumber; and they pressed their fingers to their lips.
Then I knew that shore was the dwelling of Rest, where spirits held their Sabbath,
And it seemed they would have told me much, but they might not break that silence;
For the law of their being was mystery: they glided on, hushing as they went.
Yet further, under the sun, at the roots of purple mountains,
I noted a blaze of glory, as the night-fires on northern skies;
And I heard the hum of joy, as it were a sea of melody;
And far as the eye could reach, were millions of happy creatures
Basking in the golden light; and I knew that land was Heaven.
Then the hill whereon I stood split asunder, and a crater yawned at my feet,
Black and deep and dreadful, fenced round with ragged rocks;
Dimly was the darkness lit up by spires of distant flame:
And I saw below a moving mass of life, like reptiles bred in corruption,
Where all was terrible unrest, shrieks and groans and thunder.

So I woke, and I thought upon my dream; for it seemed of wisdom's ministration.
What man is he that findeth rest, though he hunt for it year after year?
As a child he had not yet been wearied, and cared not then to court it;
As a youth he loved not to be quiet, for excitement spurred him into strife;
As a man he tracketh rest in vain, toiling painfully to catch it,
But still is he pulled from the pursuit, by the strong compulsion of his fate:
So he hopeth to have peace in old age, as he cannot rest in manhood,
But troubles thicken with his years, till Death hath dodged him to the grave.
There remaineth a rest for the spirit on the shadowy side of life;
But unto this world's pilgrim no rest for the sole of his foot:
Ever, from stage to stage, he travelleth wearily forward,

And though he pluck flowers by the way, he may not sleep among
 the flowers.
Mind is the perpetual motion; for it is a running stream
From an unfathomable source, the depth of the divine Intelli-
 gence:
And though it be stopped in its flowing, yet hath it a current
 within,
The surface may sleep unruffled, but underneath are whirlpools of
 contention.
Seekest thou rest, O mortal?—seek it no more on earth,
For destiny will not cease from dragging thee through the rough
 wilderness of life;
Seekest thou rest, O immortal?—hope not to find it in Heaven,
For sloth yieldeth not happiness: the bliss of a spirit is action.
Rest dwelleth only on an island in the midst of the ocean of
 existence,
Where the world-weary soul for a while may fold its tired wings,
Until, after short sufficient slumber, it is quickened unto deathless
 energy,
And speedeth in eagle flight to the Sun of unapproachable per-
 fection.

OF HUMILITY.

VICE is grown aweary of her gawds, and donneth russet garments,
Loving for change to walk as a nun, beneath a modest veil:
For Pride hath noted how all admire the fairness of Humility,
And to clutch the praise he coveteth, is content to be drest in hair-
 cloth;
And wily Lust tempteth the young heart, that is proof against the
 bravery of harlots,
With timid tears and retiring looks of an artful seeming maid;
And indolent Apathy, sleepily ashamed of his dull lack-lustre
 face,
Is glad of the livery of meekness, that charitable cloak and cowl;
And Hatred hideth his demon frown beneath a gentle mask;
And Slander, snake-like, creepeth in the dust, thinking to escape
 recrimination.
But the world hath gained somewhat from its years, and is quick
 to penetrate disguises,

Neither in all these is it easily deceived, but rightly divideth the
 true from the false.
Yet there is a meanness of spirit, that is fair in the eyes of most men,

Yea, and seemeth fair unto itself, loving to be thought Humility.
Its choler is not roused by insolence, neither do injuries disturb it:
Honest indignation is strange unto its breast, and just reproof unto
 its lip.
It shrinketh, looking fearfully on men, fawning at the feet of the
 great;
The breath of calumny is sweet unto its ear, and it courteth the
 rod of persecution.
But what! art thou not a man, deputed chief of the creation?
Art thou not a soldier of the right, militant for God and good?
Shall virtue and truth be degraded, because thou art too base to
 uphold them?
Or Goliath be bolder in blaspheming for want of a David in the
 camp?
I say not, avenge injuries; for the ministry of vengeance is not
 thine:
But wherefore rebuke not a liar? wherefore do dishonour to thy-
 self?
Wherefore let the evil triumph, when the just and the right are on
 thy side?
Such Humility is abject, it lacketh the life of sensibility,
And that resignation is but mock, where the burden is not felt:
Suspect thyself and thy meekness: thou art mean and indifferent
 to sin;
And the heart that should grieve and forgive, is case-hardened and
 forgetteth.

Humility mainly becometh the converse of man with his Maker,
But oftentimes it seemeth out of place in the intercourse of man
 with man;
Yea, it is the cringer to his equal, that is chiefly seen bold to his
 God,
While the martyr, whom a world cannot brow-beat, is humble as
 a child before Him.
Render unto all men their due, but remember thou also art a man,
And cheat not thyself of the reverence which is owing to thy
 reasonable being,

Be courteous, and listen, and learn: but teach and answer if thou
    canst:
Serve thee of thy neighbour's wisdom, but be not enslaved as to a
    master.
Where thou perceivest knowledge, bend the ear of attention and
    respect;
But yield not further to the teaching, than as thy mind is war-
    ranted by reasons.
Better is an obstinate disputant, that yieldeth inch by inch,
Than the shallow traitor to himself, who surrendereth to half an
    argument.

Modesty winneth good report, but scorn cometh close upon ser-
    vility;
Therefore, use meekness with discretion, casting not pearls before
    swine.
For a fool will tread upon thy neck, if he seeth thee lying in the
    dust;
And there be companies and seasons where resolute bearing is but
    duty.
If a good man discloseth his secret failings unto the view of the
    profane,
What doeth he but harm unto his brother, confirming him in his
    sin?
There is a concealment that is right, and an open-mouthed humi-
    lity that erreth;
There is a candour near akin to folly, and a meekness looking like
    shame.
Masculine sentiments, vigorously holden, well become a man;
But a weak mind hath a timorous grasp, and mistaketh it for ten-
    derness of conscience.
Many are despised for their folly, who put it to the account of
    their religion,
And because men treat them with contempt, they look to their
    God for glory;
But contempt shall still be their reward, who betrayed their
    Master unto ridicule,
Reflecting on Him in themselves, meanness and ignorance and
    cowardice.
A Christian hath a royal spirit, and need not be ashamed but unto
    One:

Among just men walketh he softly, but the world should see him
    as a champion :
His humbleness is far unlike the shame that covereth the profligate
    and weak,
When the sober reproof of virtue hath touched their tingling ears ;
It is born of love and wisdom, and is worthy of all honour,
And the sweet persuasion of its smile changeth contempt into
    reverence.

A man of a haughty spirit is daily adding to his enemies.
He standeth as the Arab in the desert, and the hands of all men
    are against him :
A man of a base mind daily subtracteth from his friends ;
For he holdeth himself so cheaply, that others learn to despise
    him :
But where the meekness of self-knowledge veileth the front of self-
    respect,
There look thou for the man, whom none can know but they will
    honour.
Humility is the softening shadow before the stature of Excellence,
And lieth lowly on the ground, beloved and lovely as the violet :
Humility is the fair-haired maid, that calleth Worth her brother,
The gentle silent nurse, that fostereth infant virtues:
Humility bringeth no excuse; she is welcome to God and man :
Her countenance is needful unto all, who would prosper in either
    world :
And the mild light of her sweet face is mirrored in the eyes of her
    companions,
And straightway stand they accepted, children of penitence and
    love.
As when the blind man is nigh unto a rose, its sweetness is the
    herald of its beauty,
So when thou savourest humility, be sure thou art nigh unto merit.
A gift rejoiceth the covetous, and praise fatteneth the vain,
And the pride of man delighteth in the humble bearing of his
    fellow ;
But to the tender benevolence of the unthanked Almoner of good,
Humility is queen among the graces, for she giveth Him occasion
    to bestow.

OF PRIDE.

DEEP is the sea, and deep is hell, but Pride mineth deeper;
It is coiled as a poisonous worm about the foundations of the soul.
If thou expose it in thy motives, and track it in thy springs of thought,
Complacent in its own detection, it will seem indignant virtue;
Smoothly will it gratulate thy skill, O subtle anatomist of self,
And spurn at its very being, while it nestleth the deeper in thy bosom.
Pride is a double traitor, and betrayeth itself to entrap thee,
Making thee vain of thy self-knowledge; proud of thy discoveries of pride.
Fruitlessly thou strainest for humility, by darkly diving into self;
Rather look away from innate evil, and gaze upon extraneous good:
For in sounding the deep things of the heart, thou shalt learn to be vain of its capacities,
But in viewing the heights above thee, thou shalt be taught thy littleness:
Could an emmet pry into itself, it might marvel at its own anatomy,
But let it look on eagles, to discern how mean a thing it is.
And all things hang upon comparison; to the greater, great is small:
Neither is there anything so vile, but somewhat yet is viler:
On all sides is there an infinity: the culprit at the gallows hath his worse,
And the virgin martyr at the stake need not look far for a better.
Therefore see thou that thine aim reacheth unto higher than thyself:
Beware that the standard of thy soul wave from the loftiest battlement:
For pride is a pestilent meteor, flitting on the marshes of corruption,
That will lure thee forward to thy death, if thou seek to track it to its source:
Pride is a gloomy bow, arching the infernal firmament,
That will lead thee on, if thou wilt hunt it, even to the dwelling of despair.
Deep calleth unto deep, and mountain overtoppeth mountain,
And still shalt thou fathom to no end the depth and the height of pride:

For it is the vast ambition of the soul, warped to an idol object,
And nothing but a Deity in Self can quench its insatiable thirst.

Be aware of the smiling enemy, that openly sheatheth his weapon,
But mingleth poison in secret with the sacred salt of hospitality:
For pride will lie **dormant in thy heart, to snatch** its secret **opportunity,**
Watching, as a **lion-ant,** in the bottom of its toils.
Stay not to parley with thy foe, for his tongue is more potent **than** his arm,
But be wiser, fighting against pride in the simple panoply of prayer.
As one also of the poets hath said, let not the Proteus escape thee;
For he will blaze forth as fire, and quench himself in likeness **of** water;
He will fright thee as a roaring beast, or charm thee as a subtle reptile.
Mark, **amid all his transformations, the** complicate deceitfulness of pride,
And the more he striveth to elude thee, bind him the closer in thy toils.
Prayer is the net that snareth him; prayer is the fetter that holdeth him:
Thou canst not nourish **pride, while** waiting as an almsman on thy God,—
Waiting in sincerity and trust, or pride **shall meet thee** even there;
Yea, from the palaces of Heaven, **hath** pride cast **down** his millions.
Root up the **mandrake from thy heart, though** it cost thee blood and groans,
Or the **cherished garden of thy** graces will fade and perish utterly.

OF EXPERIENCE.

I KNEW that age was enriched with the hard-earned wages of knowledge,
And I saw that hoary wisdom **was** bred in the school of disappointment:

OF EXPERIENCE.

I noted that the wisest **of youth,** though provident and cautious of evil,
Yet sailed along unsteadily, as lacking some ballast of the mind:
And the cause seemed to lie in this, that while they considered around them,
And warded off all dangers from without, they forgat **their** own weakness within.
So **steer** they in self-confidence, until, from the multitude of perils,
They begin to be wary of themselves, and learn the first lesson of Experience.
I knew that in the morning of life, before its wearisome journey,
The youthful soul doth expand, in the simple luxury of being;
It hath not contracted its wishes, nor set a limit to its hopes;
The wing of fancy is unclipt, and sin hath not seared the feelings:
Each feature is stamped with immortality, for all its desires are infinite,
And it seeketh an ocean of happiness, **to fill the** deep hollow within.
But the old and the grave look on, pitying that generous youth,
For they also have tasted long ago the bitterness of hope destroyed
They pity him, and are sad, remembering the days that are past,
But they know he must taste for himself, or he will not give ear to their **wisdom.**
For Experience hath another lesson, which **a man will do well if he learn,**
By checking the flight of expectation, to cheat disappointment **of** its pain.

Experience teacheth many things, and all men are his scholars:
Yet is he a strange tutor, unteaching that which he hath taught.
Youth is confident, manhood wary, and old age confident again:
Youth is kind, manhood cold, and age returneth unto kindness.
For youth suspecteth nought, till manhood, bitterly learned,
Mistrusteth **all,** overleaping the mark; and age correcteth his **excess.**
Suspicion **is** the scaffold unto faith, a temporary needful eyesore,
By which the strong man's dwelling is slowly builded up behind;
But soon as the top-stone hath been set to the well-proved goodly edifice,
The scaffold is torn down, and well-timed trust taketh its long leave of suspicion.

A thousand volumes in a thousand tongues enshrine the lessons of
    Experience,
Yet a man shall read them all, and go forth none the wiser:
For self-love lendeth him a glass, to colour all he conneth,
Lest in the features of another he find his own complexion.
And we secretly judge of ourselves as differing greatly from all
    men,
And love to challenge causes to show how we can master their
    effects:
Pride is pampered in expecting that we need not fear a common
    fate,
Or wrong-headed prejudice exulteth, in combating old experience;
Or perchance caprice and discontent are the spurs that goad us
    into danger,
Careless, and half in hope to find there an enemy to joust with.
Private experience is an unsafe teacher, for we rarely learn both
    sides,
And from the gilt surface reckon not on steel beneath:
The torrid sons of Guinea think scorn of icy seas,
And the frostbitten Greenlander disbelieveth suns too hot.
But thou, student of Wisdom, feed on the marrow of the matter;
If thou wilt suspect, let it be thyself; if thou wilt expect, let it not
    be gladness.

OF ESTIMATING CHARACTER.

RASHLY, nor ofttimes truly, doth man pass judgment on his
    brother;
For he seeth not the springs of the heart, nor heareth the reasons
    of the mind.
And the world is not wiser than of old, when justice was meted by
    the sword,
When the spear avenged the wrong, and the lot decided the right,
When the footsteps of blinded innocence were tracked by burning
    ploughshares,
And the still condemning water delivered up the wizard to the
    stake:
For we wait, like the sage of Salamis, to see what the end will be,
Fixing the right or the wrong, by the issues of failure or success.
Judge not of things by their events; neither of character by pro-
    vidence;

OF ESTIMATING CHARACTER.

And count not a man more evil, because he is more unfortunate:
For the blessings of a better covenant lie not in the sunshine of prosperity,
But pain and chastisement the rather show the wise Father's love.

Behold that daughter of the world: she is full of gaiety and gladness;
The diadem of rank is on her brow, uncounted wealth is in her coffers:
She tricketh out her beauty like Jezebel, and is welcome in the courts of kings;
She is queen of the fools of fashion, and ruleth the revels of luxury:
And though she sitteth not as Tamar, nor standeth in the ways as Rahab,
Yet in the secret of her chamber, she shrinketh not from dalliance and guilt.
She careth not if there be a God, or a soul, or a time of retribution,
Pleasure is the idol of her heart: she thirsteth for no purer heaven.
And she laugheth with light good humour, and all men praise her gentleness;
They are glad in her lovely smile, and the river of her bounty filleth them.
So she prospered in the world: the worship and desire of thousands;
And she died even as she had lived, careless and courteous and liberal.
The grave swallowed up her pomp, the marble proclaimed her virtues,
For men esteemed her excellent, and charities sounded forth her praise;
But elsewhere far other judgment setteth her—with infidels and harlots!
She abused the trust of her splendour: and the wages of her sin shall be hereafter.

Look again on this fair girl, the orphan of a village pastor
Who is dead, and hath left her his all,—his blessing and a name unstained.

And friends, with busy zeal, that their purses be not taxed,
Place the sad mourner in a home, poor **substitute for that she hath** lost.
A stranger among strange faces she drinketh the wormwood **of** dependence;
She is marked as a child of want; and the world hateth poverty
Prayer **is not heard in that** house; **the** day she **hath loved** to hallow
Is noted **but** by deeper dissipation, **the** riot of luxury and gaming:
And wantonness is in her master's eye, and she hath no where to **flee** to;
She is cared for **by none** upon earth, and her God seemeth to forsake her;
Then cometh, in **fair show, the promise and the** feint of affection,
And her heart, long unused to kindness, remembereth her father, and loveth.
And the villain hath wronged her trust, and mocked, and flung **her** from him,
And men point at her and laugh: and women hate her as an outcast:
But elsewhere far other judgment seateth her—among the martyrs!
And the Lord, who seemed to forsake, giveth double glory to the fallen.

Once more, in the matter of wealth; **if** thou throw thine all **on a** chance,
Men will come around thee, and wait, and watch the turning **of the** wheel:
And if, **in** the lottery of life, thou hast drawn a splendid prize,
What foresight hadst thou, and skill! yea, what enterprize and wisdom!
But if it fall out against thee, and thou fail in thy perilous endeavour,
Behold, the simple did sow, and hath reaped the right harvest of his folly:
And the world will be gladly excused, nor will reach **out a finger** to help;
For why should this speculative dullard be a whirlpool **to all around** him?

Go to, let him sink by himself: we knew what the end of it
would be:—
For the man hath missed his mark, and his fellows look no
further.

Also, touching guilt and innocence: a man shall walk in his up-
rightness
Year after year without reproach, in charity and honesty with all:
But in one evil hour the enemy shall come in like a flood;
Shall track him, and tempt him, and hem him,—till he knoweth
not whither to fly.
Perchance his famishing little ones shall scream in his ears for
bread,
And, maddened by that fierce cry, he rusheth as a thief upon the
world;
The world that hath left him to starve, itself wallowing **in**
plenty,—
The world, that denieth him his rights,—he daringly robbeth it of
them.
I say not, such an one is innocent; but, small is the measure of
his guilt
To that of his wealthy neighbour, who would not help him at his
need;
To that of the selfish epicure, who turned away with coldness from
his tale;
To that of unsuffering thousands, who look with complacence on
his fall.

Or perchance the continual dropping of the venomed words of
spite,
Insult and injury and scorn, hath galled and pierced his heart;
Yet, **with** all long-suffering and meekness, he forgiveth unto
seventy times seven:
Till, in some weaker moment, tempted beyond endurance,
He striketh, more in anger than in hate; and, alas! for his heavy
chance,
He hath smitten unto instant death his spiteful life-long enemy!
And none was by to **see** it; and all men knew of their contentions:
Fierce voices shout for his blood, and rude hands hurry him to
judgment;
Then man's verdict cometh,—Murderer, with forethought malice;

And his name is a note of execration; his guilt is too black for
    devils:
But to the Righteous Judge, seemeth he the suffering victim;
For his anger was not unlawful, but became him as a Christian
    and a man;
And though his guilt was grievous when he struck that heavy
    bitter blow,
Yet light is the sin of the smiter, and verily kicketh the beam,
To the weight of that man's wickedness, whose slow relentless
    hatred
Met him at every turn, with patient continuance in evil.
Doubtless, eternal wrath shall be heaped upon that spiteful enemy.

It is vain, it is vain, saith the preacher; there be none but the
    righteous and the wicked,
Base rebels, and staunch allies, the true knight, and the traitor:
And he beareth strong witness among men, There is no neutral
    ground,
The broad highway and narrow path map out the whole domain;
Sit here among the saints, these holy chosen few,
Or grovel there a wretch condemned, to die among the million.
And verily for ultimate results, there be but good and bad;
Heaven hath no dusky twilight; hell is not gladdened with a
    dawn;
Yet looking round among his fellows, who can pass righteous
    judgment,
Such an one is holy and accepted, and such an one reprobate and
    doomed?
There is so much of good among the worst, so much of evil in the
    best,
Such seeming partialities in providence, so many things to lessen
    and expand,
Yea, and with all man's boast, so little real freedom of his
    will,—
That, to look a little lower than the surface, garb or dialect or
    fashion,
Thou shalt feebly pronounce for a saint, and faintly condemn for a
    sinner.
Over many a good heart and true, fluttereth the Great King's
    pennant;
By many an iron hand, the pirate's black banner is unfurled

But there be many more besides, in the yacht and the trader and
  the fishing-boat,
In the feathered war canoe, and the quick mysterious gondola :
And the army of that Great King hath no stated uniform ;
Of mingled characters and kinds goeth forth the countless host ;
There is the turbaned Damascene, with his tattooed Zealand
  brother,
There the slim bather in the Ganges, with the sturdy Russian
  boor,
The sluggish inmate of a Polar cave, with the fire-souled daughter
  of Brazil,
The embruted slave from Cuba, and the Briton of gentle birth,
For all are His inheritance, of all He taketh tithe :
And the church, His mercy's ark, hath some of every sort.
Who art thou, O man, that art fixing the limits of the fold ?
Wherefore settest thou stakes to spread the tent of heaven ?
Lay not the plummet to the line : religion hath no landmarks :
No human keenness can discern the subtle shades of faith :
In some it is as earliest dawn, the scarce diluted darkness ;
In some as dubious twilight, cold and grey and gloomy :
In some the ebon east is streaked with flaming gold :
In some the dayspring from on high breaketh in all its praise.
And who hath determined the when, separating light from dark-
  ness ?
Who shall pluck from earliest dawn the promise of the day ?
Leave that care to the Husbandman, lest thou garner tares ;
Help thou the shepherd in his seeking, but to separate be his ;
For I have often seen the noble erring spirit
Wrecked on the shoals of passion, and numbered of the lost ;
Often the generous heart, lit by unhallowed fire,
Counted a brand among the burning, and left uncared-for, in his
  sin :
Yet I waited a little year, and the mercy thou hadst forgotten
Hath purged that noble spirit, washing it in waters of repentance ;
That glowing generous heart, having burnt out all its dross,
Is as a golden censer, ready for the aloes and cassia :
While thou, hard-visaged man, unlovely in thy strictness,
Who turned from him thy sympathies with self-complacent pride,
How art thou shamed by him ! his heart is a spring of love,
While the dry well of thine affections is choked with secret mam-
  mon.

Sometimes at a glance thou judgest well; years could add little to
 thy knowledge:
When charity gloweth on the cheek, or malice is lowering in the
 eye,
When honesty's open brow, or the weasel-face of cunning is before
 thee,
Or the loose lip of wantonness, or clear bright forehead of reflec-
 tion.
But often, by shrewd scrutiny, thou judgest to the good man's
 harm:
For it may be his hour of trial, or he slumbereth at his post,
Or he hath slain his foe, but not yet levelled the stronghold,
Or barely recovered of the wounds, that fleshed him in his fray
 with passion.
Also, of the worst, through prejudice, thou loosely shalt think
 well:
For none is altogether evil, and thou mayest catch him at his
 prayers:
There may be one small prize, though all beside be blanks;
A silver thread of goodness in the black sergecloth of crime.

There is to whom all things are easy: his mind, as a master-key
Can open, with intuitive address, the treasuries of art and science:
There is to whom all things are hard; but industry giveth him a
 crow-bar,
To force, with groaning labour, the stubborn lock of learning:
And often, when thou lookest on an eye, dim in native dulness,
Little shalt thou wot of the wealth diligence hath gathered to its
 gaze;
Often, the brow that should be bright with the dormant fire of
 genius,
Within its ample halls, hath ignorance the tenant.
Yet are not the sons of men cast as in-moulds by the lot?
The like in frame and feature have much alike in spirit;
Such a shape hath such a soul, so that a deep discerner
From his make will read the man, and err not far in judgment:
Yea, and it holdeth in the converse, that growing similarity of
 mind
Findeth or maketh for itself an apposite dwelling in the body:
Accident may modify, circumstance may bevil, externals seem to
 change it,

But still the primitive crystal is latent in its many variations:
For the map of the face, and the picture of the eye, are traced by
    the pen of passion;
And the mind fashioneth a tabernacle suitable for itself.
A mean spirit boweth down the back, and the bowing fostereth
    meanness;
A resolute purpose knitteth the knees, and the firm tread nourish-
    eth decision;
Love looketh softly from the eye, and kindleth love by looking;
Hate furroweth the brow, and a man may frown till he hateth.
For mind and body, spirit and matter, have reciprocities of
    power,
And each keepeth up the strife; a man's works make or mar him.

There be deeper things than these, lying in the twilight of truth;
But few can discern them aright, from surrounding dimness of
    error.
For perchance, if thou knewest the whole, and largely with
    comprehensive mind
Couldst read the history of character, the chequered story of a
    life,
And into the great account, which summeth a mortal's destiny,
Wert to add the forces from without, dragging him this way and
    that,
And the secret qualities within, grafted on the soul from the
    womb,
And the might of other men's example, among whom his lot is
    cast,
And the influence of want, or wealth, of kindness or harsh ill-
    usage,
Of ignorance he cannot help, and knowledge found for him by
    others,
And first impressions, hard to be effaced, and leadings to right or
    to wrong,
And inheritance of likeness from a father, and natural human
    frailty,
And the habit of health or disease, and prejudices poured into his
    mind,
And the myriad little matters none but Omniscience can know,
And accidents that steer the thoughts, where none but Ubiquity
    can trace them;—

If thou couldst compass all these, and the consequents flowing from them,
And the scope to which they tend, and the necessary fitness of all things,
Then shouldst thou see as He seeth, who judgeth all men equal,—
Equal, touching innocence and guilt; and different alone in this,
That one acknowledgeth his evil, and looketh to his God for mercy;
Another boasteth of his good, and calleth on his God for justice;
So He, that sendeth none away, is largely munificent to prayer,
But, in the heart of presumption, sheatheth the sword of vengeance.

OF HATRED AND ANGER.

Blunted unto goodness is the heart which anger never stirreth,
But that which hatred swelleth, is keen to carve out evil.
Anger is a noble infirmity, the generous failing of the just,
The one degree that riseth above zeal, asserting the prerogatives of virtue:
But hatred is a slow continuing crime, a fire in the bad man's breast,
A dull and hungry flame, for ever craving insatiate.
Hatred would harm another; anger would indulge itself:
Hatred is a simmering poison; anger, the opening of a valve:
Hatred destroyeth as the upas-tree; anger smiteth as a staff:
Hatred is the atmosphere of hell; but anger is known in heaven.
Is there not a righteous wrath, an anger just and holy,
When goodness is sitting in the dust, and wickedness enthroned on Babel?
Doth pity condemn guilt?—is justice not a feeling but a law
Appealing to the line and to the plummet, incognizant of moral sense?
Thou that condemnest anger, small is thy sympathy with angels,
Thou that hast accounted it for sin, cold is thy communion with heaven.

Beware of the angry in his passion; but fear not to approach him afterward;
For if thou acknowledge thine error, he himself will be sorry for his wrath:

Beware of the hater in his coolness; for he meditateth evil against
    thee:
Commending the resources of his mind calmly to work thy ruin.
Deceit and treachery skulk with hatred, but an honest spirit flieth
    with anger:
The one lieth secret, as a serpent; the other chaseth, as a
    leopard.
Speedily be reconciled in love, and receive the returning offender,
For wittingly prolonging anger, thou tamperest unconsciously with
    hatred.
Patience is power in a man, nerving him to rein his spirit:
Passion is as palsy to his arm, while it yelleth on the coursers to
    their speed:
Patience keepeth counsel, and standeth in solid self-possession,
But the weakness of sudden passion layeth bare the secrets of the
    soul.
The sentiment of anger is not ill, when thou lookest on the
    impudence of vice,
Or savourest the breath of calumny, or hast earned the hard wages
    of injustice,
But see that thou curb it in expression, rendering the mildness of
    rebuke,
So shalt thou stand without reproach, mailed in all the dignity of
    virtue.

OF GOOD IN THINGS EVIL.

I HEARD the man of sin reproaching the goodness of Jehovah,
Wherefore, if he be Almighty Love, permitteth he misery and
    pain?
I saw the child of hope vexed in the labyrinth of doubt,
Wherefore, O holy One and just, is the horn of thy foul foe so high
    exalted?—
And, alas! for this our groaning world, for that grief and guilt are
    here;
Alas! for that Earth is the battle-field, where good must combat
    with evil:
Angels look on and hold their breath, burning to mingle in the
    conflict,

But the troops of the Captain of Salvation may be none but the
    soldiers of the cross:
And that slender band must fight alone, and yet shall triumph
    gloriously,
Enough shall they be for conquest, and the motto of their standard
    is, ENOUGH.
Thou art sad, O denizen of earth, for pains and diseases and death,
But remember, thy hand hath earned them; grudge not at the
    wages of thy doings:
Thy guilt, and thy fathers' guilt, must bring many sorrows in their
    company,
And if thou wilt drink sweet poison, doubtless it shall rot thee to
    the core.
What art thou but the heritor of evil, with a right to nothing
    good?
The respite of an interval of ease were a boon which Justice might
    deny thee:
Therefore lay thy hand upon thy mouth, O man much to be
    forgiven,
And wait, thou child of hope, for time shall teach thee all things.

Yet hear, for my speech shall comfort thee: reverently, but with
    boldness,
I would raise the sable curtain, that hideth the symmetry of
    Providence.
Pain and sin are convicts, and toil in their fetters for good;
The weapons of evil are turned against itself, fighting under better
    banners:
The leech delighteth in stinging, and the wicked loveth to do
    harm,
But the wise Physician of the Universe useth that ill tendency for
    health.
Verily, from others' griefs are gendered sympathy and kindness;
Patience, humility, and faith, spring not seldom from thine own:
An enemy, humbled by his sorrows, cannot be far from thy
    forgiveness,
A friend, who hath tasted of calamity, shall fan the dying incense
    of thy love:
And for thyself, is it a small thing, so to learn thy frailty,
That from an aching bone thou savest the whole body?
The furnace of affliction may be fierce, but if it refineth thy soul,

The good of one meek thought shall outweigh years of torment.
Nevertheless, wretched man, if thy bad heart be hardened in the flame,
Being earth-born, as of clay, and not of moulded wax,
Judge not the hand that smiteth, as if thou wert visited in wrath:
Reproach thyself, for He is Justice; repent thee, for He is Mercy.

Cease, fond caviller at wisdom, to be satisfied that everything is wrong:
Be sure there is good necessity, even for the flourishing of evil.
Would the eye delight in perpetual noon? or the ear in unqualified harmonies?
Hath winter's frost no welcome, contrasting sturdily with summer?
Couldst thou discern benevolence, if there were no sorrows to be soothed?
Or discover the resources of contrivance, if nothing stood opposed to the means?
What were power without an enemy? or mercy without an object?
Or truth, where the false were impossible? or love, where love were a debt?
The characters of God were but idle, if all things around him were perfection,
And virtues might slumber on like death, if they lacked the opportunities of evil.
There is one all-perfect, and but one; man dare not reason of His essence:
But there must be deficiencies in heaven, to leave room for progression in bliss:
A realm of unqualified BEST were a stagnant pool of being,
And the circle of absolute perfection, the abstract cipher of indolence.
Sin is an awful shadow, but it addeth new glories to the light;
Sin is a black foil, but it setteth off the jewelry of heaven:
Sin is the traitor that hath dragged the majesty of mercy into action;
Sin is the whelming argument, to justify the attribute of vengeance.
It is a deep dark thought, and needeth to be diligently studied,
But perchance evil was essential, that God should be seen of his creatures:
For where perfection is not, there lacketh possible good,

And the absence of better that might be, taketh from the praise of it is well:
And creatures must be finite, and finite cannot be perfect:
Therefore, though in small degree, creation involveth evil,
He chargeth his angels with folly, and the heavens are not clean in His sight:
For every existence in the universe hath either imperfection or Godhead:
And the light that blazeth but in One, must be softened with shadow for the many.
There is then good in evil; or none could have known his Maker;
No spiritual intellect or essence could have gazed on his high perfections,
No angel harps could have tuned the wonders of his wisdom,
No ransomed souls have praised the glories of his mercy,
No howling fiends have shown the terrors of his justice,
But God would have dwelt alone, in the fearful solitude of holiness.

Nevertheless, O sinner, harden not thine heart in evil;
Nor plume thee in imaginary triumph, because thou art not valueless as vile;
Because thy dark abominations add lustre to the clarity of Light;
Because a wonder-working alchemy draineth elixir out of poisons;
Because the same fiery volcano that scorcheth and ravageth a continent,
Hath in the broad blue bay cast up some petty island;
Because to the full demonstration of the qualities and accidents of good,
The swarthy legions of the Devil have toiled as unwitting pioneers.
For sin is still sin; so hateful Love doth hate it;
A blot on the glory of creation, which justice must wipe out.
Sin is a loathsome leprosy, fretting the white robe of innocence;
A rottenness, eating out the heart of the royal cedars of Lebanon;
A pestilential blast, the terror of that holy pilgrimage;
A rent in the sacred veil, whereby God left his temple.
Therefore, consider thyself, thou that dost not sorrow for thy guilt:
Fear evil, or face its enemy: dread sin, or dare justice.

Yea, saith the Spirit, and their works do follow them;
Habits, and thoughts, and deeds, are shadows and satellites of self.

What! shall the claimant to a throne stand forward with a rabble
    rout,—
Meanness, impiety, and lust; riot and indolence and vanity?
Nay, man! the train wherewith thou comest attend whither thou
    shalt go:
A throne for a king's son, but an inner dungeon for the felon.
For a man's works do follow him: bodily, standing in the judg-
    ment,
Behold the false accuser, behold the slandered saint;
The slave, and his bloody driver; the poor and his generous
    friend;
The simple dupe, and the crafty knave: the murderer, and—his
    victim!
Yet all are in many characters; the best stand guilty at the bar;
And he that seemed the worst may have most of real excuse.
The talents unto which a man is born, be they few or many,
Are dropped into the balance of account, working unlooked-for
    changes;
And perchance the convict from the galleys may stand above the
    hermit from his cell,
For that the obstacles in one outweigh the propensions in the
    other.
There be, who have made themselves friends, yea, by unrighteous
    mammon,—
Friends, ready waiting as an escort to those everlasting habitations;
Embodied in living witnesses, thronging to meet them in a cloud,
Charity, meekness and truth, zeal, sincerity and patience.
There be, who have made themselves foes, yea, by honest gain,
Foes, whose plaint must have its answer, before the bright portal
    is unbarred:
Pride, and selfishness, and sloth, apathy, wrath and falsehood,
Bind to their everlasting toil many that must weary in the fires.
Love hath a power and a longing to save the gathered world,
And rescue universal man from the hunting hell-hounds of his
    doings:
Yet few, here one and there one, scanty as the gleaning after
    harvest,
Are glad of the robes of praise which Mercy would fling around
    the naked;
But wrapping closer to their skin the poisoned tunic of their works,
They stand in self-dependence, to perish in abandonment of God.

OF PRAYER.

A WICKED man scorneth prayer, in the shallow sophistry of reason,
He derideth the silly hope that God can be moved by supplication:—
Can the unchangeable be changed, or waver in his purpose?
Can the weakness of pity affect him? Should he turn at the bidding of a man?
Methought he ruled all things, and ye called his decrees immutable,
But if thus he listeneth to words, wherein is the firmness of his will?—
So I heard the speech of the wicked, and, lo, it was smoother than oil;
But I knew that his reasonings were false, for the promise of the Scripture is true:
Yet was my soul in darkness, for his words were too hard for me;
Till I turned to my God in prayer: for I know He heareth always.
Then I looked abroad on the earth, and, behold, the Lord was in all things;
Yet saw I not his hand in aught, but perceived that He worketh by means;
Yea, and the power of the mean proveth the wisdom that ordained it,
Yea, and no act is useless, to the hurling of a stone through the air.
So I turned my thoughts to supplication, and beheld the mercies of Jehovah,
And I saw sound argument was still the faithful friend of godliness:
For as the rock of the affections is the solid approval of reason,
Even so the temple of Religion is founded on the basis of Philosophy.

Scorner, thy thoughts are weak, they reach not the summit of the matter;
Go to, for the mouth of a child might show thee the mystery of prayer:
Verily, there is no change in the counsels of the Mighty Ruler:
Verily, his purpose is strong, and rooted in the depths of necessity:

But who hath shown thee **his purpose,** who hath made known to thee his will?
When, O gainsayer! hast thou been schooled in the secrets of wisdom?
Fate is a creature of God, and all things move in their orbits,
And that which shall surely happen is known **unto him from** eternity;
But as, in the field of nature, he useth the sinews of the ox,
And commandeth diligence and toil, himself giving the increase;
So, in the kingdom of his grace, granteth he omnipotence to prayer,
For he knoweth what thou wilt ask, and what thou wilt ask aright.
No man can pray **in** faith, whose prayer is not grounded on a promise:
Yet a good man commendeth all things to the righteous wisdom of his God:
For those, who pray in faith, trust the immutable Jehovah,
And they, who ask blessings unpromised, **lean** on uncovenanted mercy.

Man, regard thy prayers as a purpose of love to thy soul;
Esteem the providence that led to them as an index of God's good will;
So shalt thou pray aright, and thy words **shall** meet with acceptance.
Also, in pleading for others, be thankful for the fulness of thy prayer:
For if thou art ready to ask, the Lord is more ready to bestow.
The salt preserveth the sea, and the saints uphold the earth;
Their prayers are the thousand pillars that prop the canopy of nature.
Verily, an hour without prayer, from some terrestrial mind,
Were a curse in the calendar **of** time, a spot of the blackness of darkness.
Perchance the terrible day, when the world must rock into ruins,
Will be one unwhitened by prayer,—shall He find faith on the earth?
For there is an economy of mercy, as of wisdom, and power, and means;
Neither is one blessing granted, unbesought from the treasury of good:

And the charitable heart of the Being, to depend upon whom is
  happiness,
Never withholdeth a bounty, so long as his subject prayeth;
Yea, ask what thou wilt, to the second throne in heaven,
It is thine, for whom it was appointed; there is no limit unto
  prayer:
But and if thou cease to ask, tremble, thou self-suspended
  creature,
For thy strength is cut off as was Samson's: and the hour of thy
  doom is come.

Frail art thou, O man, as a bubble on the breaker,
Weak and governed by externals, like a poor bird caught in the
  storm;
Yet thy momentary breath can still the raging waters,
Thy hand can touch a lever that may move the world.
O Merciful, we strike eternal covenant with thee,
For man may take for his ally the King who ruleth kings;
How strong, yet how most weak, in utter poverty how rich,
What possible omnipotence to good is dormant in a man!
Behold that fragile form of delicate transparent beauty,
Whose light-blue eye and hectic cheek are lit by the bale-fires of
  decline,
All droopingly she lieth, as a dew-laden lily,
Her flaxen tresses, rashly luxuriant, dank with unhealthy moisture;
Hath not thy heart said of her, Alas! poor child of weakness?
Thou hast erred; Goliath of Gath stood not in half her strength:
Terribly she fighteth in the van as the virgin daughter of Orleans,
She beareth the banner of heaven, her onset is the rushing cata-
  ract,
Seraphim rally at her side, and the captain of that host is God,
And the serried ranks of evil are routed by the lightning of her
  eye;
She is the King's remembrancer, and steward of many blessings,
Holding the buckler of security over her unthankful land:
For that weak fluttering heart is strong in faith assured,
Dependence is her might, and behold—she prayeth.

Angels are round the good man, to catch the incense of his
  prayers,
And they fly to minister kindness to those for whom he pleadeth;

For the altar of his heart is lighted, and burneth before God continually,
And he breatheth, conscious of his joy, the native atmosphere of heaven:
Yea, though poor, and contemned, and ignorant of this world's wisdom,
Ill can his fellows spare him, though they know not of his value.
Thousands bewail a hero, and a nation mourneth for its king,
But the whole universe lamenteth the loss of a man of prayer.
Verily, were it not for One, who sitteth on His rightful throne,
Crowned with a rainbow of emerald, the green memorial of earth,—
For one, a mediating man, that hath clad His Godhead with mortality,
And offereth prayer without ceasing, the royal priest of Nature,
Matter and life and mind had sunk into dark annihilation,
And the lightning frown of Justice withered the world into nothing.

Thus, O worshipper of reason, thou hast heard the sum of the matter:
And woe to his hairy scalp that restraineth prayer before God.
Prayer is a creature's strength, his very breath and being;
Prayer is the golden key that can open the wicket of Mercy;
Prayer is the magic sound that saith to Fate, so be it;
Prayer is the slender nerve that moveth the muscles of Omnipotence:
Wherefore, pray, O creature, for many and great are thy wants;
Thy mind, thy conscience, and thy being, thy rights commend thee unto prayer,
The cure of all cares, the grand panacea for all pains,
Doubt's destroyer, ruin's remedy, the antidote to all anxieties.

So then, God is true, and yet He hath not changed:
It is He that sendeth the petition, to answer it according to His will.

THE LORD'S PRAYER.

INQUIREST thou, O man, wherewithal may I come unto the Lord?
And with what wonder-working sounds may I move the majesty of heaven?

There is a model to thy hand; upon that do **thou frame** thy supplication;
Wisdom hath measured its words; and redemption urgeth thee to use them.
Call thy God thy Father, and yet not thine alone,
For thou art **but one of many, thy** brotherhood is with all:
Remember his high estate, that he dwelleth King of Heaven;
So shall thy thoughts be humbled, nor love be unmixed with reverence:
Be thy first petition unselfish, the honour of Him who made thee,
And that in the depths of thy heart **his memory** be shrined in holiness:
Pray for that blessed **time,** when good shall triumph over evil,
And one universal temple echo the perfections of Jehovah:
Bend thou to his good will, and subserve his holy purposes,
Till in thee, and those around thee, grow a little heaven **upon earth:**
Humbly, as a grateful almsman, beg thy bread of God,—
Bread for thy triple estate, for thou hast a trinity of nature:
Humility smootheth the way, and gratitude softeneth the heart,
Be then thy prayer for pardon mingled with the tear of penitence;
Yea, and while, all unworthy, thou leanest on the hand that should smite,
Thou canst not from thy fellows withhold thy less forgiveness;
To thy Father thy weaknesses are known, and thou hast not hid thy sin,
Therefore ask him, in all trust, to lead thee from the dangers of temptation;
While the last petition of the soul, that breathed on the confines of prayer,
Is deliverance from sin and the evil one, the miseries of earth and hell.
And wherefore, child of hope, should the rock of thy confidence be sure?
Thou knowest that God heareth, and promiseth an answer of peace;
Thou knowest that he is King, and none can stay his hand;
Thou knowest his power to be boundless, for there is none other:
And to Him thou givest glory, **as a creature of** his workmanship and favour,
For the never-ending **term of thy saved and** bright **existence.**

OF DISCRETION.

For what then was I born?—to fill the circling year
With daily toil for daily bread, with sordid pains and pleasures?—
To walk this chequered world, alternate light and darkness,
The day-dreams of deep thought followed by the night-dreams of fancy?—
To be one in a full procession?—to dig my kindred clay?—
To decorate the gallery of art?—to clear a few acres of forest?—
For more than these, my soul, thy God hath lent thee life.
Is then that noble end to feed this mind with knowledge,
To mix for mine own thirst the sparkling wine of wisdom,
To light with many lamps the caverns of my heart,
To reap, in the furrows of my brain, good harvest of right reasons?—
For more than these, my soul, thy God hath lent thee life.
Is it to grow stronger in self-government, to check the chafing will,
To curb with tightening rein the mettled steeds of passion,
To welcome with calm heart, far in the voiceless desert,
The gracious visitings of heaven that bless my single self?—
For more than these, my soul, thy God hath lent thee life.
To aim at thine own happiness, is an end idolatrous and evil;
In earth, yea in heaven, if thou seek it for itself, seeking thou shalt not find.
Happiness is a road-side flower, growing on the highway of Usefulness;
Plucked, it shall wither in thy hand; passed by, it is fragrance to thy spirit:
Love not thine own soul, regard not thine own weal,
Trample the thyme beneath thy feet; be useful, and be happy!
Thus unto fair conclusions argueth generous youth,
And quickly he starteth on his course, knight-errant to do good.
His sword is edged with arguments, his vizor terrible with censures;
He goeth full mailed in faith, and zeal is flaming at his heart.
Yet one thing he lacketh, the Mentor of the mind,
The quiet whisper of Discretion—Thy time is not yet come.
For he smiteth an oppressor; and vengeance for that smiting
Is dealt in doubled stripes on the faint body of the victim:
He is glad to give and to distribute; and clamorous pauperism feasteth,

While honest labour, pining, hideth his sharp ribs:
He challengeth to a fair field that subtle giant Infidelity,
And, worsted in the unequal fight, strengtheneth the hands of error;
He hasteth to teach and preach, as the war-horse rusheth to the battle,
And to pave a way for truth, would break up the Apennines of prejudice:
He wearieth by stale proofs, where none looked for a reason,
And to the listening ear will urge the false argument of feeling.
So hath it often been, that, judging by results,
The hottest friends of truth have done her deadliest wrong.
Alas! for there are enemies without, glad enough to parley with a traitor,
And a zealot will let down the drawbridge, to prove his own prowess:
Yea, from within will he break away a breach in the citadel of truth,
That he may fill the gap, for fame, with his own weak body.

Zeal without judgment is an evil, though it be zeal unto good;
Touch not the ark with unclean hand, yea, though it seem to totter.
There are evil who work good, and there are good who work evil,
And foolish backers of wisdom have brought on her many reproaches.
Truth hath more than enough to combat in the minds of all men,
For the mist of sense is a thick veil, and sin hath warped their wills;
Yet doth an officious helper awkwardly prevent her victory,—
These thy wounded hands were smitten in the house of friends:—
To point out a meaning in her words, he will blot those words with his finger;
And winnow chaff into the eyes, before he hath wheat to show:
He will heap sturdy logs on a faint expiring fire,
And with a room in flames, will cast the casement open;
By a shoulder to the wheel downhill harasseth the labouring beast,
And where obstruction were needed, will harm by an ill-judged thrusting-on.

A vessel foundereth at sea, if a storm have unshipped the rudder;
And a mind with much sail shall require heavy ballast.
Take a lever by the middle, thou shalt seem to prove it powerless,
Argue for truth indiscreetly, thou shalt toil for falsehood.
There is plenty of room for a peaceable man in the most thronged
    assembly;
But a quarrelsome spirit is straitened in the open field:
Many a teacher, lacking judgment, hindereth his own lessons;
And the savoury mess of pottage is spoiled by a bitter herb:
The garment woven of a piece is rashly torn by schism,
Because its unwise claimants will not cast lots for its possession.

Discretion guide thee on thy way, noble-minded youth,
Help thee to humour infirmities, to wink at innocent errors,
To take small count of forms, to bear with prejudice and fancy:
Discretion guard thine asking, discretion aid thine answer,
Teach thee that well-timed silence hath more eloquence than
    speech,
Whisper thee, thou art Weakness, though thy cause be Strength,
And tell thee, the key-stone of an arch can be loosened with least
    labour from within.
The snows of Hecla lie around its troubled smoking Geysers;
Let the cool streams of prudence temper the hot spring of zeal:
So shalt thou gain thine honourable end, nor lose the midway
    prize:
So shall thy life be useful, and thy young heart happy.

OF TRIFLES.

YET once more, saith the fool, yet once, and is it not a little
    one?
Spare me this folly yet an hour, for what is one among so many?
And he blindeth his conscience with lies, and stupifieth his heart
    with doubts;—
Whom shall I harm in this matter? and a little ill breedeth much
    good;
My thoughts, are they not mine own? and they leave no mark
    behind them;
And if God so pardoneth crime, how should these petty sins affect
    him?—

So he transgresseth yet again, and falleth by little and little,
Till the ground crumble beneath him, and he sinketh in the gulf despairing.
For there is nothing in the earth so small that it may not produce great things,
And no swerving from a right line, that may not lead eternally astray.
A landmark tree was once a seed; and the dust in the balance maketh a difference;
And the cairn is heaped high by each one flinging a pebble:
The dangerous bar in the harbour's mouth is only grains of sand;
And the shoal that hath wrecked a navy is the work of a colony of worms:
Yea, and a despicable gnat may madden the mighty elephant;
And the living rock is worn by the diligent flow of the brook.
Little art thou, O man, and in trifles thou contendest with thine equals,
For atoms must crowd upon atoms, ere crime groweth to be a giant.
What, is thy servant a dog?—not yet wilt thou grasp the dagger,
Not yet wilt thou laugh with the scoffers, not yet betray the innocent;
But, if thou nourish in thy heart the reveries of injury or passion,
And travel in mental heat the mazy labyrinths of guilt,
And then conceive it possible, and then reflect on it as done,
And use, by little and little, thyself to regard thyself a villain,
Not long will crime be absent from the voice that doth invoke him to thy heart,
And bitterly wilt thou grieve, that the buds have ripened into poison.

A spark is a molecule of matter, yet may it kindle the world:
Vast is the mighty ocean, but drops have made it vast.
Despise not thou a small thing, either for evil or for good;
For a look may work thy ruin, or a word create thy wealth:
The walking this way or that, the casual stopping or hastening,
Hath saved life, and destroyed it, hath cast down and built up fortunes.
Commit thy trifles unto God, for to him is nothing trivial;
And it is but the littleness of man that seeth no greatness in a trifle.

All things are infinite in parts, and the moral is as the material,
Neither is anything vast, but it is compacted of atoms.
Thou art wise, and shalt find comfort, if thou study thy pleasure in trifles,
For slender joys, often repeated, fall as sunshine on the heart:
Thou art wise, if thou beat off petty troubles, nor suffer their stinging to fret thee;
Thrust not thine hand among the thorns, but with a leathern glove.
Regard nothing lightly which the wisdom of Providence hath ordered;
And therefore, consider all things that happen unto thee or unto others.
The warrior that stood against a host, may be pierced unto death by a needle;
And the saint that feareth not the fire, may perish the victim of a thought:
A mote in the gunner's eye is as bad as a spike in the gun;
And the cable of a furlong is lost through an ill-wrought inch.
The streams of small pleasures fill the lake of happiness;
And the deepest wretchedness of life is continuance of petty pains.
A fool observeth nothing, and seemeth wise unto himself;
A wise man heedeth all things, and in his own eyes is a fool:
He that wondereth at nothing hath no capabilities of bliss;
But he that scrutinizeth trifles hath a store of pleasure to his hand.
If pestilence stalk through the land, ye say, This is God's doing;
Is it not also his doing when an aphis creepeth on a rose-bud?—
If an avalanche roll from its Alp, ye tremble at the will of Providence:
Is not that will concerned when the sear leaves fall from the poplar?—
A thing is great or little only to a mortal's thinking,
But abstracted from the body, all things are alike important:
The Ancient of Days noteth in his book the idle converse of a creature,
And happy and wise is the man to whose thought existeth not a trifle.

OF RECREATION

To join advantage to amusement, to gather profit with pleasure.
Is the wise man's necessary aim, when he lieth in the shade of recreation.
For he cannot fling aside his mind, nor bar up the floodgates of his wisdom ;
Yea, though he strain after folly, his mental monitor shall check him :
For knowledge and ignorance alike have laws essential to their being,—
The sage studieth amusements, and the simple laugheth in his studies.
Few, but full of understanding, are the books of the library of God,
And fitting for all seasons are the gain and the gladness they bestow :
The volume of mystery and Grace, for the hour of deep communings,
When the soul considereth intensely the startling marvel of itself:
The book of destiny and Providence, for the time of sober study,
When the mind gleaneth wisdom from the olive grove of history :
And the cheerful pages of Nature, to gladden the pleasant holiday,
When the task of duty is complete, and the heart swelleth high with satisfaction.
The soul may not safely dwell too long with the deep things of futurity ;
The mind may not always be bent back, like the Parthian, straining at the past :
And, if thou art wearied with wrestling on the broad arena of science,
Leave awhile thy friendly foe, half vanquished in the dust,
Refresh thy jaded limbs, return with vigour to the strife,—
Thou shalt easier find thyself his master, for the vacant interval of leisure.

That which may profit and amuse is gathered from the volume of creation,
For every chapter therein teemeth with the playfulness of wisdom.
The elements of all things are the same, though nature hath mixed them with a difference,

And Learning delighteth to discover the affinity of seeming opposites:
So out of great things and small draweth he the secrets of the universe,
And argueth the cycles of the stars, from a pebble flung by a child.
It is pleasant to note all plants, from the rush to the spreading cedar,
From the giant king of palms, to the lichen that staineth its stem;
To watch the workings of instinct, that grosser reason of brutes,—
The river-horse browsing in the jungle, the plover screaming on the moor,
The cayman basking on a mud-bank, and the walrus anchored to an iceberg,
The dog at his master's feet, and the milch-kine lowing in the meadow;
To trace the consummate skill that hath modelled the anatomy of insects,
Small fowls that sun their wings on the petals of wild flowers;
To learn a use in the beetle, and more than a beauty in the butterfly;
To recognize affections in a moth, and look with admiration on a spider.
It is glorious to gaze upon the firmament, and see from far the mansions of the blest,
Each distant shining world, a kingdom for one of the redeemed;
To read the antique history of earth, stamped upon those medals in the rocks
Which Design hath rescued from decay, to tell of the green infancy of time;
To gather from the unconsidered shingle mottled starlike agates,
Full of unstoried flowers in the bubbling bloom-chalcedony;
Or gay and curious shells, fretted with microscopic carving,
Corallines, and fresh seaweeds, spreading forth their delicate branches.
It is an admirable lore, to learn the cause in the change,
To study the chemistry of Nature, her grand but simple secrets,
To search out all her wonders, to track the resources of her skill,
To note her kind compensations, her unobtrusive excellence.
In all it is wise happiness to see the well-ordained laws of Jehovah,

The harmony that filleth all his mind, the justice that tempereth
  his bounty,
The wonderful all-prevalent analogy that **testifieth one** Creator,
The broad arrow of the Great King, carved on all the stores of his
  arsenal.
But beware, O worshipper of God, thou forget **not him in his
  dealings,**
Though the **bright emanations of his power** hide him **in created
  glory**;
For if, **on the sea of knowledge,** thou regardest not the pole-star of
  religion,
Thy bark will miss her port, and run upon the sandbar of folly:
And if, enamoured of the means, thou considerest not the scope to
  which they tend,
Wherein art thou wiser than the child, **that is pleased with toys
  and** baubles?
Verily, a trifling scholar, thou heedest but the letter of instruction:
For, as motive is spirit unto action, as memory endeareth place,
As the sun doth fertilize the earth, as affection quickeneth the
  heart,
So is **the remembrance of God in** the varied wonders of creation.

Man hath **found out inventions,** to cheat him of the weariness of
  life,
To help him to forget realities, and hide the misery of guilt.
For love of praise, and hope of gain, for passion and delusive hap-
  piness,
He joineth **the circle of folly, and heapeth on the fire of excite-
  ment;**
Oftentimes sadly out of heart at the tiresome insipidity of pleasure,
Oftentimes labouring in vain, convinced of the palpable deceit:
Yet a man speaketh to his brother, in the voice of glad congratu-
  lation,
And thinketh **others** happy, though he himself be wretched:
And hand **joineth** hand to help in the **toil of amusement,**
While the secret aching heart is vacant **of** all but disappointment.
The cheapest pleasures are the best; **and** nothing is more costly
  than sin;
Yet we mortgage futurity, counting it but little **loss:**
Neither can a man delight in that which breedeth sorrow,
Yet do we hunt for joy even in the fires that consume it.

Whoso would find gladness may meet her in the hovel of poverty,
Where benevolence hath scattered around the gleanings of the horn of plenty;
Whoso would sun himself in peace, may be seen of her in deeds of mercy,
When the pale lean cheek of the destitute is wet with grateful tears.
If the mind is wearied by study, or the body worn with sickness,
It is well to lie fallow for a while, in the vacancy of sheer amusement;
But when thou prosperest in health, and thine intellect can soar untired,
To seek uninstructive pleasure is to slumber on the couch of indolence.

THE TRAIN OF RELIGION.

Stay awhile, thou blessed band, be entreated, daughters of heaven!
While the chance-met scholar of Wisdom learneth your sacred names:
He is resting a little from his toil, yet a little on the borders of earth,
And fain would he have you his friends, to bid him glad welcome hereafter.
Who among the glorious art thou, that walkest a Goddess and a Queen,
Thy crown of living stars, and a golden cross thy sceptre?
Who among flowers of loveliness is she, thy seeming herald,
Yet she boasteth not thee nor herself, and her garments are plain in their neatness?
Wherefore is there one among the train, whose eyes are red with weeping,
Yet is her open forehead beaming with the sun of ecstasy?
And who is that blood-stained warrior, with glory sitting on his crest?
And who that solemn sage, calm in majestic dignity?
Also, in the lengthening troop see I some clad in robes of triumph,
Whose fair and sunny faces I have known and loved on earth:
Welcome, ye glorified Loves, Graces, and Sciences, and Muses,
That, like sisters of charity, tended in this world's hospital;

Welcome, for verily I knew, ye could not but be children of the
 light,
Though earth hath soiled your robes, and robbed you of half your
 glory;
Welcome, chiefly welcome, for I find I have friends in heaven,
And some I might scarce have looked for, as thou, light-hearted
 Mirth;
Thou also, star-robed Urania; and thou, with the curious glass,
That rejoicedst in tracking wisdom where the eye was too dull to
 note it:
And art thou too among the blessed, mild much-injured Poetry?
Who quickenest with light and beauty the leaden face of matter,
Who not unheard, though silent, fillest earth's gardens with
 music,
And not unseen, though a spirit, dost look down upon us from the
 stars,—
That hast been to me for oil and for wine, to cheer and uphold
 my soul,
When wearied, battling with the surge, the stunning surge of life:
Of thee, for well have I loved thee, of thee may I ask in hope,
Who among the glorious is she, that walketh a Goddess and a
 Queen?
And who that fair-haired herald, and who that weeping saint?
And who that mighty warrior, and who that solemn sage?

Son, happy art thou that Wisdom hath led thee hitherward:
For otherwise never hadst thou known the joy-giving name of our
 Queen.
Behold her, the life of men, the anchor of their shipwrecked
 hopes:
Behold her, the shepherdess of souls, who bringeth back the
 wanderers to God.
And for that modest herald, she is named on earth Humility:
And hast thou not known, my son, the tearful face of Repentance?
Faith is yon time-scarred hero, walking in the shade of his
 laurels:
And Reason, the serious sage, who followeth the footsteps of
 Faith:
And we, all we, are but handmaids, ministers of minor bliss,
Who rejoice to be counted servants in the train of a Queen so
 glorious:

But for her name, son of man, it is strange to the language of
 heaven,
For those who have never fallen need not and may not learn it :
Ligeance we swear to our God, and ligeance well have we kept ;
It is only the band of the redeemed who can tell thee the fulness
 of that name :
Yet will I **comfort** thee, my son, for the love wherewith thou hast
 loved me,
And thou shalt touch for thyself the golden sceptre of Religion.

So that blessed train passed by me ; but the vision was sealed
 upon my soul ;
And its memory is shrined in fragrance, for the promise of the
 Spirit was true :
I learn from the silent poem of all creation round me,
How beautiful their feet, who **follow in that train.**

OF A TRINITY.

Despise not, shrewd reckoner, the God of a good man's worship,
Neither let thy calculating folly gainsay the unity of three :
Nor scorn another's creed, although he **cannot** solve thy doubts ;
Reason is the follower of faith, where he may not be precursor :
It is written, and so we believe, waiting not for outward proof,
Inasmuch as mysteries inscrutable are the clear prerogatives of
 Godhead.
Reason hath nothing positive, **faith hath nothing doubtful ;**
And the height of unbelieving wisdom is to question all things.
When there is marvel in a doctrine, faith **is** joyful and adoreth ;
But when all is clear, what place is left for faith ?
Tell me the sum of thy knowledge,—is it yet assured of anything?
Despise not what is wonderful, when all things are wonderful
 around thee.
From the multitude of like effects, thou sayest, behold a law :
And the matter thou art baffled in unmaking is to thy mind an
 element :
Then look abroad, I pray thee, for analogy holdeth everywhere,
And the Maker hath stamped his name on every creature of his
 hand :

I know not of a matter or a spirit, that is not three in one,
And truly should account it for a marvel, a coin without the image of its Cæsar.

Man talketh of himself as ignorant, but judgeth by himself as wise:
His own guess counteth he truth, but the notions of another are his scorn.
But bear thou yet with a brother, whose thought may be less subtle than thine own,
And suffer the passing speculation suggested by analogies to faith.
Like begetteth like, and the great sea of Existence
In each of its uncounted waves holdeth up a mirror to its Maker:
Like begetteth like, and the spreading tree of being
With each of its trefoil leaves pointeth at the trinity of God.
Let him whose eyes have been unfilmed, read this homily in all things,
And thou, of duller sight, despise not him that readeth:
There be three grand principles; life, generation, and obedience;
Shadowing in every creature, the Spirit, and the Father, and the Son:
There be three grand unities, variously mixed in trinities,
Three catholic divisors of the million sums of matter:
Yea, though science hath not seen it, climbing the ladder of experiment,
Let faith, in the presence of her God, promulgate the mighty truth;
Of three sole elements all nature's works consist:
The pine, and the rock to which it clingeth, and the eagle sailing around it:
The lion, and the northern whale, and the deeps wherein he sporteth;
The lizard sleeping in the sun; the lightning flashing from a cloud;
The rose, and the ruby, and the pearl; each one is made of three;
And the three be the like ingredients, mingled in diverse measures.
Thyself hast within thyself body, and life, and mind:
Matter, and breath, and instinct, unite in all beasts of the field;
Substance, coherence, and weight, fashion the fabrics of the earth;
The will, the doing, and the deed, combine to frame a fact:
The stem, the leaf, and the flower; beginning, middle, and end;

Cause, circumstance, consequent: and every three is one:
Yea, the very breath of man's life consisteth of a trinity of vapours,
And the noonday light is a compound, the triune shadow of Jehovah.

Shall all things else be in mystery, and God alone be understood?
Shall finite fathom infinity, though it sound not the shallows of creation?
Shall a man comprehend his Maker, being yet a riddle to himself?
Or time teach the lesson that eternity cannot master?
If God be nothing more than one, a child can compass the thought;
But seraphs fail to unravel the wondrous unity of three.
One verily He is, for there can be but one who is all mighty;
Yet the oracles of nature and religion proclaim Him three in one.
And where were the value to thy soul, O miserable denizen of earth,
Of the idle pageant of the cross, where hung no sacrifice for thee?
Where the worth to thine impotent heart, of that stirred Bethesda,
All numbed and palsied as it is, by the scorpion stings of sin?
No, thy trinity of nature, enchained by treble death,
Helplessly craveth of its God, Himself for three salvations:
The soul to be reconciled in love, the mind to be glorified in light,
While this poor dying body leapeth into life.
And if indeed for us all the costly ransom hath been paid,
Bethink thee, could less than Deity have owned so vast a treasure?
Could a man contend with God, and stand against the bosses of His buckler,
Rendering the balance for guilt, atonement to the uttermost?
Thou art subtle to thine own thinking, but wisdom judgeth thee a fool,
Resolving thou wilt not bow the knee to a Being thou canst not comprehend:
The mind that could compass perfection were itself perfection's equal;
And reason refuseth its homage to a God who can be fully understood.

Thou that despisest mystery, yet canst expound nothing,
Wherefore rejectest thou the fact that solveth the enigma of all things?

Wherefore veilest thou thine eyes, lest the light of revelation sun them,
And puttest aside the key that would open the casket of truth?
The mind and the nature of God are shadowed in all his works,
And none could have guessed of his essence, had He not uttered it Himself.
Therefore, thou child of folly, that scornest the record of his wisdom,
Learn from the consistencies of nature the needful miracle of Godhead:
Yea, let the heathen be thy teacher, who adoreth many gods,
For there is no wide-spread error that hath not truth for its beginning.
Be content; thine eye cannot see all the sides of a cube at one view,
Nor thy mind in the self-same moment follow two ideas:
There are now many marvels in thy creed, believing what thou seest,
Then let not the conceit of intellect hinder thee from worshipping mystery.

OF THINKING.

REFLECTION is a flower of the mind, giving out wholesome fragrance,
But reverie is the same flower, when rank and running to seed.
Better to read little with thought, than much with levity and quickness;
For mind is not as merchandize, which decreaseth in the using,
But liker to the passions of man, which rejoice and expand in exertion:
Yet live not wholly on thine own ideas, lest they lead thee astray;
For in spirit, as in substance, thou art a social creature;
And if thou leanest on thyself, thou rejectest the guidance of thy betters,
Yea, thou contemnest all men,—Am I not wiser than they?—
Foolish vanity hath blinded thee, and warped thy weak judgment;
For, though new ideas flow from new springs, and enrich the treasury of knowledge,
Yet listen often, ere thou think much; and look around thee ere thou judgest.

Memory, the daughter of **Attention**, is the teeming mother of
 Wisdom,
And safer is he that storeth knowledge, than he that would make
 it for himself.

Imagination is not thought, neither is fancy reflection :
Thought paceth like a hoary sage, but imagination hath wings as
 an eagle ;
Reflection sternly considereth, nor is sparing to condemn evil,
But fancy lightly laugheth, in the sun-clad gardens of amusement.
For the shy game of the fowler the quickest shot is the surest :
But with slow care and measured aim the gunner pointeth his
 cannon :
So for all less occasions, the surface-thought is best,
But to be master of the great take thou heavier metal.
It is a good thing, and a wholesome, to search out bosom sins,
But to be the hero of selfish imaginings, is the subtle poison of
 pride :
At night, in the stillness of thy chamber, guard and curb thy
 thoughts,
And in recounting the doings of the day, beware that thou do it
 with prayer,
Or thinking will be an idle pleasure, and retrospect yield no
 fruit.
Steer the bark of thy mind from the syren isle of reverie,
And let a watchful spirit mingle with the glance of recollection :
Also, in examining thine heart, in sounding the fountain of thine
 actions,
Be more careful of the evil than of the good ; and humble thyself
 in thy sin.

The root of all wholesome thought is knowledge of thyself,
For thus only canst thou learn the character of God toward thee.
He made thee, and thou art ; he redeemed thee, and thou wilt be
Thou art evil, yet he loveth thee : thou sinnest, yet he pardoneth
 thee.
Though thou canst not perceive him, yet is he in all his works,
Infinite in grand outline, infinite in minute perfection :
Nature is the chart of God, mapping out all his attributes ;
Art is the shadow of his wisdom, and copieth his resources.
Thou knowest the laws of matter to be emanations of his will,

And thy best reason for aught is this,—thou, **Lord**, wouldst have
    it so.
Yea, what is any law but an absolute **decree of God**?
Or the properties of matter and mind, but the arbitrary fiats of
    Jehovah?
He made and ordained necessity; he forged the **chain** of reason;
And holdeth in **his** own right hand the first of the golden links.
A fool regardeth **mind as** the spiritual essence of matter,
And not **rather matter as** the gross accident of mind.
Can finite govern infinite, or a part exceed the whole,
Or the wisdom of God sit down at the feet of innate necessity?
Necessity is a creature of his hand: for he can never change;
And chance hath no existence where everything is needful.

Canst **thou measure** Omnipotence, canst thou conceive **Ubiquity,**
Which guideth the meanest reptile, and quickeneth the brightest
    seraph,
Which **steereth the particle of dust,** and commandeth the path of
    the comet?
To **Him all things are** equal, for all things are necessary:
The **smith was** weary at his forge, and welded the metal carelessly,
And the anchor breaketh in its bed; and the vessel foundereth
    with her crew:
A word of anger **is muttered,** engendering the midnight **murder;**
The sun bursteth from **a** cloud, and maddeneth the toiling hus-
    bandman:
Shall these things **be, and God not know it?**
Shall he know, **and not be in them?** shall he see, and not be
    among them?
And how can they be otherwise than as he knoweth?
Truly, the Lord is in all things; verily, he worketh in all.
Think thus, and thy thoughts are firm, ascribing each circumstance
    to Him;
Yet know surely, and believe **the** truth, that God willeth not evil;
For adversities are blessings in disguise, and wickedness the Lord
    abhorreth:
That he is in all things is an axiom, and that he is righteous in all:
Ascribe holiness to Him, while thou musest on the mystery of sin,
For infinite can grasp that, which finite cannot compass.

In works of art, think justly: what praise canst thou render unto man?

For he made not his own mind, nor is he the source of contrivance.
If a cunning workman make an engine that fashioneth curious works,
Which hath the praise, the machine or its maker,—the engine, or he that framed it?
And could he frame it so subtly as to give it a will and freedom,
Endow it with complicated powers, and a glorious living soul,
Who, while he admireth the wondrous understanding creature,
Will not pay deeper homage to the Maker of master minds?
Otherwise, thou art senseless as the pagan, that adoreth his own handy-work;
Yea, while thou boastest of thy wisdom, thy mind is as the mind of the savage,
For he boweth down to his idols, and thou art a worshipper of self,
Giving to the reasoning machine the credit due to its creator.

The key-stone of thy mind, to give thy thoughts solidity,
To bind them as in an arch, to fix them as the world in its sphere,
Is to learn from the book of the Lord, to drink from the well of his wisdom.
Who can condense the sun, or analyse the fulness of the Bible,
So that its ideas be gathered, and the harvest of its wisdom be brought in?
That book is easy to the man who setteth his heart to understand it,
But to the careless and profane it shall seem the foolishness of God;
And it is a delicate test to prove thy moral state;
To the humble disciple it is bread, but a stone to the proud and unbelieving:
A scorner shall find nothing but the husks, wherewith to feed his hunger,
But for the soul of the simple, it is plenty of full-ripe wheat.
The Scripture abideth the same, in the sober majesty of truth;
And the differing aspects of its teaching proceed from diversity in minds.
He that would learn to think may gain that knowledge there;
For the living word, as an angel, standeth at the gate of wisdom,
And publisheth, This is the way, walk ye surely in it.
Religion taketh by the hand the humble pupil of repentance,

And teacheth him lessons of mystery, solving the questions of
 doubt;
She maketh man worthy of himself, of his high prerogative of
 reason,
Threadeth all the labyrinths of thought, and leadeth him to his
 God.

Come hither, child of meditation, upon whose high fair forehead
Glittereth the star of mind in its unearthly lustre:
Hast thou nought to tell us of thine airy joys,—
When, borne on sinewy pinions, strong as the western condor,
The soul, after soaring for a while round the cloud-capped Andes
 of reflection,
Glad in its conscious immortality, leaveth a world behind,
To dare at one bold flight the broad Atlantic to another?
Hast thou no secret pangs to whisper common men,
No dread of thine own energies, still active day and night,
Lest too ecstatic heat sublime thyself away,
Or vivid horrors, sharp and clear, madden thy tense fibres?
In half-shaped visions of sleep hast thou not feared thy flittings.
Lest reason, like a raking hawk, return not to thy call:
Nor waked to work-day life with throbbing head and heart,
Nor welcomed early dawn to save thee from unrest?
For the wearied spirit lieth as a fainting maiden,
Captive and borne away on the warrior's foam-covered steed,
And sinketh down wounded, as a gladiator on the sand,
While the keen faulchion of Intellect is cutting through the scab-
 bard of the brain.
Imagination, like a shadowy giant looming on the twilight of the
 Hartz,
Shall overwhelm judgment with affright, and scare him from his
 throne:
In a dream thou mayest be mad, and feel the fire within thee;
In a dream thou mayest travel out of self, and see thee with the
 eyes of another;
Or sleep in thine own corpse: or wake as in many bodies;
Or swell, as expanded to infinity; or shrink, as imprisoned to a
 point;
Or among moss-grown ruins mayest wander with the sullen dis-
 embodied,
And gaze upon their glassy eyes until thy heart blood freeze.

Alone must thou stand, O man! alone at the bar of judgment;
Alone must thou bear thy sentence, alone must thou answer for thy deeds:
Therefore it is well thou retirest often to secresy and solitude,
To feel that thou art accountable separately from thy fellows:
For a crowd hideth truth from the eyes, society drowneth thought,
And being but one among many, stifleth the chidings of conscience.
Solitude bringeth woe to the wicked, for his crimes are told out in his ear;
But addeth peace to the good, for the mercies of his God are numbered.
Thou mayest know if it be well with a man,—loveth he gaiety or solitude?
For the troubled river rusheth to the sea, but the calm lake slumbereth among the mountains.
How dear to the mind of the sage are the thoughts that are bred in loneliness;
For there is as it were music at his heart, and he talketh within him as with friends:
But guilt maddeneth the brain, and terror glareth in the eye,
Where, in his solitary cell, the malefactor wrestleth with remorse.
Give me but a lodge in the wilderness, drop me on an island in the desert,
And thought shall yield me happiness, though I may not increase it by imparting:
For the soul never slumbereth, but is as the eye of the Eternal,
And mind, the breath of God, knoweth not ideal vacuity.
At night, after weariness and watching, the body sinketh into sleep,
But the mental eye is awake, and thou reasonest in thy dreams:
In a dream thou mayest live a lifetime, and all be forgotten in the morning;
Even such is life, and so soon perisheth its memory.

OF SPEAKING.

SPEECH is the golden harvest that followeth the flowering of thought;
Yet oftentimes runneth it to husk, and the grains be withered and scanty:

Speech is reason's brother, and a kingly prerogative of man,
That likeneth him to his Maker, who spake, and it was done:
Spirit may mingle with spirit, but sense requireth a symbol;
And speech is the body of a thought, without which it were not seen.
When thou walkest, musing with thyself, in the green aisles of the forest,
Utter thy thinkings aloud, that they take a shape and being;
For he that pondereth in silence crowdeth the store-house of his mind,
And though he hath heaped great riches, yet he is hindered in the using.
A man that speaketh too little, and thinketh much and deeply,
Corrodeth his own heart-strings, and keepeth back good from his fellows:
A man that speaketh too much, and museth but little and lightly,
Wasteth his mind in words, and is counted a fool among men:
But thou, when thou hast thought, weave charily the web of meditation,
And clothe the ideal spirit in the suitable garments of speech.

Uttered out of time, or concealed in its season, good savoureth of evil;
To be secret looketh like guilt, to speak out may breed contention:
Often have I known the honest heart, flaming with indignant virtue,
Provoke unneeded war by its rash ambassador the tongue:
Often have I seen the charitable man go so slily on his mission,
That those who met him in the twilight, took him for a skulking thief:
I have heard the zealous youth telling out his holy secrets
Before a swinish throng, who mocked him as he spake;
And I considered, his openness was hardening them that mocked,
Whereas a judicious keeping back might have won their sympathy:
I have judged rashly and harshly the hand, liberal in the dark,
Because in the broad daylight, it hath holden it a virtue to be close;
And the silent tongue have I condemned, because reserve hath chained it,
That it hid, yea from a brother, the kindness it had done by comforting.

No need to sound a trumpet, but less to hush a footfall:
Do thou thy good openly, not as though the doing were a crime.
Secresy goeth cowled, and Honesty demandeth wherefore?
For he judgeth,—judgeth he not well?—that nothing need be hid
　　but guilt.
Why should thy good be evil spoken of, through thine unrighteous
　　silence?
If thou art challenged, speak, and prove the good thou doest.
The free example of benevolence, unobtruded, yet unhidden,
Sounded in the ears of sloth, Go, and do thou likewise:
And I wot the hypocrite's sin to be of darker dye,
Because the good man, fearing, thereby hideth his light:
But neither God nor man hath bid thee cloak thy good,
When a seasonable word would set thee in thy sphere, that all
　　might see thy brightness.
Ascribe the honour to thy Lord, but be thou jealous of that
　　honour,
Nor think it light and worthless, because thou mayest not wear it
　　for thyself:
Remember, thy grand prerogative is free unshackled utterance,
And suffer not the flood-gates of secresy to lock the full river of
　　thy speech.

Come, I will show thee an affliction, unnumbered among this
　　world's sorrows,
Yet real and wearisome and constant, embittering the cup of life.
There be, who can think within themselves, and the fire burneth
　　at their heart,
And eloquence waiteth at their lips, yet they speak not with their
　　tongue:
There be, whom zeal quickeneth, or slander stirreth to reply,
Or need constraineth to ask, or pity sendeth as her messengers;
But nervous dread and sensitive shame freeze the current of their
　　speech;
The mouth is sealed as with lead, a cold weight presseth on the
　　heart,
The mocking promise of power is once more broken in perform-
　　ance,
And they stand impotent of words, travailing with unborn
　　thoughts:
Courage is cowed at the portal; wisdom is widowed of utterance;

He that went to comfort is pitied; he that should rebuke, is
    silent:
And fools who might listen and learn, stand by to look and
    laugh;
While friends, with kinder eyes, wound deeper by compassion:
And thought, finding not a vent, smouldereth, gnawing at the
    heart,
And the man sinketh in his sphere, for lack of empty sounds.
There be many cares and sorrows thou hast not yet considered,
And well may thy soul rejoice in the fair privilege of speech;
For at every turn to want a word,—thou canst not guess that
    want;
It is as lack of breath or bread: life hath no grief more galling.

Come, I will tell thee of a joy, which the parasites of pleasure
    have not known,
Though earth and air and sea have gorged all the appetites of
    sense.
Behold, what fire is in his eye, what fervour on his cheek!
That glorious burst of winged words! how bound they from his
    tongue!
The full expression of the mighty thought, the strong triumphant
    argument,
The rush of native eloquence, resistless as Niagara,
The keen demand, the clear reply, the fine poetic image,
The nice analogy, the clenching fact, the metaphor bold and free,
The grasp of concentrated intellect wielding the omnipotence of
    truth,
The grandeur of his speech in his majesty of mind!
Champion of the right,—patriot, or priest, or pleader of the in-
    nocent cause,
Upon whose lips the mystic bee hath dropped the honey of per-
    suasion,
Whose heart and tongue have been touched, as of old by the live
    coal from the altar,
How wide the spreading of thy peace, how deep the draught of
    thy pleasures!
To hold the multitude as one, breathing in measured cadence,
A thousand men with flashing eyes, waiting upon thy will;
A thousand hearts kindled by thee with consecrated fire,
Ten flaming spiritual hecatombs offered on the mount of God:

And now a pause, a thrilling pause,—they live but in thy words,—
Thou hast broken the bounds of self, as the Nile at its rising,
Thou art expanded into them, one faith, one hope, one spirit,
They breathe but in thy breath, their minds are passive unto thine,
Thou turnest the key of their love, bending their affections to thy purpose,
And all, in sympathy with thee, tremble with tumultuous emotions:
Verily, O man, with truth for thy theme, eloquence shall throne thee with archangels.

OF READING.

ONE drachma for a good book, and a thousand talents for a true friend ;—
So standeth the market, where scarce is ever costly:
Yea, were the diamonds of Golconda common as shingles on the shore,
A ripe apple would ransom kings before a shining stone:
And so, were a wholesome book as rare as an honest friend,
To choose the book be mine: the friend let another take.
For altered looks and jealousies and fears have none entrance there:
The silent volume listeneth well, and speaketh when thou listest:
It praiseth thy good without envy, it chideth thine evil without malice,
It is to thee thy waiting slave, and thine unbending teacher.
Need to humour no caprice, need to bear with no infirmity;
Thy sin, thy slander, or neglect, chilleth not, quencheth not, its love:
Unalterably speaketh it the truth, warped nor by error nor interest;
For a good book is the best of friends, the same to-day and for ever.

To draw thee out of self, thy petty plans and cautions,
To teach thee what thou lackest, to tell thee how largely thou art blest,
To lure thy thought from sorrow, to feed thy famished mind,
To graft another's wisdom on thee, pruning thine own folly.

Choose discreetly, and well digest, the volume most suited to thy
case,
Touching not religion with levity, nor deep things when thou art
wearied,
Thy mind is freshened by morning air, grapple with science and
philosophy;
Noon hath unnerved thy thoughts, dream for a while on fictions:
Grey evening sobereth thy spirit, walk thou then with worship-
pers:
But reason shall dig deepest in the night, and fancy fly most free.

O books, ye monuments of mind, concrete wisdom of the wisest;
Sweet solaces of daily life; proofs and results of immortality;
Trees yielding all fruits, whose leaves are for the healing of the
nations;
Groves of knowledge, where all may eat, nor fear a flaming
sword:
Gentle comrades, kind advisers; friends, comforts, treasures;
Helps, governments, diversities of tongues; who can weigh your
worth?—
To walk no longer with the just; to be driven from the porch of
science;
To bid long adieu to those intimate ones, poets, philosophers, and
teachers;
To see no record of the sympathies which bind thee in communion
with the good;
To be thrust from the feet of Him who spake as never man spake;
To have no avenue to heaven but the dim aisle of superstition;
To live as an Esquimaux, in lethargy; to die as the Mohawk, in
ignorance:
O what were life, but a blank? what were death, but a terror?
What were man, but a burden to himself? what were mind, but
misery?
Yea, let another Omar burn the full library of knowledge,
And the broad world may perish in the flames, offered on the
ashes of its wisdom!

OF WRITING.

The pen of a ready writer, whereunto shall it be likened?
Ask of the scholar, he shall know,—to the chains that bind a Proteus:
Ask of the poet, he shall say,—to the sun, the lamp of heaven:
Ask of thy neighbour, he can answer,—to the friend that telleth my thought:
The merchant considereth it well, as a ship freighted with wares;
The divine holdeth it a miracle, giving utterance to the dumb,
It fixeth, expoundeth, and disseminateth sentiment;
Chaining up a thought, clearing it of mystery, and sending it bright into the world.
To think rightly is of knowledge; to speak fluently, is of nature;
To read with profit, is of care; but to write aptly, is of practice.
No talent among men hath more scholars, and fewer masters:
For to write is to speak beyond hearing, and none stand by to explain.
To be accurate, write; to remember, write; to know thine own mind, write;
And a written prayer is a prayer of faith: special, sure, and to be answered.
Hast thou a thought upon thy brain, catch it while thou canst;
Or other thoughts shall settle there, and this shall soon take wing:
Thine uncompounded unity of soul, which argueth and maketh it immortal,
Yieldeth up its momentary self to every single thought;
Therefore, to husband thine ideas, and give them stability and substance,
Write often for thy secret eye; so shalt thou grow wiser.
The commonest mind is full of thoughts; some worthy of the rarest:
And could it see them fairly writ, would wonder at its wealth.

O precious compensation to the dumb, to write his wants and wishes;
O dear amends to the stammering tongue, to pen his burning thoughts!
To be of the college of Eloquence, through these silent symbols;
To pour out all the flowing mind without the toil of speech;
To show the babbling world how it might discourse more sweetly;

And labour to build up by penury that which extravagance threw
down :
Even so, with most men, do riches earn themselves a double
curse ;
They are ill-got by tight dealing : they are ill-spent by loose
squandering.
Give me enough, saith Wisdom ;—for he feareth to ask for more ;
And that by the sweat of my brow, addeth stout-hearted Independence :
Give me enough, and not less, for want is leagued with the
tempter ;
Poverty shall make a man desperate, and hurry him ruthless into
crime :
Give me enough, and not more, saving for the children of distress ;
Wealth ofttimes killeth, where want but hindereth the budding :
There is green glad summer near the pole, though brief and after
long winter,
But the burnt breasts of the torrid zone yield never kindly nourishment.
Wouldst thou be poor, scatter to the rich,—and reap the tares of
ingratitude ;
Wouldst thou be rich, give unto the poor ;—thou shalt have thine
own with usury :
For the secret hand of Providence prospereth the charitable all
ways,
Good luck shall he have in his pursuits, and his heart shall be glad
within him ;
Yet perchance he never shall perceive, that, even as to earthly
gains,
The cause of his weal, as of his joy, hath been small givings to the
poor.

In the plain of Benares is there found a root that fathereth a forest,
Where round the parent banian-tree drop its living scions ;
Thirstily they strain to the earth, like stalactites in a grotto,
And strike broad roots, and branch again, lengthening their cool
arcades :
And the dervish madly danceth there, and the faquir is torturing
his flesh,
And the calm brahmin worshippeth the sleek and pampered bull ;
At the base lean jackalls coil, while from above depending

With dull malignant stare watcheth the branch-like boa.
Even so, in man's heart is a sin that is the root of all evil;
Whose fibres strangle the affections, whose branches overgrow the mind:
And oftenest beneath its shadow thou shalt meet distorted piety,—
The clenched and rigid fist, with the eyes upturned to heaven,
Fanatic zeal with miserly severity, a mixture of gain with godliness,
And him, against whom passion hath no power, kneeling to a golden calf·
The hungry hounds of extortion are there, the bond, and the mortgage, and the writ,
While the appetite for gold, unslumbering, watcheth to glut its maw:—
And the heart, so tenanted and shaded, is cold to all things else;
It seeth not the sunshine of heaven, nor is warmed by the light of charity.

For covetousness disbelieveth God, and laugheth at the rights of men;
Spurring unto theft and lying, and tempting to the poison and the knife;
It sundereth the bonds of love, and quickeneth the flames of hate;
A curse that shall wither the brain, and case the heart with iron.
Content is the true riches, for without it there is no satisfying,
But a ravenous all-devouring hunger gnaweth the vitals of the soul.
The wise man knoweth where to stop, as he runneth in the race of fortune,
For experience of old hath taught him, that happiness lingereth midway;
And many in hot pursuit have hasted to the goal of wealth,
But have lost, as they ran, those apples of gold,—the mind and the power to enjoy it.

There is no greater evil among men than a testament framed with injustice:
Where caprice hath guided the boon, or dishonesty refused what was due.
Generous is the robber on the highway, in the open daring of his guilt,

To the secret coward, whose malice liveth and harmeth after him;
Who smoothly sank into the tomb, with the smile of fraud upon his face,
And the last black deed of his existence was injury without redress:
For deaf is the ear of the dead, and can hear no palliating reasons;
The smiter is not among the living, and Right pleadeth but in vain.
Yet shall the curse of the oppressed be as blight upon the grave of the unjust;
Yea, bitterly shall that hand-writing testify against him at the judgment.
I saw the humble relation that tended the peevishness of wealth,
And ministered, with kind hand, to the wailings of disease and discontent:
I noted how watchfulness and care were feeding on the marrow of her youth,
How heavy was the yoke of dependence, loaded by petty tyranny;
Yet I heard the frequent suggestion,—It can be but a little longer,
Patience and mute submission shall one day reap a rich reward.
So, tacitly enduring much, waited that humble friend,
Putting off the lover of her youth until the dawn of wealth:
And it came, that day of release, and the freed heart could not sorrow,
For now were the years of promise to yield their golden harvest:
Hope, so long deferred, sickly sparkled in her eye,
The miserable past was forgotten, as she looked for the happier future,
And she checked, as unworthy and ungrateful, the dark suspicious thought
That perchance her right had been the safer, if not left alone with honour:
But, alas, the sad knowledge soon came, that her stern taskmaster's will
Hath rewarded her toil with a jibe, her patience with utter destitution!—
Shall not the scourge of justice lash that cruel coward,
Who mingled the gall of ingratitude with the bitterness of disappointment?
Shall not the hate of men, and vengeance, fiercely pursuing,
Hunt down the wretched being that sinneth in his grave?
He fancied his idol self safe from the wrath of his fellows,

But Hades rose as he came in, to point at him the finger of scorn;
And again must he meet that orphan-maid to answer her face to face,
And her wrongs shall cling around his neck, to hinder him from
 rising with the just:
For his last most solemn act hath linked his name with liar,
And the crime of Ananias is branded on his brow!

A good man commendeth his cause to the one great Patron of
 innocence,
Convinced of justice at the last, and sure of good meanwhile.
He knoweth he hath a Guardian, wise and kind and strong,
And can thank Him for giving, or refusing, the trust or the curse
 of riches:
His confidence standeth as a rock; he dreadeth not malice nor
 caprice,
Nor the whisperings of artful men, nor envious secret influence;
He scorneth servile compromise, and the pliant mouthings of
 deceit;
He maketh not a show of love where he cannot concede esteem;
He regardeth ill-got wealth, as the root most fruitful of wretched-
 ness,
So he walketh in straight integrity, leaning on God and his right.

No gain, but by its price: labour, for the poor man's meal,
Ofttimes heart-sickening toil, to win him a morsel for his hunger:
Labour, for the chapman at his trade, a dull unvaried round,
Year after year, unto death; yea, what a weariness is it!
Labour, for the pale-faced scribe, drudging at his hated desk,
Who bartereth for needful pittance the untold gold of health;
Labour, with fear, for the merchant, whose hopes are ventured on
 the sea;
Labour, with care, for the man of law, responsible in his gains;
Labour, with envy and annoyance, where strangers will thee
 wealth;
Labour, with indolence and gloom, where wealth falleth from a
 father;
Labour unto all, whether aching thews, or aching head, or
 spirit,—
The curse on the sons of men, in all their states, is labour.
Nevertheless, to the diligent, labour bringeth blessing:
The thought of duty sweeteneth toil, and travail is as pleasure;

And time spent in doing hath a comfort that is not for the idle,
The hardship is transmuted into joy by the dear alchemy of Mercy.
Labour is good for a man, bracing up his energies to conquest,
And without it life is dull, the man perceiving himself useless:
For wearily the body groaneth, like a door on rusty hinges,
And the grasp of the mind is weakened, as the talons of a caged vulture.
Wealth hath never given happiness, but often hastened misery:
Enough hath never caused misery, but often quickened happiness:
Enough is less than thy thought, O pampered creature of society,
And he that hath more than enough, is a thief of the rights of his brother.

OF INVENTION.

MAN is proud of his mind, boasting that it giveth him divinity,
Yet with all its powers can it originate nothing;
For the great God into all his works hath largely poured out Himself,
Saving one special property, the grand prerogative,—Creation.
To improve and expand is ours, as well as to limit and defeat;
But to create a thought or a thing is hopeless and impossible.
Can a man make matter?—and yet this would-be god
Thinketh to make mind, and form original idea:
The potter must have his clay, and the mason his quarry,
And mind must drain ideas from everything around it.
Doth the soil generate herbs, or the torrid air breed flies,
Or the water frame its monads, or the mist its swarming blight?—
Mediately, through thousand generations, having seed within themselves,
All things, rare or gross, own one common Father.
Truly spake Wisdom, There is nothing new under the sun:
We only arrange and combine the ancient elements of all things.
Invention is activity of mind, as fire is air in motion;
A sharpening of the spiritual sight, to discern hidden aptitudes:
From the basket and acanthus, is modelled the graceful capital;
The shadowed profile on the wall helpeth the limner to his likeness;
The footmarks, stamped in clay, lead on the thoughts to printing;

The strange skin garments cast upon the shore suggest another
    hemisphere:
A falling apple taught the sage pervading gravitation;
The Huron is certain of his prey, from tracks upon the grass;
And shrewdness, guessing out the hint, followeth on the trail:
But the hint must be given, the trail must be there, or the keenest
    sight is as blindness.

Behold the barren reef, which an earthquake hath just left dry;
It hath no beauty to boast of, no harvest of fair fruits:
But soon the lichen fixeth there, and, dying, diggeth its own grave,
And softening suns and splitting frosts crumble the reluctant
    surface;
And cormorants roost there, and the snail addeth its slime,
And efts, with muddy feet, bring their welcome tribute;
And the sea casteth out her dead, wrapped in a shroud of weeds;
And orderly nature arrangeth again the disunited atoms;
Anon, the cold smooth stone is warm with feathery grass,
And the light sporules of the fern are dropped by the passing
    wind,
The wood-pigeon, on swift wing, leaveth its crop-full of grain,
The squirrel's jealous care planteth the fir-cone and the filbert:
Years pass, and the sterile rock is rank with tangled herbage;
The wild-vine clingeth to the briar, and ivy runneth green among
    the corn,
Lordly beeches are studded on the down, and willows crowd
    around the rivulet,
And the tall pine and hazel-thicket shade the rambling hunter.
Shall the rock boast of its fertility? shall it lift the head in
    pride?—
Shall the mind of man be vain of the harvest of its thoughts?
The savage is that rock; and a million chances from without,
By little and little acting on the mind, heap up the hotbed of
    society;
And the soul, fed and fattened on the thoughts and things around
    it,
Groweth to perfection, full of fruit, the fruit of foreign seeds:
For we learn upon a hint, we find upon a clue,
We yield an hundred-fold; but the great sower is Analogy.
There must be an acrid sloe before a luscious peach,
A boll of rotting flax before the bridal veil,

An egg before an eagle, a thought before a thing,
A spark **struck** into tinder to light **the lamp** of knowledge,
A slight suggestive nod to guide the watching mind,
A **half-seen** hand upon the wall, pointing to the balance of Comparison.
By culture man may do all things, short of the miracle,—Creation;
Here is the limit of thy power,—here let thy pride be stayed:
The soil may be rich, and the mind may be active, but neither yield unsown;
The eye cannot make light, nor the mind make spirit:
Therefore it is wise in man to name all novelty invention;
For it is to find out things that are, **not to create** the unexisting:
It is to cling to contiguities, to be keen in catching likeness,
And with energetic elasticity to leap the gulfs of contrast.
The globe knoweth not increase, either of matter or spirit;
Atoms and thoughts are used again, mixing in varied combinations;
And though, by moulding them anew, thou makest them thine own,
Yet **have** they served thousands, and all their merit is of God.

OF RIDICULE.

SEAMS of thought for **the sage's brow,** and laughing lines for the fool's face;
For all things leave their track in the mind; and the glass of the mind is faithful.
Seest thou much mirth upon the cheek? there is then little exercise of virtue;
For he that looketh on the world, cannot be glad and good:
Seest **thou much gravity in** the eye? **be** not assured of finding wisdom;
For she hath **too** great praise, not **to get many mimics.**
There is a grave-faced folly; **and** verily, a laughter-loving wisdom;
And what, if surface-judges account it vain frivolity?
There is indeed an evil in excess, and a field may lie fallow too long;

Yet merriment is often as a froth, that mantleth on the strong
  mind:
And note thou this for a verity,—the subtlest thinker when alone,
From ease of thoughts unbent, will laugh the loudest with his
  fellows:
And well is the loveliness of wisdom mirrored in a cheerful coun-
  tenance,
Justly the deepest pools are proved by dimpling eddies;
For that, a true philosophy commandeth an innocent life,
And the unguilty spirit is lighter than a linnet's heart:
Yea, there is no cosmetic like a holy conscience;
The eye is bright with trust, the cheek bloomed over with affec-
  tion,
The brow unwrinkled by a care, and the lip triumphant in its
  gladness.

And for yon grave-faced folly, need not far to look for her;
How seriously on trifles dote those leaden eyes,
How ruefully she sigheth after chances long gone by,
How sulkily she moaneth over evils without cure!
I have known a true-born mirth, the child of innocence and
  wisdom,
I have seen a base-born gravity, mingled of ignorance and guilt:
And again, a base-born mirth, springing out of carelessness and
  folly,
And again, a true-born gravity, the product of reflection and right
  fear.
The wounded partridge hideth in a furrow, and a stricken con-
  science would be left alone;
But when its breast is healed, it runneth gladly with its fellows:
Whereas the solitary heron, standing in the sedgy fen,
Holdeth aloof from the social world, intent on wiles and death.

Need but of light philosophy to dare the world's dread laugh;
For a little mind courteth notoriety, to illustrate its puny self:
But the sneer of a man's own comrades trieth the muscles of
  courage,
And to be derided in his home is as a viper in the nest:
The laugh of a hooting world hath in it a notion of sublimity,
But the tittering private circle stingeth as a hive of wasps.
Some have commended ridicule, counting it the test of truth,

But neither wittily nor wisely; for truth must prove ridicule:
Otherwise a blunt bulrush is to pierce the proof armour of argument,
Because the stolidity of ignorance took it for a barbed shaft.
Softer is the hide of the rhinoceros, than the heart of deriding unbelief,
And truth is idler there, than the Bushman's feathered reed:
A droll conceit parrieth a thrust, that should have hit the conscience,
And the leering looks of humour tickle the childish mind;
For that the matter of a man is mingled most with folly,
Neither can he long endure the searching gaze of wisdom.
It is pleasanter to see a laughing cheek than a serious forehead,
And there liveth not one among a thousand whose idol is not pleasure.
Ridicule is a weak weapon, when levelled at a strong mind:
But common men are cowards, and dread an empty laugh.
Fear a nettle, and touch it tenderly, its poison shall burn thee to the shoulder;
But grasp it with a bold hand,—is it not a bundle of myrrh?
Betray mean terror of ridicule, thou shalt find fools enough to mock thee;
But answer thou their laughter with contempt, and the scoffers will lick thy feet.

OF COMMENDATION.

The praise of holy men is a promise of praise from their Master;
A fore-running earnest of thy welcome,—Well done, faithful servant;
A rich preludious note, that droppeth softly on thine ear,
To tell thee the chords of thy heart are in tune with the choirs of heaven.
Yet is it a dangerous hearing, for the sweetness may lull thee into slumber,
And the cordial quaffed with thirst may generate the fumes of presumption.
So seek it not for itself, but taste, and go gladly on thy way,
For the mariner slacketh not his sail, though the sandal-groves of Araby allure him;

And the fragrance of that incense would harm thee, as when, on a
　　summer evening,
The honied yellow flowers of the broom oppress thy charmed
　　sense :
And a man hath too much of praise, for he praiseth himself con-
　　tinually ;
Neither lacketh he at any time self-commendation or excuse.

Praise a fool, and slay him : for the canvas of his vanity is spread ;
His bark is shallow in the water, and a sudden gust shall sink it :
Praise a wise man, and speed him on his way ; for he carrieth the
　　ballast of humility,
And is glad when his course is cheered by the sympathy of brethren
　　ashore.
The praise of a good man is good, for he holdeth up the mirror of
　　Truth,
That virtue may see her own beauty, and delight in her own fair
　　face :
The praise of a bad man is evil, for he hideth the deformity of
　　Vice,
Casting the mantle of a queen around the limbs of a leper.
Praise is rebuke to the man whose conscience alloweth it not :
And where conscience feeleth it her due, no praise is better than a
　　little.
He that despiseth the outward appearance, despiseth the esteem
　　of his fellows ;
And he that overmuch regardeth it, shall earn only their con-
　　tempt :
The honest commendation of an equal no one can scorn, and be
　　blameless,
Yet even that fair fame no one can hunt for, and be honoured :
If it come, accept it and be thankful, and be thou humble in
　　accepting ;
If it tarry, be not thou cast down ; the bee can gather honey out
　　of rue ;
And is thine aim so low, that the breath of those around thee
Can speed thy feathered arrow, or retard its flight ?
The child shooteth at a butterfly, but the man's mark is an eagle ;
And while his fellows talk, he hath conquered in the clouds
Ally thee to truth and godliness, and use the talents in thy
　　charge ;

So shalt thou walk in peace, deserving, if not having.
With a friend, praise him when thou canst; for many a friendship hath decayed,
Like a plant in a crowded corner, for want of sunshine on its leaves:
With another, praise him not often—otherwise he shall despise thee;
But be thou frugal in commending; so will he give honour to thy judgment:
For thou that dost so zealously commend, art acknowledging thine own inferiority,
And he, thou so highly hast exalted, shall proudly look down on thy esteem.

Wilt thou that one remember a thing?—praise him in the midst of thy advice;
Never yet forgat man the word whereby he hath been praised.
Better to be censured by a thousand fools, than approved but by one man that is wise;
For the pious are slower to help right, than the profane to hinder it:
So, where the world rebuketh, there look thou for the excellent,
And be suspicious of the good, which wicked men can praise.
The captain bindeth his troop, not more by severity than kindness,
And justly, should recompense well-doing, as well as be strict with an offender:
The laurel is cheap to the giver, but precious in his sight who hath won it,
And the heart of the soldier rejoiceth in the approving glance of his chief.
Timely-given praise is even better than the merited rebuke of censure,
For the sun is more needful to the plant than the knife that cutteth out a canker;
Many a father hath erred, in that he hath withheld reproof,
But more have mostly sinned, in withholding praise where it was due:
There be many such as Eli among men; but these be more culpable than Eli,
Who chill the fountain of exertion by the freezing looks of indifference:

Ye call a man easy and good, yet he is as a two-edged sword;
He rebuketh not vice, and it is strong; he comforteth not virtue, and it fainteth.
There is nothing more potent among men than a gift timely bestowed;
And a gift kept back where it was hoped, separateth chief friends:
For what is a gift but a symbol, giving substance to praise and esteem?
And where is a sharper arrow than the sting of unmerited neglect?

Expect not praise from the mean, neither gratitude from the selfish;
And to keep the proud thy friend, see thou do him not a service:
For, behold, he will hate thee for his debt: thou hast humbled him by giving;
And his stubbornness never shall acknowledge the good he hath taken from thy hand:
Yea, rather will he turn and be thy foe, lest thou gather from his friendship
That he doth account thee creditor, and standeth in the second place.
Still, O kindly feeling heart, be not thou chilled by the thankless,
Neither let the breath of gratitude fan thee into momentary heat:
Do good for good's own sake, looking not to worthinesss nor love;
Fling thy grain among the rocks, cast thy bread upon the waters,
His claim be strongest to thy help, who is thrown most helplessly upon thee,—
So shalt thou have a better praise, and reap a richer harvest of reward.

If a man hold fast to thy creed, and fit his thinking to thy notions,
Thou shalt take him for a man right-minded, yea, and excuse his evil:
But seest thou not, O bigot, that thy zeal is but a hunting after praise,
And the full pleasure of a proselyte lieth in the flattering of self?
A man of many praises meeteth many welcomes,
But he, who blameth often, shall not keep a friend;
The velvet-coated apricot is one thing, and the spiked horse-chesnut is another,
A handle of smooth amber is pleasanter than rough buck-horn.
Show me a popular man; I can tell thee the secret of his power;

He hath soothed them with glozing words, lulling their ears with flattery,
The smile of seeming approbation is ever the companion of his **presence**,
And courteous looks, **and warm** regards, earn him **all their hearts**.

Nothing but may be better, and every better might **be** best;
The **blind** may discern, and the simple prove, fault or want in **all** things;
And **a little mind looketh on** the lily with a microscopic eye,
Eager and glad to pry out specks on its robe of purity;
But a great mind gazeth on the sun, glorying in his brightness,
And taking large knowledge of his good, in the broad prairie of creation:
What, though he hatch basilisks? what, though spots are **on the** sun?
In **fulness is his** worth, in fulness be his praise!

OF SELF-ACQUAINTANCE.

KNOWLEDGE holdeth by the hilt, and heweth out a road to conquest;
Ignorance graspeth the blade, and is wounded by its own good sword:
Knowledge distilleth health from the virulence of opposite poisons;
Ignorance mixeth wholesomes unto the breeding of disease:
Knowledge is leagued with the **universe,** and findeth a friend **in all** things;
But ignorance is everywhere a stranger; unwelcome, ill at ease, and out of place.
A man is helpless and unsafe up to the measure of his ignorance,
For he lacketh perception of the aptitudes commending such a matter **to his use;**
Clutching at the horn of danger, while he judgeth it the handle of security,
Or casting his anchor so widely, that the granite reef is just within the tether.
Untaught in science, he is but **half alive**, stupidly taking note of nothing,
Or listening with dull wonder to the crafty saws of an empiric!

OF SELF-ACQUAINTANCE.   103

Simple in the world, he trusteth unto knaves; and then to make
    amends for folly,
Dealeth so shrewdly **with** the honest, they cannot but suspect him
    for a thief:
With an unknown God, he maketh mock of reason, fathering con-
    trivance on chance,
Or doting with superstitious dread on some crooked image of his
    fancy:
But ignorant of Self, he is weakness at heart; the **keystone**
    crumbleth into sand,
There is panic in the general's tent, the oak is hollow as hemlock;
Though the warm sap creepeth up its bark, filling out the sheaf of
    leaves,
Though knowledge of all things beside add proofs of seeming
    vigour,
Though the master-mind of the royal sage feast on the mysteries of
    wisdom,
Yet ignorance of self shall bow down the spirit of a Solomon to
    idols;
The storm of temptation, sweeping by, shall snap that oak like a
    reed,
And the proud luxuriance of its tufted crown drag it the sooner to
    the dust.

Youth, confident in self, tampereth with dangerous dalliance,
Till the vice his heart once hated hath locked him in her foul em-
    brace:
Manhood, through **zeal of doing good**, seeketh high place for **its**
    occasions,
Unwitting that the bleak mountain **air** will nip the tender budding
    of his motives:
Or painfully, for love of truth, he climbeth the ladder of science,
Till pride of intellect heating his heart, warpeth it aside to
    delusion:
The maiden, to give shadow to her fairness, plaiteth her **raven**
    hair,
Heedlessly weaving for her soul the silken net of vanity:
The grey-beard looketh on his gold, till he loveth its yellow smile,
Unconscious of the bright **decoy** which **is** luring his heart unto
    avarice:
Wrath avoideth no quarrel, jealousy counteth its suspicions,

Pining envy gazeth still, and melancholy seeketh solitude,
The sensitive broodeth on his slights, the fearful poreth over horrors,
The train of wantonness is fired, the nerves of indecision are unstrung;
Each special proneness unto harm is pampered by ignorant indulgence,
And the man, for want of warning, yieldeth to the apt temptation.

A smith at the loom, and a weaver at the forge, were but sorry craftsmen;
And a ship that saileth on every wind never shall reach her port:
Yet there be thousands among men who heed not the leaning of their talents,
But cutting against the grain, toil on to no good end:
And the light of a thoughtful spirit is quenched beneath the bushel of commerce,
While meaner plodding minds are driven up the mountain of philosophy:
The cedar withereth on a wall, while the house-leek is fattening in a hot-bed,
And the dock with its rank leaves hideth the sun from violets.
To everything a fitting place, a proper honourable use;
The humblest measure of mind is bright in its humble sphere:
The glow-worm, creeping in the hedge, lighteth her evening torch,
And her far-off mate, on gossamer sail, steereth his course by that star:
But ignorance mocketh at proprieties, bringing out the glow-worm at noon;
And setteth the faults of mediocrity in the full blaze of wisdom.
Ravens croaking in darkness, and a sky-lark trilling to the sun,
The voice of a screech-owl from a ruin, and the blackbird's whistle in a wood,
A cushion-footed camel for the sands, and a swift reindeer for the snows,
A naked skin for Ethiopia, and rich soft furs for the Pole:
In all things is there a fitness: discord with discord hath its music;
And the harmony of nature is preserved by each one knowing his place.

The blind at an easel, the palsied with a graver, the halt making for the goal,
The deaf ear tuning psaltery, the stammerer discoursing eloquence,—
What wonder if all fail? the shaft flieth wide of the mark
Alike if itself be crooked, or the bow be strung awry;
And the mind which were excellent in one way, but foolishly toileth in another,
What is it but an ill-strung bow, and its aim a crooked arrow?
By knowledge of self, thou provest thy powers: put not the racer to the plough,
Nor goad the toilsome ox to wager his slowness with the fleet:
Consider thy failings, heed thy propensities, search out thy latent virtues,
Analyze the doubtful, cultivate the good, and crush the head of evil;
So shalt thou catch with quick hand the golden ball of opportunity,
The warrior armed shall be ready for the fray, beside his bridled steed;
Thou shalt ward off special harms, and have the sway of circumstance,
And turn to thy special good the common current of events;
Choosing from the wardrobe of the world, thou shalt suitably clothe thy spirit,
Nor thrust the white hand of peace into the gauntlet of defiance:
The shepherd shall go with a staff, and conquer by sling and stone;
The soldier shall let alone the distaff, and the scribe lay down the sword·
The man unlearned shall keep silence, and earn one attribute of wisdom,
The sage be sparing of his lessons before unhearing ears:
Calm shalt thou be, as a lion in repose, conscious of passive strength,
And the shock that splitteth the globe, shall not unthrone thy self-possession.

Acquaint thee with thyself, O man! so shalt thou be humble:
The hard hot desert of thy heart shall blossom with the lily and the rose;

The frozen cliffs of pride shall melt, as an iceberg in the tropics;
The bitter fountains of self-seeking be sweeter than the waters of
 the Nile.
But if thou lack that wisdom,—thy frail skiff is doomed,
On stronger eddy whirling to the dreadful gorge;
Untaught in that grand lore, thou standest, cased in steel,
To dare with mocking unbelief the thunderbolts of heaven.
For look now around thee on the universe, behold how all things
 serve thee;
The teeming soil, and the buoyant sea, and undulating air,
Golden crops, and bloomy fruits, and flowers, and precious gems,
Choice perfumes and fair sights, soft touches and sweet music:
For thee, shoaling up the bay, crowd the finny nations,
For thee, the cattle on a thousand hills live, and labour, and die:
Light is thy daily slave, darkness inviteth thee to slumber;
Thou art served by the hands of Beauty, and Sublimity kneeleth
 at thy feet:
Arise, thou sovereign of creation, and behold thy glory!
Yet more, thou hast a mind; intellect wingeth thee to heaven,
Tendeth thy state on earth, and by it thou divest down to hell;
Thou hast measured the belt of Saturn, thou hast weighed the
 moons of Jupiter,
And seen, by reason's eye, the centre of thy globe;
Subtly hast thou numbered by billions the leagues between sun
 and sun,
And noted in thy book the coming of their shadows;
With marvellous unerring truth, thou knowest to an inch and to an
 instant,
The where and the when of the comet's path that shall seem to
 rush by at thy command:
Arise, thou king of mind, and survey thy dignity!
Yet more,—for once believe religion's flattering tale;
Thou hast a soul, aye, and a God,—but be not therefore humbled;
Thy Maker's self was glad to live and die—a man;
The brightest jewel in his crown is voluntary manhood;
By deep dishonour, and great price, bought he that envied
 freedom,
But thou wast born an heir of all, thy Master scarce could earn.
O climax unto pride, O triumph of humanity,
O triple crown upon thy brow, most high and mighty Self!
Arise, thou Lord of all, thou greater than a God!—

How saidst thou, wretched being?—cast thy glance within;
Regard that painted sepulchre, the hovel of thy heart:
Ha! with what fearful imagery swarmeth that small chamber;
The horrid eye of murder, scowling in the dark,
The bony hand of avarice, filching from the poor,
The lurid fires of lust, the idiot face of folly,
The sickening deed of cruelty, the foul fierce orgies of the drunken,
Weak contemptible vanity, stubborn stolid unbelief,
Envy's devilish sneer, and the vile features of ingratitude,—
Man, hast thou seen enough? or are these full proof
That thou art a miracle of mercy, and all thy dignity is dross?

Well said the wisdom of earth, O mortal, know thyself;
But better the wisdom of heaven, O man, learn thou thy God:
By knowledge of self thou art conusant of evil, and mailed in panoply to meet it;
By knowledge of God cometh knowledge of good, and universal love is at thy heart.
Every creature knoweth its capacities, running in the road of instinct,
And reason must not lag behind, but serve itself of all proprieties:
The swift to the race, and the strong to the burden, and the wise for right direction;
For self-knowledge filleth with acceptance its niche in the temple of utility:
But vainly wilt thou look for that knowledge, till the clue of all truth is in thy hand,
For the labyrinth of man's heart windeth in complicate deceivings:
Thou canst not sound its depths with the shallow plumb-line of reason,
Till religion, the pilot of the soul, have lent thee her unfathomable coil:
Therefore, for this grand knowledge, and knowledge is the parent of dominion,
Learn God, thou shalt know thyself; yea, and shalt have mastery of all things.

OF CRUELTY TO ANIMALS.

Shame upon thee, savage Monarch man, proud monopolist of reason :
Shame upon Creation's lord, the fierce ensanguined despot :
What, man! are there not enough, hunger, and diseases, and fatigue,—
And yet must thy goad or thy thong add another sorrow to existence?
What! art thou not content thy sin hath dragged down suffering and death
On the poor dumb servants of thy comfort, and yet must thou rack them with thy spite?
The prodigal heir of creation hath gambled away his all,—
Shall he add torment to the bondage that is galling his forfeit serfs?
The leader in nature's pæan himself hath marred her psaltery,
Shall he multiply the din of discord by overstraining all the strings?
The rebel hath fortified his strong-hold, shutting in his vassals with him,—
Shall he aggravate the woes of the besieged by oppression from within?
Thou twice deformed image of thy Maker, thou hateful representative of Love,
For very shame be merciful, be kind unto the creatures thou hast ruined ;
Earth and her million tribes are cursed for thy sake,
Earth and her million tribes still writhe beneath thy cruelty :
Liveth there but one among the million that shall not bear witness against thee,
A pensioner of land or air or sea, that hath not whereof it will accuse thee?
From the elephant toiling at a launch, to the shrew-mouse in the harvest-field,
From the whale which the harpooner hath stricken, to the minnow caught upon a pin,
From the albatross wearied in its flight, to the wren in her covered nest,
From the death-moth and lace-winged dragon-fly, to the lady-bird and the gnat,

OF CRUELTY TO ANIMALS.

The verdict of all things is unanimous, finding their master cruel:
The dog, thy humble friend, thy trusting, honest friend;
The ass, thine uncomplaining slave, drudging from morn to even;
The lamb, and the timorous hare, and the labouring ox at plough;
The speckled trout, basking in the shallow, and the partridge, gleaning in the stubble,
And the stag at bay, and the worm in thy path, and the wild bird pining in captivity,
And all things that minister alike to thy life and thy comfort and thy pride,
Testify with one sad voice that man is a cruel master.

Verily, they are all thine: freely mayst thou serve thee of them all:
They are thine by gift for thy needs, to be used in all gratitude and kindness;
Gratitude to their God and thine,—their Father and thy Father,
Kindness to them who toil for thee, and help thee with their all:
For meat, but not by wantonness of slaying: for burden, but with limits of humanity;
For luxury, but not through torture; for draught, but according to the strength:
For a dog cannot plead his own right, nor render a reason for exemption,
Nor give a soft answer unto wrath, to turn aside the undeserved lash;
The galled ox cannot complain, nor supplicate a moment's respite;
The spent horse hideth his distress, till he panteth out his spirit at the goal;
Also, in the winter of life, when worn by constant toil,
If ingratitude forget his services, he cannot bring them to remembrance;
Behold, he is faint with hunger; the big tear standeth in his eye;
His skin is sore with stripes, and he tottereth beneath his burden;
His limbs are stiff with age, his sinews have lost their vigour,
And pain is stamped upon his face, while he wrestleth unequally with toil;
Yet once more mutely and meekly endureth he the crushing blow;
That struggle hath cracked his heart-strings,—the generous brute is dead!
Liveth there no advocate for him? no judge to avenge his wrongs?

No voice that shall be heard in his defence? no sentence to be
    passed on his oppressor?
Yea, the sad eye of the tortured pleadeth pathetically for him;
Yea, all the justice in heaven is roused in indignation at his woes;
Yea, all the pity upon earth shall call down a curse upon the
    cruel;
Yea, the burning malice of the wicked is their own exceeding
    punishment.
The Angel of Mercy stoppeth not to comfort, but passeth by on
    the other side,
And hath no tear to shed, when a cruel man is damned.

OF FRIENDSHIP.

As frost to the bud, and blight to the blossom, even such is self-
    interest to friendship:
For Confidence cannot dwell where Selfishness is porter at the
    gate.
If thou see thy friend to be selfish, thou canst not be sure of his
    honesty;
And in seeking thine own weal, thou hast wronged the reliance of
    thy friend.
Flattery hideth her varnished face when friendship sitteth at his
    board;
And the door is shut upon suspicion, but candour is bid glad
    welcome:
For friendship abhorreth doubt, its life is in mutual trust,
And perisheth, when artful praise proveth it is sought for a
    purpose.
A man may be good to thee at times, and render thee mighty
    service,
Whom yet thy secret soul could not desire as a friend;
For the sum of life is in trifles, and though, in the weightier
    masses,
A man refuse thee not his purse, nay his all in thine utmost need,
Yet if thou canst not feel that his character agreeth with thine
    own,
Thou never wilt call him friend, though thou render him a heartful
    of gratitude.
A coarse man grindeth harshly the finer feelings of his brother;

A common mind will soon depart from the dull companionship of
    wisdom;
A weak soul dareth not to follow in the track of vigour and
    decision;
And the worldly regardeth with scorn the seeming foolishness of
    faith.
A mountain is made up of atoms, and friendship of little matters,
And if the atoms hold not together, the mountain is crumbled
    into dust.

Come, I will show thee a friend; I will paint one worthy of thy
    trust:
Thine heart shall not weary of him: thou shalt not secretly
    despise him.
Thou art long in learning him, in unravelling all his worth;
And he dazzleth not thine eyes at first, to be darkened in thy
    sight afterward,
But riseth from small beginnings, and reacheth the height of thine
    esteem.
He remembereth that thou art only man; he expecteth not great
    things from thee;
And his forbearance toward thee silently teacheth thee to be con-
    siderate unto him.
He despiseth not courtesy of manner, nor neglecteth the decencies
    of life;
Nor mocketh the failings of others, nor is harsh in his censures
    before thee:
For so, how couldst thou tell, if he talketh not of thee in
    ridicule?
He withholdeth no secret from thee, and rejecteth not thine in
    turn;
He shareth his joys with thee, and is glad to bear part in thy
    sorrows.
Yet one thing, he loveth thee too well to show thee the corrup-
    tions of his heart:
For as an ill example strengtheneth the hands of the wicked,
So to put forward thy guilt, is a secret poison to thy friend:
For the evil in his nature is comforted, and he warreth more
    weakly against it,
If he find that the friend whom he honoureth, is a man more sinful
    than himself.

I hear the communing of friends; ye speak out the fulness of your souls,
And being but men, as men, ye own to all the sympathies of manhood:
Confidence openeth the lips, indulgence beameth from the eye,
The tongue loveth not boasting, the heart is made glad with kindness:
And one standeth not as on a hill, beckoning to the other to follow,
But ye toil up hand in hand, and carry each other's burdens.
Ye commune of hopes and aspirations, the fervent breathings of the heart,
Ye speak with pleasant interchange the treasured secrets of affection,
Ye listen to the voice of complaint, and whisper the language of comfort,
And as in a double solitude, ye think in each other's hearing.

Choose thy friend discreetly, and see thou consider his station,
For the graduated scale of ranks accordeth with the ordinance of heaven:
If a low companion ripen to a friend, in the full sunshine of thy confidence,
Know, that for old age thou hast heaped up sorrow:
For thou sinkest to that level, and thy kin shall scorn thee,
Yea, and the menial thou hast pampered haply shall neglect thee in thy death;
And if thou reachest up to high estates, thinking to herd with princes,
What art thou but a footstool, though so near a throne?
O rush among the lilies, be taught thou art a weed,
O briar among the cedars, hot contempt shall burn thee.
But thou, friend and scholar, select from thine own caste,
And make not an intimate of one, thy servant or thy master;
For only friendship among men is the true republic,
Where all have equality of service, and all have freedom of command.
And yet, if thou wilt take my judgment, be shy of too much openness with any,
Lest thou repent hereafter, should he turn and rend thee;

For many an apostate friend hath abused unguarded confidence,
And bent to selfish ends the secret of the soul.

Absence strengtheneth friendship, where the last recollections were kindly;
But it must be good wine at the last, or absence shall weaken it daily.
A rare thing is faith, and friendship is a marvel among men,
Yet strange faces call they friends, and say they believe when they doubt.
Those hours are not lost that are spent in cementing affection;
For a friend is above gold, precious as the stores of the mind.
Be sparing of advice by words, but teach thy lesson by example:
For the vanity of man may be wounded, and retort unkindly upon thee.
There be some that never had a friend, because they were gross and selfish;
Worldliness, and apathy, and pride, leave not many that are worthy:
But one who meriteth esteem, need never lack a friend:
For as thistledown flieth abroad, and casteth its anchor in the soil,
So philanthropy yearneth for a heart, where it may take root and blossom.

Yet I hear the child of sensibility moaning at the wintry cold,
Wherein the mists of selfishness have wrapped the society of men:
He grieveth, and hath deep reasons; for falsehood hath wronged his trust,
And the breaches in his bleeding heart have been filled with the briars of suspicion.
For, alas, how few be friends, of whom charity hath hoped well!
How few there be among men who forget themselves for other!
Each one seeketh his own, and looketh on his brethren as rivals,
Masking envy with friendship, to serve his secret ends;
And the world, that corrupteth all good, hath wronged that sacred name,
For it calleth any man friend, who is not known for an enemy;
And such be as the flies of summer, while plenty sitteth at thy board;
But who can wonder at their flight from the cold denials of want?

Such be as vultures round a carcase assembled together for the feast;
But a sudden noise scareth them, and forthwith are they specks among the clouds.
There be few, O child of sensibility, who deserve to have thy confidence;
Yet weep not, for there are some, and such some live for thee:
To them is the chilling world a drear and barren scene,
And gladly seek they such as thou art, for seldom find they the occasion:
For, though no man excludeth himself from the high capability of friendship,
Yet verily the man is a marvel whom truth can write a friend.

OF LOVE.

THERE is a fragrant blossom, that maketh glad the garden of the heart;
Its root lieth deep: it is delicate, yet lasting, as the lilac crocus of autumn:
Loneliness and thought are the dews that water it morn and even;
Memory and Absence cherish it, as the balmy breathings of the south:
Its sun is the brightness of Affection, and it bloometh in the borders of Hope;
Its companions are gentle flowers, and the briar withereth by its side.
I saw it budding in beauty; I felt the magic of its smile;
The violet rejoiced beneath it, the rose stooped down and kissed it;
And I thought some cherub had planted there a truant flower of Eden,
As a bird bringeth foreign seeds, that they may flourish in a kindly soil.
I saw and asked not its name; I knew no language was so wealthy,
Though every heart of every clime findeth its echo within.
And yet what shall I say? Is a sordid man capable of Love?
Hath a seducer known it? Can an adulterer perceive it?
Or he that seeketh strange women, can he feel its purity?

Or he that changeth often, can he know its truth?
Longing for another's happiness, yet often destroying its own;
Chaste, and looking up to God, as the fountain of tenderness and
    joy;
Quiet, yet flowing deep, as the Rhine among rivers;
Lasting, and knowing not change—it walketh with Truth and
    Sincerity.

Love:—what a volume in a word, an ocean in a tear,
A seventh heaven in a glance, a whirlwind in a sigh,
The lightning in a touch, a millenium in a moment,
What concentrated joy or woe in blest or blighted love!
For it is that native poetry springing up indigenous to Mind,
The heart's own-country music thrilling all its chords,
The story without an end that angels throng to hear,
The word, the king of words, carved on Jehovah's heart!
Go, call thou snake-eyed malice mercy, call envy honest praise,
Count selfish craft for wisdom, and coward treachery for prudence,
Do homage to blaspheming unbelief as to bold and free philo-
    sophy,
And estimate the recklessness of license as the right attribute of
    liberty,—
But with the world, thou friend and scholar, stain not this pure
    name;
Nor suffer the majesty of Love to be likened to the meanness of
    desire:
For love is no more such, than seraphs' hymns are discord,
And such is no more Love, than Etna's breath is summer.

Love is a sweet idolatry enslaving all the soul,
A mighty spiritual force, warring with the dullness of matter,
An angel-mind breathed into a mortal, though fallen yet how
    beautiful!
All the devotion of the heart in all its depth and grandeur.
Behold that pale geranium, pent within the cottage window;
How yearningly it stretcheth to the light its sickly long-stalked
    leaves,
How it straineth upward to the sun, coveting his sweet influences,
How real a living sacrifice to the god of all its worship!
Such is the soul that loveth; and so the rose-tree of affection
Bendeth its every leaf to look on those dear eyes,

Its every blushing petal basketh in their light,
And all its gladness, all its life, is hanging on their love.

If the love of the heart is blighted, it buddeth not again :
If that pleasant song is forgotten, it is to be learnt no more :
Yet often will thought look back, and weep over early affection ;
And the dim notes of that pleasant song will be heard as a reproachful spirit,
Moaning in Æolian strains over the desert of the heart,
Where the hot siroccos of the world have withered its one oasis.

OF MARRIAGE.

Seek a good wife of thy God, for she is the best gift of his providence ;
Yet ask not in bold confidence that which he hath not promised :
Thou knowest not his good will :—be thy prayer then submissive thereunto ;
And leave thy petition to his mercy, assured that He will deal well with thee.
If thou art to have a wife of thy youth, she is now living on the earth ;
Therefore think of her, and pray for her weal ; yea, though thou hast not seen her.
They that love early become like-minded and the tempter toucheth them not :
They grow up leaning on each other, as the olive and the vine.
Youth longeth for a kindred spirit, and yearneth for a heart that can commune with his own ;
He meditateth night and day, doting on the image of his fancy.
Take heed that what charmeth thee is real, nor springeth of thine own imagination ;
And suffer not trifles to win thy love ; for a wife is thine unto death
The harp and the voice may thrill thee,—sound may enchant thine ear,
But consider thou, the hand will wither, and the sweet notes turn to discord :

The eye, so brilliant at even, may be red with sorrow in the morning;
And the sylph-like form of elegance must writhe in the crampings of pain.

O happy lot, and hallowed, even as the joy of angels,
Where the golden chain of godliness is entwined with the roses of love:
But beware, thou seem not to be holy, to win favour in the eyes of a creature,
For the guilt of the hypocrite is deadly, and winneth thee wrath elsewhere.
The idol of thy heart is as thou, a probationary sojourner on earth;
Therefore be chary of her soul, for that is the jewel in her casket:
Let her be a child of God, that she bring with her a blessing to thy house,—
A blessing above riches, and leading contentment in its train:
Let her be an heir of heaven; so shall she help thee on thy way:
For those who are one in faith, fight double-handed against evil.
Take heed lest she love thee before God; that she be not an idolator:
Yet see thou that she love thee well; for her heart is the heart of woman;
And the triple nature of humanity must be bound by a triple chain,
For soul and mind and body—godliness, esteem, and affection.

How beautiful is modesty! it winneth upon all beholders:
But a word or a glance may destroy the pure love that should have been for thee.
Affect not to despise beauty: no one is freed from its dominion;
But regard it not a pearl of price:—it is fleeting as the bow in the clouds.
If the character within be gentle, it often hath its index in the countenance:
The soft smile of a loving face is better than splendour that fadeth quickly.
When thou choosest a wife, think not only of thyself,
But of those God may give thee of her, that they reproach thee not for their being:

See that he hath given her health, lest thou lose her early and weep :

See that she springeth of a wholesome stock, that thy little ones perish not before thee :

For many a fair skin hath covered a mining disease,

And many a laughing cheek been bright with the glare of madness.

Mark the **converse of one** thou lovest, that it be simple and sincere ;

For an artful or false woman shall set thy pillow with thorns.

Observe her deportment with **others, when she** thinketh not that thou art nigh,

For with thee will **the blushes of love** conceal the true colour of her mind.

Hath she learning ? it is good, so that modesty go with it :

Hath she wisdom ? it is precious, but beware that thou exceed ;

For woman must be subject, and the true mastery is of the mind.

Be joined to thine equal in rank, **or the foot of** pride will kick at thee ;

And look not only for riches, lest thou be mated with misery :

Marry not without means ; for so shouldst thou tempt Providence ;

But wait not for more than enough ; for marriage is **the DUTY of** most men :

Grievous indeed **must be the burden that shall outweigh innocence** and health,

And a well-assorted marriage hath not many cares.

In the day of thy **joy consider the poor**: thou shalt reap a rich harvest of blessing ;

For these be the pensioners of One who filleth thy cup with pleasures :

In the day of thy joy be thankful : He hath well deserved thy praise :

Mean and **selfish** is the heart that seeketh Him only in sorrow.

For her sake who leaneth on thine arm, court not the notice of the world,

And remember that sober privacy is comelier than public display.

If thou marriest, thou art allied unto strangers ; see they be not such as shame thee :

If thou marriest, thou leavest thine own ; see that it be not done in anger.

Bride and bridegroom, pilgrims of life, henceforward to travel together,
In this the beginning of **your journey, neglect not** the favour of heaven:
Let the day of hopes fulfilled be blest by many prayers,
And at even-tide kneel ye together, that your joy be **not unhallowed**:
Angels that are round you will be glad, those loving ministers of mercy,
And the richest blessings of your God shall be poured on his favoured children.
Marriage is a figure and an earnest of holier things unseen,
And reverence well becometh the symbol of dignity and glory.
Keep thy heart pure, lest thou do dishonour to thy state;
Selfishness is base and hateful; **but love** considereth not itself.
The wicked turneth good into evil, for his mind is warped within him;
But the heart of the righteous is chaste: his conscience casteth off sin.
If thou wilt be loved, render implicit confidence;
If thou wouldst not suspect, receive full confidence in turn:
For where trust is not reciprocal, the love that trusted withereth.
Hide not your grief nor your gladness; **be open one with the other**;
Let bitterness be strange unto your **tongues, but** sympathy a dweller in your hearts:
Imparting halveth the evils, while it doubleth the pleasures of life,
But sorrows breed and thicken in the gloomy bosom of Reserve.

Young wife, be not froward, nor forget that modesty becometh thee:
If it be discarded now, **who will not hold it** feigned before?
But be not as a timid girl,—there is honour due to thine estate;
A matron's modesty is dignified: she blusheth not, neither is she bold.
Be kind to the friends of thine husband, for the love they have to him:
And gently bear with his infirmities: hast thou **no need of his** forbearance?
Be not always in each other's company; it is often good to be alone;

And if there be too much sameness, ye cannot but grow weary of each other :
Ye have each a soul to be nourished, and a mind to be taught in wisdom,
Therefore, as accountable for time, help one another to improve it.
If ye feel love to decline, track out quickly the secret cause ;
Let it not rankle for a day, but confess and bewail it together :
Speedily seek to be reconciled, for love is the life of marriage ;
And be ye co-partners in triumph, conquering the peevishness of self.

Let no one have thy confidence, O wife, saving thine husband :
Have not a friend more intimate, O husband, than thy wife.
In the joy of a well-ordered home be warned that this is not your rest ;
For the substance to come may be forgotten in the present beauty of the shadow.
If ye are blessed with children, ye have a fearful pleasure,
A deeper care and a higher joy, and the range of your existence is widened :
If God in wisdom refuse them, thank Him for an unknown mercy :
For how can ye tell if they might be a blessing or a curse?
Yet ye may pray, like Hannah, simply dependent on his will :
Resignation sweeteneth the cup, but impatience dasheth it with vinegar :
Now this is the sum of the matter :—if ye will be happy in marriage,
Confide, love, and be patient : be faithful, firm, and holy.

OF EDUCATION.

A BABE in a house is a well-spring of pleasure, a messenger of peace and love :
A resting place for innocence on earth ; a link between angels and men :
Yet is it a talent of trust, a loan to be rendered back with interest ;
A delight, but redolent of care ; honey-sweet, but lacking not the bitter.
For character groweth day by day, and all things aid it in unfolding,

And the bent unto good or evil may be given in the hours of
  infancy:
Scratch the green rind of a sapling, or wantonly twist it in the soil,
The scarred and crooked oak will tell of thee for centuries to
  come;
Even so mayst thou guide the mind to good, or lead it to the
  marrings of evil,
For disposition is builded up by the fashioning of first impressions:
Wherefore, though the voice of Instruction waiteth for the ear of
  reason,
Yet with his mother's milk the young child drinketh Education.
Patience is the first great lesson; he may learn it at the breast:
And the habit of obedience and trust may be grafted on his mind
  in the cradle:
Hold the little hands in prayer, teach the weak knees their
  kneeling;
Let him see thee speaking to thy God; he will not forget it after-
  ward:
When old and grey will he feelingly remember a mother's tender
  piety,
And the touching recollection of her prayers shall arrest the strong
  man in his sin.

Select not to nurse thy darling one that may taint his innocence,
For example is a constant monitor, and good seed will die among
  the tares.
The arts of a strange servant have spoiled a gentle disposition:
Mother, let him learn of thy lips, and be nourished at thy breast.
Character is mainly moulded by the cast of the minds that sur-
  round it:
Let then the playmates of thy little one be not other than thy
  judgment shall approve:
For a child is in a new world, and learneth somewhat every
  moment,
His eye is quick to observe, his memory storeth in secret,
His ear is greedy of knowledge, and his mind is plastic as soft
  wax.
Beware then that he heareth what is good, that he feedeth not on
  evil maxims,
For the seeds of first instruction are dropt into the deepest
  furrows.

That which immemorial use hath sanctioned, seemeth to be right and true ;

Therefore, let him never have to recollect the time when good things were strangers to his thought.

Strive not to centre in thyself, fond mother, all his love ;

Nay, do not thou so selfishly, but enlarge his heart for others ;

Use him to sympathy betimes, that he learn to be sad with the afflicted ;

And check not a child in his merriment,—should not his morning be sunny ?

Give him not all his desire, so shalt thou strengthen him in hope ;

Neither stop with indulgence the fountain of his tears, so shall he fear thy firmness.

Above all things graft on him subjection, yea in the veriest trifle ;

Courtesy to all, reverence to some, and to thee unanswering obedience.

Read thou first, and well approve, the books thou givest to thy child ;

But remember the weakness of his thought, and that wisdom for him must be diluted :

In the honied waters of infant tales, let him taste the strong wine of truth :

Pathetic stories soften the heart ; but legends of terror breed midnight misery ;

Fairy fictions cram the mind with folly, and knowledge of evil tempteth to like evil :

Be not loath to curb imagination, nor be fearful that truths will depress it ;

And for evil, he will learn it soon enough ; be not thou the devil's envoy.

Induce not precocity of intellect, for so shouldst thou nourish vanity ;

Neither can a plant, forced in the hot-bed, stand against the frozen breath of winter.

The mind is made wealthy by ideas, but the multitude of words is a clogging weight :

Therefore be understood in thy teaching, and instruct to the measure of capacity.

Analogy is milk for babes, but abstract truths are strong meat ;

Precepts and rules are repulsive to a child, but happy illustration winneth him:
In vain shalt thou preach of industry and **prudence,** till he learn of the bee and the ant;
Dimly will he think **of his soul,** till the acorn and **the chrysalis** have taught him;
He will fear God in thunder, and worship his loveliness in flowers;
And parables shall charm his heart, while doctrines seem **dead** mystery;
Faith shall he learn of the husbandman casting good corn into the soil;
And if thou train him to trust thee, he will not withhold his reliance from the Lord.
Fearest thou the dark, poor child? I would not have thee left to thy terrors;
Darkness is the semblance of evil, and nature regardeth it with dread:
Yet know thy father's God is with thee still, to guard thee;
It is a simple lesson of dependence; let thy tost mind anchor upon Him.
Did a sudden noise affright thee? lo, this or that hath caused it:
Things undefined are full of dread, and stagger stouter nerves.
The seeds of misery and madness have been sowed in the nights of infancy;
Therefore be careful that ghastly fears be not the **night companions** of thy child.

Lo, thou art a land-mark on a hill; thy little ones copy thee **in all** things:
Let, then, thy religion be perfect: so shalt thou be honoured in thy house.
Be instructed in all wisdom, and communicate that thou knowest,
Otherwise thy learning is hidden, and thus thou seemest unwise.
A sluggard **hath no respect;** an epicure commandeth **not reverence;**
Meanness is always despicable, and folly provoketh contempt.
Those parents are best honoured whose characters best deserve it;
Show me a child undutiful, I shall know where to look for a foolish father:
Never hath a father done his duty, and lived to be despised of his son.

But how can that son reverence an example he dare not follow?
Should he imitate thee in thine evil? his scorn is thy rebuke.
Nay, but bring him up aright, in obedience to God and to thee;
Begin betimes, lest thou fail of his fear; and with judgment, that
    thou lose not his love:
Herein use good discretion, and govern not all alike,
Yet, perhaps, the fault will be in thee, if kindness prove not all-
    sufficient:
By kindness, the wolf and the zebra become docile as the spaniel
    and the horse;
The kite feedeth with the starling, under the law of kindness:
That law shall tame the fiercest, bring down the battlements of
    pride,
Cherish the weak, control the strong, and win the fearful spirit.
Be obeyed when thou commandest; but command not often:
Let thy carriage be the gentleness of love, not the stern front of
    tyranny.
Make not one child a warning to another; but chide the offender
    apart:
For self-conceit and wounded pride rankle like poisons in the soul.
A mild rebuke in the season of calmness, is better than a rod in
    the heat of passion;
Nevertheless, spare not, if thy word hath passed for punishment;
Let not thy child see thee humbled, nor learn to think thee false;
Suffer none to reprove thee before him, and reprove not thine own
    purposes by change;
Yet speedily turn thou again, and reward him where thou canst,
For kind encouragement in good cutteth at the roots of evil.

Drive not a timid infant from his home, in the early spring-time
    of his life,
Commit not that treasure to an hireling, nor wrench the young
    heart's fibres:
In his helplessness leave him not alone, a stranger among strange
    children,
Where affection longeth for thy love, counting the dreary hours;
Where religion is made a terror, and innocence weepeth unheard;
Where oppression grindeth without remedy, and cruelty delighteth
    in smiting.
Wherefore comply with an evil fashion? Is it not to spare thee
    trouble?

Can he gather no knowledge at thy mouth? Wilt thou yield thine
 honour to another?
What can he gain in learning, to equal what he loseth in
 innocence?
Alas! for the price above gold, by which such learning cometh!
For emulative pride and envy are the specious idols of the diligent,
Oaths and foul-mouthed sin burn in the language of the idle:
Bolder in that mimic world of boys stareth brazen-fronted vice,
Than thereafter in the haunts of men, where society doth shame
 her into corners.
My soul, look well around thee, ere thou give thy timid infant unto
 sorrows.
There be many that say, We were happiest in days long past,
When our deepest care was an ill-conned book,
And when we sported in that merry sunshine of our life,
Sadness a stranger to the heart, and cheerfulness its gay inhabitant.
True, ye are now less pure, and therefore are more wretched:
But have ye quite forgotten how sorely ye travailed at your
 tasks,
How childish griefs and disappointments bowed down the childish
 mind?
How sorrow sat upon your pillow, and terror hath waked you up
 betimes,
Dreading the strict hand of justice, that will not wait for a reason,
Or the whims of petty tyrants, children like yourselves,
Or the pestilent extract of evil poured into the ear of innocence?
Behold the coral island, fresh from the floor of the Atlantic,
It is dinted by every ripple, and a soft wave can smooth its
 surface;
But soon its substance hardeneth in the winds and tropic sun,
And weakly the foaming billows break against its adamantine
 wall:
Even thus, though sin and care dash upon the firmness of man-
 hood,
The timid child is wasted most by his petty troubles;
And seldom, when life is mature, and the strength proportioned to
 the burden,
Will the feeling mind, that can remember, acknowledge to deeper
 anguish,
Than when, as a stranger and a little one, the heart first ached
 with anxiety,

And the sprouting buds of sensibility were bruised by the harshness of a school.
My soul, look well around thee, ere thou give thine infant unto sorrows.
Yet there be boisterous tempers, stout nerves, and stubborn hearts,
And there is a riper season, when the mind is well disciplined in good,
And a time, when youth may be bettered by the wholesome occasions of knowledge,
Which rarely will he meet with so well, as among the congregation of his fellows.
Only for infancy, fond mother, rend not those first affections;
Only for the sensitive and timorous, consign not thy darling unto misery.

A man looketh on his little one, as a being of better hope;
In himself ambition is dead, but it hath a resurrection in his son:
That vein is yet untried,—and who can tell if it be not golden?
While his, well-nigh worked out, never yielded aught but lead:
And thus is he hurt more sorely, if his wishes are defeated there,
He hath staked his all upon a throw, and lo! the dice have foiled him.
All ways, and at all times, men follow on in flocks,
And the rife epidemic of the day shall tincture the stream of education.
Fashion is a foolish watcher posted at the tree of knowledge,
Who plucketh its unripe fruit to pelt away the birds:
But, for its golden apples,—they dry upon the boughs,
And few have the courage or the wisdom to eat in spite of fashion:
One while, the fever is to learn, what none will be wiser for knowing,
Exploded errors in extinct tongues, and occasions for their use are small;
And the bright morning of life, for years of misspent time,
Wasted in following sounds, hath tracked up little sense,
Till at noon a man is thrown upon the world, with a mind expert in trifles,
Having yet everything to learn that can make him good or useful:
The curious spirit of youth is crammed with unwholesome garbage,
While starving for the mother's milk the breasts of nature yield;

And high-coloured fables of depravity lure with their classic
    varnish,
While truth is holding out in vain her mirror much despised.

Of olden time, the fashion was for arms, to make an accomplished
    slayer,
And set gregarious man a-tilting with his fellows;
Thereafter, occult sciences, and mystic arts, and symbols,
How to exorcise a wizard, and how to lay a ghost;
Anon, all for gallantry and presence, the minuet, the palfrey, and
    the foil,
And the grand aim of education was to produce a coxcomb;
Soon came scholastical dispute with hydra-headed argument,
And the true philosophy of mind confounded in a labyrinth of
    words;
Then the Pantheon, and its orgies, initiating docile childhood,
While diligent youth strove hard to render his all unto Cæsar;
And now is seen the passion for utility, when all things are ac-
    counted by their price,
And the wisdom of the wise is busied in hatching golden
    eggs.
Perchance, not many moons to come, and all will again be for
    abstrusity,
Unravelling the figured veil that hideth Egypt's gods;
Or in those strange Avatars seeking benignant Vishnu,
Kali, and Kamala the fair, and much invoked Ganesa.

The mines of knowledge are oft laid bare through the forked
    hazelwand of chance,
And in a mountain of quartz we find a grain of gold.
Of a truth, it were well to know all things, and to learn them all
    at once,
And what, though mortal insufficiency attain to small knowledge of
    any?
Man loveth exclusions, delighting in the sterile trodden path,
While the broad green meadow is jewelled with wild flowers:
And whether it is better with the many to follow a beaten track,
Or by eccentric wanderings to cull unheeded sweets?

When his reason yieldeth fruit, make thy child thy friend;
For a filial friend is a double gain, a diamond set in gold.

As an infant, thy mandate was enough, but now let him see thy reasons;

Confide in him, but with discretion: and bend a willing ear to his questions.

More to thee than to all beside, let him owe good counsel and good guidance;

Let him feel his pursuits have an interest, more to thee than to all beside.

Watch his native capacities; nourish that which suiteth him the readiest;

And cultivate early those good inclinations wherein thou fearest he is most lacking:

Is he phlegmatic and desponding? let small successes comfort his hope:

Is he obstinate and sanguine? let petty crosses accustom him to life:

Showeth he a sordid spirit? be quick, and teach him generosity:

Inclineth he to liberal excess? prove to him how hard it is to earn.

Gather to thy hearth such friends as are worthy of honour and attention;

For the company a man chooseth is a visible index of his heart:

But let not the pastor whom thou hearest be too much a familiar in thy house,

For thy children may see his infirmities, and learn to cavil at his teaching.

It is well to take hold on occasions, and render indirect instruction;

It is better to teach upon a system, and reap the wisdom of books:

The history of nations yieldeth grand outlines: of persons, minute details:

Poetry is polish to the mind, and high abstractions cleanse it.

Consider the station of thy son, and breed him to his fortune with judgment:

The rich may profit in much which would bring small advantage to the poor.

But with all thy care for thy son, with all thy strivings for his welfare,

Expect disappointment, and look for pain: for he is of an evil stock, and will grieve thee.

OF TOLERANCE.

A WISE man in a crowded street winneth his way with gentleness,
Nor rudely pusheth aside the stranger that standeth in his path;
He knoweth that blind hurry will but hinder, stirring up contention against him,
Yet holdeth he steadily right on, with his face to the scope of his pursuit:
Even so, in the congress of opinions, the bustling highway of intelligence,
Each man should ask of his neighbour, and yield to him again concession.
Terms ill-defined, and forms misunderstood, and customs, where their reasons are unknown,
Have stirred up many zealous souls to fight against imaginary giants;
But wisdom will hear the matter out, and often, by keenness of perception,
Will find in strange disguise the precious truth he seeketh;
So he leaveth unto prejudice or taste the garb and the manner of her presence,
Content to see so nigh the mistress of his love.
There is no similitude in nature that owneth not also to a difference,
Yea, no two berries are alike, though twins upon one stem;
No drop in the ocean, no pebble on the beach, no leaf in the forest, hath its counterpart,
No mind in its dwelling of mortality, no spirit in the world unseen:
And therefore, since capacity and essence differ alike with accident,
None but a bigot partizan will hope for impossible unity.
Wilt thou ensue peace, nor buffet with the waters of contention,
Wilt thou be counted wise and gain the love of men,
Let unobtruded error escape the frown of censure,
Nor lift the glass of truth alway before thy fellows:
I say not, compromise the right, I would not have thee countenance the wrong,
But hear with charitable heart the reasons of an honest judgment;
For thou also hast erred, and knowest not when thou art most right,

Nor whether to-morrow's wisdom may not prove thee simple to-day:

Perchance thou art chiding in another what once thou wast thyself;

Perchance thou sharply reprovest what thou wilt be hereafter.

A man that can render a reason, is a man worthy of an answer;

But he that argueth for victory, deserveth not the tenderness of Truth.

Whiles a man liveth he may mend: count not thy brother reprobate;

When he is dead his chance is gone: remember not his faults in bitterness:

A man, till he dieth, is immortal in thy sight; and then he is as nothing;

Make not the living thy foe, nor take weak vengeance of the dead:

For life is as a game of chess, where least causeth greatest,

And an ill move bringeth loss, and a pawn may ensure victory.

Dost thou suspect? seek out certainty: for now, by self-inflicted pain,

Or ill-directed wrath, thou wrongest thyself or thy neighbour;

Suspicion is an early lesson, taught in the school of experience,

Neither shalt thou easily unlearn it, though charity ply thee with her preaching;

Yet look thou well for reasons, or ever mistrust hath marred thee,

Or fear curdled thy blood, or jealousy goaded thee to madness;

For a look, or a word, or an act, may be taken well or ill

As construed by the latitude of love, or the closeness of cold suspicion.

Better is the wrong with sincerity, rather than the right with falsehood:

And a prudent man will not lay siege to the strong hold of ignorant bigotry.

To unsettle a weak mind were an easy inglorious triumph,

And a strong cause taketh little count of the worthless suffrage of a fool:

Lightly he held to the wrong, loosely will he cling to the right;

Weakness is the essence of his mind, and the reed cannot yield an acorn.

Dogged obstinacy is oftentimes the buttress that proppeth an unstable spirit,

But a candid man blusheth not to **own,** he is wiser to-day than yesterday.
A man of a little wisdom is a sage among fools;
But himself is chief among the fools, if he look for admiration from them.
A heresy is an evil thing, for its shame is its pride:
Its necessary difference of error is the character it most esteemeth:
Give a man all things short of liberty, thou shalt have no thanks,
And little wilt thou speed with thine opponent, by proving **points he** will concede.
The tost sand darkeneth the waves; and **clear had** been the pages of truth,
Had not the **glosses** of men obscured **the** simplicity of faith.
In all things consider thine own ignorance, and gladly take occasion to be taught;
But suffer not excess of liberality to neutralize thy mental independence.

The faults and follies of most men make their deaths a gain:
But thou also art a man, full of faults and follies:
Therefore sorrow for the dead, or none shall weep for thee,
For the measure of charity thou dealest, shall be poured into thine own bosom.
That which vexeth thee now, provoking thee **to hate thy brother,**
Bear with it; the annoyance passeth, and may not return for ever:
The same combinations and results which aggravate thy soul to-day,
May not meet again for centuries in the kaleidoscope of circumstance;
For men and matters change, new elements mixing in continually,
And, as with chemical magic, the sour is transmuted into sweetness:
A little explained, a little endured, a little passed over as a foible,
And lo, the jagged atoms fit like smooth mosaic.
Thou canst not shape another's mind to suit thine own body,
Think not, **then,** to be furnishing his brain with thy special notions.

Charity walketh with a high step, and stumbleth not at a trifle:
Charity hath keen eyes, but the lashes half conceal them:
Charity is praised of all, and fear not thou that praise,
God will not love thee less, because men love thee more.

OF SORROW.

I SAID, I will seek out Sorrow, and minister the balm of pity,
So I sought her in the house of mourning; but peace followed in her train.
Then I marked her brooding silently in the gloomy cavern of Regret;
But a sunbeam of heavenly hope gleamed on her folded wing.
So I turned to the cabin of the poor, where famine dwelt with disease:
But the bed of the sick was smoothed, and the ploughman whistled at his labour.
So I stopt, and mused within myself, to remember where sorrow dwelt,
For I sought to see her alone, uncomforted, uncompanioned.
I went to the prison, but penitence was there, and promise of better times;
I listened at the madman's cell, but it echoed with deluded laughter.
Then I turned me to the rich and noble; I noted the sons of fashion:
A smile was on the languid cheek, that had no commerce with the heart;
Unhallowed thoughts, like fires, gleamed from the window of the eye,
And sorrow lived with those whose pleasures add unto their sins.

His infancy wanted not guilt; his life was continued evil:
He drew in pride with his mother's milk, and a father's lips taught him cursing.
I marked him as the wayward boy; I traced the dissolute youth;
I saw him betray the innocent, and sacrifice affection to his lust;
I saw him the companion of knaves, and a squanderer of ill-got gain:
I heard him curse his own misery, while he hugged the chains that galled him:
For well had experience declared the bitterness of guilty pleasure,
But habit, with its iron net, involved him in its folds.
Behind him loured the thunder-storm, which the caldron of his wickedness had brewed;

Before him was the smooth steep cliff, whose base is ruin and despair.
So he rushed madly on, and tried to forget his being:
The noisy revel and the low debauch, and fierce excitement of play,
With dreary interchange of palling pleasures filled the dull round of existence:
Memory was to him as a foe, so he flew for false solace to the wine-cup,
And stunned his enemy at even; but she rent him as a giant in the morning.

I turned aside to weep; I lost him a little while:
I looked, and years had past; he was hoar with the winter of his age.
And what was now his hope? where was the balm for his sadness?
The memory of the past was guilt: the feeling of the present, remorse.
Then he set his affections on gold, he worshipped the shrine of Mammon,
And to lay richer gifts before his idol, he starved his own bowels;
So, the youth spent in profligacy ended in the gripings of want:
The miser grudged himself husks to take deeper vengeance of the prodigal.
And I said, this is sorrow, but pity cannot reach it;
This is to be wretched indeed, to be guilty without repentance.

OF JOY.

My soul was sickened within me, so I sought the dwelling place of Joy:
And I met it not in laughter; I found it not in wealth or power;
But I saw it in the pleasant home, where religion smiled upon content,
And the satisfied ambition of the heart rejoiced in the favour of its God.
Behold the happy man, his face is rayed with pleasure,
His thoughts are of calm delight, and none can know his blessedness:

I have watched him from his infancy, and seen him in the grasp of death,

Yet, never have I noted on his brow the cloud of desponding sorrow.

He hath knelt beside his cradle; his mother's hymn lulled him to sleep:

In childhood he hath loved holiness, and drank from that fountainhead of peace.

Wisdom took him for her scholar, guiding his steps in purity:

He lived unpolluted by the world; and his young heart hated sin.

But he owned not the spurious religion engendered of faction and moroseness,

Neither were the sproutings of his soul seared by the brand of superstition.

His love is pure and single, sincere, and knoweth not change;

For his manhood hath been blest with the pleasant choice of his youth:

Behold his one beloved, she leaneth on his arm,

And he looketh on the years that are past, to review the dawn of her affection.

Memory is sweet unto him, as a perfect landscape to the sight;

Each object is lovely in itself, but the whole is the harmony of nature.

Behold his little ones around him, they bask in the warmth of his smile;

And infant innocence and joy lighten their happy faces;

He is holy, and they honour him: he is loving, and they love him:

He is consistent, and they esteem him: he is firm, and they fear him.

His friends are the excellent among men; and the bands of their friendship are strong;

His house is the palace of peace: for the Prince of Peace is there.

As the wearied man to his couch, as the thoughtful man to his musings,

Even so, from the bustle of life, he goeth to his well-ordered home:

And though he often sin, he returneth with weeping eyes:

For he feeleth the mercies of forgiveness, and gloweth with warmer gratitude.

Thus did he walk in happiness, and sorrow was a stranger to his soul;
The light of affection sunned his heart, the tear of the grateful bedewed his feet,
He put his hand with constancy to good, and angels knew him as a brother,
And the busy satellites of evil trembled as at God's ally:
He used his wealth as a wise steward, making him friends for futurity:
He bent his learning to religion, and religion was with him at the last:
For I saw him after many days, when the time of his release was come,
And I longed for a congregated world, to behold that dying saint.
As the aloe is green and well-liking, till the last best summer of its age,
And then hangeth out its golden bells, to mingle glory with corruption;
As a meteor travelleth in splendour, but bursteth in dazzling light;
Such was the end of the righteous; his death was the sun at its setting.

Look on this picture of joy, and remember that portrait of sorrow:
Behold the beauty of holiness, behold the deformity of sin!
How long, ye sons of men, will ye scorn the words of wisdom?
How long will ye hunt for happiness in the caverns that breed despair?
Will ye comfort yourselves in misery, by denying the existence of delight,
And from experience in woe, will ye reason that none are happy?
Joy is not in your path, for it loveth not that bleak broad road,
But its flowers are hung upon the hedges that line a narrower way;
And there the faint travellers of earth may wander and gather for themselves,
To soothe their wounded hearts with balm from the amaranths of heaven.

ΘΕΩ ΔΟΞΑ.

SECOND SERIES.

INTRODUCTORY.

Come again, and greet me as a friend, fellow-pilgrim upon life's highway,
Leave awhile the hot and dusty road, to loiter in the greenwood of Reflection.
Come unto my cool dim grotto, that is watered by the rivulet of truth,
And over whose time-stained rock climb the fairy flowers of content.
Here, upon this mossy bank of leisure fling thy load of cares,
Taste my simple store, and rest one soothing hour.

Behold, I would count thee for a brother, and commune with thy charitable soul;
Though wrapt within the mantle of a prophet, I stand mine own weak scholar.
Heed no disciple for a teacher, if knowledge be not found upon his tongue;
For vanity and folly were the lessons these lips untaught could give:
The precious staple of my merchandise cometh from a better country,
The harvest of my reaping sprang of foreign seed

And this poor pensioner of Mercy, should he boast of merit?
The grafted stock,—should that be proud of apples not its own?
Into the bubbling brook I dip my hermit shell;
Man receiveth as a cup, but Wisdom is the river.

Moreover, for this fillagree of fancy, this Oriental garnish of similitude,
Alas, the world is old,—and all things old within it:
I walk a trodden path, I love the good old way ;
Prophets, and priests, and kings have tuned the harp I faintly touch.
Truth, in a garment of the past, is my choice and simple theme ;
No truth is new to-day: and the mantle was another's.

Still, there is an insect swarm, the buzzing cloud of imagery,
Mote-like steaming on my sight, and thronging my reluctant mind;
The memories of studious culling, and multiplied analogies of nature,
Fresh feelings unrepressed, welling from the heart spontaneous,
Facts, and comparisons, and meditative atoms, gathered on the heap of combination,
Mingle in the fashion of my speech with gossamer dreams of Reverie.
I need not beat the underwood for game; my pheasants flock upon the lawn,
And gamboling hares disport fearless in my dewy field;
I roam no heath-empurpled hills, wearily watching for a covey,
But thoughts fly swift to my decoy, eager to be caught ;
I sit no quiet angler, lingering patiently for sport,
But spread my nets for a draught, and take the glittering shoal ;
I chase no solitary stag, tracking it with breathless toil,
But hunt with Aureng-zebe, and spear surrounded thousands.

What then,—count ye this a boast?—sweet charity, think it other;
For the dog-fish and poisonous ray are captured in the mullet-haul:
The crane and the kite are of my thoughts, alike with the partridge and the quail,
And unclean meats as of the clean hang upon my Seric shambles.
—How saith he? shall a man deceive, dressing up his jackal as a lion?

Or colour in staid hues of fact the changing vest of falsehood?—
Brother, unwittingly he may; doubtless, unwillingly he doth:
For men are full of fault, and how should he be righteous?
Carefully my garden hath been weeded, yet shall it be foul with thistle;
My grapery is diligently thinned, and yet many berries will be sour:
From my nets have I flung the bad away, to my small skill and caution
Yet may some slimy snake have counted for an eel.
The rudder of Man's best hope cannot always steer himself from error:
The arrow of Man's straightest aim flieth short of truth.
Thus, the confession of sincerity visit not as if it were presumption:
Nor own me for a leader, where thy reason is not guide.

OF CHEERFULNESS.

TAKE courage, prisoner of time, for there be many comforts,
Cease thy labour in the pit, and bask awhile with truants in the sun
Be cheerful, man of care, for great is the multitude of chances,
Burst thy fetters of anxiety, and walk among the citizens of ease:
Wherefore dost thou doubt? if present good is round thee,
It may be well to look for change, but to trust in a continuance is better;
Whilst, at the crisis of adversity, to hope for some amends were wisdom,
And cheerfully to bear thy cross in patient strength is duty:
I speak of common troubles, and the petty plagues of life,
The phantom-spies of Unbelief, that lurk about his outposts
Sharp suspicion, dull distrust, and sullen stern moroseness
Are captains in that locust swarm to lead the cloudy host.
Thou hast need of fortitude and faith, for the adversaries come on thickly,
And he that fled hath added wings to his pursuing foes;
Fight them, and the cravens flee; thy boldness is their panic;
Fear them, and thy treacherous heart hath lent the ranks a legion:
Among their shouts of victory resoundeth the wail of Heraclitus,
While Democrite, confident and cheerful, hath plucked up the standard of their camp.

Not few nor light are the burdens of life; **then load** it not with heaviness of **spirit**;
Sicknesses, and penury, **and** travail,—there be **real ills enow**:
We are wandering benighted, with a waning moon; plunge not rashly into jungles,
Where cold and poisonous damps will quench the torch **of hope**:
The tide is strong against us; good oarsmen, pull or perish,—
If your **arms be** slack for fear, ye shall not stem the torrent.
A wise traveller goeth on cheerily, through fair weather or foul;
He knoweth that his journey must be sped, so he carrieth his sunshine with him.
Calamities come not as a curse,—nor prosperity for other than a trial;
Struggle,—thou art **better for the strife,** and the very energy shall hearten thee.
Good is taught in a Spartan school,—hard lessons and a rough discipline,
But evil cometh idly of itself, in the luxury of Capuan holidays;
And wisdom will go bravely forth to meet the chastening scourge,
Enduring with a thankful heart that punishment of Love.

There be **three chief rivers** of despondency; **sin, sorrow, fear**;
Sin is the deepest, sorrow hath its shallows, and fear is **a noisy rapid**:
But even to **the darkest holes in** guilt's profoundest river
Hope can pierce with quickening ray, and all those depths are lightened;
So long as there is mercy in a God, hope is the privilege of creatures,
And so soon as there is penitence in creatures, that hope is exalted into duty.
Verily, consider this for courage; that the fearful and the unbelieving
Are classed with idolators and liars, because they trusted not in God:
For it is none other than selfish sin, a hard and proud ingratitude,
Where seeming repentance is herald of despair, instead of hope's forerunner.

Moreover, in thy day of grief,—for friends, **or** fame, or fortune,
Well I wot the heart shall ache, and mind be numbed in torpor;

Let nature weep; leave her alone; the freshet of her sorrow must run off;
And sooner will the lake be clear, relieved of turbid floodings.
Yet see that her license hath a limit; with the novelty her agony is over;
Hasten in that earliest calm, to tie her in the leash with Reason.
For regrets are an enervating folly, and the season for energy is come,
Yea rather, that the future may repair with diligence the ruins of the past.

Again, for empty fears, the harassings of possible calamity;
Pray, and thou shalt prosper; trust in God, and tread them down.
Yield to the phantasy,—thou sinnest; resist it, He will aid thee:
Out of Him there is no help, nor any sober courage.
Feeble is the comfort of the faithless, a man without a God;
Who dare counsel such an one to fling away his fears?
Fear is the heritage of him, a portion wise and merciful,
To drive the trembler into safety, if haply he may turn and flee:
Nevertheless, let him reckon an he will, that all he counteth casual
May as well be for him as against him; dice have many sides:
And, even as in ailments of the body, diseases follow closely upon dreads,
So, with infirmities of mind, is fear the pallid harbinger of failure.
It were wise to walk undaunted even in an accidental chaos,
For the brave man is at peace, and free to get the mastery of circumstance.
The stoutest armour of defence is that which is worn within the bosom,
And the weapon that no enemy can parry, is a bold and cheerful spirit:
Catapults in old war worked like Titans, crushing foes with rocks;
So doth a strong-springed heart throw back every load on its assailants.

I went heavily for cares, and fell into the trance of sorrow;
And behold, a vision in my trance, and my ministering angel brought it.
There stood a mountain huge and steep, the awful Rock of Ages;

The sun upon its summit, and storms midway, and deep ravines at
    foot.
And, as I looked, a dense black cloud, suddenly dropping from the
    thunder,
Filled, like a cataract with yeasty foam, a narrow smiling valley:
Close and hard that vaporous mass seemed to press the ground,
And lamentable sounds came up, as of some that were smothering
    beneath.
Then, as I walked upon the mountain, clear in summer's noon,
For charity I called aloud, Ho! climb up hither to the sunshine.
And even like a stream of light my voice had pierced the mist;
I saw below two families of men, and knew their names of old:
Courage, struggling through the darkness, stout of heart and glad-
    some,
Ran up the shining ladder which the voice of hope had made;
And tripping lightly by his side, a sweet-eyed helpmate with him,
I looked upon her face to welcome pleasant Cheerfulness;
And a babe was cradled in her bosom, a laughing little prattler,
The child of Cheerfulness and Courage,—could his name be other
    than Success?
So, from his happy wife, when they both stood beside me on the
    mountain,
The fond father took that babe, and set him on his shoulder in the
    sunshine.

Again I peered into the valley, for I heard a gasping moan,
A desolate weak cry, as muffled in the vapours.
So down that crystal shaft into the poisonous mine
I sped for charity to seek and save,—and those I sought fled from
    me.
At length, I spied, far distant, a trembling withered dwarf
Who crouched beneath the cloak of a tall and spectral mourner:
Then I knew Cowardice and Gloom, and followed them on in
    darkness
Guided by their rustling robes and moans and muffled cries,
Until in a suffocating pit the wretched pair had perished,—
And lo, their whitening bones were shaping out an epitaph of
    Failure.

So I saw that despondency was death, and flung my burdens from
    me,

And, lightened by that effort, I was raised above the world;
Yea, in the strangeness of my vision, I seemed to soar on wings,
And the names they called my wings were Cheerfulness and
    Wisdom.

OF YESTERDAY.

SPEAK, poor almsman of to-day, whom none can assure of a to-
    morrow,
Tell out, with honest heart, the price thou settest upon yesterday.
Is it then a writing in the dust, traced by the finger of idleness,
Which Industry, clean housewife, can wipe away for ever?
Is it as a furrow on the sand, fashioned by the toying waves,
Quickly to be trampled then again by the feet of the returning
    tide?
Is it as the pale blue smoke, rising from a peasant's hovel,
That melted into limpid air, before it topped the larches?
Is it but a vision, unstable and unreal, which wise men soon for-
    get?
Is it as the stranger of a night,—gone, we heed not whither?
Alas! thou foolish heart, whose thoughts are but as these,
Alas! deluded soul, that hopeth thus of Yesterday.

For, behold,—those temples of Ellora, the Brahmin's rock-built
    shrine,
Behold—yon granite cliff, which the North Sea buffeteth in vain,—
That stout old forest fir,—these waking verities of life,
This guest abiding ever, not strange, nor a servant, but a son,—
Such, O man, are vanity and dreams, transient as a rainbow on the
    cloud,
Weighed against that solid fact, thine ill-remembered Yesterday.

Come, let me show thee an ensample, where Nature shall instruct
    us;
Luxuriantly the arguments for truth spring native in her gardens.
Seek we yonder woodman of the plain; he is measuring his axe to
    the elm,
And anon the sturdy strokes ring upon the wintry air·
Eagerly the village school-boys cluster on the tightened rope,
Shouting, and bending to the pull, or lifted from the ground
    elastic;

The huge tree boweth like Sisera, boweth to its foes with faint-
 ness,—
Its sinews crack,—deep **groans declare the** reeling anguish of
 Goliath,
The wedge is driven home,—and the saw is at its heart,—and lo,
 with solemn slowness,
The shuddering monarch riseth from his throne,—toppled with a
 crash,—and is fallen!

Now, shall the mangled stump teach proud man a lesson?
Now, can we from that elm-tree's sap distil the wine of Truth.
Heed ye those hundred rings, concentric from the core,
Eddying in various waves to the red-bark's shore-like rim?
These be the gatherings of yesterdays, present all to-day,
This is the tree's judgment, self-history that cannot be gainsaid:
Seven years agone there was a drought,—and the seventh ring is
 narrowed;
The fifth from hence **was half a deluge**,—the fifth is cellular and
 broad:
Thus, Man, thou art a result, the growth of many yesterdays,
That stamp thy secret soul with marks of weal or woe:
Thou art an almanack of self, the living record of thy deeds;
Spirit hath its scars as well as body, sore and aching in **their**
 season:
Here is a knot,—it was a crime; there is a canker,—selfishness;
Lo, here, the heart-wood rotten, lo, there, perchance, the sap-wood
 sound.
Nature teacheth not in vain; thy works are in thee, of thee;
Some present **evil** bent hath grown of older errors:
And what if thou be walking now uprightly? Salve not thy wounds
 with poison,
As if a petty goodness of to-day hath blotted out the sin of yester-
 day:
It is well, thou hast life and light; and the Hewer showeth mercy,
Dressing the root, pruning the branch, and looking for thy tardy
 fruits;
But, even here as thou standest, cheerful belike and careless,
The stains of ancient evil are upon **thee, the record** of thy wrong
 is in thee:
For, a curse of many yesterdays is thine, many yesterdays of sin,
That, haply little heeded now, shall blast thy many morrows.

Shall then a man reck nothing, but hurl mad defiance at his Judge,
Knowing that less than an Omnipotent cannot make the has been,
    not been?
He ought,—so Satan spake; he must,—so Atheism urgeth;
He may,—it was the libertine's thought; he doth,—the bad world
    said it.
But thou of **humbler heart,** thou student wiser for simplicity,
While Nature warneth thee betimes, heed the loving counsel of
    Religion.
True, this change is good, and penitence most precious;
But trust not thou thy change, nor rest upon repentance;
For all we are corrupted at the core, smooth as surface seemeth;
What health can bloom in a beautiful skin, when rottenness hath
    fed upon the bones?
And guilt is parcel of us all; not thou, sweet nursling of affection,
Art spotless, though so passing fair,—nor thou, mild patriarch of
    virtue.

Behold then the better Tree of Life, free unto us all for grafting,
Cut thee from the hollow root of self, to be budded on a richer
    Vine.
Be desperate, O man, as of evil, so of good; tear that **tunic** from
    thee;
The past **can never** be retrieved, be the present what it may.
Vain is the penance and the scourge, vain **the fast and vigil:**
The fencer's cautious skill to-day, can this erase his scars?
It is Man's to famish as a faquir, it is **Man's to** die a devotee,
Light **is** the torture and the **toil,** balanced with the wages of
    Eternity:
But, it is God's to yearn in love, on the humblest, the poorest, and
    the worst,
For he giveth freely, as a king, asking only thanks for mercy.
Look upon this noble-hearted Substitute; seeing thy woes, he
    pitied thee,
Bowed beneath the mountain of thy sin, and perished—but for
    Godhead;
There stood the Atlas in his power, and Prometheus in his love is
    there,
Emptying on wretched men the blessings earned from heaven:
Put them not away, hide them in thy heart, poor and penitent
    receiver,

Be gratitude thy counsellor to good, and wholesome fear unto
    obedience;
Remember, the pruning-knife is keen, cutting cankers even from
    the vine;
Remember, twelve were chosen, and one among them liveth—in
    perdition.

Yea,—for standing unatoned, the soul is a bison on the prairie,
Hunted by those trooping wolves, the many sinful yesterdays:
And it speedeth a terrified Deucalion, flinging back the pebble in
    his flight,
The pebble that must add one more to those pursuing ghosts.
O man, there is a storm behind should drive thy bark to haven;
The foe, the foe is on thy track, patient, certain, and avenging;
Day by day, solemnly, and silently, followeth the fearful past,—
His step is lame, but sure; for he catcheth the present in eternity:
And how to escape that foe, the present-past in future?
How to avert that fate, living consequence of causes unexistent?—
Boldly we must overleap his birth, and date above his memories,
Grafted on the living Tree, that WAS before a yesterday:
No refuge of a younger birth than one that saw creation
Can hide the child of time from still condemning yesterday:
There, is the Sanctuary-city, mocking at the wrath of thine
    Avenger,
Close at hand, with the wicket on the latch; haste for thy life,
    poor hunted one!
The gladiator, Guilt, fighteth as of old, armed with net and
    dagger;
Snaring in the mesh of yesterdays, stabbing with the poignard of
    to-day:
Fly, thy sword is broken at the hilt; fly, thy shield is shivered;
Leap the barriers, and baffle him: the arena of the past is his.
The bounds of Guilt are the cycles of Time: thou must be safe
    within Eternity;
The arms of God alone shall rescue thee from Yesterday.

OF TO-DAY.

Now, is the constant syllable ticking from the clock of time,
Now, is the watchword of the wise, Now, is on the banner of the
    prudent.

Cherish thy to-day and prize it well, or ever it be gulphed into the
    past;
Husband it, for who can promise, if it shall have a morrow?
Behold, thou art,—it is enough; that present care be thine;
Leave thou the past to thy Redeemer, entrust the future to thy
    Friend;
But for to-day, child of man, tend thou charily the minutes,
The harvest of thy yesterday, the seed-corn of thy morrow.

Last night died its day; and the deeds thereof were judged:
Thou didst lay thee down as in a shroud, in darkness and death-
    like slumber:
But at the trumpet of this morn, waking the world to resurrection,
Thou didst arise, like others, to live a new day's life:
Fear, lest folly give thee cause to mourn its passing presence,
Fear, that to-morrow's sigh be not, would God it had not dawned!

For, To-day the lists are set, and thou must bear thee bravely,
Tilting for honour, duty, life, or death without reproach:
To-day, is the trial of thy fortitude, O dauntless Mandan chief;
To-day, is thy watch, O sentinel; to-day, thy reprieve, O cap-
    tive:
What more? to-day is the golden chance wherewith to snatch
    fruition,—
Be glad, grateful, temperate: there are asps among the figs.
For the potter's clay is in thy hands,—to mould it or to mar it at
    thy will,
Or idly to leave it in the sun, an uncouth lump to harden.

O bright presence of To-day, let me wrestle with thee, gracious
    angel,
I will not let thee go, except thou bless me; bless me, then, To-
    day:
O sweet garden of To-day, let me gather of thee, precious Eden;
I have stolen bitter knowledge, give me fruits of life To-day:
O true temple of To-day, let me worship in thee, glorious Zion:
I find none other place nor time, than where I am To-day:
O living rescue of To-day, let me run into thee, ark of refuge:
I see none other hope nor chance, but standeth in To-day:
O rich banquet of To-day, let me feast upon thee, saving manna;
I have none other food nor store, but daily bread To-day!

Behold, thou art pilot of the ship, and owner of that freighted
    galleon,
Competent, with all thy weakness, to steer into safety or be lost:
Compass and chart are in thy hand; roadstead and rocks thou
    knowest;
Thou art warned of reefs and shallows; thou beholdest the harbour
    and its lights.
What? shall thy wantonness or sloth drive the gallant vessel on
    the breakers?
What? shall the helmsman's hand wear upon the black lee shore?
Vain is that excuse; thou canst escape: thy mind is responsible
    for wrong:
Vain that murmur; thou mayst live: thy soul is debtor for the
    right.
To-day, in the voyage of thy life down the dark tide of time,
Stand boldly to thy tiller, guide thee by the pole-star, and be safe;
To-day, passing near the sunken rocks, the quicksands and whirl-
    pools of probation,
Leave awhile the rudder to swing round, give the wind its heading,
    and be wrecked.

The crisis of man's destiny is Now, a still recurring danger;
Who can tell the trials and temptations coming with the coming
    hour?
Thou standest a target-like Sebastian, and the arrows whistle near
    thee;
Who knoweth when he may be hit? for great is the company of
    archers.
Each breath is burdened with a bidding, and every minute hath its
    mission;
For spirits, good and bad, cluster on the thickly-peopled air:
Sin may blast thee, grace may bless thee, good or ill this hour:
Chance, and change, and doubt, and fear, are parasites of all.
A man's life is a tower, with a staircase of many steps,
That, as he toileth upward, crumble successively behind him:
No going back; the past is an abyss; no stopping, for the present
    perisheth;
But ever hasting on, precarious on the foothold of To-day;
Our cares are all To-day; our joys are all To-day;
And in one little word, our life, what is it, but—To-day?

OF TO-MORROW.

THERE is a floating island, forward, on the stream of time,
Buoyant with fermenting air, and borne along the rapids;
And on that island is a siren, singing sweetly as she goeth,
Her eyes are bright with invitation, and allurement lurketh in her cheeks;
Many lovers, vainly pursuing, follow her beckoning finger,
Many lovers seek her still, even to the cataract of death.
To-morrow is that island, a vain and foolish heritage,
And, laughing with seductive lips, Delusion hideth there.
Often, the precious present is wasted in visions of the future,
And coy To-morrow cometh not with prophecies fulfilled.

There is a fairy skiff, plying on the sea of life,
And charitably toiling still to save the shipwrecked crews;
Within, kindly patient, sitteth a gentle mariner,
Piloting, through surf and strait, the fragile barks of men:
How cheering is her voice, how skilfully she guideth,
How nobly leading onward yet, defying even death!
To-morrow is that skiff, a wise and welcome rescue,
And, full of gladdening words and looks, that mariner is Hope.
Often, the painful present is comforted by flattering the future,
And kind To-morrow beareth half the burdens of To-day.

To-morrow, whispereth weakness: and To-morrow findeth him the weaker;
To-morrow, promiseth conscience, and behold, no to-day for a fulfilment.
O name of happy omen unto youth, O bitter word of terror to the dotard,
Goal of folly's lazy wish, and sorrow's ever-coming friend,
Fraud's loophole,—caution's hint,—and trap to catch the honest,—
Thou wealth to many poor, disgrace to many noble,
Thou hope and fear, thou weal and woe, thou remedy, thou ruin,
How thickly swarms of thought are clustering round To-morrow.
The hive of memory increaseth, to every day its cell;
There is the labour stored, the honey or corruption;
Each morn the bees fly forth, to fill the growing comb,
And levy golden tribute of the uncomplaining flowers:

To-morrow is their care; they toil for rest to-morrow;
But man deferreth duty's task, and loveth ease to-day.

To-morrow is that lamp upon the marsh, which a traveller never
    reacheth;
To-morrow, the rainbow's cup, coveted prize of ignorance;
To-morrow, the shifting anchorage, dangerous trust of mariners;
To-morrow, the wrecker's beacon, wily snare of the destroyer.
Reconcile convictions with delay, and To-morrow is a fatal lie;
Frighten resolutions into action, To-morrow is a wholesome truth;
I must, for I fear To-morrow; this is the Cassava's food;
Why should I? let me trust To-morrow,—this is the Cassava's
    poison.

Lo, it is the even of To-day,—a day so lately a To-morrow;
Where are those high resolves, those hopes of yesternight?
O faint fond heart, still shall thy whisper be, To-morrow,
And must the growing avalanche of sin roll down that easy slope?
Alas, it is ponderous, and moving on in might, that a Sisyphus
    may not stop it;
But haste thee with the lever of a prayer, and stem its strength To-
    day:
For its race may speedily be run, and this poor hut, thyself,
Be whelmed in death and suffocating guilt, that dreary Alpine
    snow-wreath.

Pensioner of life, be wise, and heed a brother's counsel;
I also am a beadsman, with scrip and staff as thou:
Wouldest thou be bold against the past, and all its evil memories,
Wouldest thou be safe amid the present, its dangers and tempta-
    tions,
Wouldest thou be hopeful of the future, vague though it be and
    endless?
Haste thee, repent, believe, obey! thou standest in the courage of
    a legion.
Commend the Past to God, with all its irrevocable harm,
Humbly, but in cheerful trust, and banish vain regrets;
Come to him, continually come, casting all the Present at his feet,
Boldly, but in prayerful love, and fling off selfish cares;
Commit the Future to his will, the viewless fated future;
Zealously go forward with integrity, and God will bless thy faith.

For that, feeble as thou art, there is with thee a mighty Conqueror,
Thy friend, the same for ever, yesterday, to-day, and to-morrow;
That friend, changeless as eternity, himself shall make thee friends
Of those thy foes transformed, yesterday, to-day, and to-morrow.

OF AUTHORSHIP.

GREAT is the dignity of Authorship: I magnify mine office;
Albeit in much feebleness I hold it thus unworthily.
For it is to be one of a noble band, the welfare of the world,
Whose haunt is on the lips of men, whose dwelling in their hearts,
Who are precious in the retrospect of Memory, and walk among
    the visions of Hope,
Who commune with the good for everlasting, and call the wisest,
    brother,
Whose voice hath burst the Silence, and whose light is flung upon
    the Darkness,
—Flashing jewels on a robe of black, and harmony bounding out
    of chaos,—
Who gladden empires with their wisdom, and bless to the farthest
    generation,
Doers of illimitable good, gainers of inestimable glory!—
We speak but of the Magnates, we heed none humbler than the
    highest,
We take no count of sorry scribes, nor waste one thought upon the
    groundlings;
Our eyes are lifted from the multitude, groping in the dark with
    candles,
To gaze upon that firmament of praise, the constellated lamps of
    learning.
Everduring witnesses of mind, undisputed evidence of Power,
Goodly volumes, living stones, build up their author's temple:
Though of low estate, his rank is above princes,—though needy he
    hath worship of the rich,
When Genius unfurleth on the winds his banner as a mighty
    leader.
Just in purpose, and self-possessed in soul, lord of many talents,
The mental Croesus goeth forth, rejoicing in his wealth;
Keen and clear perception gloweth on his forehead like a sunbeam,
He readeth men at a glance, and mists roll away before him;

The wise have set him as their captain, the foolish are rebuked at
    his presence,
The excellent bless him with their prayers, and the wicked praise
    him by their curses ;
His voice, mighty in operation, stirreth up the world as a trumpet,
And kings account it honour to be numbered of his friends.

Rare is the worthiness of Authorship: I justify mine office :
Albeit fancies weak as mine credit not the calling.
For it addeth immortality to dying facts, that are ready to vanish
    away,
Embalming as in amber the poor insects of an hour ;
Shedding upon stocks and stones the tender light of interest,
And illumining dark places of the earth, with radiance of classic
    lustre.
It hath power to make past things present, and availeth for the
    present in the future,
Delivering thoughts, and words, and deeds, from the outer dark-
    ness of oblivion.
Where are the sages and the heroes, giants of old time ?—
Where are the mighty kings, that reigned before Agamemnon ?—
Alas, they lie unwept, unhonoured, hidden in the midnight ;
Alas, for they died unchronicled : their memorial perished with
    them.
Where are the nobles of Nineveh, and mitred rulers of Babylon ?
Where are the lords of Edom, and the royal pontiffs of The-
    bais ?
The golden Satrap, and the Tetrarch,—the Hun, and the Druid,
    and the Celt ?
The merchant princes of Phœnicia, and the minds that fashioned
    Elephanta ?
Alas, for the poet hath forgotten them ; and lo ! they are out-
    casts of Memory ;
Alas, that they are withered leaves, sapless and fallen from the
    chaplet of fame.
Speak, Etruria, whose bones be these, entombed with costly
    care,—
Tell out, Herculaneum, the titles that have sounded in those thy
    palaces,—
Lycian Xanthus, thy citadels are mute, and the honour of their
    architects hath died ;

Copan and Palenque, **dreamy ruins in** the West, the forest hath
    swallowed up your sculptures ;
Syracuse,—how silent of the past !—Carthage, thou art blotted
    from remembrance,—
Egypt, wondrous shores, ye are buried in the sand-hills of forget-
    fulness !
Alas,—for in your glorious youth, Time himself was young,
And none durst wrestle with that Angel, iron-sinewed bridegroom
    of Space ;
So he flew by, strong upon the wing, nor dropped **one** failing
    feather,
Wherewith some hoary scribe might register **your** honour and
    renown.
Beyond the broad Atlantic, in the regions of the setting sun,
Ask of the plume-crowned Incas, that ruled **in** old Peru,—
Ask of grand Caciques, and priests of the pyramids in Mexico,—
Ask **of a** thousand painted tribes, high nobility of Nature,
Who, once, could roam their own Elysian plains, free, generous,
    and happy,
Who now, degraded and in exile, having sold their fatherland for
    nought,
Sink and are extinguished in the western seas, even as the sun they
    follow,—
Where is the record of their deeds, their prowess worthy of
    Achilles,
Nestor's wisdom, the chivalry of Manlius, the native eloquence of
    Cicero,
The skill of Xenophon, the spirit of Alcibiades, the firmness of a
    Maccabæan mother,
Brotherly love that Antigone might envy, the honour and the forti-
    tude of Regulus ?
Alas, their glory and their praise have vanished like a summer
    cloud ;
Alas ! that they are dead indeed ; they are not written down in
    the Book of the living.

High is the privilege **of** Authorship **:** I purify **mine office ;**
Albeit earthly stains pollute it in my **hands.**
For it is to the world a teacher and **a** guide, Mentor of that gay
    Telemachus ;
Warning, comforting, and helping,—a lover and friend of Man.

Heaven's almoner, Earth's health, patient minister of goodness,
With kind and zealous pen, the wise religious blesseth:
Nature's worshipper, and neophyte of grace, rich in tender sympathies,
With kindled soul and flashing eye, the poet poureth out his heartful:
Priest of truth, champion of innocence, warder of the gates of praise,
Carefully with sifting search laboureth the pale historian:
Error's enemy, and acolyte of science, firm in sober argument,
The calm philosopher marshalleth his facts, noting on his page their principles.
These pour mercies upon men; and others, little less in honour,
By cheerful wit and graphic tale refreshening the harassed spirit.
But, there be other some beside, buyers and sellers in the temple,
Who shame their high vocation, greedy of inglorious gain;
There be, who fabricating books, heed of them meanly as of merchandise;
And seek nor use, nor truth, nor fame, but sell their minds for lucre:
O false brethren! ye wot indeed the labour, but are witless of the love;
O lying prophets, chilled in soul, unquickened by the life of inspiration!—
And there be, who, frivolous and vain, seek to make others foolish,
Snaring Youth by loose sweet Song, and Age by selfish maxim:
Cleverly heartless, and wittily profane, they swell the river of corruption:
Brilliant satellites of sin,—my soul, be not found among their company.
And there be, who, haters of religion, toil to prove it priestcraft,
Owning none other aim nor hope, but to confound the good:
Woe unto them! for their works shall live; yea, to their utter condemnation:
Woe! for their own handwriting shall testify against them for ever.

Pure is the happiness of Authorship: I glorify mine office;
Albeit lightly having sipped the cup of its lower pleasures.
For it is to feel with a father's heart, when he yearneth on the child of his affections;

To rejoice in a man's own miniature world, gladdened by its rare arrangement.
The poem, is it not a fabric of mind? we love what we create:
That choice and musical order,—how pleasant is the toil of composition!
Yea, when the volume of the universe was blazoned out in beauty by its Author,
God was glad, and blessed his work; for it was very good.
And shall not the image of his Maker be happy in his own mind's doing,
Looking on the structure he hath reared, gratefully with sweet complacence?
Shall not the Minerva of his brain, panoplied and perfect in proportions,
Gladden the soul and give light unto the eyes, of him the travailing parent?
Go to the sculptor, and ask him of his dreams,—wherefore are his nights so moonlit?
Angel faces, and beautiful shapes, fascinate the pale Pygmalion:
Go to the painter, and trace his reveries,—wherefore are his days so sunny?
Choice design and skilful colouring charm the flitting hours of Parrhasius:
Even so, walking in his buoyancy, intoxicate with fairy fancies,
The young enthusiast of authorship goeth on his way rejoicing:
Behold,—he is gallantly attended; legions of thrilling thoughts
Throng about the standard of his mind, and call his Will their captain;
Behold,—his court is as a monarch's; ideas, and grand imaginations
Swell, with gorgeous cavalcade, the splendour of his Spiritual State;
Behold,—he is delicately served: for oftentimes, in solitary calmness,
Some mental fair Egeria smileth on her Numa's worship;
Behold,—he is happy; there is gladness in his eye, and his heart is a sealed fountain,
Bounding secretly with joys unseen, and keeping down its ecstasy of pleasure!

Yea: how dignified, and worthy, full of privilege and happiness,

Standeth in majestic independence the self-ennobled Author!
For God hath blessed him with a mind, and cherished it in tenderness and purity,
Hath taught it in the whisperings of wisdom, and added all the riches of content:
Therefore, leaning on his God, a pensioner for soul and body,
His spirit is the subject of none other, calling no man Master,
His hopes are mighty and eternal, scorning small ambitions:
He hideth from the pettiness of praise, and pitieth the feebleness of envy.
If he meet honours, well; it may be his humility to take them:
If he be rebuked, better; his veriest enemy shall teach him.
For the master-mind hath a birthright of eminence; his cradle is an eagle's eyrie:
Need but to wait till his wings are grown, and Genius soareth to the sun:
To creeping things upon the mountain leaveth he the gradual ascent,
Resting his swiftness on the summit only for a higher flight.
Glad in clear good-conscience, lightly doth he look for commendation;
What, if the prophet lacketh honour? for he can spare that praise:
The honest giant careth not to be patted on the back by pigmies;
Flatter greatness, he brooketh it good-humouredly: blame him,—thou tiltest at a pyramid:
Yet, just censure of the good never can he hear without contrition;
Neither would he miss one wise man's praise, for scarce is that jewel and costly:
Only for the herd of common minds, and the vulgar trumpetings of fame,
If aught he heedeth in the matter, his honour is sought in their neglect:
Slender is the marvel, and little is the glory, when round his luscious fruits
The worm and the wasp and the multitude of flies are gathered as to banquet;
Fashion's freak, and the critical sting, and the flood of flatteries he scorneth;
Cheerfully asking of the crowd the favour to forget him:
The while his blooming fruits ripen in richer fragrance,
A feast for the few,—and the many yet unborn,—who still shall love their savour.

So then, humbly with his God, and proudly independent of his
 fellows,
Walketh, in pleasures multitudinous, the man ennobled by his
 pen :
He hath built up, glorious architect, a monument more durable
 than brass ;
His children's children shall talk of him in love, and teach their
 sons his honour :
His dignity hath set him among princes, the universe is debtor to
 his worth,
His privilege is blessing for ever, his happiness shineth now,
For he standeth of that grand Election, each man one among a
 thousand,
Whose sound is gone out into all lands, and their words to the end
 of the world !

OF MYSTERY.

ALL things being are in mystery; we expound mysteries by mys-
 teries ;
And yet the secret of them all is one in simple grandeur :
All intricate, yet each path plain, to those who know the way ;
All unapproachable, yet easy of access, to them that hold the key :
We walk among labyrinths of wonder, but thread the mazes with a
 clue ;
We sail in chartless seas, but behold ! the pole-star is above us.
For, counting down from God's good will, thou meltest every
 riddle into Him,
The axiom of reason is an undiscovered God, and all things live in
 his ubiquity :
There is only one great secret ; but that one hideth everywhere.
How should the infinite be understood in Time, when it stretcheth
 on ungrasped for ever ?
Can a halting Œdipus of earth guess that enigma of the universe ?
Not one : the sword of faith must cut the Gordian knot of nature.

God, pervading all, is in all things the mystery of each ;
The wherefore of its character and essence, the fountain of its vir-
 tues and its beauties.
The child asketh of its mother,—Wherefore is the violet so sweet

The mother answereth her babe,—Darling, God hath willed it.
And sages, diving into science, have but a profundity of words,
They track for some few links the circling chain of consequence,
And then, after doubts and disputations, are left where they began,
At the bald conclusion of a clown, things are because they are.
Wherefore are the meadows green, is it not to gratify the eye?
But why should greenness charm the eye? such is God's good will.
Wherefore is the ear attuned to a pleasure in musical sounds,
And who set a number to those sounds, and fixed the laws of harmony?
Who taught the bird to build its nest, or lent the shrub its life,
Or poised in the balances of order the power to attract and to repel?
Who continueth the worlds, and the sea, and the heart, in motion?
Who commanded gravitation to tie down all upon its sphere?—
For even as a limestone cliff is an aggregate of countless shells,
One riddle concrete of many, a mystery compact of mysteries,
So God, cloudcapped in immensity, standeth the cohesion of all things,
And secrets, sublimely indistinct, permeate that Universe, Himself:
As is the whole, so are the parts, whether they be mighty or minute,
The sun is not more unexplained than the tissue of an emmet's wing.

Thus then, omnipresent Deity worketh his unbiassed mind,
A mind, one in moral, but infinitely multiplied in means:
And the uniform prudence of his will cometh to be counted law,
Till mutable man fancieth volition stirring in the potter's clay:
God, a wise father, showeth not his reasons to his babes;
But willeth in secresy and goodness: for causes generate dispute:
Then we, his darkling children, watch that invariable purpose,
And invest the passive creature with its Maker's energy and skill.
Therefore, they of old time stopped short of God in idols,
Therefore, in these latter days, we heed not the Jehovah in his works.
Mystery is God's great name; He is the mystery of goodness:
Some other, from the hierarchs of heaven, usurped the mystery of sin.

God is the King, yea, even of himself; he crowned himself with holiness;
The burning circlet of iniquity another found and wore.
God is separate, even from his attributes; but **he** willed eternally the good;
Therefore freely, **though unchangeably,** is wise, righteous, and loving:
But ambition, open unto angels, saw the evil, flung aside from the beginning,
It was Lucifer that saw, and nothing loathed those black unclaimed regalia,
So he coveted and stole, to be counted for a king, antagonist of God,
But when he touched the **leprous robes,** behold, a cheated traitor.

For self-existence, charactered **with love,** with power, wisdom, and ubiquity,
Could not dwell alone, but willed and worked creation:
Thus, in continual exhalation, darkening the void with matter,
Sprang from prolific Deity the creatures of his skill:
And beings living on his breath, were needfully less perfect than himself,
Therefore less capable of bliss, **whereat His** benevolence was bounded;
So to make the capability expand, intensely progressive to eternity,
He suffered **darkness to illustrate the light,** and pain to heighten pleasure:
To heap up happiness on souls he loved, allowed he sin and sorrow,
And then to guilt and grief and shame, he brought unbidden amnesty:
Sinless, **none had** been redeemed, nor wrapt again in God:
Sorrowless, no conflict had been known, and Heaven had been mulcted of its comfort:
Yea, with evil unexhibited, probationary toils unfelt,
Men had not appreciated good, nor angels valued their security.
Herein, to reason's **eye,** is revealed the **mystery** of goodness
Blessing, through permitted woe, and **teaching by the** mystery **of** sin.

O Christian, whose chastened curiosity loveth things mysterious,

Accounting them shadows and eclipses of Him the one great light,
Look now, satisfied with faith, on minds that judge by sense,
And, dull from contemplating matter, take small heed of spirit.
Toiling feebly upward, their argument tracketh from below,
They catch the latest consequent, and prove the nearest cause:
What is this? that a seed produced a seed, and so for a thousand
    seasons;
Ascend a thousand steps, thy ladder leaveth thee in air:
Thou canst not climb to God, and short of Him is nothing;
There is no cause for aught we see, but in his present will.
Begin from the Maker, thou carriest down his attributes to reptiles,
The sharded beetle and the lizard live and move in Him:
Begin from the creature, corruption and infirmity mar thy foolish
    toil,
Heap Ossa on Olympus, how much art thou nearer to the stars?
It is easy running from a mountain's top down to the valleys at its
    foot,
But difficult and steep the laborious ascent, and feebly shalt thou
    reach it;
Yet man, beginning from himself, that first deluding mystery,
Hopeth from the pit of lies to struggle up to truth;
So, taxing knowledge to its strength, he pusheth one step further,
And fancieth complacently that much is done by reaching a remote
    effect:
Then he maketh answer to himself, as a silly nurse to her little
    one,
Evading, in a mist of words, hard things he cannot solve;
Till, like an ostrich in the desert, he burieth his head in atoms,
Thinking that, if he is blind, no sun can shine in heaven.

Therefore cometh it to pass, that an atheist is ever the most
    credulous,
Snatching at any foolish cause, that may dispel his doubts;
And, even as it were for ridicule, a spectacle to men and angels,
The captious and cautious unbeliever is of all men weakest to
    believe:
Cut from the anchorage of God, his bark is a plaything of the
    billows;
The compass of his principle is broken, the rudder of his faith un-
    shipped:
Chance and Fate, in a stultified antagonism, govern all for him;

Truth sprang from the conflict of falsities, and the multitude of
 accidents hath bred design !
Where is the imposture so gross, that shall not entrap his curiosity ?
What superstition is so abject, that it doth not blanch his cheek ?
Whereof can he be sure, with whom Chaos is substitute for Order ?
How should his silly structure stand, a pyramid built upon its
 apex ?—
Yea, I have seen grey-headed men, the bastard slips of science,
Go for light to glow-worms, while they scorn the sun at noon :
Men, who fear no God, trembling at a gipsy's curse,
Men, who jest at revelation, clinging to a madman's prophecy !

There is a pleasing dread in the fashion of all mysteries,
For hope is mixed therein and fear ; who shall divine their issues ?
Even the orphan, wandering by night, lost on dreary moors,
Is sensible of some vague bliss amidst his shapeless terrors ;
The buoyancy of instant expectation, spurring on the mind to
 venture,
Overbeareth, in its energy, the cramp and the chill of apprehen-
 sion.
There is a solitary pride, when the heart, in new importance,
Writeth gladly on its archives, the secrets none other men have
 seen :
And there is a caged terror, evermore wrestling with the mind,
When crime hath whispered his confession, and the secrets are
 written there in blood :
The village maiden is elated at a tenderly confided tale :
The bandit's wife with sickening fear guessed the premeditated
 murder :
The sage, with triumph on his brow, hideth up his deep discovery ;
The idlest clown shall delve all day, to find a hidden treasure.

For mystery is man's life ; we wake to the whisperings of novelty :
And what, though we lie down disappointed ? we sleep, to wake
 in hope.
The letter, or the news, the chances and the changes, matters that
 may happen,
Sweeten or embitter daily life with the honey-gall of mystery.
For we walk blindfold,—and a minute may be much,—a step may
 reach the precipice ;
What earthly loss, what heavenly gain, may not this day produce ?

Levelled of Alps and Andes, without its valleys and ravines,
How dull the face of earth, unfeatured of both beauty and sublimity:
And so, shorn of mystery, beggared in its hopes and fears,
How flat the prospect of existence, mapped by intuitive foreknowledge.
Praise God, creatures of earth, for the mercies linked with secresy,
That spices of uncertainty enrich the cup of life;
Praise God, his hosts on high, for the mysteries that make all joy;
What were intelligence, with nothing more to learn, or heaven, in eternity of sameness?

To number every mystery were to sum the sum of all things;
None can exhaust a theme, whereof God is example and similitude:
Nevertheless, take a garland from the garden, a handful from the harvest,
Some scattered drops of spray from the ceaseless mighty cataract:
Whence are we,—whither do we tend,—how do we feel, and reason?
How strange a thing is man, a spirit saturating clay!
When doth soul make embryos immortal,—how do they rank hereafter,—
And will the unconscious idiot be quenched in death as nothing?
In essence immaterial, are these minds, as it were, thinking machines?
For, to understand may but rightly be to use a mechanism all possess,
So that in reading or hearing of another, a man shall seem unto himself
To be recollecting images or arguments, native and congenial to his mind:
And yet, what shall we say,—who can arede the riddle?
The brain may be clockwork, and mind its spring, mechanism quickened by a spirit.

Who so shrewd as rightly to divide life, instinct, reason;
Trees, zoophytes, creatures of the plain, and savage men among them?
Hath the mimosa instinct,—or the scallop more than life,—
Or the dog less than reason,—or the brute-man more than instinct?
What is the cause of health,—and the gendering of disease?

I.

Why should arsenic kill, and whence is the potency of antidotes?
Behold, a morsel,—eat and die: the term of thy probation is expired:
Behold, a potion,—drink and be alive; the limit of thy trial is enlarged.
Who can expound beauty? or explain the character of nations?
Who will furnish a cause for the epidemic force of fashion?
Is there a moral magnetism living in the light of example?
Is practice electricity?—Yet all these are but names.
Doth normal Art imprison, in its works, spirit translated into substance,
So that the statue, the picture, or the poem, are crystals of the mind?
And doth Philosophy with sublimating skill shred away the matter,
Till rarefied intelligence exudeth even out of stocks and stones?

O mysteries, ye all are one, the mind of an inexplicable Architect
Dwelleth alike in each, quickening and moving in them all.
Fields, and forests, and cities of men, their woes and wealth and works,
And customs, and contrivances of life, with all we see and know,
For a little way, a little while, ye hang dependent on each other,
But all are held in one right-hand, and by his will ye are.
Here is answer unto mystery, an unintelligible God,
This is the end and the beginning, it is reason that He be not understood.
Therefore it were probable and just, even to a man's weak thinking,
To have one for God who always may be learnt, yet never fully known:
That He, from whom all mysteries spring, in whom they all converge,
Throned in his sublimity beyond the grovellings of lower intellect,
Should claim to be truer than man's truest, the boasted certainty of numbers,
Should baffle his arithmetic, confound his demonstrations, and paralyse the might of his necessity,
Standing supreme as the mystery of mysteries, everywhere, yet impersonate,
Essential one in three, essential three in one!

OF GIFTS.

I HAD a seeming friend ;—I gave him gifts, and he was gone
I had an open enemy ;—I gave him gifts, and won him :
Common friendship standeth on equalities, and cannot bear a debt ;
But the very heart of hate melteth at a good man's love :
Go to, then, thou that sayest,—I will give and rivet the links :
For pride shall kick at obligation, and push the giver from him
The covetous spirit may rejoice, revelling in thy largess,
But chilling selfishness will mutter,—I must give again :
The vain heart may be glad, in this new proof of man's esteem,
But the same idolatry of self abhorreth thoughts of thanking.

Nevertheless, give ; for it shall be a discriminating test
Separating honesty from falsehood, weeding insincerity from friendship.
Give, it is like God ; thou weariest the bad with benefits ·
Give, it is like God ; thou gladdenest the good by gratitude.
Give to thy near of kin, for providence hath stationed thee his helper :
Yet see that he claim not as his right, thy freewill offering of duty.
Give to the young, they love it ; neither hath the poison of suspicion
Spoilt the flavour of their thanks, to look for latent motives.
Give to merit, largely give ; his conscious heart will bless thee :
It is not flattery, but love,—the sympathy of men his brethren.
Give, for encouragement in good ; the weak desponding mind
Hath many foes, and much to do, and leaneth on its friends.
Yet heed thou wisely these ; give seldom to thy better ;
For such obtrusive boon shall savour of presumption ;
Or, if his courteous bearing greet thy proffered kindness,
Shall not thine independent honesty be vexed at the semblance of a bribe ?
Moreover, heed thou this ; give to thine equal charily,
The occasion fair and fitting, the gift well chosen and desired :
Hath he been prosperous and blest ? a flower may show thy gladness ;
Is he in need ? with liberal love, tender him the well filled purse :
Disease shall welcome friendly care in grapes and precious unguents ;

And where a darling child hath died, give praise, and hope, and
 sympathy.
Yet once more, heed thou this ; give to the poor discreetly,
Nor suffer idle sloth to lean upon thy charitable arm :
To diligence give, as to an equal, on just and fit occasion ;
Or he bartereth his hard-earned self-reliance for the casual lottery
 of gifts.
The timely loan hath added nerve, where easy liberality would
 palsy ;
Work and wages make a light heart ; but the mendicant asked
 with a heavy spirit.
A man's own self-respect is worth unto him more than money,
And evil is the charity that humbleth, and maketh man less
 happy.

There are who sow liberalities, to reap the like again ;
But men accept his boon, scorning the shallow usurer :
I have known many such a fisherman lose his golden baits ;
And oftentimes the tame decoy escapeth with the flock.
Yea, there are who give unto the poor, to gain large interest of
 God,—
Fool,—to think His wealth is money, and not mind :
And haply after thine alms, thy calculated givings,
The hurricane shall blast thy crops, and sink the homeward ship ;
Then shall thy worldly soul murmur that the balances were false,
Thy trader's mind shall think of God,—He stood not to his bar-
 gain !

Give, saith the preacher, be large in liberality, yield to the holy
 impulse,
Tarry not for cold consideration, but cheerfully and freely scatter.
So, for complacency of conscience, in a gush of counterfeited
 charity,
He that hath not wherewith to be just, selfishly presumeth to be
 generous :
The debtor, and the rich by wrong, are known among the band of
 the benevolent ;
And men extol the noble hearts, who rob that they may give.
Receivers are but little prone to challenge rights of giving,
Nor stop to test, for conscience' sake, the righteousness of mam-
 mon :

And the zealot in a cause is a receiver, at the hand which bettereth
 his cause;
And thus an unsuspected bribe shall blind the good man's judg-
 ment:
It is easy to excuse greatness, and the rich are readily forgiven:
What, if his gains were evil, sanctified by using them aright?
O shallow flatterer, self-interest is thy thought,
Heedless of partaking in the like, thou too wouldest scorn the giver.

Money hath its value; and the scatterer thereof his thanks:
Few men, drinking at a rivulet, stop to consider its source.
The hand that closeth on an alm, be it for necessities or zeal,
Hath small scruple whence it came: Vespasian rejoiceth in his
 tribute.
Therefore have colleges and hospitals risen upon orphans' wrongs,
Chapels and cathedrals have thriven on the welcome wages of
 iniquity,
And fraud, in evil compensation, hath salved his guilty conscience,
Not by restoring to the cheated, but by ostentatious giving to the
 grateful.

So, those who reap rejoice; and reaping, bless the sower:
No one is eager to discover, where discovery tendeth unto loss:
Yet, if knowledge of a theft made gainers thereby guilty,
Can he be altogether innocent, who never asked the honesty of
 gain?
Therefore, O preacher, zealous for charity, temper thy warm ap-
 peal,—
Warning the debtor and unjustly rich, they may not dare to give:
To do good is a privilege and guerdon: how shouldest thou re-
 joice
If ill-got gifts of presumptuous fraud be offered on the altar?
The question is not of degrees; unhallowed alms are evil;
Discourage and reject alike the obolus, or talent, of iniquity.

Yet more, be careful that, unworthily, thou gain not an advantage
 over weakness,
Unstable souls, fervent and profuse, fluttered by the feeling of the
 moment;
For eloquence swayeth to its will the feeble and the conscious of
 defect:

Rashly give they, and afterward are sad,—a gift that doubly erred.
It was the worldliness of priestcraft that accounted almsgiving for charity;
And many a father's penitence **hath** steeped his **son in** penury;
Yet, considered he lightly the guilt of a death-bed selfishness
That strove to take with him, for gain, the gold no longer his;
So **he died in a** false peace, and dying robbed his kindred:
The cunning **friar at** his side having cheated both the living and the dead.

Charity sitteth on a fair hill-top, blessing far and near,
But **her** garments drop ambrosia, chiefly, on the violets around her:
She gladdeneth indeed the maplike scene, stretching **to the** verge of the horizon,
For her angel face is lustrous and beloved, even as the moon in heaven:
But the light of that beatific vision gloweth in serener concentration
The nearer to her heart, and nearer to her home,—that hill-top where she sitteth:
Therefore is she kind unto her kin, yearning in affection on her neighbours,
Giving gifts to those around, who know and love her well.
But the counterfeit of charity, an hypocrite of earth, **not** a grace of heaven,
Seeketh not to bless at home, for her nearer aspect is ill-favoured:
Therefore hideth she for shame, counting that pride humility,
And none of those around her hearth are gladdened by her gifts:
Rather, with an overreaching zeal, flingeth she her bounty to the **stranger,**
And scattered prodigalities abroad compensate for meanness in her home:
For benefits showered on the distant shine in unmixed beauty,
So **that even she may reap** their undiscerning praise:
Therefore native want **hath** pined, where foreign need **was fattened:**
Woman been crushed by the tyrannous hand that upheld the flag of liberality;
Poverty been prisoned up and starved, by hearts that are maudlin **upon** crime;

And freeborn babes been manacled by men, who liberate the
   sturdy slave.

Policy counselleth a gift, given wisely and in season,
And policy afterwards approveth it, for great is the **influence of
   gifts.**
The lover, unsmiled upon before, is welcome for his **jewelled
   bauble;**
The righteous cause without a fee, must yield to bounteous guilt:
How fair is a man in thine esteem, whose just discrimination
   seeketh thee,
And so, discerning merit, honoureth it with gifts!
Yea, **let** the cause appear sufficient, and the **motive clear** and **un-
   suspicious,**
As given unto one who cannot help, or proving honest thanks,
There liveth not one among a million, who is proof against the
   charm of liberality,
And flattery, that boon of praise, hath power with the wisest.

Man is of three natures, craving all for charity:
It is not enough to give him meats, withholding other comfort;
For the mind starveth, and the soul is scorned, and so the human
   animal
Eateth his unsatisfying pittance, a thankless, heartless pauper:
Yet would he bless thee and be grateful, didst thou feed his spirit,
And **teach him** that thine almsgivings are charities, are loves:
—I saw a beggar in the street, and another beggar pitied him;
Sympathy sank into his soul, and the pitied one felt happier:
Anon passed by a cavalcade, children of wealth and gaiety;
They laughed and looked upon the beggar, and the gallants flung
   him gold;
He, poor spirit-humbled wretch, gathered up their givings with a
   curse,
And went—to **share it with his** brother, the beggar who had
   pitied him.

OF BEAUTY.

Thou mightier than Manoah's son, whence is thy great strength,
And wherein the secret of thy craft, O charmer charming wisely?—

For thou art strong in weakness, and in artlessness well-skilled,
Constant in the multitudes of change, and simple amidst intricate
    complexity.
Folly's shallow lip can ask the deepest question,
And many wise in many words should answer, what is beauty?—
Who shall separate the hues that flicker on a dying dolphin,
Or analyse the jewelled lights that deck the peacock's train,
Or shrewdly mix upon a pallette the tints of an iridescent spar,
Or set in rank the wandering shades about a watered silk?

For beauty is intangible, vague, ill to be defined;
She hath the coat of a chameleon, changing while we watch it.
Strangely woven is the web, disorderly yet harmonious,
A glistering robe of mingled mesh, that may not be unravelled.
It is shot with heaven's blue, the soul of summer skies,
And twisted strings of light, the mind of noonday suns,
And ruddy gleams of life, that roll along the veins;
A coat of many colours, running curiously together.
There is threefold beauty for man; twofold beauty for the animal;
And the beauty of inanimates is single: body, temper, spirit.
Multiplied in endless combination, issue the changeable results;
Each class verging on the other twain, with imperceptible grada-
    tion;
And every individual in each having his propriety of difference,
So that the meanest of creation bringeth in a tribute of the beau-
    tiful.
Yea, from the worst in favour shineth out a fitness of design,
The patent mark of beauty, its Maker's name imprest.
For the great Creator's seal is set to all his works;
Its quarterings are Attributes of praise, and all the shield is beauty:
So, that heraldic blazon is Creation's common signet;
And the universal family of life goeth in the colours of its Lord:
But each one, as a several son, shall bear those arms with a dif-
    ference:
Beauty, various in phase, and similar in seeming oppositions.
The coins of old Rome were struck with a diversity for each,
Barely two be found alike, in every Cæsar's image:
So, note thou the seals, ranged round the charters of the Uni-
    verse,
The finger of God is the stamp upon them all, but each hath its
    separate variety.

Beauty, theme of innocence, how may guilt discourse thee?
Let holy angels sing thy praise, for man hath marred thy visage.
Still the maimed torso of a Theseus can gladden taste with its proportions;
Though sin hath shattered every limb, how comely are the fragments!
And **music leaveth** on the ear a memory of sweet sounds,
And broken arches charm the sight with hints of fair completeness.
So, while **humbled at the ruin, be thou** grateful for the relics;
Go forth, and look on all around with kind uncaptious eye:
Freely let us wander through these unfrequented ways,
And talk of glorious beauty filling all the world.

For beauty hideth everywhere, that Reason's child may seek **her**,
And having found the gem of price, may set it in God's crown.
Beauty nestleth in the rosebud, or walketh the firmament with planets,
She is heard in the beetle's evening hymn, and shouteth in the matins of the sun;
The cheek of the peach is glowing with her smile, her splendour blazeth in the lightning,
She is the dryad of the woods, the naiad of the streams;
Her golden hair hath tapestried the silkworm's silent chamber,
And to her measured harmonies the wild waves beat in time;
With tinkling feet at eventide she danceth in the meadow,
Or, like a **Titan**, lieth stretched athwart the ridgy Alps;
She is rising, in her veil of mist, a Venus from the waters,—
Men gaze upon the loveliness,—and lo, it is beautiful exceedingly;
She, with the might of a Briareus, is dragging down the clouds upon the mountain,—
Men look upon the grandeur,—and lo, it is excellent in glory.
For I judge that beauty and sublimity be but the lesser and the great,
Sublime as magnified to giants, and beautiful, diminished into fairies.
It were a false fancy to solve all beauty by desire,
It were a lowering thought to expound sublimity by dread.
Cowardly men with trembling hearts have feared the furious storm,
Nor felt its thrilling beauty; but is it then not beautiful?
And careless men, at summer's eve, have loved the dimpled waves;

O that smile upon the seas,—hath it no sublimity?
Dost thou nothing know of this,—to be awed at woman's beauty?
Nor, with exhilarated heart, to hail the crashing thunder?
Thou hast much to learn, that never found a fearfulness in flowers;
Thou hast missed of joy, that never basked in beauties of the terrible.

Show me an enthusiast in aught; he hath noted one thing narrowly,
And lo, his keenness hath detected the one dear hiding-place of beauty:
Then he boasteth, simple soul, flattered by discovery,
Fancying that no science else can show so fair and precious:
He hath found a ray of light, and cherisheth the treasure in his closet,
Mocking at those larger minds, that bathe in floods of noon;
Lo, what a jewel hath he gotten,—this is the monopolist of beauty,—
And lightly heeding all beside, he poured his yearnings thitherward:
Be it for love, or for learning, habit, art, or nature,
Exclusive thought is all the cause of this particular zeal.
But the like intensity of fitness, kind and skilful beauty,
So pleasant to his mind in one thing, filleth all beside:
From the waking minute of a chrysalis, to the perfect cycle of chronology,
From the centipede's jointed armour, to the mammoth's fossil ribs,
From the kingfisher's shrill note, to the cataract's thundering bass,
From the greensward's grateful hues, to the fascinating eye of woman,
Beauty, various in all things, setteth up her home in each,
Shedding graciously around an omnipresent smile.

There is beauty in the rolling clouds, and placid shingle beach,
In feathery snows, and whistling winds, and dun electric skies;
There is beauty in the rounded woods, dank with heavy foliage,
In laughing fields, and dinted hills, the valley and its lake;
There is beauty in the gullies, beauty on the cliffs, beauty in sun and shade,
In rocks and rivers, seas and plains,—the earth is drowned in beauty.

Beauty coileth with the watersnake, and is cradled in the shrewmouse's nest,
She flitteth out with evening bats, and the soft mole hid her in his tunnel;
The limpet is encamped upon the shore, and beauty not a stranger to his tent;
The silvery dace and golden carp thread the rushes with her:
She saileth into clouds with an eagle, she fluttereth into tulips with a humming bird;
The pasturing kine are of her company, and she prowleth with the leopard in his jungle.

Moreover, for the reasonable world, its words, and acts, and speculation,
For frail and fallen manhood, in his every work and way,
Beauty, wrecked and stricken, lingereth still among us,
And morsels of that shattered sun are dropt upon the darkness.
Yea, with savages and boors, the mean, the cruel, and besotted,
Ever, in extenuating grace hide some relics of the beautiful.
Gleams of kindness, deeds of courage, patience, justice, generosity,
Truth welcomed, knowledge prized, rebukes taken with contrition,
All, in various measure, have been blest with some of these,
And never yet hath lived the man, utterly beggared of the beautiful.

Beauty is as crystal in the torchlight, sparkling on the poet's page;
Virgin honey of Hymettus, distilled from the lips of the orator;
A savour of sweet spikenard, anointing the hands of liberality;
A feast of angel's food set upon the tables of religion.
She is seen in the tear of sorrow, and heard in the exuberance of mirth;
She goeth out early with the huntsman, and watcheth at the pillow of disease.
Science in his secret laws hath found out latent beauty,
Sphere and square, and cone and curve, are fashioned by her rules:
Mechanism met her in his forces, fancy caught her in its flittings,
Day is lightened by her eyes, and her eyelids close upon the night.

Beauty is dependence in the babe, a toothless tender nurseling;
Beauty is boldness in the boy, a curly rosy truant;
Beauty is modesty and grace in fair retiring girlhood,

Beauty is openness and strength in pure highminded youth;
Man, the noble and intelligent, gladdeneth earth in beauty,
And woman's beauty sunneth him, as with a smile from heaven.

There is none enchantment against beauty, Magician for all time,
Whose potent spells of sympathy have charmed the passive world;
Verily, she reigneth a Semiramis; there is no might against her;
The lords of every land are harnessed to her triumph.
Beauty is conqueror of all, nor ever yet was found among the nations
That iron-moulded mind, full proof against her power.
Beauty, like a summer's day, subdueth by sweet influences;
Who can wrestle against Sleep?—yet is that giant, very gentleness.

Ajax may rout a phalanx, but beauty shall enslave him single-handed;
Pericles ruled Athens, yet is he the servant of Aspasia:
Light were the labour, and oftentold the tale, to count the victories of beauty,—
Helen, and Judith, and Omphale, and Thais, many a trophied name.
At a glance the misanthrope was softened, and repented of his vows,
When beauty asked, he gave, and banned her—with a blessing;
The cold ascetic loved the smile that lit his dismal cell,
And kindly stayed her step, and wept when she departed:
The bigot abbess felt her heart gush with a mother's feeling,
When looking on some lovely face beneath the cloister's shade;
Usury freed her without ransom; the buccaneer was gentle in her presence;
Madness kissed her on the cheek, and Idiotcy brightened at her coming:
Yea, the very cattle in the field, and hungry prowlers of the forest
With fawning homage greeted her, as beauty glided by.
A welcome guest unbidden, she is dear to every hearth;
A glad spontaneous growth of friends is springing round her rest:
Learning sitteth at her feet, and Idleness laboureth to please her;
Folly hath flung aside his bells, and leaden Dullness gloweth;
Prudence is rash in her defence; Frugality filleth her with riches;
Despair came to her for counsel; and Bereavement was glad when she consoled;

Justice putteth up his sword at the tear of supplicating beauty,
And Mercy, with indulgent haste, hath pardoned beauty's sin.

For beauty is the substitute for all things, satisfying every absence,
The rich delirious cup to make all else forgotten :
She also is the zest unto all things, enhancing every presence,
The rare and precious ambergris, to quicken each perfume.
O beauty, thou art eloquent ; yea, though slow of tongue,
Thy breast, fair Phryne, pleaded well before the dazzled judge :
O beauty, thou art wise ; yea, though teaching falsely,
Sages listen, sweet Corinna, to commend thy lips ;
O beauty, thou art ruler ; yea, though lowly as a slave,
Myrrha, that imperial brow is monarch of thy lord ;
O beauty, thou art winner ; yea, though halting in the race,
Hippodame, Camilla, Atalanta,—in gracefulness ye fascinate your umpires ;
O beauty, thou art rich ; yea, though clad in russet,
Attalus cannot boast his gold against the wealth of beauty ;
O beauty, thou art noble ; yea, though Esther be an exile,
Set her up on high, ye kings, and bow before the majesty of beauty !

Friend and scholar, who, in charity, hast walked with me thus far,
We have wandered in a wilderness of sweets, tracking beauty's footsteps.
And ever as we rambled on among the tangled thicket,
Many a startled thought hath tempted further roaming :
Passion, sympathetic influence, might of imaginary haloes,—
Many the like would lure aside, to hunt their wayward themes.
And, look you,—from his ferny bed in yonder hazel coppice,
A dappled hart hath flung aside the boughs and broke away ;
He is fleet and capricious as the zephyr, and with exulting bounds
Hieth down a turfy lane between the sounding woods ;
His neck is garlanded with flowers, his antlers hung with chaplets,
And rainbow-coloured ribbons stream adown his mottled flanks :
Should we follow?—foolish hunters, thus to chase afoot,—
Who can track the airy speed and doubling wiles of Taste ?

For the estimates of human beauty, dependent upon time and clime,

Manifold and changeable, are multiplied the more by strange gre-
    garious fashion :
And notable ensamples in the great turn to epidemics in the lower,
So that a nation's taste shall vary with its rulers.
Stern Egypt, humbled to the Greek, fancied softer idols,
Greece, the Roman province, nigh forgat her classic sculpture,
Rome, crushed beneath the Goth, loved his barbarian habits,
And Alaric, with his ruffian horde, is tamed by silken Rome.
Columbia's flattened head, and China's crumpled feet,—
The civilized tapering waist,—and the pendulous ears of the
    savage,—
The swollen throat among the mountains, and an ebon skin
    beneath the tropics,—
These shall all be reckoned beauty: and for weighty cause.
First, for the latter: Providence in mercy tempereth taste by cir-
    cumstance,
So that Nature's must shall hit her creature's liking ;
Second, for the middle: though the foolishness of vanity seek to
    mar proportion,
Still, defects in those we love shall soon be counted praise ;
Third, for the first ; a chief, and a princess, maimed or distorted
    from the cradle,
Shall coax the flattery of slaves to imitate the great in their defor-
    mity :
Hence groweth habit : and habits make a taste,
And so shall servile zeal deface the types of beauty
Whiles Alexander conquered, crookedness was comely :
And followers learn to praise the scars upon their leader's brow.
Youth hath sought to flatter age by mimicking grey hairs ;
Age plastereth her wrinkles, and is painted in the ruddiness of
    Youth.
Fashion, the parasite of Rank, apeth faults and failings,
Until the general Taste depraved hath warped its sense of beauty.

Each man hath a measure for himself, yet all shall coincide in
    much ;
A perfect form of human grace would captivate the world :
Be it manhood's lustre, or the loveliness of woman, all would own
    its beauty,
The Caffre and Circassian, Russians and Hindoos, the Briton, the
    Turk, and Japanese.

Not all alike, nor all at once, but each in proportion to intelligence;
His purer state in morals, **and a lesser** grade **in guilt:**
For **the** high standard **of the beautiful** is fixed in Reason's forum,
And sins, and customs, and caprice, have failed to break **it down:**
And reason's standard for the creature pointeth three perfections,
Frame, knowledge, and the feeling heart, well **and kindly**
    mingled:
A **fair** dwelling, furnished wisely, **with a** gentle tenant in it,
This is the glory of humanity: thou hast seen it seldom.

There is a beauty for the body; the superficial polish of a statue,
The symmetry of form and feature delicately carved and painted.
How bright in **early** bloom the Georgian sitteth at her lattice,
How softened **off** in graceful curves her young and gentle shape:
Those dark eyes, lit by curiosity, flash beneath the lashes,
And still her velvet cheek is dimpled with a smile.
Dost thou count her beautiful?—even as a mere fair figure,
A plastic image, **little** more,—the outer garb of woman:
Yea,—and thus far it is well; but Reason's hopes are higher,—
Can he sate his soul on a scantling third of beauty?

Yet is this the pleasing trickery, that cheateth **half the world,**
Nature's wise deceit to make up waste in life;
And few be they that rest uncaught, for many a twig is **limed;**
Where is the wise among a million, that took not form for beauty?
But **watch it** well: for vanity and sin, malice, hate, suspicion,
Louring as clouds upon **the countenance,** will disenchant its
    charms.
The needful complexity of beauty claimeth mind and soul,
Though many coins of foul alloy pass current for the true:
And albeit fairness in the creature shall **often co-exist** with excel-
    lence,
Yet hath many an angel shape been tenanted by fiends.
A man, **spiritually keen,** shall detect in surface beauty
Those **marring specks of** evil which the sensual cannot see;
Therefore **is he proof** against a face, unlovely to his likings,
And **common minds** shall scorn the taste, that shrunk from sin's
    distortion.
There is a beauty of the reason; grandly independent of externals,
It looketh from the windows of the house, shining in the man
    triumphant.

I have seen the broad blank face of some misshapen dwarf
Lit on a sudden as with glory, the brilliant light of mind :
Who then imagined him deformed? intelligence is blazing on his forehead,
There is empire in his eye, and sweetness on his lip, and his brown cheek glittereth with beauty :
And I have known some Nireus of the camp, a varnished paragon of chamberers,
Fine, elegant, and shapely, moulded as the master-piece of Phidias,—
Such an one, with intellects abased, have I noted crouching to the dwarf,
Whilst his lovers scorn the fool, whose beauty hath departed !

And there is a beauty of the spirit ; mind in its perfect flowering,
Fragrant, expanded into soul, full of love and blessed.
Go to some squalid couch, some famishing death-bed of the poor ;
He is shrunken, cadaverous, diseased ;—there is here no beauty of the body :
Never hath he fed on knowledge, nor drank at the streams of science,
He is of the common herd, illiterate ;—There is here no beauty of the reason :
But lo ! his filming eye is bright with love from heaven,
In every look it beameth praise, as worshipping with seraphs ;
What honeycomb is hived upon his lips, eloquent of gratitude and prayer,—
What triumph shrined serene upon that clammy brow,
What glory flickering transparent under those thin cheeks,—
What beauty in his face !—Is it not the face of an angel ?

Now, of these three, infinitely mingled and combined,
Consisteth human beauty, in all the marvels of its mightiness :
And forth from human beauty springeth the intensity of Love ;
Feeling, thought, desire, the three deep fountains of affection.
Son of Adam, or daughter of Eve, art thou trapped by nature,
And is thy young eye dazzled with the pleasant form of beauty ?
This is but a lower love ; still it hath its honour ;
What God hath made and meant to charm, let not man despise.
Nevertheless, as reason's child, look thou wisely farther,
For age, disease, and care, and sin, shall tarnish all the surface :

Reach a loftier love : be lured by the comeliness of mind,—
Gentle, kind, and calm, or lustrous in the livery of knowledge :
And more, there is a higher grade ; force the mind to its perfection,—
Win those golden trophies of consummate love :
Add unto riches of the reason, and a beauty moulded to thy liking,
The precious things of nobler grace that well adorn a soul ;
Thus, be thou owner of a treasure, great in earth and heaven,
Beauty, wisdom, goodness, in a creature like its God.

So then, draw we to an end ; with feeble step and faltering,
I follow Beauty through the universe, and find her home Ubiquity :
In all that God hath made, in all that man hath marred,
Lingereth beauty, or its wreck, a broken mould and castings.
And now, having wandered long time, freely and with desultory feet,
To gather in the garden of the world a few fair sample flowers,
With patient scrutinizing care let us cull the conclusion of their essence,
And answer to the riddle of Zorobabel, Whence the might of beauty?

Ugliness is native unto nothing, but an attribute of concrete evil ;
In everything created, at its worst, lurk the dregs of loveliness ;
We be fallen into utter depths, yet once we stood sublime,
For man was made in perfect praise, his Maker's comely image :
And so his new-born ill is spiced with older good,
He carrieth with him, yea to crime, the withered limbs of beauty.
Passions may be crooked generosities ; the robber stealeth for his children ;
Murder was avenger of the innocent, or wiped out shame with blood.
Many virtues, weighted by excess, sink among the vices ;
Many vices, amicably buoyed, float among the virtues.
For, albeit sin is hate, a foul and bitter turpitude,
As hurling back against the Giver all his gifts with insult,
Still when concrete in the sinner, it will seem to partake of his attractions,
And in seductive masquerade shall cloak its leprous skin ;
His broken lights of beauty shall illumine its utter black,
And those refracted rays glitter on the hunch of its deformity.

M

Verily the fancy may be false, yet hath it met me in my musings,
(As expounding the pleasantness of pleasure, but no ways extenuating licence,)
That even those yearnings after beauty, in wayward wanton youth,
When, guileless of ulterior end, it craveth but to look upon the lovely,
Seem like struggles of the soul, dimly remembering pre-existence,
And feeling in its blindness for a long-lost god, to satisfy its longing;
As if the sucking babe, tenderly mindful of his mother,
Should pull a dragon's dugs, and drain the teats of poison.
Our primal source was beauty, and we pant for it ever and again;
But sin hath stopped the way with thorns; we turn aside, wander, and are lost.

God, the undiluted good, is root and stock of beauty,
And every child of reason drew his essence from that stem.
Therefore, it is of intuition, an innate hankering for home,
A sweet returning to the well, from which our spirit flowed,
That we, unconscious of a cause, should bask these darkened souls
In some poor relics of the light that blazed in primal beauty;
And, even like as exiles of idolatry, should quaff from the cisterns of creation
Stagnant draughts, for those fresh springs that rise in the Creator.

Only, being burdened with the body, spiritual appetite is warped,
And sensual man, with taste corrupted, drinketh of pollutions:
Impulse is left, but indiscriminate; his hunger feasteth upon carrion;
His natural love of beauty doateth over beauty in decay:
He still thirsteth for the beautiful; but his delicate ideal hath grown gross,
And the very sense of thirst hath been fevered from affection into passion.
He remembereth the blessedness of light, but it is with an old man's memory,
A blind old man from infancy, that once hath seen the sun,
Whom long experience of night hath darkened in his cradle recollections,
Until his brightest thought of noon is but a shade of black.

This then is thy charm, O beauty all pervading;

And this thy wondrous strength, O beauty, conqueror of all:
The outline of our shadowy best, the pure and comely creature,
That winneth on the conscience with a saddening admiration:
And some untutored thirst for God, the root of every pleasure,
Native to creatures, yea in ruin, and dating from the birthday of
    the soul.
For God sealeth up the sum, confirmed exemplar of proportions,
Rich in love, full of wisdom, and perfect in the plenitude of
    Beauty.

OF FAME.

BLOW the trumpet, spread the wing, fling thy scroll upon the sky,
Rouse the slumbering world, O Fame, and fill the sphere with
    echo!
—Beneath thy blast they wake, and murmurs come hoarsely on
    the wind,
And flashing eyes and bristling hands proclaim they hear thy
    message:
Rolling and surging as a sea, that upturned flood of faces
Hasteneth with its million tongues to spread the wondrous tale;
The hum of added voices groweth to the roaring of a cataract,
And rapidly from wave to wave is tossed that exaggerated story,
Until those stunning clamours, gradually diluted in the distance,
Sink ashamed, and shrink afraid of noise, and die away.
Then brooding Silence, forth from his hollow caverns,
Cloaked and cowled, and gliding along, a cold and stealthy
    shadow,
Once more is mingled with the multitude, whispering as he
    walketh,
And hushing all their eager ears, to hear some newer Fame.

So all is still again; but nothing of the past hath been forgotten;
A stirring recollection of the trumpet ringeth in the hearts of men:
And each one, either envious or admiring, hath wished the chance
    were his
To fill as thus the startled world with fame, or fear, or wonder.
This lit thy torch of sacrilege, Ephesian Eratostratus,
This dug thy living grave, Pythagoras, the traveller from Hades;
For this, dived Empedocles into Etna's fiery whirlpool;

For this conquerors, regicides, and rebels, have dared their perilous crimes.
In all men, from the monarch to the menial, lurketh lust of fame;
The savage and the sage alike regard their labours proudly:
Yea, in death, the glazing eye is illumined by the hope of reputation,
And the stricken warrior is glad, that his wounds are salved with glory.

For fame is a sweet self-homage, an offering grateful to the idol,
A spiritual nectar for the spiritual thirst, a mental food for mind,
A pregnant evidence to all of an after immaterial existence,
A proof that soul is scatheless, when its dwelling is dissolved.
And the manifold pleasures of fame are sought by the guilty and the good:
Pleasures, various in kind, and spiced to every palate:
The thoughtful loveth fame as an earnest of better immortality,
The industrious and deserving, as a symbol of just appreciation,
The selfish, as a promise of advancement, at least to a man's own kin,
And common minds, as a flattering fact that men have been told of their existence.

There is a blameless love of fame, springing from desire of justice,
When a man hath featly won and fairly claimed his honours:
And then fame cometh as encouragement to the inward consciousness of merit,
Gladdening by the kindliness and thanks, wherewithal his labours are rewarded:
But there is a sordid imitation, a feverish thirst for notoriety,
Waiting upon vanity and sloth, and utterly regardless of deserving:
And then fame cometh as a curse; the fire-damp is gathered in the mine:
The soul is swelled with poisonous air, and a spark of temptation shall explode it.

Idle causes, noised awhile, shall yield most active consequents,
And therefore it were ill upon occasion to scorn the voice of rumour.
Ye have seen the chemist in his art mingle invisible gases;
And lo, the product is a substance, a heavy dark precipitate:

Even so fame, hurtling on the quiet with many meeting tongues,
Can out of nothing bring forth fruits, and blossom on a nourishment of air:
For many have earned honour, and thereby rank and riches,
From false and fleeting tales, some casual mere mistake;
And many have been wrecked upon disgrace, and have struggled with poverty and scorn,
From envious hints and ill reports, the slanders cast on innocence.
Whom may not scandal hit? those shafts are shot at a venture:
Who standeth not in danger of suspicion? that net hath caught the noblest.
Cæsar's wife was spotless, but a martyr to false fame;
And Rumour, in temporary things, is gigantic as a ruin or a remedy:
Many poor and many rich have testified its popular omnipotence,
And many a panic-stricken army hath perished with the host of the Assyrians.

Nevertheless, if opportunity be nought, let a man bide his time;
So the matter be not merchandize nor conquest, fear thou less for character.
If a liar accuseth thee of evil, be not swift to answer:
Yea, rather give him licence for awhile; it shall help thine honour afterward:
Never yet was calumny engendered, but good men speedily discerned it,
And innocence hath burst from its injustice, as the green world rolling out of Chaos.
What, though still the wicked scoff,—this also turneth to his praise;
Did ye never hear that censure of the bad is buttress to a good man's glory?
What, if the ignorant still hold out, obstinate in unkind judgment,—
Ignorance and calumny are paired; we affirm by two negations:
Let them stand round about, pushing at the column in a circle,
For all their toil and wasted strength, the foolish do but prop it.
And note thou this; in the secret of their hearts, they feel the taunt is false,
And cannot help but reverence the courage, that walketh amid calumnies unanswering:

He standeth as a gallant chief, unheeding shot or shell;
He trusted in God his Judge: **neither** arrows nor the **pestilence shall harm him.**

A high heart is a sacrifice to heaven; should **it stoop among the** creepers in **the** dust,
To **tell them that what God** approved, is worthy of their praise?
Never shall **it heed the** thought; but flaming on in triumph to the skies,
And **quite forgetting** fame, shall find it added as a trophy.
A great mind is an altar on a hill: should the priest descend from **his** altitude,
To canvass offerings and worship from dwellers on the plain?
Rather, with majestic perseverance **will he** minister in solitary grandeur,
Confident **the** time will come, when pilgrims shall be flocking **to the shrine.**
For fame is the birthright of genius; and he recketh not how long it be delayed;
The heir need not hasten to his heritage, when he knoweth that his **tenure is eternal.**
The careless poet of Avon, was he troubled for his fame,
Or the deep-mouthed chronicler of Paradise, heeded he the suffrage of his equals?
Mæonides took no thought, committing all his **honours to the** future,
And Flaccus, standing on his watch-tower, spied the praise of ages.

Smoking flax will breed a flame, and the flame may illuminate a world;
Where **is he who scorned** that smoke as foul and murky vapour?
The village stream swelled to a river, and the river was a kingdom's wealth,
Where is he **who** boasted he could step across that stream?
Such are the beginnings of the famous: little in the judgment of their peers,
The juster verdict of posterity shall fix them in the **orbits of the** Great.
Therefore dull Zoilus, clamouring ascendant of the hour,
Will soon **be** fain to hide his hate, and bury up his bitterness for **shame;**

Therefore mocking Momus, offended at the steps of Beauty,
Shall win the prize of his presumption, and be hooted from his
    throne among the stars.
For, as the shadow of a mountain lengtheneth before the setting
    sun,
Until that screening Alp have darkened all the canton,—
So, Fame groweth to its great ones; their images loom larger in
    departing;
But the shadow of mind is light, and earth is filled with its glory.

And thou, student of the truth, commended to the praise of God,
Wouldst thou find applause with men?—seek it not, nor shun it.
Ancient fame is roofed in cedar, and her walls are marble;
Modern fame lodgeth in a hut, a slight and temporary dwelling:
Lay not up the treasures of thy soul within so damp a chamber,
For the moth of detraction shall fret thy robe, and drop its eggs
    upon thy motive:
Or the rust of disheartening reserve shall spoil the lustre of thy
    gold,
Until its burnished beauty shall be dim as tarnished brass;
Or thieves, breaking through to steal, shall claim thy jewelled
    thoughts,
And turn to charge the theft on thee, a pilferer from them!

There is a magnanimity in recklessness of fame, so fame be well
    deserving,
That rusheth on in fearless might, the conscious sense of merit:
And there is a littleness in jealousy of fame, looking as aware of
    weakness,
That creepeth cautiously along, afraid that its title will be
    challenged.
The wild boar, full of beechmast, flingeth him down among the
    brambles:
Secure in bristly strength, without a watch, he sleepeth:
But the hare, afraid to feed, croucheth in his own soft form;
Wakefully with timid eyes, and quivering ears, he listeneth.
Even so, a giant's might is bound up in the soul of Genius,
His neck is strong with confidence, and he goeth tusked with
    power:
Sturdily he roameth in the forest, or sunneth him in fen and field,
And scareth from his marshy lair a host of fearful foes.

But there is a mimic Talent, whose safety **lieth in** its quickness,
A timorous thing of doubling guile, that **scarce can face a** friend :
This **one is captious** of reproof, **provident to snatch** occasion,
Greedy of applause, and **vexed to lose one tittle of the glory.**
He is a poor warder of his **fame,** who is ever on the watch to keep
    it spotless ;
Such care argueth debility, **a** garrison relying on its sentinel
Passive strength shall scorn excuses, patiently waiting a reaction,
He wotteth well **that** truth is great, and must prevail at **last** :
But fretful weakness hasteth to explain, anxiously dreading **preju-**
    dice,
And ignorant that perishable falsehood dieth as a branch **cut off.**

Purity of motive and nobility of mind shall rarely condescend
To prove its rights, and prate of wrongs, **or** evidence its worth to
    others :
And it shall be small care to the high and happy conscience
What jealous friends, or envious foes, or common fools may judge.
Should the lion turn and rend every snarling jackal,
Or an **eagle be stopt** in **his career to** punish **the** petulance of spar-
    rows ?
Should the palm tree bend **his crown to** chide the briar at his feet,
Nor kindly help its climbing, if it hope, and be ambitious ?
Should the nightingale account it worth her pains to vindicate her
    music,
Before some sorry finches, that affect to judge of **song ?**
No : many an injustice, many a sneer, and slur,
Is passed aside with noble scorn by lovers of true fame :
For well they wot that glory shall be tinctured good or evil,
By the character of those who give it, as wine is flavoured by the
    wine-skin :
So that **worthy** fame floweth only from a worthy fountain,
But from an ill-conditioned troop the best report is worthless.
And if the sensibility **of** genius count his injuries in secret,
Wisely will he hide the pains a hardened herd would mock :
For the great mind well may be sad to note such littleness in
    brethren,
The while he is comforted and happy in the firmest assurance of
    desert.

Cease awhile, gentle scholar ;—seek other thoughts and themes ;

Or dazzling Fame with wildfire light will lure us on for ever.
For look, all subjects of the mind may range beneath his banner,
And time would fail and patience droop, to count that numerous
    host.
The mine is deep, and branching wide,—and who can work it
    out?
Years of thought would leave untold the boundless topic, Fame.
Every matter in the universe is linked in suchwise unto others,
That a deep full treatise upon one thing might reach to the history
    of all things:
And before some single thesis had been followed out in all its
    branches,
The wandering thinker would be lost in the pathless forest of
    existence.
What were the matter or the spirit, that hath no part in Fame?
Where were the fact irrelevant, or the fancy out of place?
For the handling of that mighty theme should stretch from past
    to future,
Catching up the present on its way, as a traveller burdened with
    time;
All manner of men, their deeds, hopes, fortunes, and ambitions,
All manner of events and things, climate, circumstance, and
    custom,
Wealth and war, fear and hope, contentment, jealousy, devotion,
Skill and learning, truth, falsehood, knowledge of things gone and
    things to come,
Pride and praise, honour and dishonour, warnings, ensamples,
    emulations,
The excellent in virtues, and the reprobate in vice, with the cloud
    of indifferent spectators,—
Wave on wave with flooding force throng the shoals of thought,
Filling that immeasurable theme, the height and depth of Fame.
With soul unsatisfied and mind dismayed, my feet have touched
    the threshold,
Fain to pour these flowers and fruits an offering on that altar:
Lo, how vast the temple,—there are clouds within the dome!
Yet might the huge expanse be filled, with volumes writ on Fame.

OF FLATTERY.

Music is commended of the deaf:—but is that praise despised?
I trow not: with flattered soul the musician heard him gladly.
Beauty is commended of the blind:—but is that compliment misliking?
I trow not: though false and insincere, woman listened greedily.
Vacant Folly talketh high of Learning's deepest reason:
Is she hated for her hollowness?—learning held her wiser for the nonce.
The worldly and the sensual, to gain some end, did homage to religion:
And the good man gave thanks as for a convert, where others saw the hypocrite.

Yet none of these were cheated at the heart, nor steadily believed those flatteries;
They feared the core was rotten, while they hoped the skin was sound:
But the fruits have so sweet fragrance, and are verily so pleasant to the eyes,
It were an ungracious disenchantment to find them apples of Sodom.
So they laboured to think all honest, winking hard with both their eyes;
And hushed up every whisper that could prove that praise absurd:
They willingly regard not the infirmities that make such worship vain,
And palliate to their own fond hearts the faults they will not see.
For the idol rejoiceth in his incense, and loveth not to shame his suppliants,
Should he seek to find them false, his honours die with theirs:
An offering is welcome for its own sake, set aside the giver,
And praise is precious to a man, though uttered by the parrot or the mocking-bird.

The world is full of fools; and sycophancy liveth on the foolish:
So he groweth great and rich, that fawning supple parasite.
Sometimes he boweth like a reed, cringing to the pompousness of pride,

Sometimes he strutteth as a gallant, pampering the fickleness of
    vanity:
I have known him listen with the humble, enacting silent mar-
    veller,
To hear some purse-proud dunce expound his poverty of mind;
I have heard him wrangle with the obstinate, vowing that he will
    not be convinced,
When some weak youth hath wisely feared the chance of ill
    success:
Now, he will barely be a winner,—to magnify thy triumphs after-
    ward;
Now, he will hardly be a loser,—but cannot cease to wonder at thy
    skill:
He laudeth his own worth, that the leader may have glory in his
    follower;
He meekly confesseth his unworthiness, that the leader may have
    glory in himself.
Many wiles hath he, and many modes of catching,
But every trap is selfishness, and every bait is praise.

Come, I would forewarn thee and forearm thee; for keen are
    the weapons of his warfare;
And, while my soul hath scorned him, I have watched his skill
    from far.
His thoughts are full of guile, deceitfully combining contrarieties,
And when he doeth battle in a man, he is leagued with traitorous
    Self-love.
Strange things have I noted, and opposite to common fancy;
We leave the open surface, and would plumb the secret depths.
For he will magnify a lover, even to disparaging his mistress;
So much wisdom, goodness, grace,—and all to be enslaved?
Till the Narcissus, self-enamoured, whelmed in floods of flattery,
Is cheated from the constancy and fervency of love by friendship's
    subtle praise.
Moreover, he will glorify a parent, even to the censure of his
    child,—
O degenerate scion, of a stock so excellent and noble!
Scant will he be in well earned praise of a son before his father;
And rarely commendeth to a mother her daughter's budding beauty:
Yet shall he extol the daughter to her father, and be warm about
    the son before his mother;

Knowing that self-love entereth not, to resist applause with
    jealousies.
Wisely is he sparing of hyperbole where vehemence of praise
    would humble,
For many a father liketh ill to be counted second to his son:
And shrewdly the flatterer hath reckoned on a self still lurking in
    the mother,
When his tongue was slow to speak of graces in the daughter.
But if he descend a generation, to the grandsire his talk is of the
    grandson,
Because in such high praise he hideth the honours of the son;
And the daughter of a daughter may well exceed, in beauty, love,
    and learning,
For unconsciously old age perceived—she cannot be my rival.
These are of the deep things of flattery: and many a shallow syco-
    phant
Hath marvelled ill that praise of children seldom won their
    parents.
This therefore note, unto detection: flattery can sneer as well as
    smile;
And a master in the craft wotteth well, that his oblique thrust is
    surest.

Flattery sticketh like a burr, holding to the soil with anchors,
A vital, natural, subtle seed, everywhere hardy and indigenous.
Go to the storehouse of thy memory, and take what is readiest to
    thy hand,—
The noble deed, the clever phrase, for which thy pride was
    flattered:
Oh, it hath been dwelt upon in solitude, and comforted thy heart
    in crowds,
It hath made thee walk as in a dream, and lifted up the head
    above thy fellows;
It hath compensated months of gloom, that minute of sweet sun-
    shine,
Drying up the pools of apathy, and kindling the fire of ambition:
Yea, the flavour of that spice, mingled in the cup of life,
Shall linger even to the dregs, and still be tasted with a welcome;
The dame shall tell her grandchild of her coy and courted youth,
And the greybeard prateth of a stranger, who praised his task at
    school.

Ofttimes to the sluggard and the dull, flattery hath done good
    service,
Quickening the mind to emulation, and encouraging the heart that
    failed.
Even so, a stimulating poison, wisely tendered by the leech,
Shall speed the pulse, and rally life, and cheat astonished death.
For, as a timid swimmer ventureth afloat with bladders,
Until self-confidence and growth of skill have made him spurn
    their aid,
Thus commendation may be prudent where a child hath ill de-
    served it;
But praise unmerited is flattery, and the cure will bring its cares:
For thy son may find thee out, and thou shalt rue the remedy:
Yea, rather, where thou canst not praise, be honest in rebuke.

I have seen the objects of a flatterer mirrored clearly on the surface,
Where self-love scattereth praise, to gather praise again.
This is a commodity of merchandize, words put out at interest:
A scheme for canvassing opinions, and tinging them all with par-
    tiality.
He is but a harmless fool; humour him with pitiful good-nature:
If a poetaster quote thy song, be thou tender to his poem:
Did the painter praise thy sketch? be kind, commend his picture;
He looketh for a like return; then thank him with thy praise.
In these small things with these small minds count thou the syco-
    phant a courtier,
And pay back, as blindly as ye may, the too transparent honour.

Also, where the flattery is delicate, coming unobtrusive and in
    season,
Though thou be suspicious of its truth, be generous at least to its
    gentility:
The skilful thief of Lacedæmon had praise before his judges,
And many caitiffs win applause for genius in their callings
Moreover, his meaning may be kind,—and thou art a debtor to his
    tongue;
Hasten well to pay the debt, with charity and shrewdness.
He must not think thee caught, nor feel himself discovered,
Nor find thine answering compliment as hollow as his own.
Though he be a smiling enemy, let him heed thee as the fearless
    and the friendly;

A searching look, a poignant word, may prove thou art aware:
Still, with compassion to the frail, though keen to see his soul,
Let him not fear for thy discretion: see thou keep his secret, and
    thine own.

However, where the flattery is gross, a falsehood clear and ful-
    some,
Crush the venomous toad, and spare not for a jewel in his head.
Tell the presumptuous in flattery, that or ever he bespatter thee
    with praise,
It might be well to stop and ask how little it were worth:
Thou hast not solicited his suffrage,—let him not force thee to
    refuse it;
Look to it, man, thy fence is foiled,—and thus we spoil the plot.
Self-knowledge goeth armed, girt with many weapons,
And carrieth whips for flattery, to lash it like a slave:
But the dunce in that great science goeth as a greedy tunny,
To gorge both bait and hook, unheeding all but appetite:
He smelleth praise and swalloweth,—yea, though it be palpable
    and plain,
Say unto him, Folly, thou art Wisdom,—he will bless thee for thy
    lie.

Flatterer, thou shalt rue thy trade, though it have many present
    gains;
Those varnished wares may sell apace, yet shall they spoil thy
    credit.
Thine is the intoxicating cup, which whoso drinketh it shall
    nauseate:
Thine is trickery and cheating; but deception never pleased for
    long.
And though while fresh thy fragrance seemed even as the dews of
    charity,
Yet afterwards it fouled thy censer, as with savour of stale smoke.
For the great mind detected thee at once, answering thine empti-
    ness with pity,
He saw thy self-interested zeal, and was not cozened by vain-glory:
And the little mind is bloated with the praise, scorning him who
    gave it,
A fool shall turn to be thy tyrant, an thou hast dubbed him great:
And the medium mind of common men, loving first thy music,

After, when the harmonies are done, shall feel small comfort in
    their echoes :
For either he shall know thee false, conscious of contrary deserv-
    ings,
And, hating thee for falsehood, soon will scorn himself for truth
Or, if in aught to toilsome merit honest praise be due,
Though for a season, belike, his weakness hath been raptured at
    thy witching,
Shall he not speedily perceive, to the vexing of his disappointed
    spirit,
That thine exaggerative tongue hath robbed him of fair fame?
Thou hast paid in forger's coins, and he had earned true money:
For the substance of just praise, thou hast put him off with shadows
    of the sycophant :
Thou art all things to all men, for ends false and selfish,
Therefore shalt be nothing unto any one, when those thine ends
    are seen.

Turn aside, young scholar, turn from the song of Flattery !
She hath the Siren's musical voice, to ravish and betray.
Her tongue droppeth honey, but it is the honey of Anticyra ;
Her face is a mask of fascination, but there hideth deformity
    behind ;
Her coming is the presence of a queen, heralded by courtesy and
    beauty,
But, going away, her train is held by the hideous dwarf, Disgust.

Know thyself, thine evil as thy good, and flattery shall not harm
    thee :
Yea, her speech shall be a warning, a humbling and a guide.
For wherein thou lackest most, there chiefly will the sycophant
    commend thee,
And then most warmly will congratulate, when a man hath least
    deserved.
Behold, she is doubly a traitor ; and will underrate her victim's
    best,
That, to the comforting of conscience, she may plead his worse for
    better.

Therefore, is she dangerous,—as every lie is dangerous :
Believe her tales, and perish : if thou act upon such counsel,

Her aims are thine not thee, thy wealth and not thy welfare,
Thy suffrage not thy safety, thine aid and not thine honour.
Moreover, with those aims insured, ceaseth all her glozing;
She hath used thee as a handle,—but her hand was wise to turn it:
Thus will she glorify her skill, that it deftly caught thy kindness,
Thus will she scorn thy kindness, so pliable and easy to her skill.
And then, the flatterer will turn to be thy foe, the bitterest and hottest,
Because he oweth thee much hate to pay off many humblings.
Thinkest thou now that he is high, he loveth the remembrance of his lowliness,
The servile manner, the dependent smile, the conscience self-abased?
No, this hour is his own, and the flatterer will be found a busy mocker;
He that hath salved thee with his tongue, shall now gnash upon thee with his teeth:
Yea, he will be leader in the laugh,—silly one, to listen to thy loss,
We scarce had hoped to lime and take another of the fools of flattery.

At the last; have charity, young scholar,—yea, to the sycophant convicted;
Be not a Brutus to thyself, nor stern in thine own cause.
Pardon exaggerated praise; for there is a natural impulse,
Spurring on the nobler mind, to colour facts by feelings:
Take an indulgent view of each man's interest in self,
Be large and liberal in excuses; is not that infirmity thine own?
Search thy soul and be humble; and mercy abideth with humility;
So that, yea, the insincere may find thee pitiful, and love thee.
Mildly put aside, without rudeness of repulse, the pampering hand of flattery,
For courtesy and kindness have gone beneath its guise, and ill shouldst thou rebuke them.

Thou art incapable of theft: but flowers in the garden of a friend
Are thine to pluck with confidence, and it were unfriendliness to hesitate:
Thou abhorrest flattery: but a generous excess in praise

Is thine to yield with honest heart, and false were the charity to
    doubt it :
The difference lieth in thine aim ; kindliness and good are of
    charity,
But selfish, harmful, vile, and bad, is Flattery's evil end.

OF NEGLECT.

GENEROUS and righteous is thy grief, slighted child of sensibility,
For kindliness enkindleth love, but the waters of indifference
    quench it :
Thy soul is athirst for sympathy, and hungereth to find affection,
The tender scions of thy heart yearn for the sunshine of good feel-
    ing ;
And it is an evil thing and bitter, when the cheerful face of
    Charity,
Going forth gaily in the morning to woo the world with smiles,
Is met by those wayfaring men with coldness, suspicion, and re-
    pulse,
And turneth into hard dead stone at the Gorgon visage of Neglect.
O brother, warm and young, covetous of others' favour,
I see thee checked and chilled, sorrowing for censure or forgetful-
    ness :
Let coarse and common minds despise—that wounding of thy
    vanity,
Alas, I note a sorer cause, the blighting of thy love ;
Let the callous sensual deride thee,—disappointed of thy praise,
Alas, thou hast a juster grief, defrauded of their kindness :
It is a theme for tears to feel the soft heart hardening,
The frozen breath of apathy sealing up the fountain of affection ;
It is a pang, keen only to the best, to be injured well-deserving,
And slumbering Neglect is injury,—Could ye not watch one hour ?
When God himself complained, it was that none regarded,
And indifference bowed to the rebuke, Thou gavest Me no kiss
    when I came in.

Moreover, praise is good ; honour is a treasure to be hoarded ;
A good man's praise foreshadoweth God's, and in His smile is
    heaven :
But men walk on in hardihood, steeling their sinfulness to censure,

And when rebuke is ridiculed, the love of praise were an infirmity;
The judge thou heedest not in fear, cannot have deep homage of
 thy hope,
And who then is the wise of this world, that will own he trembleth
 at his fellows?
Calm, careless, and insensible, he mocketh blame or calumny,
Neither should his dignity be humbled to some pittance of their
 praise:
The rather, let false pride affect to trample on the treasure
Which evermore in secret strength unconquered Nature prizeth;
Rather, shall he stifle now the rising bliss of triumph,
Lest after, in the world's Neglect, he must acknowledge bitterness.

For lo, that world is wide, a huge and crowded continent,
Its brazen sun is mammon, and its iron soil is care:
A world full of men, where each man clingeth to his idol;
A world full of men, where each man cherisheth his sorrow;
A world full of men, multitude shoaling upon multitude;
A surging sea, where every wave is burdened with an argosy of
 self;
A boundless beach, where every stone is a separate microscopic
 world;
A forest of innumerable trees, where every root is independent.

What then is the marvel or the shame, if units be lost among the
 million?
Canst thou reasonably murmur, if a a leaf drop off unnoticed?
Wondrous in architecture, intricate and beautiful, delicately tinged
 and scented,
Exquisite of feeling and mysterious in life, none cared for its
 growth, or its decay.
None? yea,—no one of its fellows,—nor cedar, palm, nor
 bramble,—
None? its twinborn brother scarcely missed it from the spray;
None?—if none indeed, then man's neglect were bitterness;
And Life a land without a sun, a globe without a God!
Yea, flowers in the desert, there be that love your beauty;
Yea, jewels in the sea, there be that prize your brightness;
Children of unmerited oblivion, there be that watch and woo you,
And many tend your sweets, with gentle ministering care:
Thronging spirits of the happy, and the everpresent Good One

Yearning seek those precious things, **man hath** not heart to love,
Gems of the humblest **or the highest, pure and** patient in their
    kind,
The souls unhardened by ill usage, and uncorrupt by luxury.

And ye, poor desolates unsunned, toilers in the dark damp mine,
Wearied daughters of oppression, crushed beneath the car of ava-
    rice,
There be that **count your tears,—He hath** numbered the hairs of
    thy head,—
There be that can forgive your ill, with kind considerate pity:
Count ye this for comfort, **Justice** hath **her** balances,
And yet another world can compensate for all:
The daily martyrdom of patience shall not be wanting of reward;
Duty is a prickly **shrub, but its** flower will **be** happiness and glory.

Ye too, the friendless, yet dependent, that find nor home nor lover,
Sad imprisoned hearts, captive to the net of circumstance,—
And ye, too harshly judged, noble unappreciated intellects,
Who, capable of highest, lowlier fix **your** just ambition in con-
    tent,—
And chiefest, **ye, famished infants of** the poor, toiling for your
    parents' bread,
Tired, and sore, and uncomforted the **while,** for want **of love** and
    learning,
Who struggle with the pitiless machine in dull continuous conflict,
Tasked by iron men, who care for nothing but your labour,—
Be ye long-suffering and courageous: abide the will of Heaven;
God is on your side; all things are tenderly remembered:
His servants here shall help you; and where **those fail** you through
    Neglect,
His kingdom still hath **time and space** for ample discriminative
    Justice:
Yea, though utterly on this bad earth ye lose both right and
    mercy,
The tears that we forgat to note, our God shall wipe away.

Nevertheless, kind spirit, susceptible and guileless,
Meek uncherished dove, in a carrion flock of fowls,
Sensitive mimosa, shrinking from the **winds** that help to root
    the fir,

Fragile nautilus, shipwrecked in the gale whereat the conch is glad,
Thy sharp peculiar grief is uncomforted by hope of compensation,
For it is a delicate and spiritual wound, which the probe of pity bruiseth :
Yet hear how many thoughts extenuate its pain ;
Even while a kindred heart can sorrow for its presence.
For the sting of neglect is in this,—that such as we are all, forget us,
That men and women, kith and kin, so lightly heed of other :
Sympathy is lacking from the guilty such as we, even where angels minister,
And souls of fine accord must prize a fellow-sinner's love ;
For the worst love those who love them, and the best claim heart for heart,
And it is a holy thirst to long for love's requital :
Hard it will be, hard and sad, to love and be unloved ;
And many a thorn is thrust into the side of him that is forgotten.
The oppressive silence of reserve, the frost of failing friendship,
Affection blighted by repulse, or chilled by shallow courtesy,
The unaided struggle, the unconsidered grief, the unesteemed self-sacrifice,
The gift, dear evidence of kindness, long due, but never offered,
The glance estranged, the letter flung aside, the greeting ill received,
The services of unobtrusive care unthanked, perchance unheeded,
These things, which hard men mock at, rend the feelings of the tender,
For the delicate tissue of a spiritual mind is torn by those sharp barbs ;
The coldness of a trusted friend, a plenitude ending in vacuity,
Is as if the stable world had burst a hollow bubble

But consider, child of sensibility ; the lot of men is labour,
Labour for the mouth, or labour in the spirit, labour stern and individual.
Worldly cares and worldly hopes exact the thoughts of all,
And there is a necessary selfishness, rooted in each mortal breast.
The plans of prudence, or the whisperings of pride, or all-absorbing reveries of love,
Ambition, grief, or fear, or joy, set each man for himself ;

Therefore, the centre **of a circle, whereunto** all the universe convergeth,
Is seen in fallen **solitude, the naked selfish heart** :
Stripped of conventional deceptions, untrammelled **from the** harness of society,
We all may read one little word engraved on all we do ;
Other men, what are they unto us? the age, the mass, the million,—
We segregate, distinct from generalities, that isolated particle, a **self** :
It is the very law of our life, a law for soul and body,
An earthly law for earthly men, toiling in responsible probation.
For each is the all unto himself, disguise it as we may,
Each infinite, each most precious ; yet even as a nothing to his neighbour.
O consider, **we be crowding up** an avenue, trapped in the **decoy of time,**
Behind us the irrevocable past, before us the illimitable future :
What wonder is there, if the traveller, wayworn, hopeful, fearful,
Burdened himself, so lightly heed the burden of his brother ?
How shouldst thou marvel and be sad, that the pilgrims trouble not to learn thee,
When each hath **to** master for himself the lessons of life and immortality ?

Moreover, what art thou,—so vainly impatient of Neglect,
Where then is thy worthiness, that so **thou claimest** honour ?
Let the true judgment of humility reckon up thine ill deserts,
How little is there to be **loved,** how much to stir up scorn !
The double heart, the bitter tongue, the rash and erring spirit,
Be these, ye purest among men, your passports unto favour ?
It is mercy in the Merciful, and justice in the Just, to be jealous of his creature's love,
But how should evil or duplicity arrogate affection to itself ?
Where **love is** happiness and duty, **to** be jealous of that love is godlike,
But who can reverence the guilty ? who findeth pleasure in the mean ?
Check the presumption of thy hopes : thankfully take **refuge in** obscurity
Or, if thou claimest merit, thy sin shall be proclaimed upon the housetops.

Yet again: consider them of old, **the good**, the great, the learned,
Who have blessed the world by wisdom, and glorified their God
by purity.
Did those speed in favour? were **they the loved and** the admired?
Was every prophet had in honour? and every deserving one
remembered to his praise?
What shall I say of yonder band, a glorious cloud of witnesses,
The scorned, defamed, insulted,—but the excellent of earth?
It were weariness to count up noble names, neglected in their lives,
Whom none esteemed, nor cared to love, till death had sealed
them his.
For good men are the health of the world, valued only when it
perisheth,
Like water, light, and air, all precious in **their absence**.
Who hath considered the blessing of his breath, till the poison of
an asthma struck him?
Who hath regarded the just **pulses of his heart, till spasm or par-
alysis have stopped them?**
Even thus, an unobserved routine of daily grace and wisdom,
When no more here, had worship of a world, whose penitence
atoned for its neglect,
And living genius is seen among infirmities, wherefrom the com-
moner are free;
And other rival men of mind crowd this arena of contention;
And there be many cares; and a man knoweth little of his brother;
Feebly we **appreciate a motive, and** slowly keep pace with a
feeling:
And social difference is much; and experience teacheth **sadly,**
How great the treachery of friends, how dangerous the courtesy of
enemies.
So, the sum of all these things operateth largely upon all men,
Hedging us about with thorns, to cramp our yearning sympathies,
And we grow materialized in mind, forgetting what we see not,
But, immersed in perceptions of the present, keep things absent
out of thought:
Thus, where ingratitude, **and guilt, and labour,** and selfishness
would harden,
Humbly will the good man bow, unmurmuring, to Neglect.

Yet once more, griever at Neglect, hear **me to** thy comfort, or
rebuke;

For, after all thy just complaint, the world is full of love.
O heart of childhood, tender, trusting, and affectionate,
O youth, warm youth, full of generous attentions,
O woman, self-forgetting woman, poetry of human life,
And not less thou, O man, so often the disinterested brother,
Many a smile of love, many a tear of pity,
Many a word of comfort, many a deed of magnanimity,
Many a stream of milk and honey pour ye freely on the earth,
And many a rosebud of love rejoiceth in the dew of your affection.
Neglect? O liberal world, for thine are many prizes :
Neglect? O charitable world, where thousands feed on bounty ;
Neglect? O just world, for thy judgments err not often ;
Neglect? O libel on a world where half that world is woman !
Where is the afflicted, whose voice, once heard, stirreth not a host of comforters ?
Where is the sick untended, or in prison, and they visited him not ?
The hungry is fed, and the thirsty satisfied, till ability set limits to the will,
And those who did it unto them, have done it unto God !
For human benevolence is large, though many matters dwarf it,
Prudence, ignorance, imposture, and the straitenings of circumstance and time.
And if to the body, so to the mind, the most of men are generous ;
Their estimate, who know us best, is seldom seen to err ;
Be sure the fault is thine, as pride, or shallowness, or vanity,
If all around thee, good and bad, neglect thy seeming merit :
No man yet deserved, who found not some to love him ;
And he, that never kept a friend, need only blame himself :
Many for unworthiness will droop and die, but all are not unworthy ;
It must indeed be cold clay soil, that killeth every seed.
Therefore, examine thy state, O self-accounted martyr of Neglect,
It may be, thy merit is a cubit, and thy measure thereof a furlong ;
But grant it greater than thy thoughts, and grant that men thy fellows
For pleasure, business, or interest, misuse, forget, neglect thee,—
Still be thou conqueror in this, the consciousness of high deservings ;
Let it suffice thee to be worthy ; faint not thou for praise ;

For that thou art, be grateful; go humbly even in thy confidence;
And set thy foot upon the neck of an enemy so harmless as Neglect.

OF CONTENTMENT.

GODLINESS with Contentment,—these be the pillars of felicity,
Jachin, wherewithal it is established, and Boaz, in the which is strength:
And upon their capitals is lily-work, the lotus fruit and flower,
Those fair and fragrant types of holiness, innocence, and beauty;
Great gain pertaineth to the pillars, nets and chains of wreathen gold,
And they stand up straight in the temple porch, the house where Glory dwelleth.

The body craveth meats, and the spirit is athirst for peacefulness,
He that hath these, hath enough; for all beyond is vanity.
Surfeit vaulteth over pleasure to light upon the hither side of pain;
And great store is great care, the rather if it mightily increaseth.
Albeit too little is a trouble, yet too much shall swell into an evil,
If wisdom stand not nigh to moderate the wishes:
For covetousness never had enough, but moaneth at its wants for ever,
And rich men have commonly more need to be taught contentment than the poor.
That hungry chasm in their market-place gapeth still unsatisfied,
Yea, fling in all the wealth of Rome,—it asketh higher victims;
So, when the miser's gold cannot fill the measure of his lust,
Curtius must leap into the pit, and avarice shall close upon his life.

Behold Independence in his rags, all too easily contented,
Careful for nothing, thankful for much, and uncomplaining in his poverty:
Such an one have I somewhiles seen earn his crust with gladness;
He is a gatherer of simples, culling wild herbs upon the hills;
And now, as he sitteth on the beach, with his motherless child beside him,

To rest them in the cheerful sun, and sort their mints and horehound,—
Tell me, can ye find upon his forehead the cloud of covetous anxiety,
Or note the dull unkindled eyes of sated sons of pleasure?—
For there is more joy of life with that poor picker of the ditches,
Than among the multitude of wealthy who wed their gains to discontent.

I have seen many rich, burdened with the fear of poverty,
I have seen many poor, buoyed with all the carelessness of wealth:
For the rich had the spirit of a pauper, and the moneyless a liberal heart;
The first enjoyeth not for having, and the latter hath nothing but enjoyment.
None is poor but the mean in mind, the timorous, the weak, and unbelieving;
None is wealthy but the affluent in soul, who is satisfied and floweth over.
The poor-rich is attenuate for fears, the rich-poor is fattened upon hopes;
Cheerfulness is one man's welcome, and the other warneth from him by his gloom.
Many poor have the pleasures of the rich, even in their own possessions;
And many rich miss the poor man's comforts, and yet feel all his cares.
Liberty is affluence, and the Helots of anxiety never can be counted wealthy;
But he that is disenthralled from fear, goeth for the time a king;
He is royal, great, and opulent, living free of fortune,
And looking on the world as owner of its good, the Maker's child and heir:
Whereas, the covetous is slavish, a very Midas in his avarice,
Full of dismal dreams, and starved amongst his treasures:
The ceaseless spur of discontent goaded him with instant apprehension,
And his thirst for gold could never be quenched, for he drank with the throat of Crassus.

Vanity, and dreary disappointment, care, and weariness, and envy;

Vanity is graven upon all things; wisely spake the preacher.
For ambition is a burning mountain, thrown up amid the turbid sea,
A Stromboli in sullen pride above the hissing waves;
And the statesman climbing there, forgetful of his patriot intentions,
Shall hate the strife of each rough step, or ever he hath toiled midway:
And every truant from his home, the happy home of duty,
Shall live to loathe his eminence of cares, that seething smoke and lava.
Contentment is the temperate repast, flowing with milk and honey:
Ambition is the drunken orgy, fed by liquid flames:
A black and bitter frown is stamped upon the forehead of Ambition,
But fair Contentment's angel-face is rayed with winning smiles.

There was in Tyre a merchant, the favourite child of fortune,
An opulent man with many ships, to trade in many climes;
And he rose up early to his merchandize, after feverish dreaming,
And lay down late to his hot unrest, overwhelmed with calculated cares:
So, day by day, and month by month, and year by year, he gained;
And grew grey, and waxed great; for money brought him all things.
All things?—verily, not all; the kernel of the nut is lacking,—
His mind was a stranger to content, and as for Peace, he knew her not:
Luxuries palled upon his palate, and his eyes were satiate with purple;
He could coin much gold, but buy no happiness with it.
And on a day, a day of dread, in the heat of inordinate ambition,
When he threw with a gambler's hand, to lose or to double his possessions,
The chance hit him,—he had speculated ill,—and men began to whisper;—
Those he trusted, failed; and their usuries had bribed him deeply;
One ship foundered out at sea,—and another met the pirate,—
And so, with broken fortunes, men discreetly shunned him.
He was a stricken stag, and went to hide away in solitude,
And there in humility, he thought,—he resolved, and promptly acted:
From the wreck of all his splendours, from the dregs of the goblet of affluence,

He saved with management a morsel and a drop, for his daily cup
    and platter :
And lo, that little was enough, and in enough was competence ;
His cares were gone,—he slept by night, and lived at peace by
    day ;
Cured of his guilty selfishness,—money's love, envy, competition,—
He lived to be thankful in a cottage that he had lost a palace :
For he found in his abasement, what he vainly had sought in high
    estate,
Both mind and body well at ease, though robed in the russet of
    the lowly.

Once more, a certain priest, happy in his high vocation,
With faith, and hope, and charity, well served his village altar ;
As men count riches, he was poor ; but great were his treasures in
    heaven,
And great his joys on earth, for God's sake doing good :
He had few cares and many consolations, one of the welcome
    everywhere ;
The labourer accounted him his friend, and magnates did him
    honour at their table :
With a large heart and little means he still made many grateful,
And felt as the centre of a circle, of comfort, calmness, and
    content.
But, on a weaker sabbath,—for he preached both well and wisely,—
Some casual hearer loudly praised his great neglected talents :
Why should he be buried in obscurity, and throw these pearls to
    swine?
Could he not still be doing good,—the whilst he pushed his for-
    tunes?
Then came temptation, even on the spark of discontent ;
The neighbouring town had a pulpit to be filled ; hotly did he
    canvass, and won it :
Now was he popular and courted, and listened to the spell of
    admiration,
And toiled to please the taste, rather than to pierce the conscience.
Greedily he sought, and seeking found, the patronizing notice of
    the great ;
He thirsted for emoluments and honours, and counted rich men
    happy ;
So he flattered, so he preached ; and gold and fame flowed in ;

They flowed in,—he was reaping his reward, and felt himself a
 fool.
Alas, what a shadow was he following,—how precious was the
 substance he had left!
Man for God, gold for good, this was his miserable bargain.
The village church, its humble flock, and humbler parish priest,
Zeal, devotion, and approving heaven,—his books, and simple life,
His little farm and flower-beds,—his recreative rambles with a
 friend,
And haply, at eventide, the leaping trouts, to help their humble
 fare,
All these wretchedly exchanged for what the world called fortune,
With the harrowing conscience of a state relapsed to vain ambi-
 tions.
Then,—for God was gracious to his soul,—his better thoughts
 returned,
And better aims with better thoughts, his holy walk of old.
Sickened of style, and ostentation, and the dissipative fashions of
 society,
He deserted from the ranks of Mammon, and renewed his allegiance
 to God:
For he found that the praises of men, and all that gold can give,
Are not worthy to be named, against godliness and calm content-
 ment.

OF LIFE.

A CHILD was playing in a garden, a merry little child,
Bounding with triumphant health, and full of happy fancies;
His kite was floating in the sunshine,—but he tied the string to a
 twig
And ran among the roses to catch a new-born butterfly;
His horn-book lay upon a bank, but the pretty truant hid it,
Buried up in gathered grass, and moss, and sweet wild-thyme;
He launched a paper boat upon the fountain, then wayward turned
 aside,
To twine some fragrant jessamines about the dripping marble:
So, in various pastime shadowing the schemes of manhood,
That curly-headed boy consumed the golden hours:
And I blessed his glowing face, envying the merry little child,

As he shouted with the ecstasy of being, clapping his hands for
    joyfulness :
For I said, Surely, O Life, **thy name** is happiness **and hope,**
Thy days are bright, thy flowers are sweet, and pleasure the con-
    dition of thy gift.

A youth was walking in the moonlight, walking not alone,
For a fair and gentle maid leant on his trembling arm :
Their whispering **was still** of beauty, and the light of love was in
    their eyes,
Their twin young hearts had not a thought unvowed to love and
    beauty :
The stars and the sleeping world, and the guardian **eye of God,**
The murmur of the distant waterfall, and nightingales warbling in
    the thicket,
Sweet speech **of years to come,** and promises of fondest hope,
And more, a present gladness in each other's trust,
All these fed their souls with the hidden manna of affection,
While their faces shone beatified in the radiance of reflected Eden :
I gazed on that fond youth, and coveted his heart,
Attuned to holiest symphonies, with music in its strings :
For I said, Surely, O Life, thy name is love and beauty,
Thy joys are full, thy looks most fair, thy feelings **pure and
    sensitive.**

A man sat beside his merchandize, **a careworn altered man,**
His waking hope, his nightly fear, were money, and its losses :
Rarely was the laugh upon his cheek, **except** in bitter scorn,
For his foolishness of heart, and the lie of its romance, counting
    Love a treasure.
His talk is of stern Reality, chilling unimaginative facts,
The dull material accidents of this sensual body ;
Lucreless honour were contemptible, impoverished affection but a
    pauper's riches,
Duty, struggling unrewarded, **the** bargain of a cheated fool ;
The market **value of** a fancy must be measured by **the gain it
    bringeth,**
No man is fed or clothed by fame, or love, or **duty :—**
So toiled he day by day, that cold and joyless man ;
I gazed upon his haggard face, and sorrowed for the change :
For I said, Surely, O Life, thy name is care and weariness,

Thy soil is parched, thy winds are fierce, and the suns above thee
 hardening.

A withered elder lay upon his bed, a desolate man and feeble:
His thoughts were of the past, the early past, the byegone days of
 youth:
Bitterly repented he the years stolen by the god of this world,
Remembering the maiden of his love, and the heart-stricken wife
 of his selfishness.
For the sunshiny morning of life came again to him a vivid truth,
But the years of toil as a long dim dream, a clouded blighted noon:
He saw the nutting schoolboy, but forgat the speculative mer-
 chant;
The callous calculating husband was shamed by the generous lover:
He knew that the weeds of worldliness, and the smoky breath of
 Mammon
Had choked and killed those tender shoots, his yearnings after
 honour and affection;
So was he sick at heart, and my pity strove to cheer him,
But a deep and dismal gulph lay between comfort and his soul.
Then I said, Surely, O Life, thy name is vanity and sorrow,
Thy storms at noon are many, and thine eventide is clouded by
 remorse.

Now, when I thought upon these things, my heart was grieved
 within me:
I wept, with bitterness of speech, and these were the words of my
 complaining:
"Wherefore then must happiness and love wither into care and
 vanity,—
Wherefore is the bud so beautiful, but flower and fruit so
 blighted?
Hard is the lot of man; to be lured by the meteor of romance,
Only to be snared, and to sink, in the turbid mudpool of reality."

Suddenly, a light,—and a rushing presence,—and a consciousness
 of Something near me,—
I trembled, and listened, and prayed: then I knew the Angel of
 Life:
Vague, and dimly visible, mine eye could not behold him,
As, calmly unimpassioned, he looked upon an erring creature;

Unseen, my spirit apprehended him; though he spake not, yet I heard:
For a sympathetic communing with Him flashed upon my mind electric.

Pensioner of God, be grateful; the gift of Life is good:
The life of heart, and life of soul, mingled with life for the **body**.
Gladness and beauty are its just inheritance,—the beauty thou hast counted **for** romance:
And guardian spirits weep that selfishness and sorrow should destroy it.
Thou hast seen the natural blessing marred into a curse by man;
Come then, **in favour will I** show thee the proper excellence of life;
Keep thou purity, and watch against suspicion,—love shall never perish;
Guard thine innocency spotless, and the buoyancy of childhood shall remain.
Sweet ideals feed the soul, thoughts of loveliness delight it,
The chivalrous affection of uncalculating youth lacketh not honourable wisdom.
Charge not folly on invisibles, that render thee happier and purer,
The fair frail visions of **Romance** have a use **beyond the maxims of the Real.**

Behold a patriarch of years, who leaneth on the staff of religion;
His heart is fresh, quick to feel, a bursting fount of generosity:
He, playful in his wisdom, is gladdened in his children's gladness,
He, pure in his experience, loveth in his son's first love:
Lofty aspirations, deep affections, holy hopes are his delight;
His abhorrence is to strip from Life its charitable garment of Idea.
The cold and callous sneerer, who heedeth of the merely practical,
And mocketh at good uses in imaginary things, that man is his scorn:
The hard unsympathizing modern, filled with facts and figures,
Cautious, and coarse, and materialized in mind, that man **is his** pity.
Passionate thirst for gain never hath burnt **within his bosom,**
The leading chains of that dull lust have not bound him prisoner:
The shrewd world laughed at him for honesty, the vain world mouthed at him for honour,

The false world hated him for truth, the cold world despised him
    for affection :
Still, he kept his treasure, the warm and **noble heart**,
And in that happy wise old man survive the child and lover.
For human Life is as Chian wine, flavoured unto him who drinketh it,
Delicate fragrance comforting the soul, as needful substance for the
    body :
Therefore, see thou art pure and guileless ; so shall thy Realities of
    Life
Be sweetened and tempered, and gladdened by the wholesome
    spirit of Romance.

Dost thou live, man, dost thou live,—or only breathe and labour?
Art thou free, or enslaved to a routine, the daily machinery of
    habit ?
For one man is quickened into Life, where thousands exist as in
    a torpor,
Feeding, toiling, sleeping, an insensate weary round :
The plough, or the ledger, or the trade, with animal cares and in-
    dolence,
Make the mass of **vital years** a heavy lump unleavened.
Drowsily lie down in thy dulness, fettered with the irons of circum-
    stance,
Thou wilt **not wake to think and feel a minute in a month**.
The epitome of common life is seen in the common epitaph,
Born on such a day, and dead on such **another, with an** interval of
    threescore years.
For time hath been wasted on the senses, to the hourly diminishing
    of spirit :
Lean is the soul and pineth, in the midst of abundance for the body :
He forgat the worlds to which he tended, and a creature's true
    nobility,
Nor wished that hope and wholesome fear should stir him from his
    hardened satisfaction.
And this is death in life ; to be sunk beneath the waters of the
    Actual,
Without one feebly-struggling sense of an airier spiritual realm :
Affection, fancy, feeling—dead ; imagination, conscience, faith,
All wilfully expunged, till they leave the man mere carcase.
See thou livest, whiles thou art : for heart must live, and soul,
But care and sloth and sin and self, combine to kill that life.

A man will grow to an automaton, an appendage to the counter or
    the desk,
If mind and spirit be not roused, to raise the plodding groveller :
Then praise God for sabbaths, for books, and dreams and pains,
For the recreative face of nature, and the kindling charities of home ;
And remember, thou that labourest,—thy leisure is not loss,
If it help to expose and undermine that solid falsehood, the
    Material.

Life is a strange avenue of various trees and flowers ;
Lightsome at commencement, but darkening to its end in a distant
    massy portal.
It beginneth as a little path, edged with the violet and primrose,
A little path of lawny grass and soft to tiny feet :
Soon, spring thistles in the way, those early griefs of school,
And fruit-trees ranged on either hand show holiday delights :
Anon, the rose and the mimosa hint at sensitive affection,
And vipers hide among the grass, and briars are woven in the
    hedges :
Shortly, staked along in order, stand the tender saplings,
While hollow hemlock and tall ferns fill the frequent interval :
So advancing, quaintly mixed, majestic line the way
Sturdy oaks, and vigorous elms, the beech and forest-pine :
And here the road is rough with rocks, wide, and scant of herbage,
The sun is hot in heaven, and the ground is cleft and parched :
And many-times a hollow trunk, decayed, or lightning-scathed,
Or in its deadly solitude, the melancholy upas ;
But soon, with closer ranks, are set the sentinel trees,
And darker shadows hover amongst Autumn's mellow tints ;
Ever and anon, a holly,—junipers, and cypresses, and yews ;
The soil is damp ; the air is chill ; night cometh on apace :
Speed to the portal, traveller,—lo, there is a moon,
With smiling light to guide thee safely through the dreadful shade :
Hark,—that hollow knock,—behold, the warder openeth,
The gate is gaping, and for thee ;—those are the jaws of Death !

OF DEATH.

KEEP silence, daughter of frivolity,—for Death is in that chamber !
Startle not with echoing sound the strangely solemn peace.

Death is here in spirit, watcher of a marble corpse,—
That eye is fixed, that heart is still,—how dreadful in its stillness!
Death, new tenant of the house, pervadeth all the fabric;
He waiteth at the head, and he standeth at the feet, and hideth in
 the caverns of the breast:
Death, subtle leech, hath anatomized soul from body,
Dissecting well in every nerve its spirit from its substance:
Death, rigid lord, hath claimed the heriot clay,
While joyously the youthful soul hath gone to take his heritage:
Death, cold usurer, hath seized his bonded debtor;
Death, savage despot, hath caught his forfeit serf;
Death, blind foe, wreaketh petty vengeance on the flesh;
Death, fell cannibal, gloateth on his victim,
And carrieth it with him to the grave, that dismal banquet-hall,
Where in foul state the Royal Goul holdeth secret orgies.

Hide it up, hide it up, draw the decent curtain:
Hence! curious fool, and pry not on corruption:
For the fearful mysteries of change are being there enacted,
And many actors play their part on that small stage, the tomb.
Leave the clay, that leprous thing, touch not the fleshly garment:
Dust to dust, it mingleth well among the sacred soil:
It is scattered by the winds, it is wafted by the waves, it mixeth
 with herbs and cattle,
But God hath watched those morsels, and hath guided them in
 care;
Each waiting soul must claim his own, when the archangel
 soundeth,
And all the fields, and all the hills, shall move a mass of life;
Bodies numberless crowding on the land, and covering the trampled
 sea,
Darkening the air precipitate, and gathered scatheless from the
 fire;
The Himalayan peaks shall yield their charge, and the desolate
 steppes of Siberia,
The Maelström disengulph its spoil, and the iceberg manumit its
 captive:
All shall teem with life, the converging fragments of humanity.
Till every conscious essence greet his individual frame;
For in some dignified similitude, alike, yet different in glory,
This body shall be shaped anew, fit dwelling for the soul:

The hovel hath grown to a palace, the bulb hath burst into the flower,
Matter hath put on incorruption, and is at peace with spirit.

Amen,—and so it shall be :—but now, the scene is drear,—
Yea, though promises and hope strive to cheat its sadness ;
Full of grief, though faith herself is strong to speed the soul,
For the partner of its toil is left behind to endure an ordeal of change,
Dear partner, dear and frail, my loved though humble home,—
Should I cast thee off without a pang, as a garment flung aside ?
Many years, for joy and sorrow, have I dwelt in thee,
How shall I be reckless of thy weal, nor hope for thy perfection ?—
This also, He that lent thee for my uses in mortality,
Shall well fulfil with boundless praise on that returning day :
Behold, thou shalt be glorified : thou, mine abject friend,
And should I meanly scorn thy state, until it rise to greatness ?
Far be it, O my soul, from thine expectant essence,
To be heedless, if indignity or folly desecrate those thine ashes :
Keep them safe with careful love ; and let the mound be holy ;
And, thou that passest by, revere the waiting dead.

Naples sitteth by the sea, keystone of an arch of azure,
Crowned by consenting nations peerless queen of gaiety :
She laugheth at the wrath of Ocean, she mocketh the fury of Vesuvius,
She spurneth disease and misery and famine, that crowd her sunny streets :
The giddy dance, the merry song, the festal glad procession,
The noonday slumber and the midnight serenade,—all these make up her Life
Her Life ?—and what her Death ?—look we to the end of life,—
Solon, and Tellus the Athenian, wisely have ye pointed to the grave.
For behold yon dreary precinct,—those hundreds of stone wells,
A pit for a day, a pit for a day,—a pit to be sealed for a year :
And in the gloom of night, they raise the year-closed lid,—
Look in,—for gnawing lime hath half consumed the carcases ;
Thus they hurl the daily dead into that horrible pit,
The dead that only died this day,—as unconsidered offal !
There, a stark white heap, unwept, unloved, uncared for,

Old men and maidens, young men and infants, mingle in hideous
 corruption ;
Fling in the gnawing lime,—seal up the charnel for a year ;
For lo, a morrow's dawn hath tinged the mountain summit.
O fair false city, thou gay and gilded harlot,
Woe, for thy wanton heart, woe, for thy wicked hardness :
Woe unto thee, that the lightsomeness of Life, beneath Italian suns,
Should meet the solemnity of Death, in a sepulchre so foul and
 fearful.

For that, even to the best, the wise and pure and pious,
Death, repulsive king, thine iron rule is terrible :
Yea, and even at the best, in company of buried kindred,
With hallowing rites, and friendly tears, and the dear old
 country church,
Death, cold and lonely, thy frigid face is hateful,
The bravest look on thee with dread, the humblest curse thy
 coming.
Still, ye unwise among mankind, your foolishness hath added fears ;
The crowded cemetery, the catacomb of bones, the pestilential
 vault,
With fancy's gliding ghost at eve, her moans and flaky footfalls,
And the gibbering train of terror to fright your coward hearts.
We speak not here of sin, nor the phantoms of a bloody conscience,
Nor of solaces, and merciful pardon : we heed but the inevitable
 grave,
The grave, the wage of guilt, that due return to dust,
The grave, the goal of earth, and starting-post for Heaven.

Plant it with laurels, sprinkle it with lilies, set it upon yonder
 dewy hill,
Midst holy prayers, and generous grief, and consecrating blessings :
Let Sophocles sleep among his ivy, green perennial garlands,
Let olives shade their Virgil, and roses bloom above Corinne ;
To his foster-mother, Ocean, entrust the mariner in hope,
The warrior's spirit, let it rise on high from the flaming fragrant
 pyre:
But heap not coffins and corruption to infect the mass of living,
Nor steal from odious realities the charitable poetry of Death.
It is wise to gild uncomeliness, it is wise to mask necessity,
It is wise from cheerful sights and sounds to draw their gentle uses :

Hide the facts, the bitter facts, the foul and fearful facts,
Tend the body well in hope, this were praise and wisdom:
But to plunge in gloom the parting soul, that hath loved its clay
    tenement so long,
This were vanity and folly, the counsel of moroseness and de-
    spair.
Not thus, the Scythian of old time welcomed Death with songs;
Not thus, the shrewd Egyptian decorated Death with braveries;
Not thus, on his funeral tower sleepeth the sun-worshipping Parsee;
Not thus, the Moslem saint lieth in his arabesque mausoleum;
Not thus, the wild red Indian, hunter of the far Missouri,
In flowering trees hath nested up his forest-loving ancestry;
Not thus, the Switzer mountaineer scattereth ribboned garlands
About the rustic cross that halloweth the bed of his beloved;
Not thus, the village maiden wisheth she may die in spring,
With store of violets and cowslips to be sprinkled on her snow
    white shroud;
Not thus, the dying poet asketh a cheerful grave,—
Lay him in the sunshine, friends, nor sorrow that a Christian hath
    departed!

Yea; it is the poetry of Death, an Orpheus gladdening Hades,
To care with mindful love for all so dear—and dead;
To think of them in hope, to look for them in joy, and—but for its
    simple vanity—
To pray with all the earnestness of nature for souls who cannot
    change.
For the tree is felled, and boughed, and bare, and the Measurer
    standeth with his line;
The chance is gone for ever, and is past the reach of prayer:
For men and angels, good and ill, have rendered all their witness;
The trial is over, the jury are gone in, and none can now be heard;
Well are they agreed upon the verdict, just, and fixt, and final,
And the sentence showeth clear, before the Judge hath spoken:
Now,—while resting matter is at peace within the tomb,
The conscious spirit watcheth in unspeakable suspense;
Racked with a fearful looking-forward, or blissfully feeding on the
    foretaste,
Waiting souls in eager expectation pass the solemn interval:
They slumber not at death, but awaken, quickened to the terrors
    of the judgment;

They lie not insensate among darkness, but exult, looking forward
   to the light :
Idiotcy, brightening on the instant, when that veil is torn,
Is grateful that his torpor here hath left him as an innocent :
The young child, stricken as he played, and guileless babes unborn,
Freed from fetters of the flesh, burst into mind immediate :
Madness judgeth wisely and the visions of the lunatic are gone,
And each hasteneth to praise the mercy that made him irresponsible.
For the soul is one, though manifold in act, working the machinery
   of brain,
Reason, fancy, conscience, passion, are but varying phases ;
If, in God's wise purpose, the machine were shattered or confused,
Still is soul the same, though it exhibit with a difference :
Therefore, dissipate the brain, and set its inmate free,
Behold, the maniacs and embryos stand in their place intelligent.
That solvent eateth away all dross, leaving the gold intact :
Matter lingereth in the retort, spirit hath flown to the receiver.
And lo, that recipient of the spirits, it is some aerial world,
An oasis midway on the desert space, separating earth from heaven,
A prison house for essences incorporate, a limbus vague and wide,
Tartarus for evil, and Paradise for good, that intermediate Hades.

O Death, what art thou ? a Lawgiver that never altereth,
Fixing the consummating seal, whereby the deeds of life become
   established :
O Death, what art thou ? a stern and silent usher,
Leading to the judgment for Eternity, after the trial scene of Time :
O Death, what art thou ? the Husbandman, that reapeth always,
Out of season, as in season, with a sickle in his hand :
O Death, what art thou ? the shadow unto every substance,
In the bower as in the battle, haunting night and day :
O Death, what art thou ? Nurse of dreamless slumbers
Freshening the fevered flesh to a wakefulness eternal :
O Death, what art thou ? strange and solemn Alchymist,
Elaborating life's elixir from these clayey crucibles :
O Death, what art thou ? Antitype of Nature's marvels,
The seed and dormant chrysalis bursting into energy and glory.
Thou calm safe anchorage for the shattered hulls of men,—
Thou spot of gelid shade, after the hot-breathed desert,—
Thou silent waiting-hall, where Adam meeteth with his children,—
How full of dread, how full of hope, loometh inevitable Death :

Of dread, for all have sinned; of hope, for One hath saved:
The dread is drowned in joy, the hope is filled with immortality!
—Pass along, pilgrim of life, go to thy grave unfearing,
The terrors are but shadows now, that haunt the vale of Death.

OF IMMORTALITY.

GIRD up thy mind to contemplation, trembling inhabitant of earth;
Tenant of a hovel for a day,—thou art heir of the universe for ever!
For, neither congealing of the grave, nor gulphing waters of the firmament,
Nor expansive airs of heaven, nor dissipative fires of Gehenna,
Nor rust of rest, nor wear, nor waste, nor loss, nor chance, nor change,
Shall avail to quench or overwhelm the spark of soul within thee!

Thou art an imperishable leaf on the evergreen bay-tree of Existence;
A word from wisdom's mouth, that cannot be unspoken;
A ray of Love's own light; a drop in Mercy's sea;
A creature, marvellous and fearful, begotten by the fiat of Omnipotence.
I, that speak in weakness, and ye, that hear in charity,
Shall not cease to live and feel, though flesh must see corruption;
For the prison-gates of matter shall be broken, and the shackled soul go free,
Free, for good or ill, to satisfy its appetence for ever:
For ever,—dreadful doom, to be hurried on eternally to evil,—
For ever,—happy fate, to ripen into perfectness—for ever!

And is there a thought within thy heart, O slave of sin and fear,
A black and harmful hope, that erring spirit dieth?
That primal disobedience hath ensured the death of soul,
And separate evil sealed it thine—thy curse, Annihilation?
Heed thou this; there is a Sacrifice; the Maker is Redeemer of his creature;
Freely unto each, universally to all, is restored the privilege of essence:
Whether unto grace or guilt, all must live through Him,
Live in vital joy, or live in dying woe:

Death in Adam, Life in Christ : the curse hung upon the cross :
Who art thou that heedest of redemption, as narrower than the
  fall?
All were dead,—He died for all ; that living, they might love ;
If living souls withhold their love,—still, He hath died for them.
Eve stole the knowledge ; Christ gave the life :
Knowledge and life are the perquisites of soul, the privilege of
  Man :
Mercy stepped between and stayed the double theft ;
God gave ; and giving, bought ; and buying, asketh love :
And in such asking rendereth bliss, to all that hear and answer,
For love with life is heaven ; and life unloving, hell.

Creature of God, his will is for thy weal, eternally progressing ;
Fear not to trust a Maker's love, nor a Saviour's ransom :
He drank for all,—for thee, and me,—the poison of our deeds ;
We shall not die, but live,—and, of his grace, we love.
For, in the mysteries of Mercy, the One fore-knowing Spirit
Outstrippeth reason's halting choice, and winneth men to Him :
Who shall sound the depths? who shall reach the heights?
Freedom, in the gyves of fate ; and sovereignty, reconciled with
  justice.

If then, as annihilate by sin, the soul was ever forfeit,
Godhead paid the mighty price, the pledge hath been redeemed :
He from the waters of Oblivion raised the drowning race,
Lifting them even to Himself, the baseless Rock of Ages.
None can escape from Adam's guilt, or second Adam's guerdon :
Sin and death are thine ; thine also is interminable being :
Let it be even as thou wilt, still are we ransomed from nonentity,
The worlds of bliss and woe are peopled with immortals :
And ruin is thy blame ; for thou, the worst, art free
To take from Heaven the grace of love, as the gift of life :
Yet is not remedy thy praise ; for thou, the best, art bound
In self, and sin, and darkling sloth, until He break the chain :
None can tell, without a struggle, if that chain be broken ;
Strive to-day,—one effort more may prove that thou art free !
Here is faith and prayer, here is the Grace and the Atonement,
Here is the creature feeling for its God, and the prodigal returning
  to his Father
But, behold, His reasonable children, standing in just probation,

With ears to hear, neglect; with eyes to see, refuse:
They will not have the blessing with the life, the blessing that
 enricheth immortality;
And look for pleasures out of God, for heaven in life alone;
So, they snatch that awful prize, existence void of love,
And in their darkening exile make a needful hell of self.

Therefore fear, thou sinner, lest the huge blessing, Immortality,
Be blighted in thine evil to a curse,—it were better he had not
 been born;
Therefore hope, thou saint, for the gift of Immortality is free;
Take and live, and live in love; fear not, thou art redeemed!
The happy life, that height of hope, the knowledge of all good,
This is the blessing on obedience, obedience the child of faith;
The miserable life, that depth of all despair, the knowledge of all
 evil,
This is the curse upon impenitence, impenitence that sprung of
 unbelief.
God, from a beautiful necessity, is Love in all He doeth,
Love, a brilliant fire, to gladden or consume:
The wicked work their woe by looking upon love, and hating it:
The righteous find their joys in yearning on its loveliness for ever.

Who shall imagine Immortality, or picture its illimitable prospect?
How feebly can a faltering tongue express the vast idea!
For consider the primæval woods that bristle over broad Australia,
And count their autumn leaves, millions multiplied by millions;
Thence look up to a moonless sky from a sleeping isle of the
 Ægæan,
And add to these leaves yon starry host, sparkling on the mid-
 night numberless;
Thence traverse an Arabia, some continent of eddying sand,
Gather each grain, let none escape, add them to the leaves and to
 the stars;
Afterward gaze upon the sea, the thousand leagues of an Atlantic,
Take drop by drop, and add their sum, to the grains, and leaves,
 and stars;
The drops of ocean, the desert sands, the leaves, and stars innu-
 merable,
(Albeit, in that multitude of multitudes, each small unit were an
 age,)

All might reckon for an instant, a transient flash of Time,
Compared with this intolerable blaze, the measureless Enduring of
        eternity!

O grandest gift of the Creator,—O largess worthy of a God,—
Who shall grasp that thrilling thought, life and joy for ever?
For the sun in heaven's heaven is Love that cannot change,
And the shining of that sun is life, to all beneath its beams:
Who shall arrest it in the firmament,—or drag it from its sphere?
Or bid its beauty smile no more, but be extinct for ever?
Yea, where God hath given, none shall take away,
Nor build up limits to his love, nor bid his bounty cease;
Wide, as space is peopled, endless as the empire of heaven,
The river of the water of life floweth on in majesty for ever!

Why should it seem a thing impossible to thee, O man of many
        doubts,
That God shall wake the dead, and give this mortal immortality?
Is it that such riches are unsearchable, the bounty too profuse?
And yet, what gift, to cease or change, is worthy of the King
        Almighty!
For remember the moment thou art not, thou mightest as well not
        have been;
A millennium and an hour are equal in the gulph of that desolate
        abyss, annihilation:
If Adam had existed till to-day, and to-day had perished utterly,
What were his gain in length of a life, that hath passed away for
        ever?
No tribute of thanks can exhale from the empty censer of non-
        entity:
The Giver, with his gift reclaimed, is mulcted of all praise.

Tell me, ye that strive in vain to cramp and dwarf the soul,
Wherefore should it cease to be, and when shall essence die?
It is,—and therefore shall be,—till just obstacle opposeth:
Show no cause for change, and reason leaneth to continuance.
The body verily shall change; this curious house we live in
Never had continuing stay, but changeth every instant:
But the spiritual tenant of the house abideth in unalterable con-
        sciousness,
He may fly to many lands, but cannot flee himself.

The soil wherein ye drop the seed, by suns or rains may vary;
But the seed is the same; and soul is the seed; and flesh but its
　　anchorage to earth.

The machine may be broken, and rust corrode the springs: but
　　can rust feed on motion?
Worms may batten on the brain: but can worms gnaw the mind?
Dynamics are, and dwell apart, though matter be not made;
Spirit is, and can be separate, though a body were not:
Power is one, be it lever, screw, or wedge; but it needeth these
　　for illustration:
Mind is one, be it casual or ideal; but it is shown in these.
The creature is constructed individual, for trial of his reasonable
　　will,
Clay and soul, commingled wisely, mingled not confused:
As power is not in the spring, till somewhat give it action,
So, until spirit be infused, the organism lieth inergetic.

Or shalt thou say that mind is the delicate offspring of matter,
The bright consummate flower that must perish with its leaf?
Go to: doth weight breed lightness? is freedom the atmosphere
　　of prisons?
When did the body elevate, expand, and bud the mind?
Lo, a red hot cinder flung from the furnaces of Ætna,—
There is fire in that ash; but did the pumice make it?
Nay, cold clod, never canst thou generate a flame,
Nay, most exquisite machinery, never-more elaborate a mind;
Rather do ye battle and contend, opposite the one to the other;
Till God shall stop the strife, and call the body colleague.

Garment of flesh, and art thou then a vest, so tinged with subtle
　　poison,
(Maddening tunic of the centaur,) as to kill the soul?
Not so: fruit of disobedience, rot in dissolution, as thou must,—
The seed is in the core, its germ is safe, and life is in that germ:
Moreover, Marah shall be sweetened; and a Good Physician
Yet shall heal those gangrene wounds, the spotted plague of sin:
He, through worldly trials, and the separative cleansing of the
　　grave,
Shall change its corruptible to glory, and wash that garment
　　white.

Still, is the whisper in thy heart, that oftenest the bed of death
Seemeth but a sluggish ebb, of sinking soul and body?
Mind dwelling, long-time, sensual in the chambers of the flesh,
May slumber on in conscious sloth, and wilfully be dulled:
But is it therefore nigh to dissolution, even as the body of this death?
Ask the stricken conscience, gasping out its terrors;
Ask the dying miser, loth to leave his gold;
Ask the widowed poor, confiding her fatherless to strangers;
Ask the martyr-maid, a broken reed so strong,
That weak and tortured frame, with triumph on its brow!—
O thou gainsayer, the finger of disease may seem to reach the soul,
But it is a spiritual touch, sympathy with that which aileth:
Pain or fear may dislocate and shatter this delicate machinery of nerves;
But madness proveth mind: the fault is in the engine, not the impetus:
Dissipate the mists of matter, lo, the soul is clear:
Timour's cage bowed it in the dust; but now it goeth forth a freedman.

Yet more, there is reason in moralities, that the soul must live;
If God be king in heaven, or have care for earth.
Can wickedness have triumphed with impunity, or virtue toiled unseen?
Shall cruelty torture unavenged, and the innocent complain unheard?
Is there no recompense for woe,—must there be no other world for justice,—
No hope in setting suns of good, nor terror for the evil at its zenith?
How shall ye make answer unto this; a just God prospering iniquity,
Wisdom encouraging the foolish, and Goodness abetting the depraved!

Yet again; mine erring brother, pardon this abundance of my speech,
Yield me thy candour and thy charity, listening with a welcome:
For, even now, a thousand thoughts are trooping to my theme;

O mighty theme, O feeble thoughts! Alas! who is sufficient?
Judge not so high a cause by these poor words alone,
For lo, the advocate hath little skill: pardon, and pass on.
Certify thyself with surer proofs; fledge thine own mind for
    flight;
Think, and pray; those better proofs shall follow on with holy
    aspiration.
Yet in my humbler grade to help thy weal and comfort,
Thy weal for this and higher worlds, and comfort in thy sickness,
Suffer the multitude of fancies, walking with me still in love;
But tread in fear, it is holy ground,—remember, Immortality!

Wilt thou argue from infirmities, thine abject evil state,
As how should stricken wretched man indeed exist for ever:
The brutal and besotted, the savage and the slave, the sucking
    infant and the idiot,
The mass of mean and common minds, and all to be immortal?—
Consider every beginning, how small it is and feeble:
Ganges, and the rolling Mississippi sprung of brooks among the
    mountains;
The yew-tree of a thousand years was once a little seed;
And Nero's marble Rome, a shepherd's mudbuilt hovel:
A speck is on the tropic sky, and it groweth to the terrible
    tornado;
An apple, all too fair to see, destroyed a world of souls:
A tender babe is born,—it is Attila, scourge of the nations!
A seeming malefactor dieth,—it is Jesus, the Saviour of men!

And hive not in thy thoughts the vain and wordy notion
That nothing which was born in Time can tire out the footsteps of
    Infinity:
Reckon up a sum in numbers; where shall progression stop?
The starting-post is definite and fixed, but what is the goal of
    numeration?
So, begin upon a moment, and when shall being end?
Souls emanate from God, to travel with Him equally for ever.
Moreover, thou that objectest the unenterable circle of eternity,
That none but He from everlasting can endure, as to a future ever-
    lasting,
Consider, may it be impossible that creatures were counted in their
    Maker,

And so, that the confines of Eternity are filled by God alone?
Trust not thy soul upon a fancy: who would freight a bubble with a diamond,
And launch that priceless gem on the boiling rapids of a cataract?

If then we perish not at death, but walk in spirit through the darkness,
Waiting for a mansion incorruptible, whereof this body is the seed,
Tell me, when shall be the period? time and its ordeals are done:
The storms are passed, the night is at end, behold the Sabbath morning.
Is death to be conqueror again, and claim once more the victory,—
Can the enemy's corpse awaken into life, and bruise the Champion's head?
Evil, terrible ensample, that foil to the attributes of Good,
Is banished to its own black world, weeded out of earth and heaven:
Shall that great gulf be passed, and sin be sown again?—
We know but this, the book of truth proclaimeth gladly, Never!

There remaineth the will of our God: when He repenteth of his creature,
Made by self-suggested mercy, ransomed by self-sacrificing justice,—
When Truth, that swore unto his neighbour, disappointeth him, and cleaveth to a lie,—
When the counsels of Wisdom are confounded, and Love warreth with itself,—
When the Unchangeable is changed, and the arm of Omnipotence is broken,—
Then,—thy quenchless soul shall have reached the goal of its existence.

But it seemeth to thy notions of the merciful and just, a false and fearful thing,
To lay such a burden upon time, that eternity be built on its foundation:
As if so casual good or ill should colour all the future,
And the vanity of accident, or sternness of necessity, save or wreck a soul.
Were it casual, vain, or stern, this might pass for truth;

But all things are marshalled by Design, and carefully tended by Benevolence.
O man, thy Judge is righteous,—noting, **remembering**, and weighing ;—
Want, ignorance, diversities of state, **are cast into the balance of advantage :**
The poisonous example of a parent asketh for allowance in the child ;
Care, diseases, toils, and frailties,—all things are considered.
And again, **a** mysterious Omniscience knoweth the spirits that are His,
While the delicate tissues of Event are woven by the fingers of Ubiquity.
Should Providence be taken by surprise from the possible impinging of an accident,
One fortuitous grain might dislocate the banded universe :
The merest seeming trifle is ordered as the morning light ;
And He, that rideth **on** the hurricane, is pilot **of** the bubble on the breaker.

Once more, consider Matter, how small a thing is father to the greatest ;
Thou that lightly hast regarded the results of so-called accident.
A blade of grass took fire in the sun,—and the prairies are burnt to the horizon :
A grain of sand may blind the eye, **and** madden the **brain to** murder :
A careful fly deposited its egg in the swelling bud of an acorn,—
The sapling grew,—cankrous and gnarled,—it is yonder hollow oak :
A child touched a **spring, and** the spring **closed a** valve, and the labouring engine burst,—
A thousand lives were in that ship,—wrecked by an infant's finger!
Shall nature preach in **vain?** thy casualty, guided in its orbit,
Though less than **a** mote upon the sunbeam, saileth in **a** fleet of worlds ;
That trivial cause, watered and observed of the Husbandman day by day,
In calm undeviating strength doth **work** its large effect.
Thus, in the pettiness of life note thou seeds of grandeur,
And watch the hour-glass of Time with **the eyes** of an heir of Immortality.

There still be clouds of witnesses,—if thou art not weary of my
  speech,—
Flocks of thoughts adding lustre to the light, and pointing on to
  Life.
For reflect how Truth and Goodness, well and wisely put,
Commend themselves to every mind with wondrous intuition:
What is this? the recognition of a standard, unwritten, natural,
  uniform;
Telling of one common source, the root of Good and True.
And if thus present soul can trace descent from Deity,
Being, as it standeth, individual, a separate reasonable thing,
What should hinder that its hope may not trace gladly forward,
And, in astounding parallel, like Enoch walk with God?
Yea, the genealogy of soul, that vivifying breath of a Creator,
Breath, no transient air, but essence, energy, and reason,
Is looming on the past, and shadowing the future, sublimely as
  Melchisedek of old,
Having not beginning, nor end of days, but present in the majesty
  of Peace!

O false scholar, credulous in vanities and only sceptical of truth,
Wherefore toil to cheat thy soul of its birthright, Immortality?
Is it for thy guilt? He pardoneth: Is it for thy frailty? He will
  help:
Though thou fearest, He is love; and Mercy shall be deeper than
  Despair:
Even for thy full-blown pride, is it much to be receiver of a God?
And lo, thy rights, He made thee; thy claims, He hath redeemed.
Hath the fair aspect of affection no beauty that thou shouldst
  desire it?
And are those sorrows nothing, to thee that passest by?
For it is Fact, immutable, that God hath dwelt in Man:
With gentle generous love ennobling while He bought us.
What, though thou art false, ignorant, weak and daring,—
Can the sun be quenched in heaven—or only Belisarius be blind?

But, even stooping to thy folly, grant all these hopes are vain;
Stultify reason, wrestle against conscience, and wither up the heart:
Where is thy vast advantage?—I have all that thou hast,
The buoyancy of life as strong, and term of days no shorter;
My cup is full with gladness, my griefs are not more galling;

And thus, we walk together, even to the gates of death:
There, (if not also on my journey, blessing every step,
Gladdening with light, and quickening with love, and killing all
    my cares,)
There,—while thou art quailing, or sullenly expecting to be
    nothing,—
There,—is found my gain; I triumph where thou tremblest.
Grant all my solace is a lie, yet it is a fountain of delight,
A spice in every pleasure, and a balm for every pain:
O precious wise delusion, scattering both misery and sin,—
O vile and silly truth, depraving while it curseth!

Darkling child of knowledge, commune with Socrates and Cicero,
They had no prejudice of birth, no dull parental warpings;
See, those lustrous minds anticipate the dawning day,—
Whilst thou, poor mole, art burrowing back to darkness from the
    light.
I will not urge a revelation, mercies, miracles, and martyrs,
But, after twice a thousand years, go, learn thou of the pagan;
It were happier and wiser even among fools, to cling to the shadow
    of a hope,
Than, in the company of sages, to win the substance of despair;
But here, the sages hope; despair is with the fools,
The base bad hearts, the stolid heads, the sensual and the selfish.

And wilt thou, sorry scorner, mock the phrase, despair?
Despair for those who die and live,—for me, I live and die:
What have I to do with dread?—my taper must go out;—
I nurse no silly hopes, and therefore feel no fears:
I am hastening to an End.—O false and feeble answer:
For hope is in thee still, and fear, a racking deep anxiety.
Erring brother, listen: and take thine answer from the ancients:
Consider every end, that it is but the end of a beginning:
All things work in circles; weariness induceth unto rest,
Rest invigorateth labour, and labour causeth weariness:
War produceth peace, and peace is wanton unto war:
Light dieth into darkness, and night dawneth into day:
The rotting jungle reeds scatter fertility around;
The buffalo's dead carcass hath quickened life in millions:
The end of toil is gain, the end of gain is pleasure,
Pleasure tendeth unto waste, and waste commandeth toil.

So, is death an end,—but it breedeth an infinite beginning;
Limits are for time, and death killed time; Eternity's beginning is for ever.
Ambition, hath it any goal indeed? is not all fruition, disappointment?
A step upon the ladder, and another, and another,—we start from every end?
Look to the eras of mortality; babe, student, man,
The husband, the father, the death-bed of a saint,—and is it then an end?
That common climax, Death, shall it lead to nothing?
How strong a root of causes flowering a consequence of vapour:
That solid chain of facts, is it to be snapped for ever?
How stout a show of figures, weakly summing to nonentity.

Or haply, Death, in the doublings of thy thought, shall seem continuous ending;
A dull eternal slumber, not an end abrupt.
O most futile chrysalis, wherefore dost thou sleep?
Dreamless, unconscious, never to awake,—what object in such slumber?
If thou art still to live, it may as well be wakefully as sleeping:
How grovelling must that spirit be, to need eternal sleep!
Or was indeed the toil of life so heavy and so long,
That nevermore can rest refresh thine overburdened soul?—
Sleep is a recreance to body, but when was mind asleep?
Even in a swoon it dreameth, though all be forgotten afterward:
The muscles seek relaxing, and the irritable nerves ask peace;
But life is a constant force, spirit an unquietable impetus:
The eye may wear out as a telescope, and the brain work slow as a machine,
But soul, unwearied, and for ever, is capable of effort unimpaired.

I live, move, am conscious; what shall bar my being?
Where is the rude hand, to rend this tissue of existence?
Not thine, shadowy Death, what art thou but a phantom?
Not thine, foul Corruption, what art thou but a fear?
For death is merely absent life, as darkness absent light;
Not even a suspension, for the life hath sailed away, steering gladly somewhere.
And corruption, closely noted, is but a dissolving of the parts,

The parts remain, and nothing lost, to build a better whole.
Moreover, mind is unity, however versatile and rapid;
Thou canst not entertain two coincident ideas, although they
    quickly follow:
And Unity hath no parts, so that there is nothing to dissolve:
The element is still unchanged in every searching solvent.
Who then shall bid me be annulled?—He that gave me being?
Amen, if God so will; I know that will is love:
But love hath promised life, and therefore I shall live;
So long as he is God, I shall be his Creature!

And here, shrewd reasoner, so eager to prove that thou must perish,
I note a sneer upon thy lip, and ridicule is haply on thy tongue:
How, said he,—creature of a God, and are not all his creatures,—
The lion, and the gnat,—yea, the mushroom, and the crystal,—
    have all these a soul?
Thy fancies tend to prove too much, and overshoot the mark:
If I die not with brutes, then brutes must live with me?—
I dare not tell thee that they will, for the word is not in my com-
    mission;
But of the twain it is the likelier; continuance is the chance:
Men, dying in their sins, are likened unto beasts that perish;
They are dark, animal, insensate, but have they not a lurking soul?
The spirit of a man goeth upward, reasonable, apprehending God;
The spirit of a beast goeth downward, sensual, doting on the crea-
    ture:
Who told thee they die at dissolution?—boldly think it out,—
The multitude of flies, and the multitude of herbs, the world with
    all its beings:
Is Infinity too narrow, Omnipotence too weak, and Love so anx-
    ious to destroy,
Doth Wisdom change its plan, and a Maker cancel his created?
God's will may compass all things, to fashion and to nullify at
    pleasure:
Yet are there many thoughts of hope, that all which are shall live.
True, there is no conscience in the brute, beyond some educated
    habit,
They lay them down without a fear, and wake without a hope:
Hunger and pain is of the animal; but when did they reckon or
    compare?
They live, idealess, in instinct; and while they breathe they gain:

The master is an idol to his dog, who cannot rise beyond him;
And void of capability for God, there would seem small cause for
 an infinity.
Therefore, caviller, my poor thoughts dare not grant they live:
But is it not a great thing to assume their annihilation—and thine
 own?
Would it be much if a speck on space, this globe with all its millions,
Verily, after its pollution, were suffered to exist in purity?
Or much, if guiltless creatures, that were cruelly entreated upon
 earth,
Found some commensurate reward in lower joys hereafter?
Or much, if a Creator, prodigal of life, and filled with the profundity of love,
Rejoice in all creatures of his skill, and lead them to perfection in
 their kind?
O man, there are many marvels; yet life is more a mystery than
 death:
For death may be some stagnant life,—but life is present God!

Many are the lurking holes of evil; who shall search them out?
Who so skilled to cut away the cancer with its fibres?
For wily minds with sinuous ease escape from lie to lie;
And cowards driven from the trench steal back to hide again.
Vain were the battle, if a warrior, having slain his foes,
Shall turn and find them vital still, unharmed, yea, unashamed:
For Error, dark magician, daily cast out killed,
Quickeneth animate anew beneath the midnight moon:
Once and again, once and again, hath reason answered wisely;
But not the less with brazen front doth folly urge her questions.
It were but unprofitable toil, a stand-up fight with unbelief:
When was there candour in a caviller, and who can satisfy the
 faithless?
Too long, O truant from the fold, have I tracked thy devious
 paths;
Too long, treacherous deserter, fought thee as a noble foeman:
Haply, my small art, and an arm too weakly for its weapon,
Hath failed to pierce thine iron coat, and reach thy stricken soul:
Haply, the fervour of my speech, and too patient sifting of thy
 fancies,
Shall tend to make thee prize them more, as worthier and wiser:

Go to: be mine the gain: we measure swords no more;
Go,—and a word go with thee,—Man, thou ART Immortal!

Child of light, and student in the truth, too long have I forgotten
    thee:
Lo, after parley with an alien, let me hold sweet converse with a
    brother.
Glorious hopes, and ineffable imaginings, crowd our holy theme;
Fear hath been slaughtered on the portal, and Doubt driven back
    to darkness:
For Christ hath died, and we in Him; by faith His All is ours;
Cross and crown, and love, and life; and we shall reign in Him!
Yea, there is a fitness and a beauty in ascribing immortality to
    mind,
That its energies and lofty aspirations may have scope for inde-
    finite expansion:
To learn all things is privilege of reason, and that with a growing
    capability,
But in this age of toil and time we scarce attain to alphabets:
How hardly in the midst of our hurry, and jostled by the cares of
    life,
Shall a man turn and stop to consider mighty secrets;
With barely hours, and barely powers, to fill up daily duties,
How small the glimpse of knowledge, his wondering eye can
    catch:
And knowledge is a noting of the order wherein God's attributes
    evolve,
Therefore worthy of the creature, worthy of an angel's seeking:
Yea, and human knowledge, meagre though the harvest,
Hath its roots, both deep and strong; but the plants are exotic to
    the climate:
All we seem to know demand a longer learning,
History and science, and prophecy and art, are workings all of
    God:
And there are galaxies of globes, millions of unimagined beings,
Other senses, wondrous sounds, and thoughts of thrilling fire,
Powers of strange might, quickening unknown elements,
And attributes and energies of God which man may never guess.

Not in vain, O brother, hath soul the spurs of enterprize,
Nor aimlessly panteth for adventure, waiting at the cave of mystery:

Not in vain the cup of curiosity, sweet and richly spiced,
Is ruby to the sight, and ambrosia to the taste, and redolent with
    all fragrance :
Thou shalt drink, and deeply, filling the mind with marvels ;
Thou shalt watch no more, lingering, disappointed of thy hope ;
Thou shalt roam where road is none, a traveller untrammelled,
Speeding at a wish, emancipate, to where the stars are suns !

Count, count your hopes, heirs of immortality and love ;
And hear my kindred faith, and turn again to bless me :
For lo, my trust is strong to dwell in many worlds,
And cull of many brethren there, sweet knowledge ever new :
I yearn for realms where fancy shall be filled, and the ecstacies of
    freedom shall be felt,
And the soul reign gloriously, risen to its royal destinies :
I look to recognise again, through the beautiful mask of their per-
    fection,
The dear familiar faces I have somewhile loved on earth :
I long to talk with grateful tongue of storms and perils past,
And praise the mighty Pilot that hath steered us through the
    rapids :
HE shall be the focus of it all, the very heart of gladness,—
My soul is athirst for God, the God who dwelt in Man !
Prophet, priest, and king, the sacrifice, the substitute, the Saviour,
Rapture of the blessed in the hunted One of earth, the Pardoner
    in the victim :
How many centuries of joy concentrate in that theme,
How often a Methuselah might count his thousand years and leave
    it unexhausted !
And lo, the heavenly Jerusalem, with all its gates one pearl,
That pearl of countless price, the door by which we entered,—
Come, tread the golden streets, and join that glorious throng,
The happy ones of heaven and earth, ten thousand times ten thou-
    sand ;
Hark, they sing that song,—and cast their crowns before him ;
Their souls alight with love,—Glory, and Praise, and Immor-
    tality !—
Veil thine eyes : no son of time may see that holy vision,
And even the seraph at thy side hath covered his face with wings.

Doth he not speak parables ?—each one goeth on his way,

Ye that hear, and I that counsel, **go on** our ways forgetful.
For the terrible **realities whereto we tend, are** hidden from **our eyes ;**
We know, but heed them not, and walk as if the temporal were all things.
Vanities, buzzing on the ear, fill its drowsy chambers,
Slow to dread those coming fears, the thunder and the trumpet ;
Motes, steaming on the sight, dim our purblind **eyes,**
Dark to see the ponderous orb of nearing Immortality :
Hemmed in by hostile foes, the trifler is busied on an epigram ;
The dull ox, driven to slaughter, careth but for pasture by the way.
Alas, that the precious things of truth, and the everlasting hills,
The mighty hopes we spake of, and the consciousness we feel,—
Alas, that all the future, and its adamantine facts,
Clouded by the present with intoxicating fumes,—
Should seem even to us, the great expectant heirs,
To us, the responsible and free, fearful sons of reason,
Only as a lovely song, sweet sounds of solemn music,
A pleasant voice, and nothing more,—doth he not speak parables?

Look to thy soul, O man, for none can be surety for his brother :
Behold, for heaven—or for hell,—thou canst not escape from Immortality !

OF IDEAS.

Mind is like a volatile essence, flitting hither and thither,
A solitary sentinel of the fortress body, to show himself everywhere by turns:
Mind is indivisible and instant, with neither parts nor organs,
That it doeth, it doth quickly, but the whole mind doth it :
An **active versatile** agent, untiring in the principle of energy,
Nor space, nor time, nor rest, nor toil, can affect the tenant of the brain.
His dwelling may verily be shattered, and the furniture thereof be disarranged,
But the particle of Deity in man slumbereth not, neither can be wearied :
However swift to change, even as the field of a kaleidoscope,

It taketh in but one idea at once, moulded for the moment to its
 likeness:
Mind is as the quicksilver, which; poured from vessel to vessel,
Instantly seizeth on a shape, and as instantly again discardeth it;
For it is an apprehensive power, closing on the properties of Matter,
Expanding to enwrap a world, collapsing to prison up an atom.
As, by night, thine irritable eyes may have seen strange changing
 figures,
Now a wheel, now suddenly a point, a line, a curve, a zigzag,
A maze ever altering, as the dance of gnats upon a sunbeam,
Swift, intricate, neither to be prophesied, nor to be remembered in
 succession,
So, the mind of a man, single, and perpetually moving,
Flickereth about from thought to thought, changed with each idea;
For the passing second metamorphosed to the image of that within
 its ken,
And throwing its immediate perceptions into each cause of contem-
 plation.
It shall regard a tree; and unconsciously, in separate review,
Embrace its colour, shape, and use, whole and individual conceptions;
It shall read or hear of crime, and cast itself into the commission;
It shall note a generous deed, and glow for a moment as the doer;
It shall imagine pride or pleasure, treading on the edges of tempta-
 tion;
Or heed of God and of his Christ, and grow transformed to glory.

Wherefore, it is wise and well to guide the mind aright,
That its aptness may be sensitive to good, and shrink with
 antipathy from evil:
For use will mould and mark it, or nonusage dull and blunt it;—
So to talk of spirit by analogy with substance;
And analogy is a truer guide, than many teachers tell of,
Similitudes are scattered round, to help us, not to hurt us;
Moses, in his every type, and the Greater than Moses, in his parables,
Preach, in terms that all may learn, the philosophic lessons of
 analogy:
And here, in a topic immaterial, the likeness of analogy is just;
By habits, knit the nerves of mind, and train the gladiator shrewdly:
For thought shall strengthen thinking, and imagery speed ima-
 gination,
Until thy spiritual inmate shall have swelled to the giant of Otranto.

Nevertheless, heed well, that this Athlete, growing in thy brain,
Be a wholesome Genius, not a cursed Afrite:
And see thou discipline his strength, and point his aim discreetly;
Feed him on humility and holy things, weaned from covetous desires;
Hour by hour and day by day, ply him with ideas of excellence,
Dragging forth the evil but to loathe, as a Spartan's drunken Helot:
And win, by gradual allurements, the still expanding soul,
To rise from a contemplated universe, even to the Hand that made it.

A common mind perceiveth not beyond his eyes and ears:
The palings of the park of sense enthral this captured roebuck:
And still, though fettered in the flesh, he doth not feel his chains,
Externals are the world to him, and circumstance his atmosphere.
Therefore tangible pleasures are enough for the animal-man;
He is swift to speak and slow to think, dreading his own dim conscience;
And solitude is terrible, and exile worse than death,
He cannot dwell apart, nor breathe at a distance from the crowd.
But minds of nobler stamp, and chiefest the mint-marked of heaven,
Walk independent, by themselves, freely manumitted of externals:
They carry viands with them, and need no refreshment by the way,
Nor drink of other wells than their own inner fountain.
Strange shall it seem how little such a man will lean upon the
    accidents of life,
He is winged and needeth not a staff; if it break,—he shall not fall:
And lightly perchance doth he remember the stale trivialities
    around him,
He liveth in the realm of thought, beyond the world of things;
These are but transient Matter, and himself enduring Spirit:
And worldliness will laugh to scorn that sublimated wisdom.
His eyes may open on a prison-cell, but the bare walls glow with
    imagery;
His ears may be filled with execrations, but are listening to the
    music of sweet thoughts;
He may dwell in a hovel with a hero's heart, and canopy his
    penury with peace,
For mind is a kingdom to the man, who gathereth his pleasure
    from Ideas.

OF NAMES.

Adam gave the name, when the Lord had made his creature,
For God led them in review, to see what man would call them.
As they struck his senses, he proclaimed their sounds,
A name for the **distinguishing** of each, a numeral by which it should be known:
He specified the partridge by her cry, and the forest prowler by his roaring,
The tree by its use, and the flower by its beauty, and everything according to its truth.

There is an arbitrary name; whereunto the idea attacheth;
And there is a reasonable name, linking its fitness to idea:
Yet shall these twain run in parallel courses,
Neither shalt thou readily discern **the** habit from the nature.
For **mind is apt** and quick to wed ideas and names together,
Nor stoppeth its perception to be curious of priorities;
And there is but little in the sound, as some have vainly fancied,
The same tone in different tongues shall be suitable to opposite ideas:
Yea, take an ensample in thine own; consider similar words:
How various and contrary the thoughts those kindred **names** produce:
A house shall seem a fitting word to call a roomy dwelling,
Yet there is a like propriety in the small smooth sound, a mouse:
Mountain, as if of a necessity, is **a word** both mighty and majestic.—
What heed ye then of Fountain?—flowing silver in the sun.

Many a **fair** flower is burdened with preposterous appellatives,
Which the wiser simplicity of rustics entitled by its beauties;
And often the conceit of science, loving to be thought cosmopolite,
Shall mingle names of every clime, alike obscure to each.
There is wisdom in calling a thing fitly; name should note particulars,
Through a character **obvious to all men**, and worthy of their instant acceptation.
The herbalist had a simple cause for **every word upon his** catalogue,
But now the mouth of Botany is filled with **empty** sound;
And many a peasant hath an answer on his tongue, concerning some vexed flower,

Shrewder than the centipede phrase, wherewithal philosophers
    invest it.

For that, the foolishness of pride, and flatteries of cringing homage,
Strew with chaff the threshing-floors of science; names perplex
    them all:
The entomologist, who hath pried upon an insect, straightway shall
    endow it with his name;
It had many qualities and marks of note,—but in chief, a vain
    observer:
The geographer shall journey to the pole, through biting frost and
    desolation,
And, for some simple patron's sake, shall name that land the happy:
The fossilist hath found a bone, the rib of some huge lizard,
And forthwith standeth to it sponsor, to tack himself on reptile
    immortalities:
The sportsman, hunting at the Cape, found some strange-horned
    antelope,
The spots are new, the fame is cheap, and so his name is added.
Thus, obscurities encumber knowledge, even by the vanity of men,
Who play into each other's hand the game of giving names.

Various are the names of men, and drawn from different wells;
Aspects of body, or characters of mind, the creature's first idea:
And some have sprung of trades, and some of dignities or office;
Other some added to a father's, and yet more growing from a place:
Animal creation, with sciences, and things,—their composites, and
    near associations,
Contributed their symbollings of old, wherewith to title men:
And heraldry set upon its cresture the figured attributes as ensigns
By which, as by a name concrete, its bearer should be known.

Egypt opened on the theme, dressing up her gods in qualities;
Horns of power, feathers of the swift, mitres of catholic dominion,
The sovereign asp, the circle everlasting, the crook and thong of
    justice,
By many mystic shapes and sounds displayed the idol's name.
Thereafter, high-plumed warriors, the chieftains of Etruria and
    Troy,
And Xerxes, urging on his millions to the tomb of pride, Ther-
    mopylæ,

And Hiero with his bounding ships, all figured at the prow,
And Rome's Prætorian standards, piled with strange devices,
And stout crusaders pressing to the battle, locked in sable mail;
These all in their speaking symbols, earned, or wore, a name.
Eve, the mother of all living, and Abraham, father of a multitude,
Jacob, the supplanter, and David, the beloved, and all the worthies of old time,
Noah, who came for consolation, and Benoni, son of sorrow,
Kings and prophets, children of the East, owned each his title of significance.

There be names of high descent, and thereby storied honours:
Names of fair renown, and therein characters of merit:
But to lend the lowborn noble names, is to shed upon them ridicule and evil;
Yea, many weeds run rank in pride, if men have dubbed them cedars:
And to herald common mediocrity with the noisy notes of fame,
Tendeth to its deeper scorn; as if it were to call the mole a mammoth.
Yet shall ye find the trader's babe dignified with sounding titles,
And little hath the father guessed the harm he did his child:
For either they may breed him discontent, a peevish repining at his station,
Or point the finger of despite at the mule in the trappings of an elephant:
And it is a kind of theft to filch appellations from the famous,
A soiling of the shrines of praise with folly's vulgar herd.
Prudence hath often gone ashamed for the name they added to his father's,
If minds of mark and great achievements bore it well before:
For he walketh as the jay in the fable, though not by his own folly,
Another's fault hath compassed his misfortune, making him a martyr to his name.

Who would call the tench a whale, or style a torch, Orion?
Yet many a silly parent hath dealt likewise with his nurseling.
Give thy child a fit distinguishment, making him sole tenant of a name,
For it were a sore hindrance to hold it in common with a hundred:
In the Babel of confused identities fame is little feasible,

The felon shall detract from the philanthropist, and the sage share
 honours with the simple;
Still, in thy title of distinguishment, fall not into arrogant assumption,
Steering from caprice and affectations; and for all thou doest,
 have a reason.
He that is ambitious for his son, should give him untried names,
For those that have served other men, haply may injure by their
 evils;
Or otherwise may hinder by their glories; therefore, set him by
 himself,
To win for his individual name some clear specific praise.
There were nine Homers, all goodly sons of song, but where is
 any record of the eight?
One grew to fame, an Aaron's rod, and swallowed up his brethren:
Who knoweth? more distinctly titled, those dead eight had lived;
But the censers were ranged in a circle to mingle their sweets
 without a difference.

Art thou named of a common crowd, and sensible of high as-
 pirings?
It is hard for thee to rise,—yet strive: thou mayest be among them
 a Musæus.
Art thou named of a family, the same in successive generations?
It is open to thee still to earn for epithets, such an one, the good
 or great.
Art thou named foolishly? show that thou art wiser than thy
 fathers,
Live to shame their vanity or sin by dutiful devotion to thy sphere.
Art thou named discreetly? It is well, the course is free:
No competitor shall claim thy colours, neither fix his faults upon
 thee:
Hasten to the goal of fame between the posts of duty,
And win a blessing from the world, that men may love thy name:
Yea, that the unction of its praise, in fragrance well deserving,
May float adown the stream of time, like ambergris at sea;
So thy sons may tell their sons, and those may teach their children,
He died in goodness, as he lived;—and left us his good name.
And more than these: there is a roll whereon thy name is written;
See that, on the Book of Doom, that name is fixed in light:
Then, safe within a better home, where time and its titles are not
 found,

God will give thee his new Name, and write it on thy heart:
A Name, better than of sons, a Name dearer than of daughters,
A Name of union, peace, and praise, as numbered in thy God.

OF THINGS.

ABSTRACTED from all substance, and flying with the feathered
    flock of thoughts,
The idea of a thing hath the nature of its Soul, a separate seeming
    essence:
Intimately linked to the idea, suggesting many qualities,
The name of a thing hath the nature of its Mind, an intellectual
    recorder:
And the matter of a thing, concrete, is a Body to the perfect crea-
    ture,
Compacted three in one, as all things else within the universe.
Nothing canst thou add to them, and nothing take away, for all
    have these proportions,
The thought, the word, the form, combining in the Thing:
All separate, yet harmonizing well, and mingled each with other,
One whole in several parts, yet each part spreading to a whole:
The idea is a whole; and the meaning phrase that spake idea, a
    whole;
And the matter, as ye see it, is a whole; the mystery of true tri-
    unity:
Yea, there is even a deeper mystery,—which none, I wot, can
    fathom,
Matter, different from properties whereby the solid substance is
    described;
For, size and weight, cohesion and the like, live distinct from
    matter,
Yet who can imagine matter, unendowed with size and weight?
As in the spiritual, so in the material, man must rest with patience,
And wait for other eyes wherewith to read the books of God.

Men have talked learnedly of atoms, as if matter could be ever
    indivisible;
They talk, but ill are skilled to teach, and darken truth by fancies:
An atom by our grosser sense was never yet conceived,
And nothing can be thought so small, as not to be divided:

For an atom runneth to infinity, and never shall be caught in space,
And a molecule is no more indivisible than Saturn's belted orb.
Things intangible, multiplied by multitudes, never will amass to substance,
Neither can a thing which may be touched, be made of impalpable proportions;
The sum of indivisibles must need be indivisible, as adding many nothings,
And the building up of atoms into matter is but a silly sophism;
Lucretius, and keen Anaximander, and many that have followed in their thoughts,
(For error hath a long black shadow, dimming light for ages,)
In the foolishness of men without a God fancied to fashion Matter
Of intangibles, and therefore uncohering, indivisibles, and therefore Spirit.

Things breed thoughts; therefore at Thebes and Heliopolis,
In hieroglyphic sculptures are the priestly secrets written;
Things breed thoughts; therefore was the Athens of idolatry
Set with carved images, frequent as the trees of Academus:
Things breed thoughts; therefore the Brahmin and the Burman
With mythologic shapes adorn their coarse pantheon:
Things breed thoughts; therefore the statue and the picture,
Relics, rosaries, and miracles in act, quicken the Papist in his worship:
Things breed thoughts; therefore the lovers at their parting,
Interchanged with tearful smiles the dear reminding tokens:
Things breed thoughts; therefore when the clansman met his foe,
The blood-stained claymore in his hand revived the memories of vengeance.

Things teach with double force; through the animal eye, and through the mind,
And the eye catcheth in an instant, what the ear shall not learn within an hour.
Thence is the potency of travel, the precious might of its advantages
To compensate its dissipative harm, its toil and cost and danger.
Ulysses, wandering to many shores, lived in many cities,
And thereby learnt the minds of men, and stored his own more richly:
Herodotus, the accurate and kindly, spake of that he saw,

And reaped his knowledge on the spot, in fertile fields of Egypt:
Lycurgus culled from every clime the golden fruits of justice;
And Plato roamed through foreign lands, to feed on truth in all.
For travel, conversant with Things, bringeth them in contact with the mind;
We breathe the wholesome atmosphere about ungarbled truth:
Pictures of fact are painted on the eye, to decorate the house of intellect,
Rather than visions of fancy, filling all the chambers with a vapour.
For, in Ideas, the great mind will exaggerate, and the lesser extenuate truth;
But in Things the one is chastened, and the other quickened, to equality:
And in Names,—though a property be told, rather than some arbitrary accident,
Still shall the thought be vague or false, if none have seen the Thing:
For in Things the property with accident standeth in a mass concrete,
These cannot cheat the sense, nor elude the vigilance of spirit.
Travel is a ceaseless fount of surface education,
But its wisdom will be simply superficial, if thou add not thoughts to things:
Yet, aided by the varnish of society, things may serve for thoughts,
Till many dullards that have seen the world shall pass for scholars:
Because one single glance will conquer all descriptions,
Though graphic, these left some unsaid, though true, these tended to some error;
And the most witless eye that saw, had a juster notion of its object,
Than the shrewdest mind that heard and shaped its gathered thoughts of Things.

OF FAITH.

CONFIDENCE was bearer of the palm; for it looked like conviction of desert:
And where the strong is well assured, the weaker soon allow it.
Majesty and Beauty are commingled, in moving with immutable decision,
And well may charm the coward hearts that turn and hide for fear.

Faith, firmness, confidence, consistency,—these are well allied ;
Yea, let a man press on in aught, he shall not lack of honour :
For such an one seemeth as superior to the native instability of creatures ;
That he doeth, he doeth as a god, and men will marvel at his courage.
Even in crimes, a partial praise cannot be denied to daring,
And many fearless chiefs have won the friendship of a foe.

Confidence is conqueror of men ; victorious both over them and in them ;
The iron will of one stout heart shall make a thousand quail :
A feeble dwarf, dauntlessly resolved, will turn the tide of battle,
And rally to a nobler strife the giants that had fled ;
The tenderest child, unconscious of a fear, will shame the man to danger,
And when he dared it, danger died, and faith had vanquished fear.
Boldness is akin to power : yea, because ignorance is weakness,
Knowledge with unshrinking might will nerve the vigorous hand :
Boldness hath a startling strength ; the mouse may fright a lion,
And oftentimes the horned herd is scared by some brave cur.
Courage hath analogy with faith, for it standeth both in animal and moral ;
The true is mindful of a God, the false is stout in self :
But true or false, the twain are faith ; and faith worketh wonders :
Never was a marvel done upon the earth, but it had sprung of faith:
Nothing noble, generous, or great, but faith was the root of the achievement ;
Nothing comely, nothing famous, but its praise is faith.
Leonidas fought in human faith, as Joshua in divine :
Xenophon trusted to his skill, and the sons of Mattathias to their cause :
In faith Columbus found a path across those untried waters ;
The heroines of Arc and Saragossa fought in earthly faith :
Tell was strong, and Alfred great, and Luther wise, by faith :
Margaret by faith was valiant for her son, and Wallace mighty for his people :
Faith in his reason made Socrates sublime, as faith in his science, Galileo :
Ambassadors in faith are bold, and unreproved for boldness :
Faith urged Fabius to delays, and sent forth Hannibal to Cannæ :

Q

Cæsar at the Rubicon, Miltiades at Marathon; both were sped by faith.
I set not all in equal spheres: I number not the martyr with the patriot;
I class not the hero with his horse, because the twain have courage;
But only for ensample and instruction, that all things stand by faith;
Albeit faith of divers kinds, and varying in degree.
There is a faith towards men, and there is a faith towards God;
The latter is the gold and the former is the brass; but both are sturdy metal:
And the brass mingled with the gold floweth into rich Corinthian;
A substance bright and hard and keen, to point Achilles' spear:
So shalt thou stop the way against the foes that hem thee;
Trust in God to strengthen man;—be bold, for He doth help.

Yet more: for confidence in man, even to the worst and meanest,
Hath power to overcome his ill, by charitable good.
Fling thine unreserving trust even on the conscience of a culprit,
Soon wilt thou shame him by thy faith, and he will melt and mend:
The nest of thieves will harm thee not, if thou dost bear thee boldly;
Boldly, yea and kindly, as relying on their honour:
For the hand so stout against aggression, is quite disarmed by charity;
And that warm sun will thaw the heart case-hardened by long frost.
Treat men gently, trust them strongly, if thou wish their weal;
Or cautious doubt and bitter thoughts will tempt the best to foil thee.
Believe the well in sanguine hope, and thou shalt reap the better;
But if thou deal with men so ill, thy dealings make them worse.
Despair not of some gleams of good still lingering in the darkest,
And among veterans in crime, plead thou as with their children:
So, astonied at humanities, the bad heart long estranged,
Shall even weep to feel himself so little worth thy love;
In wholesome sorrow will he bless thee; yea, and in that spirit may repent;
Thus wilt thou gain a soul, in mercy given to thy faith.

Look aside to lack of faith, the mass of ills it bringeth:
All things treacherous, base, and vile, dissolving the brotherhood of men.

Bonds break; the cement hath lost its hold; and each is separate
    from other:
That which should be neighbourly and good, is cankered into
    bitterness and evil.
O thou serpent, fell Suspicion, coiling coldly round the heart,—
O thou asp of subtle Jealousy, stinging hotly to the soul,—
O distrust, reserve, and doubt,—what reptile shapes are here,
Poisoning the garden of a world with death among its flowers!
No need of many words, the tale is easy to be told;
A point will touch the truth, a line suggest the picture.
For if, in thine own home, a cautious man and captious,
Thou hintest at suspicion of a servant, thou soon wilt make a
    thief;
Or if, too keen in care, thou dost evidently disbelieve thy child,
Thou hast injured the texture of his honour, and smoothed to him
    the way of lying;
Or if thou observest upon friends, as seeking thee selfishly for
    interest,
Thou hast hurt their kindliness to thee, and shalt be paid with
    scorn:
Or if, O silly ones of Marriage, your foul and foolish thoughts,
Harshly misinterpreting in each the levity of innocence for sin,
Shall pour upon the lap of home pain where once was pleasure,
And mix contentions in the cup, that mantled once with comforts,
Bitterly and justly shall ye rue the punishment due to unbelief;
Ye trust not each the other, nor the mutual vows of God;
Take heed, for the pit may now be near, a pit of your own
    digging,—
Faith abused tempteth unto crime, and doubt may make its
    monster.

Man verily is vile, but more in capability than action;
His sinfulness is deep, but his transgressions may be few, even
    from the absence of temptation:
He is hanging in a gulph midway, but the air is breathable about
    him:
Thrust him not from that slight hold, to perish in the vapours
    underneath.
For, God pleadeth with the deaf, as having ears to hear,
Christ speaketh to the dead, as those that are capable of living;
And an evil teacher is that man, a tempter to much sin,

Who looketh on his hearers with distrust, and hath no confidence
  in brethren.
All may mend; and sympathies are healing: and reason hath its
  influence with the worst;
And in those worst is ample hope, if only thou hast charity, and
  faith.

Somewhiles have I watched a man exchanging the sobriety of
  faith,
Old lamps for new,—even for fanatical excitements.
He gained surface, but lost solidity; heat, in lieu of health;
And still with swelling words and thoughts he scorned his ancient
  coldness:
But, his strength was shorn as Samson's; he walked he knew not
  whither;
Doubt was on his daily path; and duties showed not certain.
Until, in an hour of enthusiasm, stung with secret fears,
He pinned the safety of his soul on some false prophet's sleeve:
And then, that sure word failed; and with it, failed his faith;
It failed, and fell; O deep and dreadful was his fall in faith!
He could not stop, with reason's rein, his coursers on the slope,
And so they dashed him down the cliff of hardened unbelief.
With overreaching grasp he had strained for visionary treasures,
But a fiend had cheated his presumption, and hurled him to
  despair.
So he lay in his blood, the victim of a credulous false faith,
And many nights, and night-like days, he dwelt in outer darkness.
But, within a while, his variable mind caught a new impression.
A new impression of the good old stamp, that sealed him when a
  child:
He was softened, and abjured his infidelity; he was wiser, and
  despised his credulity;
And turned again to simple faith more simply than before.
Experience had declared too well his mind was built of water,
And so, renouncing strength in self, he fixed his faith in God.

It is not for me to stipulate for creeds; Bible, Church, and Reason,
These three shall lead the mind, if any can, to truth.
But I must stipulate for faith; both God and man demand it:
Trust is great in either world, if any would be well.
Verily, the sceptical propensity is an universal foe;

Sneering Pyrrho never found, nor cared to find, a friend:
How could he trust another? and himself, whom would he not
 deceive?
His proper gains were all his aim, and interests clash with kindness.
So, the Bedouin goeth armed, an enemy to all,
The spear is stuck beside his couch, the dagger hid beneath his
 pillow.
For society, void of mutual trust, of credit, and of faith,
Would fall asunder as a waterspout, snapped from the cloud's
 attraction.
Faith may rise into miracles of might, as some few wise have
 shown:
Faith may sink into credulities of weakness, as the mass of fools
 have witnessed.
Therefore, in the first, saints and martyrs have fulfilled their
 mission,
Conquering dangers, courting deaths, and triumphing in all.
Therefore, in the last, the magician and the witch, victims of their
 own delusion,
Have gained the bitter wages of impracticable sins:
They believed in allegiance with Satan; they worked in that
 belief,
And thereby earned the loss and harm of guilt that might not be.
For, faith hath two hands; with the one it addeth virtue to indifferents;
Yea, it sanctified a Judith and a Jael, for what otherwise were
 treachery and murder:
With the other hand it heapeth crime even on impossibles or
 simples,
And many a wizard well deserved the faggot for his faith:
He trusted in his intercourse with evil, he sacrificed heartily to
 fiends,
He withered up with curses to the limit of his will, and was vile,
 because he thought himself a villain.

A great mind is ready to believe, for he hungereth to feed on facts,
And the gnawing stomach of his ignorance craveth unceasing to be
 filled:
A little mind is boastful and incredulous, for he fancieth all knowledge is his own,

So will he cavil at a truth; how should it be true, and he not
  know it?—
There is an easy scheme, to solve all riddles by the sensual,
And thus, despising mysteries, to feel the more sufficient:
For it comforteth the foul hard heart, to reject the pure unseen,
And relieveth the dull soft head, to hinder one from gazing upon
  vacancy.
True wisdom, labouring to expound, heareth others readily;
False wisdom, sturdy to deny, closeth up her mind to argument.
The sum of certainties is found so small, their field so wide an
  universe,
That many things may truly be, which man hath not conceived:
The characters revealed of God are a strong mind's sole assurance
That any strangeness may not stand a sober theme for faith:
Ignorance being light denied, this ought to show the stronger in
  its view,
But ignorance is commonly a double negative, both of light and
  morals:
So, adding vanity to blindness, for ease, it taketh refuge in a doubt,
And aching soon with ceaseless doubt, it finisheth the strife by
  misbelieving.

Faith, by its very nature, shall embrace both credence and obedience:
Yea, the word for both is one, and cannot be divided.
For, work void of faith, wherein can it be counted for a duty;
And faith not seen in work,—whereby can the doctrine be dis-
  covered?
Faith in religion is an instrument; a handle, and the hand to turn it:
Less a condition than a mean, and more an operation than a virtue.
A moral sickness, like to sin, must have a moral cure;
And faith alone can heal the mind, whose malady is sense.
Ye are told of God's deep love: they that believe will love him:
They that love him, will obey: and obedience hath its blessing.
Ye are taught of the soul's great price; they that believe will
  prize it,
And, prizing soul, will cherish well the hopes that make it happy.
Effects spring from feelings; and feelings grow of faith:
If a man conceive himself insulted, will not his anger smite?
Thus, let a soul believe his state, his danger, destiny, redemption,
Will he not feel eager to be safe, like him that kept the prison at
  Philippi?

A mother had an only son, and sent him out to sea :
She was a widow, and in **penury ; and he** must seek his fortunes.
How often in the wintry nights, when waves and winds were howling,
Her heart was torn with sickening dread, and bled to see her boy,
And on one **sunny morn, when** all around was comfort,
News came, that weeks agone, the vessel had been wrecked ;
Yea, wrecked, and he was dead! they had seen him perish in his agony:
Oh then, what agony was like to her's,—for she believed the **tale.**
She was bowed and broken down with sorrow, and uncomforted in prayer ;
Many nights she mourned, and pined, and had no hope but **death.**
But on a day, while sorely she was weeping, a stranger broke upon her loneliness,
He had news to tell, that **weather-beaten** man, **and** must not be denied :
And what were the wonder-working words that made this mourner joyous,
That swept her heaviness away, and filled her world with praise ?
Her son was saved,—is alive,—is near !—O did she stop to question ?
No, rushing in the force of faith, she met him at the door !

OF HONESTY.

ALL is vanity which is not honesty ;—thus is it graven on the tomb !
And there is no wisdom but in piety ;—so the dead man preacheth :
For, in a simple village church, among those classic shades
Which sylvan Evelyn loved to rear, (his praise, and my delight,)
These, the words of truth, are writ upon his sepulchre,
Who learnt much lore, and knew all trees, from the cedar to the **hyssop** on the wall ;
A just conjunction, godliness and honesty ; ministering to both worlds,
Well wed, **and ill to be divided,** a pair that God hath joined together.
I touch not now the vulgar thought, as of tricks and cheateries in trade ;
I speak of honest purpose, character, speech and action.
For an honest man hath special need of charity, and prudence,
Of a deep and humbling self-acquaintance, and of blessed commerce with his God,

So that the keennesses of truth may be freed from asperities of censure,
And the just but vacillating mind be not made the pendulum of arguments:
For a false reason, shrewdly put, can often not be answered on the instant,
And prudence looketh unto faith, content to wait solutions;
Yea, it looketh, yea, it waiteth, still holding honesty in leash,
Lest, as a hot young hound, it track not game, but vermin.
Many a man of honest heart, but ignorant of self and God,
Hath followed the marsh-fires of pestilence, esteeming them the lights of truth;
He heard a cause, which he had not skill to solve,—and so received it gladly;
And that cause brought its consequence, harm to an unstable soul.
Prudence, for a man's own sake, never should be separate from honesty;
And charity, for other's good and his, must still be joined therewith:
For the harshly chiding tongue hath neither pleasuring nor profit,
And the cold unsympathizing heart never gained a good.
Sin is a sore, and folly is a fever; touch them tenderly for healing;
The bad chirurgeon's awkward knife harmeth, spite of honesty.
Still, a rough diamond is better than the polished paste,—
That courteous flattering fool, who spake of vice as virtue:
And honesty, even by itself, though making many adversaries
Whom prudence might have set aside, or charity have softened,
Evermore will prosper at the last, and gain a man great honour
By giving others many goods, to his own cost and hindrance.

Freedom is father of the honest, and sturdy Independence is his brother;
These three, with head and hand, dwell together in unity.
The blunt yeoman, stout and true, will speak unto princes unabashed:
His mind is loyal, just and free, a crystal in its plain integrity;
What should make such an one ashamed? where courtiers kneel, he standeth;—
I will indeed bow before the king, but knees were knit for God.
And many such there be, of a high and noble conscience,
Honourable, generous, and kind, though blest with little light:

What should he barter for his Freedom? some petty gain of gold?
Free of speech, and free in act, magnates honour him for boldness:
Long may he flourish in his peace, and a stalwarth race around him,
Rooted in the soil like oaks, and hardy as the pine upon the mountains!

Yet, there be others, that will truckle to a lie, selling honesty for interest:
And do they gain?—they gain but loss; a little cash, with scorn.
Behold, the sorrowful change wrought upon a fallen nature:
He hath lost his own esteem, and other men's respect,
For the buoyancy of upright faith, he is clothed in the heaviness of cringing;
For plain truth where none could err, he hath chosen tortuous paths;
In lieu of his majesty of countenance—the timorous glances of servility;
Instead of Freedom's honest pride,—the spirit of a slave.

Nevertheless, there is something to be pleaded, even for a necessary guile,
Whilst the world, and all that is therein, lieth deep in evil.
Who can be altogether honest,—a champion never out of mail,
Ready to break a lance for truth with every crowding error?
Who can be altogether honest,—dragging out the secresies of life,
And risking to be lashed and loathed for each unkind disclosure?
Who can be altogether honest,—living in perpetual contentions,
And prying out the petty cheats that swell the social scheme?
For he must speak his instant mind,—a mind corrupt and sinful,
Exhibiting to other men's disgust its undisguised deformities:
He must utter all the hatred of his heart, and add to it the venom of his tongue;
Shall he feel, and hide his feelings? that were the meanness of a hypocrite.—
Still, O man, such hypocrisy is better, than this bold honesty to sin:
Kill the feeling, or conceal it: let shame at least do the work of charity.

O charity, thou livest not in warnings, meddling among men,
Rebuking every foolish word, and censuring small sins;
This is not thy secret,—rather wilt thou hide their multitude,

And silence the condemning tongue, and wearisome exhortation.
But for thee, thy strength and zeal shine in encouragement to good,
Lifting up the lantern of ensample, that wanderers may find the way;
That lantern is not lit to gaze on all the hatefulness of evil,
But set on high for life and light, the loveliness of good.
The hard censorious mind sitteth as a keen anatomist
Tracking up the fibres in corruption, and prying on a fearful corpse:
But the charitable soul is a young lover, enamoured little wisely,
That saw no fault in her he loved, and sought to see one less;
So, in his kind and genial light, she grew more worthy of his love;
Won to good by gentle suns, and not by frowning tempest.

Verily infirm thyself,—be slow to chide a brother's imperfections;
For many times the decent veil must hang on faults of nature:
And the rude hands, that rend it offend against the modesty of right,
While seeming zeal, with its effort to do good, is only feigned self-praise:
Often will the meannesses of life, hidden away in corners,
Prove wisdom; and the generous is glad to leave them unregarded in the shade.
The follies none are found to praise, let them die unblamed;
Thine honest strife will only tend to make some think them wise:
And small conventional deceits, let them live uncensured:
Or, if thou war with pigmies, thou shalt haply help the cranes.
Where to be blind was safety, Ovid had been wise for winking:
And when a tell-tale might do harm, be sure it is prudent to be dumb;
That which is just and fit is often found combating with honesty;
In the cause of good, be wise; and in a case indifferent, keep silence.

Let honesty's unblushing face be shaded by the mantle of humility,
So shall it shine a lamp of love, and not the torch of strife:
Otherwise the lantern of Diogenes, presumptuously thrust before the face,
If it never find an honest man, shall often make an angered.
Let honesty be companied by charity of heart, lest it walk unwelcome;
Or the mouthing censor of others and himself, soon shall sink to scorn:

Let honesty be added unto innocence of life: then a man may
 only be its martyr;
But if openness of speech be found with secresy of guilt, the martyr
 will be seen a malefactor.

There is a cunning scheme, to put on surface bluntness,
And cover still deep water, with the clamorous ripples of a shallow.
For a man, to gain his selfish ends, will make a stalking-horse of
 honesty:
And hide his poaching limbs behind, that he may cheat the
 quicker.
Such an one is loud and ostentatious, full of oaths for argument,
Boastful of honour and sincerity, and not to be put down by facts:
He is obstinate, and showeth it for firmness; he is rude, display-
 ing it for truth;
And glorieth in doggedness of temper, as if it were uncompro-
 mising justice.
Be aware of such a man; his brawling covereth designs;
This specious show of honesty cometh as the herald of a thief:
His feint is made with awkward clashing on the buckler's boss,
But meanwhile doth his secret skill ensure its fatal aim.
This is the hypocrite of honesty; ye may know him by an over-
 acted part;
Taking pains to turn and twist, where other men walk straight;
Or walking straight, he will not step aside to let another pass,
But roughly pusheth on, provoking opposition on the way;
He is full of disquietude for calmness, full of intriguing for simplicity,
Valorous with those who cannot fight, and humble to the brave:
Where brotherly advice were good, this man rudely blameth,
And on some small occasion, flattereth with coarse praise.
The craven in a lion's skin hath conquered by his character for
 courage;
Sheep's clothing helped the wolf, till he slew by his character for
 kindness.

For honesty hath many gains, and well the wise have known
This will prosper at the end, and fill their house with gold.
The phosphorus of cheatery will fade, and all its profits perish,
While honesty with growing light endureth as the moon.
Yea, it would be wise in a world of thieves, where cheating were
 a virtue,

To dare the vice of honesty, if any would be rich :
For that which by the laws of God is heightened into duty,
Ever, in the practice of a man, will be seen both policy and privilege.
Thank God, ye toilers for your bread, in that, daily labouring,
He hath suffered the bubbles of self-interest to float upon the stream of duty :
For honesty, of every kind, approved by God and man,
Of wealth and better weal is found the richest cornucopia.
Tempered by humbleness and charity, honesty of speech hath honour ;
And mingled well with prudence, honesty of purpose hath its praise :
Trust payeth homage unto truth, rewarding honesty of action :
And all men love to lean on him, who never failed nor fainted.
Freedom gloweth in his eyes, and Nobleness of nature at his heart,
And Independence took a crown and fixed it on his head :
So, he stood in his integrity, just and firm of purpose,
Aiding many, fearing none, a spectacle to angels and to men :
Yea,—when the shattered globe shall rock in the throes of dissolution,
Still, will he stand in his integrity, sublime—an honest man.

OF SOCIETY.

Better is the mass of men, Suspicion, than thy fears,
Kinder than thy thoughts, O chilling heart of Prudence,
Purer than thy judgments, ascetic tongue of Censure,
In all things worthier to love, if not also wiser to esteem ;
Yea, let the moralist condemn, there be large extenuations of his verdict,
Let the misanthrope shun men and abjure, the most are rather loveable than hateful.
How many pleasant faces shed their light on every side,
How many angels unawares have crossed thy casual way !
How often, in thy journeyings, hast thou made thee instant friends,
Found, to be loved a little while, and lost, to meet no more ;
Friends of happy reminiscence, although so transient in their converse,

Liberal, cheerful, and sincere, a crowd of kindly traits.
I have sped by land and sea, and mingled with much people,
But never yet could find a spot, unsunned by human kindness;
Some more, and some less,—but truly all can claim a little;
And a man may travel through the world, and sow it thick with friendships.

There be indeed, to say it in all sorrow, bad apostate souls,
Deserted of their ministering angels, and given up to liberty of sin,—
And other some, the miserly and mean, whose eyes are keen and greedy,
With stony hearts, and iron fists, to filch and scrape and clutch,—
And others yet again, the coarse in mind, selfish, sensual, brutish,
Seeming as incapable of softer thoughts, and dead to better deeds,—
Such, no lover of the good, no follower of the generous and gentle,
Can nearer grow to love, than may consist with pity.
Few verily are these among the mass, and cast in fouler moulds,
Few and poor in friends, and well deserving of their poverty:
Yet, or ever thou hast harshly judged, and linked their presence to disgust,
Consider well the thousand things that made them all they are.
Thou hast not thought upon the causes, ranged in consecutive necessity,
Which tended long to these effects, with sure constraining power:
For each of those unlovely ones, if thou couldst hear his story,
Hath much to urge of just excuse, at least as men count justice:
Foolish education, thwarted opportunities, natural propensities unchecked,—
Thus were they discouraged from all good, and pampered in their evil;
And, if thou wilt apprehend them well, tenderly looking on temptations,
Bearing the base indulgently, and liberally dealing with the froward,
Thou shalt discern a few fair fruits even upon trees so withered,
Thou shalt understand how some may praise, and some be found to love them.

Nevertheless for these, my counsel is, Avoid them if thou canst;

For the finer edges of thy virtues will be dulled by attrition with
    their vice.
And there is an enemy within thee; either to palliate their sin,
Until, for surface-sweetness, thou too art drawn adown the vortex;
Or, even unto fatal pride, to glorify thy purity by contrast,
Until the publican and harlot stand nearer heaven than the Phari-
    see;
Or daily strife against their ill, in subtleness may irritate thy soul,
And in that struggle thou shalt fail, even through infirmity of
    goodness;
Or, callous by continuance of injuries, thou wilt cease to pardon,
Cease to feel, and cease to care, a cold case-hardened man.
Beware of their example,—and thine own; beware the hazards of
    the battle;
But chiefly be thou ware of this, an unforgiving spirit.
Many are the dangers and temptations compassing a bad man's
    presence;
The upas hath a poisonous shade, and who would slumber there?
Wherefore, avoid them if thou canst; only, under providence and
    duty,
If thy lot be cast with Kedar, patiently and silently live to their
    rebuke.

How beautiful thy feet, and full of grace thy coming,
O better kind companion, that art well for either world!
There is an atmosphere of happiness floating round that man,
Love is throned upon his heart, and light is found within his
    dwelling:
His eyes are rayed with peacefulness, and wisdom waiteth on his
    tongue;
Seek him out, cherish him well, walking in the halo of his in-
    fluence;
For he shall be fragrance to thy soul, as a garden of sweet lilies,
Hedged and apart from the outer world, an island of the blest
    among the seas.

There is an outer world, and there is an inner centre;
And many varying rings concentric round the self:
For, first, about a man,—after his communion with heaven,—
Is found the helpmate even as himself, the wife of his vows and
    his affections;

See then that ye love in faith, scorning petty jealousies,
For Satan spoileth too much love, by souring it with doubts;
See that intimacy die not to indifference, nor anxiety sink into moroseness
And tend ye well the mutual minds bound in a copartnership for life.

Next of those concentric circles, radiating widely in circumference,
Wheel in wheel, and world in world,—come the band of children:
A tender nest of soft young hearts, each to be separately studied,
A curious eager flock of minds, to be severally tamed and tutored.
And a man, blest with these, hath made his own society,
He is independent of the world, hanging on his friends more loosely:
For the little faces round his hearth are friends enow for him,
If he seek others, it is for sake of these, and less for his own pleasure.
What companionship so sweet, yea, who can teach so well
As these pure budding intellects, and bright unsullied hearts?
What voice so musical as theirs, what visions of elegance so comely,
What thoughts and hopes and holy prayers, can others cause like these?
If ye count society for pastime,—what happier recreation than a nurseling,
Its winning ways, its prattling tongue, its innocence and mirth?
If ye count society for good,—how fair a field is here,
To guide these souls to God, and multiply thyself for heaven!

And this sweet social commerce with thy children groweth as their growth,
Unless thou fail of duty, or have weaned them by thine absence.
Keep them near thee, rear them well, guide, correct, instruct them;
And be the playmate of their games, the judge in their complainings.
So shall the maiden and the youth love thee as their sympathizing friend,
And bring their joys to share with thee, their sorrows for consoling:
Yea, their inmost hopes shall yearn to thee for counsel,
They will not hide their very loves, if thou hast won their trust:
But, even as man and woman, shall they gladly seek their father,
Feeling yet as children feel, though void of fear in honour:

And thou shalt be a **Nestor** in the camp, the **just and** good old
man,
Hearty still, though full of years, and held the friend of all;
No secret shall be kept from thee; for if ill, thy wisdom may re-
pair it;
If well, thy praise is precious: and they would not miss that prize.
O the blessing of a home, where old and young **mix kindly,**
The young unawed, **the** old unchilled, in unreserved communion!
O that refuge **from the world,** when a stricken son or daughter
May seek, with confidence of love, a father's hearth and heart;
Sure of a **welcome,** though others cast them out; of kindness,
though men scorn them;
And finding there the last to blame, the earliest to commend.
Come unto me, my son, if sin shall have tempted thee astray,
I will not chide thee like the rest, but help thee to return;
Come unto me, my son, if men rebuke and mock thee,
There always shall be one to bless,—for I am on thy side!

Alas,—and bitter is their loss, the parents, and the children,
Who, loving up **and** down the world, have missed each other's
friendship.
Haply, it had grown of careless life, for years go swiftly by;
Or sprang **of too much carefulness,** that drank up all the streams:
Haply, sullen disappointment came and quenched the fire;
Haply, sternness, or misrule, crushed or warped the feelings.
Then, ill-combined in tempers, they learnt not each the other;
The growing child grew out of love, and drew the breath of fear;
The youth, ill-trained, renounced his fears, and made a league with
cunning;
And so those hardened men were foes, that should have been chief
friends.
Where was the cause, the mutual cause? O hunt it out to kill it:
And what the cure, the simple cure?—A mutual flash of love.
For dull estrangement's daily air froze up those early sympathies
By cold continuance in apathy, or cutting winds of censure;
It was a slow process, which any fleeting hour could have melted;
But every hour duly came, and passed without the sun.
Caution, care, and dry distrust, obscured each other's minds,
Till both those gardens, rich to yield, were rank with many weeds:
And doubt, a hidden worm, gnawed **at the root** of their Society,
They lacked of mutual confidence, and lived in mutual dread.

Judge me, many fathers; and hearken to my counsel, many sons;
I come with good in either hand, to reconcile contentions;
For better friends can no man have, than those whom God hath given,
And he that hath despised the gift, thought ill of that he knew not.
Be ye wiser,—(I speak unto the sons,)—and win paternal friendships,
Cultivate their kindness, seek them out with honour, and be the screening Japheth to their failings:
And be ye wiser,—(I speak unto the fathers,)—gain those filial comrades,
Cherish their reasonable converse, and look not with coldness on your children.
For the friendship of a child is the brightest gem set upon the circlet of Society,
A jewel worth a world of pains—a jewel seldom seen

The third cycle on the waters, another of those rings upon the onyx,
A further definite broad zone, holdeth kith and kin:
A motley band of many tribes, and under various banners;
The intimate and strangers, the known and loved, or only seen for loathing:
Some, dear for their deserts, shall honour and have honour of relationship,
Some, despising duties, will add to it both burden and disgrace.
A man's nearest kin are oftentimes far other than his dearest,
Yet in the season of affliction those will haste to help him.
For, note thou this, the Providence of God hath bound up families together,
To mutual aid and patient trial; yea, those ties are strong.
Friends are ever dearer in thy wealth, but relations to be trusted in thy need,
For these are God's appointed way, and those the choice of man:
There is lower warmth in kin, but smaller truth in friends,
The latter show more surface, and the first have more of depth.
Relations rally to the rescue, even in estrangement and neglect,
Where friends will have fled at thy defeat, even after promises and kindness
For friends come and go, the whim that bound may loose them,
But none can dissever a relationship, and Fate hath tied the knot.

R

Wide, and edged with shadowy bounds, a distant boulevard to the
 city,
The common crowd of social life is buzzing round about :
That is as the outer court, with all defences levelled,
Ranged around a man's own fortress, and his father's house.
For many friends go in and out, and praise thee, finding pasture,
And some are honey-comb to-day, who turn to gall to-morrow ;
And many a garrulous acquaintance with his frequent visit
Will spend his leisure to thy cost, selling dullness dearly :
For the idle call is a heavy tax, where time is counted gold,
And even in the day of relaxation, haply he may spare his pre-
 sence,—
He found himself alone, and came to talk,—till they that hear are
 tired ;
Let the man bethink him of an errand, that his face be not unwel-
 come.

But many friends there be, both well and wisely greeted,
Gladly are they hailed upon the hills, and are chidden that they
 come so seldom.
Of such are the early recollections, school friendships that have
 thriven to grey hairs,
And veteran men are young once more, and talk of boyish pranks ;
And such, yet older on the list, are those who loved thy father,
Thy father's friend, and thine, who tendereth thee tried love :
Such also, many gentle hearts, whom thou hast known too lately,
Hastening now to learn their worth, and chary of those minutes ;
And such, thy faithful pastor, coming to thy home with peace ;—
Greet the good man heartily,—and bid thy children bless him !

Many thoughts, many thoughts,—who can catch them all?
The best are ever swiftest winged, the duller lag behind ;
For, behold, in these vast themes, my mind is as a forest of the
 West,
And flocking pigeons come in clouds, and bend the groaning
 branches ;
Here for a rest, then off and away,—they have sped to other
 climes,
And leave me to my peace once more, a holiday from thoughts.
I dare not lure them back, for the mighty subject of Society
Would tempt to many an hackneyed note in many a weary key :

Sage warnings, stout advice, **experiences** ever to be learned,
The foolish floatiness of vanity, **and solemn** trumperies of pride,—
Economy, the poor man's mint,—extravagance, the rich man's pitfall,
Harmful copings with the better, and empty-headed apings of the worse,
Circumstance and custom, sympathies, antipathies, diverse **kinds of conversation,**
Vapid pleasures, **the weariness** of gaiety, the strife and bustle of the world,
Home comforts, the miseries of style, the cobweb lines of etiquette,
The hollowness of courtesies, and substance of deceits,—idleness, business, and pastime,—
The multitude of matters **to be done**, the when, and where, and how,
And varying shades of character, to do, undo, or miss them,—
All these, and many more alike, thick converging fancies,
Flit in throngs about my theme, as honey-bees at even to their hive.
Find an end, or make one: these seeds are dragon's teeth:
Sown thoughts grow to things, and fill that field, the world:
Many wise have gone before, and used the sickle well;
Who can find a corner now, where none hath bound the sheaves?
So, other some may reap: I do but glean and gather:
My sorry handful hath been culled after the ripe harvest of Society.

OF SOLITUDE.

Who hath known his brother,—or found him in his freedom unrestrained?
Even he, whose hidden glance hath watched his deepest Solitude.
For we walk the world in domino, putting on characters and habits,
And wear a social Janus mask, while others stand around:
I speak not of the hypocrite, nor dream of meant deceptions,
But of that quick unconscious change, whereof the best know most.
For mind hath its influence on mind; and no man is free but when alone;
Yea, let a dog be watching thee, its eye will tend to thy restraint.

Self-possession cannot be so perfect, with another intellect beside
 thee,
It is not as a natural result, but rather the educated produce.
The presence of a second spirit must control thine own,
And throw it off its equipoise of peace, to balance by an effort.
The common minds of common men know of this but little;
What then? they know nothing of themselves: I speak to those
 who know.
The consciousness that some are hearing, cometh as a care,
The sense that some are watching near, bindeth thee to caution;
And the tree of tender nerves shrinketh as a touched mimosa,
Drooping like a plant in drought, with half its strength decayed.
There are antipathies warning from the many, and sympathies
 drawing to the few,
But merchant-minds have crushed the first, and cannot feel the
 latter:
Whereas to the quickened apprehension of a keen and spiritual
 intellect,
Antipathies are galling, and sympathies oppress, and solitude is
 quiet.

He that dwelleth mainly by himself, heedeth most of others,
But they that live in crowds, think chiefly of themselves.
There is indeed a selfish seeming, where the anchorite liveth alone,
But probe his thoughts,—they travel far, dreaming for ever of the
 world:
And there is an apparent generosity, when a man mixeth freely
 with his fellows;
But prove his mind, by day and night, his thoughts are all of self:
The world, inciting him to pleasures, or relentlessly provoking
 him to toil,
Is full of anxious rivals, each with a difference of interest;
So must he plan and practise for himself, even as his own best
 friend;
And the gay soul of dissipation never had a thought unselfish.
The hermit standeth out of strife, abiding in a contemplative calm-
 ness;
What shall he contemplate,—himself? a meagre theme for musing;
He hath cast off follies, and kept aloof from cares; a man of
 simple wants;
God and the soul, these are his excuse, a just excuse, for solitude:

But he carried with him to his cell the half-dead feelings of
 humanity :
There were they rested and refreshed ; and he yearned once more
 on men.

Where is the wise, or the learned, or the good, that sought not
 solitude for thinking,
And from seclusion's secret vale brought forth his precious fruits?
Forests of Aricia, your deep shade mellowed Numa's wisdom,
Peaceful gardens of Vaucluse, ye nourished Petrarch's love ;
Solitude made a Cincinnatus, ripening the hero and the patriot,
And taught De Staël self-knowledge, even in the damp Bastile ;
It fostered the piety of Jerome, matured the labours of Augustine,
And gave imperial Charles religion for ambition :
That which Scipio praised, that which Alfred practised,
Which fired Demosthenes to eloquence, and fed the mind of Milton,
Which quickened zeal, nurtured genius, found out the secret things
 of science,
Helped repentance, shamed folly, and comforted the good with
 peace,—
By all men just and wise, by all things pure and perfect,
How truly, Solitude, art thou the fostering nurse of greatness !

Enough ;—the theme is vast ; sear me these necks of Hydra :
What shall drive away the thoughts flocking to this carcase ?
Yea,—that all which man may think, hath long been said of Soli-
 tude ;
For many wise have proved and preached its evils and its good :
I cannot add,—I will not steal ; enough, for all is spoken :
Yet heed thou these for practice, and discernment among men.

There are pompous talkers, solemn, oracular, and dull :
Track them from society to solitude ; and there ye find them fools.
There are light-hearted jesters, taking up with company for pas-
 time ;
How speed they when alone ?—serious, wise, and thoughtful.
And wherefore ? both are actors, saving when in solitude,
There they live their truest life, and all things show sincere :
But the fool by pomposity of speech striveth to be counted wise,
And the wise, for holiday and pleasance, playeth with the fool's
 best bauble.

The solemn seemer, as a rule, will be found more ignorant and shallow
Than those who laugh both loud and long, content to hide their knowledge.

For thee; seek thou Solitude, but neither in excess, nor morosely;
Seek her for her precious things, and not of thine own pride.
For there, separate from a crowd, the still small voice will talk with thee,
Truth's whisper, heard and echoed by responding conscience;
There, shalt thou gather up the ravelled skeins of feeling,
And mend the nets of usefulness, and rest awhile for duties;
There, thou shalt hive thy lore, and eat the fruits of study,
For solitude delighteth well to feed on many thoughts:
There, as thou sittest peaceful, communing with fancy,
The precious poetry of life shall gild its leaden cares;
There, as thou walkest by the sea, beneath the gentle stars,
Many kindling seeds of good will sprout within thy soul;
Thou shalt weep in Solitude,—thou shalt pray in Solitude,
Thou shalt sing for joy of heart, and praise the grace of Solitude.
Pass on, pass on!—for this is the path of wisdom:
God make thee prosper on the way; I leave thee well with Solitude.

THE END.

EVERY beginning is shrouded in a mist, those vague ideas beyond,
And the traveller setteth on his journey, oppressed with many thoughts,
Balancing his hopes and fears, and looking for some order in the chaos,
Some secret path between the cliffs, that seem to bar his way:
So, he commenceth at a clue, unravelling its tangled skein,
And boldly speedeth on to thread the labyrinth before him.
Then as he gropeth in the darkness, light is attendant on his steps,
He walketh straight in fervent faith, and difficulties vanish at his presence;
The very flashing of his sword scattereth those shadowy foes;
Confident and sanguine of success, he goeth forth conquering and to conquer.

Every middle is burdened with a weariness,—to have to go as far
    again,—
And Diligence is sick at heart, and Enterprize footsore:
That which began in zeal, bursting as a fresh-dug spring,
Goeth on doggedly in toil, and hath no help of nature;
Then, is need of moral might, to wrestle with the animal re-
    action,
Still to fight, with few men left, and still though faint pursuing.
The middle is a marshy flat, whereon the wheels go heavily,
With clouds of doubt above, and ruts of discouragement below:
Press on, sturdy traveller, yet a league, and yet a league!
While every step is binding wings on thy victorious feet.

Every end is happiness, the glorious consummation of design,
The perils past, the fears annulled, the journey at its close:
And the traveller resteth in complacency, home-returned at last:
Work done may claim its wages, the goal gained hath won its
    prize:
While the labour lasted, while the race was running,
Many-times the sinews ached, and half refused the struggle:
But now, all is quietness, a pleasant hour given to repose;
Calmness in the retrospect of good, and calmness in the prospect
    of a blessing.
Hope was glad in the beginning, and fear was sad midway,
But sweet fruition cometh in the end, a harvest safe and sure.
That which is, can never not have been: facts are solid as the
    pyramids:
A thing done is written in the rock, yea, with a pen of iron.
Uncertainty no more can scare, the proof is seen complete,
Nor accident render unaccomplished, for the deed is finished.
Thus the end shall crown the work, with grace, grace, unto the
    topstone,
And the work shall triumph in its crown, with peace, peace, unto
    the builder.

I have written, as other some of old, in quaint and meaning phrase,
Of many things for either world, a crowd of facts and fancies:
And will ye judge me, men of mind?—judge in kindly calmness;
For bitter words of haste or hate have often been repented.
Deep dreaming upon surface reading; imagery crowded over argu-
    ment;

Order less considered in the multitude of thoughts: this witnessing is just.
Scripture gave the holier themes, the well-turned words and wisdom;
While Fancy on her swallow's wing skimmed those deeper waters:
And wilt thou say with shrewdness,—He hath burnished up old truths,
But where he seemed to fashion new, the novelty was false?
Alas, for us in these last days, our elders reaped the harvest:
Alas, for all men in all times, who glean so many tares!
That which is true, how should it be new? for time is old in years:
That which is new, how should it be true? for I am young in wisdom.

Nevertheless, I have spoken at my best, according to the mercies given me,
Of high, and deep, and famous things, of Evil, or of Good.
I have told of Errors near akin to Truth, and wholesomes linked with poison;
Of subtle Uses in the humblest, and the deep laid plots of Pride:
I have praised Wisdom, comforted thy Hope, and proved to thee the folly of Complainings;
Hinted at the hazard of an Influence, and turned thee from the terrors of Ambition.
I have shown thee thy captivity to Law: yet bade thee hide Humilities;
I have lifted the curtains of Memory; and smoothed the soft pillow of Rest.
Experience had his sober hour; and Character its keen appreciation;
And holy Anger stood sublime, where Hatred fell condemned.
Prayer spake the mind of God, even in His own good words:
And Zeal, with kindness warmly mixt, allied him to Discretion.
I taught thee that nothing is a Trifle, even to the laugh of Recreation;
I led thee with the Train of Religion, to be dazzled at the name of the Triune.
Thought confessed his unseen fears; and Speech declared his triumphs;
I sang the blessedness of books; and commended the prudence of a letter:

Riches found their room, either unto honour—or despising :
Inventions took their lower place, for all things come of God.
I scorned Ridicule ; nor would humble me for Praise ; for I had
    gained Self-knowledge ;
And pleaded fervently for Brutes, who suffer for man's sin.
Then, I rose to Friendship ; and bathed in all the tenderness of
    Love ;
Knew the purity of Marriage ; and blest the face of Children.
And whereas, by petulance or pride, I had haply said some evil,
Mine after-thought was Tolerance, to bear the faults of all :
Many faults, ill to bear, bred the theme of Sorrow ;
Many virtues, dear to see, induced the gush of Joy.

Thus, for awhile, as leaving thee in joy, was I loth to break that
    spell ;
I roamed to other things and thoughts, and fashioned other books.
But in a season of reflection, after many days,
A thought stood before me in its garment of the past,—and lo, a
    legion with it !
They came in thronging bands,—I could not fight nor fly them,—
And so they took me to their tent, the prisoner of thoughts.

Then, I bade thee greet me well, and heed my cheerful counsels ;
For every day we have a Friend, who changeth not with time.
Gladly did I speak of my commission, for I felt it graven on my
    heart,
And could not hold my wiser peace, but magnified mine office.
Mystery had left her echoes in my mind, and I discoursed her
    secret :
And thence I turned aside to man, and judged him for his Gifts.
Beauty, noble thesis, had a world of sweets to sing of,
And dated all her praise from God, the birthday of the soul.
Thence grew Fame ; and Flattery came like Agag ;
But this was as the nauseous dregs of that inspiring cup :
Forth from Flattery sprang in opposition harsh and dull Neglect ;
And kind Contentment's gentle face to smile away the sadness.
Life, all buoyancy and light, and Death, that sullen silence,
Sped the soul to Immortality, the final home of man.
Then, in metaphysical review, passed a triple troop,
Swift Ideas, sounding Names, and heavily armed Things :
Faith spake of her achievements even among men her brethren ;

And Honesty, with open mouth, would vindicate himself:
The retrospect of Social life had many truths to tell of,
And then I left thee to thy Solitude, learning there of Wisdom.

Friend and scholar, lover of the right, mine equal kind com-
　　　　panion,—
I prize indeed thy favour, and these sympathies are dear:
Still, if thy heart be little with me, wot thou well, my brother,
I canvass not the smiles of praise, nor dread the frowns of censure.
Through many themes in many thoughts, have we held sweet con-
　　　　verse;
But God alone be praised for mind! He only is sufficient.
And every thought in every theme by prayer had been established
Who then should fear the face of man, when God hath answered
　　　　prayer?—
I speak it not in arrogance of heart, but humbly as of justice,
I think it not in vanity of soul, but tenderly, for gratitude,—
God hath blest my mind, and taught it many truths:
And I have echoed some to thee, in weakness, yet sincerely:
Yea, though ignorance and error shall have marred those lessons
　　　　of His teaching,
I stand in mine own Master's praise, or fall to His reproof.
If thou lovest, help me with thy blessing; if otherwise, mine shall
　　　　be for thee;
If thou approvest, heed my words; if otherwise, in kindness be my
　　　　teacher.
Many mingled thoughts for self have warped my better aim;
Many motives tempted still, to toil for pride or praise:
Alas, I have loved pride and praise, like others worse or worthier;
But hate and fear them now, as snakes that fastened on my hand:
Scævola burnt both hand and crime; but Paul flung the viper on
　　　　the fire:
He shook it off, and felt no harm: so be it! I renounce them.
Rebuke then, if thou wilt rebuke,—but neither hastily nor harshly;
Or, if thou wilt commend, be it honestly, of right: I work for God
　　　　and good.

ΤΕΛΟΣ.

THIRD SERIES

PREAMBLE.

AGAIN, toward the eventide of life, I touch that rhythmic harp
Struck by the son of Sirac twenty centuries agone;
Again, I ask thy favour,—thou, my brother or my sister,
Not as a stranger might but now a friend of thirty years;
Again, I canvass for my words thy patience and thy love,
Again, I show my thoughts to thee, for sympathy and kindness:
Thoughts not stolen out of books, nor noted day by day,
But springing fresh beneath my pen, unsought and unrestrained;
Thoughts ever frankly spoken, as from brother's heart to heart,
Regardless of the jibe of fools, and proof against their spleen.
I would away with selfishness; I would forswear all vanity;
Nor write for praises, but in hope, to do a little good;
In all sincerity and singleness to work my Master's work,
While yet the day of life is lent, with leisure health and grace.

Once more then after thirty years, I come, O friend and brother,
Bringing my modern thoughts to thee in their antique disguise:
This Eastern garb is somewhat, if its ancient quaintness help
To catch thy kind attention, and to win thy willing mind.
In those thirty years, a generation is entombed,
And wondrous changes have there been, and much of good and
    evil;

And death hath **made** old friendships rare, and many have been
 the wrecks
From storm to storm as some we knew broke on the rocks of life;
And thankfulness and penitence and charity and faith,
These well become us all, O friends, remembering the past.

We have been through seas of sorrows, we have traversed a whole
 wilderness of trial,
Many sins and cares and pains and pleasures have we met.
Often in the shadow of death, often in the valley of weeping,
And rarely now and then have basked full in the prosperous sun:
Danger and adventure have been **ours**, good providences and
 strange accidents,
And well indeed if heinous sin hath **not** bedimmed our light;
Slander bespattered us at times, at times fair fame caressed us,
And now disease hath brought us down, or strong help set us up;
Many disappointments and misfortunes, yet manifold blessings and
 advancements,
Much was ours of grievous loss, yet some good gains withal:
Thousands have fallen at our side, slain in the battle of life,
Or dropping, scarcely missed, to death, through Mirza's visioned
 bridge:
And still we stand to fight the fight, if faint—thank God, pursuing,
Still is life with half its hopes and all its mercies ours:
Therefore gratitude and penitence, faith and hope and **charity**,
These well become us **each**, O friends, reviewing all that past.

To teach thy neighbour clearly, search thine own **heart** deeply,
Search impartially, with prayer, in humbleness **of mind**;
And from the bottom of that well thou shalt draw up truth,
Which, quickened by the breath of day, may flow to others' good.
Each man's heart is a mine unworked, and all are rich in metal,
Silver or copper, arsenic or iron, mercury lead or gold;
More is beneath than can ever be brought up, veins to be wrought
 for ages,
When the life of Eternity beginneth, after the death of Time.
No man knoweth his **own** wealth, his mightiness for evil or for
 good,
No man hath guessed his capabilities, **nor how he** shall expand;
No one ever writ the half, nor spoke the tithe he thinketh,
Never yet was mind exhausted, **nor** one heart dug out.

We are here for an hour to catch a fated bent, and then, direct or
 crooked,
The arrow speedeth ever, as first aimed and shot by us,
That arrow of Existence, our own unendable career,
Ever flying to its mark, the Infinite of joy or sorrow.
And every man's experience, is a lesson due to all,
For no one ever yet was taught of Heaven for selfish ends.
The trials and temptations thou hast seen, thy battles lost or won,
Were meant not for thyself alone, to strengthen only thee ;
The story of thy wreck in life, or winning the Fair Havens
Shall be the chart of safety, to thy neighbour for his bark :
Then say not thou so bitterly,—self-shewing is self-seeking,—
A fool's heart is worn upon his sleeve, for every daw to peck at :
No ! there is a generous egotism,—in wisdom genially uttered,
Frank and honest plainness, which no true man will despise.
In no self-seeking doth the Christian analyse his heart,
In no self-praising can he show the spots and wrinkles there ;
A servant, he hath much to do, and little time for doing ;
A soldier, duty is his end, with courage for the way ;
A man among his brother-men, he prizeth well their love,
And scorning no one's censure, asketh no one's praise.

A book is in no sort like a cable, to be judged by its weakest inch,
A chain to be condemned throughout, because some links are faulty ;
Neither as a hedge nor as a wall, to be measured for its usefulness
 by gaps,
But generously, honourably, fairly, averaging this and that :
If the tree have any well-ripe fruits, produce them for the banquet,
But let the sourlings be, a good tree beareth both :
It is the vice of our scribes to magnify both best and worst
In books they think to help by praise, or hope to harm by censure:
And some will read before they judge, other some will judge with-
 out the reading,
Fairness guiding those, party and prejudice these ;
Yet is your confessor of no party ; neither side can claim him ;
High, or low, narrow, or broad,—in all are good and evil ;
The Patriot, as the Christian, is found of every sect,
And moderate men will bid God-speed to Patriots and to Chris-
 tians ;—
And, for the matter of prejudice, none asketh other than strict
 justice

After honest diligence to learn an **author's mind**;
But books will **live**, and books will **die, alone for** their deservings,
And no man's fame is made or **marred**, by other than himself:
While, for better things than fame, good-doing and glad conscience,
A champion, shod in steel with these, **can** kick against the pricks;
Good doing, tokened by your love, O **world** of unseen friends,
Glad conscience, stablished **in** Thy grace, my Saviour and my God.

OF INNOCENCE AND GUILT.

HAPPY art thou, O son, if thou hast walked innocently,
Baffling corruption in thy heart, and battling the temptations **of** the world;
Happy, if thy present is not clouded with the past,—nor miserably shadowed on the future,
Happy among men art thou, **if** hitherto thy converse hath been innocent:
If there be **none of** all thy brethren whom thy greed hath wronged,
None to complain of thee for meannesses, none to charge thee with injustice,
None whom thy vindictiveness hath slandered, none by thee maligned,
No poor cruelly entreated, no rich fraudulently spoiled:
If there be none of all thy sisters, whom thy passion hath betrayed,
No foul retrospects of folly, no dark consciousness of crime,
No young unguilty face, to dim remembrance with her tears,
No lower outcast claiming thee, hereafter, soul and body:
If to thyself thou hast been true, if thou hast been mindful of thy God,
Nor ever slept, nor ever woke, without **a** prayer to Him;
If thou hast at all times done thy best, bearing trials well,
If thou hast smiled at slander, and been humble under praise,
If thou hast diligently used thy talents and occasions,
If through good doing here, thou hast laid up treasure elsewhere,
Happy art thou, and honourable; yea thy heart is peaceful,
Pleasant is thy sleep by night, **and sweet is thy** complacency by day.
Truly, an innocent life bringeth its own rewardings,
Truly, within and not without, is that better heaven.

Yet, art thou still in peril, and hast need of grace, my son,
To keep thee pure as now thou art, and save thee from a fall:
Yea, thou hast need of Angels, ministering good,
Thankfulness, humility, and fear; praying and watching always.
For, this very hour, the Philistines may be upon thee, Samson,
Delilah may mesh thee in her hair, and steal from thee thy treasure,—
Or some evil covetousness stamp thee Ananias,
Or thy soul may drain that poison, spiritual pride.
Dread thine utter weakness, trust the strength of God,
Regard thy purer past only as a gift of mercy,
Kindly raise the fallen, considering thine own corruption,
Look in fear upon the guilt that might have been thine own;
Be humble, that is safety; in thankfulness be humble,
And fling from thy clean hand the viper of self-righteousness.

And wretched art thou, O son,—though rich and gorged with pleasures,
Though rank, and wealth, and favour set thee high above thy kind,
Yea, most miserable art thou, if guilt is as a cancer on thy conscience,
In memory of evil deeds, wilful and unrepented:
If thy selfish falsehood hath broken loving hearts,
If thy coarser passions riot in the mysteries of sin,
If thou hast stolen and defrauded, if thou hast harmed through malice,
If thou hast secretly indulged, or openly professed pollution,
Yea, thou hast seeds of sorrow planted in thy heart
Enough to make its borders sad for ever and for ever;
Yea, there is need of nothing else, nor fire nor worm undying,
To make the sinner's punishment eternal and supreme;
His conscious soul aflame with all those burning memories,
This is enough for vengeance in whatever world:
Here, sharp terrors of discovery, and the pale faces of his victims,
Remorse, disease, and self contempt, despair for earth and heaven;
Hereafter, all the past become a terrible present,
Never to end and never to mend, without one hope of better;
Only misery to feed on, memory of chances gone,
Ruined good, and squandered talents, all one bitter chaos:
Such are the wages of the guilty, hourly paid him here,
And evermore to be the price of all his evil doings;
Now, to darken every noon, and frighten every night,
Then, to make eternal life an endless death to him.

Yet, is there hope, O brother,—still in life is hope,—
For He that giveth one more day, gave it for repentance.
Now, in this blest hour, put aside thy sins,
Lay thy guilt on Christ, the scapegoat for all evil :
If this word, sincerely uttered, reacheth thee in solitude,
Put it not aside, but lift thy heart in momentary prayer ;
Who knoweth, whether thy Good Angel be not now beside thee,
And did not the Father of the prodigal fall on his neck and kiss him?
If thou art in company with others, be not ashamed of Truth,
Seek to be alone awhile, and gaze upon her face :
This shall be a day to be remembered, the dawn of happy good,
The breaking of thy fetters, and the death to all thy fears :
Whatever may have been the past, however black and hideous,
It hath a present cure, repentance with amendment.
Be just in restitution where thou canst, confessing with discreetness,
And prove not so unjust to God, as to despair of grace ;
Guilt is pardoned at the word, that Heaven waiteth long to hear,
And pardoned guilt is that New Life, the next akin to innocence.

But, there are strange differences in guilt, as there is infinity toward innocence,
This last leading up to God, and those being footsteps in corruption :
And many causes of all kinds are leaven to the twain,
Birth, education, circumstance, the mysteries of partial Providence.
Far be it from any man to judge, ignorant and full of prejudice,
For the race is run with various weights, that have to be allowed for.
An orphan outcast of the streets, bred in vice and cruelty,
Whose only teachings have been theft, lying, lust and baseness,
With nought but evil round him, and his mother's taint within,
Some reprobate father's image, stunted in mind and body,—
How to compare him as to guilt, with another nurtured in piety,
Carefully taught and tended, come of a stock of saints,
With every help for either world, health and wealth and kindness,
And leanings to the good and pure through twenty generations ?
O Man, leave judgments to the Judge : it needeth an infinity of wisdom
To set those balances aright, which bless or ban a soul.

Yet there is a marvellous diversity among the characters of men,

OF INNOCENCE AND GUILT.

Heights of aspiration, and depths of degradation, with infinite
    breadths upon the level :
The many are read at a glance, neither very good nor very evil,
Changeable to either sort, and kindly weakly natured ;
The few, of infinite capacities, bent toward right or wrong,
So that thou shalt not easily gauge the saint or the sinner before
    thee :
There are higher heights in the spiritual life, than thy thought may
    reach,
There are deeper depths in wickedness, than common men can
    fathom ;
In either the immortal is perceived, the strong flight of that spirit
    is begun,
To wing its way for ever, through all good or evil worlds.
O Man, set steadily thy will to catch the breeze of Heaven,
Nor luff that iron rudder to the Maelstrom of the Lost ;
It is given to thy nature to be great, an awful Immortality,
And in thy hand is placed betimes its happiness or woe.
Needs must there be a separation, dividing the evil from the good ;
Worlds of retribution and reward, as worlds of resurrection in ex-
    perience :
So long as consciousness surviveth, so long shall memory be keen ;
And there is no crueller avenger, no tenderer rewarder than Re-
    membrance.
The Muses were daughters of Mnemosyne ; and Night the mother
    of Memory
Had likewise the Furies for her daughters, Remorse and bitter
    Shame.
Even with pardoned guilt, the scars will ache though healed :
But innocence hath no such scars, no aching if no healing :
To be well-forgiven may be joy, so to be redeemed from punish-
    ment,
Yet must that spirit recollect, painfully what evil it hath worked :
And there is a cloud upon its brow that never darkened innocence,
Whose crown of glory is not dimmed by memories of sin.

O youth, O man, O fair maid or matron,
Keep innocency,—nothing less ensureth peace at the last :
Or, if utterly thou hast lost it, let no rash despair
Provoke thee to be reckless of the Grace that yearneth to restore
    thee :

Haste with penitence and prayer: all have need of mercy;
All may ask it, if they will, and have it for the asking.

OF THIS WORLD'S AGE.

God is truth, God is light, God is right and reason;
He cannot darken nor deceive, nor cheat the sons of men:
That which He graveth on the rock, as that which He writeth in
    the Book,
Leadeth not astray, is not dangerous to seek, nor difficult to find.
Fear not thou, meek Christian, the flare from Reason's torch
Illumining the caverns of the Earth, and searching secrets there;
Be not ashamed, O Philosopher, but boldly show thy proofs
That mother Earth is old beyond all human computation;
That infinite periods are needed for her mountains made of shells,
For her saltmines dried from ancient seas, for her ores and fossil
    forests,
For the monsters living through their centuries on continents of mud,
Millions of years ere Adam was, with Eden for his home.
As leaves of some old book, inscribed with unknown characters,
The strata, folios on folios, testify to byegone histories:
Whether in the page-like slates, and schales and films of stone,
Each with its beauteous illustration, ferns and flies and fishes,
Or in the miles of massy chalk, or swathing thicknesses of clay,
Or granite where all life was fused by force of primal fires,
Or lower still where water, in the green Laurentian lime,
Preserved to our microscopic wonder, the first-born atomies of life,—
Everywhere, is manifestly written in characters that all may read
A vast antiquity for Earth scarce shorter than a past Eternity.

Moses, the wisest among men, taught by the God of wisdom,
Knew and spake of old the truths we now discover:
In the beginning of all æons, myriads of eras back,
In the beginning with the Word, who both was God and with God,
In that beginning of beginnings, He created all things,
The suns as they stand, and their planets as they roll, the universe,
    the Heavens and the Earth.
What need hath man to learn the history of all those ages?
Why should his teacher of religion heap him with the chaos of
    their facts?

Tribes of most ancient lower-life over-swarmed the desolated globe,
Preyed on each other and were whelmed, by earthquakes, deluges,
    volcanoes:
In a beautiful series of improvement, higher succeeding to the
    humbler,
As if the choice of Wisdom was Perfection by degrees:
Each wave of life congealing was a stepping-stone beyond,
Until they bridged that ancient sea with monumental death.
But why encumber our minds with lore so slightly worth
When in man's little year he scarce hath time for duties?
It were wise to leave riddles in the rocks, for science to solve
    thereafter,
But not to vex an infant race, with themes beyond its ken:
So, when this everlasting scroll, that God hath fashioned all things,
Was first and once, as by an Angel, flung across the universe of matter,
The spirit of the Book, and of the World, commandeth holy silence,
And the gulf of innumerable ages is leapt by Revelation.
Era followed era, while Earth lay ripening for man,
And multitudes of living things then served their generations:
The rocks and giant hills are full of fossil forms,
And half the crust of Earth is built of microscopic shells:
Dragons fattened in the slime, while forests, matting overhead,
Drained, from premundane sunshine, our brightest coloured tints:
And grinding cataracts of ice, and tilts of land and water
Many times wrought destruction on those pristine tribes of Earth;
Often the creation was renewed, standing on the ruins of a former,
Often, by fire or by flood, the catastrophes swept on to desolation.
Then, after many many ages, when earth stood rich in soils,
Laden with ores and fuel, stocked and stored with wealth,
Fitted, at God's behest, to bring forth food for man,
And baited with secrets for his intellect as well as with jewels for
    his pride,
Then, after some more crashing ruin, when the globe was void and
    formless,
Dashed into fragments as a potsherd, and empty of all life,
Then, the Spirit moved, on the face of drowning waters,
And God commanded order, crystallizing from those ruins.
Thus our Cosmos grew; He willed it, day by day,
(Why not a week of days, as easy as an instant or an æon?)
And, in harmonious succession, rising from the lowest to the highest,
All our humbler creatures, and their mother Earth,

Waited ready for their lord, the man whom God created.

Adam is our date,—as we are Adam's children ;
From Adam's birth six thousand years have well nigh sped on Earth.
To Adam's race alone, the Word by Moses spake,
And God was pleased Himself to live a very Son of Eve.
It may be there were earlier tribes, in some premundane eras,
Tribes analogous with man, but not of Adam's race :
Skulls in the sandstone, or the chalk, or the lias may yet be
    gathered,
To scatter sagest theory, but not harm foolish faith :
Hitherto nothing hath appeared, beyond some faint remains
Of savage men, who dwelt in caves, before our Noah's flood,
Battling wretchedly with beasts, extinct since that last deluge,
And downward sunk in misery, a whole degraded race,
Children of Cain scattered over earth, curst for their father's sake,
With his black mark set on them over all, as witnessed to this hour;
Even in the Ark of refuge, the wife of Ham was one,
And so, indelibly for ever, was multiplied that ancient stain.
Perchance, if any so-called men were in those old creations,
God may have raised their bodies, in some earlier resurrection
No trace would then be found, saving of the lower animals ;
While the absence of their lord proclaimed his higher calling :
But, what mattereth it to us, the new made race of Man,
The dynasty of Adam, formed to fill that ancient throne ?
From him, through a thousand generations, God doth give all good,
Commanding duties, promising rewards, and stirring hopes and fears;
For which our privilege is gratitude, our daily strength is Faith,
Our aim a nobler sphere, and this old world's great future.

Yea : for a bright regeneration is ripening for this Earth,
Its thousand years of days of years, according to the Scripture,
A year for a day and a day for a year, no simple thousand years ;
Three hundred threescore and five thousand make the wondrous
    sum :
Then,—and the promise is to us, to us and to our children,
Commencing with a generation that yet shall see the end,
That glorious consummation for the Earth, our longed-for age of
    glory,
Our holiday of happiness, our Sabbath of high praise,
Shall gladden all Earth's creatures, the lion as the ox,

The trees of the wood, and the flowers of the field, the hills and
  plains and valleys.

OF CIRCUMSTANCE.

Boast not, O man of much adventure, for thou canst compass
  little,
Save by steering with the tide, to catch the swing of circumstance;
Skill and courage are as nought, striving against the current,
But best are shown and used, when with it, not against it.
A wise man watcheth for his chance, to seize it on the instant,
And, to be ready for that chance, must be well prepared before-
  hand :
Therefore, a diligence in all things is the strongest fulcrum of suc-
  cess,
Therefore the many sided mind is ripe for every prize.

How mightily beyond our power, beyond our will or thought
The force of outer circumstance constraineth to obey :
Yet a man is no straw upon the hurricane; his consciousness is
  calm ;
In patience, strength, and prayer he still can stem the tempest ;
Waiting and watching his occasion, self-possessed and shrewd,
He yet may make the vortex serve him not enslave him.
If thou art master of thyself, circumstance shall harm thee little ;
But weakness sloth and sin make men as leaves on eddies.
True, some seeming accident can fell the strong man by a blow,
Decisive and inevitable, to be patiently accepted as of Providence ;
Even if the throne of Palæologus be lost through such slight cause,
Well,—it was the will of Heaven, not the whim of chance ;
Or haply an honest serf, running with the crowd of sightseers
To win a glance at his loved Prince, the Russian's Czar and father,
Blest by happy circumstance, but ready for the act
In loyal heart and daring hand, and kindliness and honour,
Stayeth the crime of the assassin ; and leapeth into instant fortune
Hero and darling of his people, ennobled and enriched.
Or haply, in the dead of night, some half-mad jealous sister
Terribly perpetrateth murder upon sleeping infant innocence ;
And the false finger of suspicion pointed at the wretched father,
Ruin swept his home, calumny and hatred crushed him,

And all through evil circumstance, that **he** could **not** escape :
Yet **had he** governed early the **wicked wayward** daughter,
Or **lived the life of** purity, that **no ill tongue could taint,**
Or **frankly** and manfully outspoken, quelling **the voice of clamour,**
He, as pitied, not condemned, **might have overmastered circum-
    stance.**
All things spring of seeds, nothing groweth but from roots,
Even calumnious suspicion **is weak** against strong character :
And many times an innocent in fact hath suffered as a criminal in
    law
Deserving all that penalty, well due to old transgressions.

Wide is the range of circumstance, but narrower the difference in
    condition,
Happiness is measured out, to most, **with equal hand.**
Innocency, rarest among men,—yet some **there be** who keep it,
Innocency **from** the great offence, clean life **with** quiet conscience,
Innocency giveth in all **states a double dole of** happiness,—
And guilt detracteth from them all the half if not the whole.
Even **disease upon** her bed, lying there year after year,
Is cheerful and contented, with religion **in her** heart ;
Even strong health upon his **hunter,** galloping **over the** uplands,
Is wretched from his **sins,** blaspheming as he leapt :
The little workhouse orphan, slave to some woman tyrant,
Singeth at her half-starved toil merrily spite of hardship ;
While yonder highbred beauty, wearied with **waltzing at the ball,**
Sobbeth on her sofa, envious, piqued, unhappy.
It is not accident of circumstance, but innate quality of soul
That addeth peace or taketh it away, **as** well with **the** highest as
    the lowest.

Many things marvellous to us, until we know their causes,
Justify the government of Providence, with those their causes known.
Sometimes the profligate father hath a pious son,
Driven to **such** happy contrariety through hate of Helot-vice ;
Sometimes a profligate son shall cheat his pious father
For morals all too stern, and ill-advised restraints
Guilt shall heap up wealth, if keenness and industry be added,—
And saints must come to poverty, if prudence be not theirs ;
Triumph is not given to the right, if vigour be wanting in its
    champion ;

And high success may crown the **wrong** through energy and skill.
Causes win consequents, **and** laws will govern universally,
Neither are they warped but **by a miracle**, that miracle born of
    prayer.
While thou canst, give diligence ; every sort of knowledge
Riseth to the surface in its turn on the eddying torrent of life :
And it is the privilege of genius, energy seizing **on** occasion,
To use all sorts of knowledge, and **make** them serve its **ends**.
I have known a **poor school teacher**, husbanding his scant **leisure**,
Studious of Chinese lore, while many mocked his folly ;
But in due time good **circumstance swept by**, an interpreter was
    wanted for a treaty,
The Chinese scholar was in quest, and lo ! a man ready with his
    learning ;
Wealth and fame and fortune came within his reach,
And so well-skilled he gathered wealth and fame and fortune.
As occasion passeth on, if thy hand pluck not quickly at its sleeve,
It walketh away, thy chance is gone, because thou wast not ready.
The soil must be well-dressed, **to** give the seed full growth,
And for the battle of life, both mind and body should be athletes.
Therefore the aim of education should be more to build up character
Than painfully to store the mind with multitude of facts :
And the training, the discipline, the grammar, these are ends as
    well as means ;
Nerving and establishing the man, for much beyond **his** classics.
Our youths have Spartan lessons, and grow thereby strong and
    patient ;
Our maidens throng the Capuan school, **for vanities and caprice**.
Mindfully, with **high conscience, true scholars study all things**,
And learn betimes to use aright all weapons in all armouries.
A wise man redeemeth his time, that he may improve his chances ;
Diligence ever winning reward upon occasion :
Never have I seen the statesman, the orator poet or preacher,
To whom **his school day lessons came not** as continual allies.
However wide the field, analogy **in all** things is so perfect,
No knowledge seemeth unavailable, no toil bringeth not its gain.
Therefore read and **mark, and think and write** for memory,
Therefore scorn no lore, for all are full **of uses** ;
The student of a shingle beach may find in stones true sermons ;
The watcher of a microscope shall win deep wisdom out of monads ;
He that knoweth to swim can save himself or another,

So earning second lives, by readiness for occasion ;
The linguist, multiplying usefulness, and fusing his ideas in other
    tongues,
Is fitted both to teach and learn, through being well prepared ;
The musician pleaseth by his skill, philosophers make rich through
    science,
But all must have given diligence, to be quick to the call of Cir-
    cumstance.

Every one of us getteth his desert, somehow, somewhen, some-
    where,
Penalties are earned as surely as rewards, pains alike with plea-
    sures :
No man gathereth grapes of thorns, neither figs of thistles ;
Everything is consequent, and nothing by a chance :
This thy torment of disease, this racking of a joint or of a nerve,
Is due to thine own foolishness, and hath been well deserved :
All things grow of seeds, accident hath no real being,
That we sow we reap, that which is is ordered.

A wise man fitteth into Circumstance, easily cheerfully and wholly,
Even as a globule of quicksilver filleth up its any little mould ;
Instantly adaptable his mind acquiesceth contentedly and bravely
In all the will of Providence, led on by Duty's clue :
For he wotteth well and shrewdly, that, let whatever happen,
Circumstance is the servant, not the master of his soul,
And that, looking still toward Heaven in his travail on the earth,
He is gradually fitted for his place, and the work he hath to do.

OF THE STARRY HEAVENS.

"The heavens declare the glory of God, and the firmament showeth
    His handy work :
"One day telleth another, and one night proclaimeth to another :
"There is neither speech nor language, where their voices are not
    heard ;
"Their sound is gone out through all the earth, and their words
    to the ends of the world."
The Spirit that sang in David, as the Mind that preached in Paul,
Knew and recorded long ago how various are the lights of heaven ;

That there is one glory of the sun and another glory of the moon,
And another glory of the stars, differing each from other:
And now doth modern science but retouch that ancient truth,
Dividing by three-angled glass those glories in proportions,
So that we calculate and prove what Paul and David saw,
And show that the Bible of the saint is equally the text-book of the
    sage.

O stars, inhabited of angels, worlds of wondrous glory,
That shine in your far stations, flaming sentinels of Space,
How full of mystery and marvel, rich in unthought wealth,
How beauteous and how vast are ye, strange islands of the Blest!
Walking in these fields by night, with dews and solitude around me,
Or on that rippled shingle, with music in the waves,
I lift my heart up with mine eyes, yearning toward the stars,
Each so different in glory, all so brilliant and enormous,
Wondering which of them is mine, my kingdom of inheritance,
Claimed through The Heir of all things, my Saviour, God and
    Brother.
Is there not for each of us his star, as those of yore declared,—
(And old tradition runneth rooted strong in earth, like couch,)
A fated realm for the immortal, made co-heir in Christ,
A waiting throne with its angel here, to guard him on the way?
Each star beckoneth on to glory, our distant twinkling goal,
Albeit this clay-cold soil of earth may clog the wayward feet;
Ever are we creeping on in darkness, with Duty for a lantern
    through it all;
Ever fighting ambushed foes, and God to fight for us;
Ever do we grope and guess, hoping where we cannot see,
And all our wisdom here the while, is walking straight in faith.

O bright candles of the Lord, searching out earth's dark corners,
Calm witnesses to many deeds that fain would hide in night;
Alas! for the evils ye behold, the wrongs and harms and sorrows,
The discords that rush up from us to your harmonic sphere!
Yea, sinner, cease from sinning, in the sight of all these eyes,
Let them not see thy guilt, for shame, to testify far off;
For thou art watched, O sinner, and thy works recorded;
Repent, return, and sin no more beneath the conscious stars.

Suns, fixed centres of bright systems, grouped with unseen planets,

All, one universe of globes careering round God's Throne,
How meanly can we estimate the glory and high grace
Hid in some sparkle, twinkling there, ten billion leagues away!
Possibly, each star-sun is the central heaven to its system;
Probably, the worlds round each are tried and purified as ours;
For, matter tendeth to corruption, and moral trials unto purity;
Exceeding broad are His commandments, filling the extremities of Space.
He spreadeth out the heavens like a curtain, woven of many lights,
A golden tissue of comets' trails, bejewelled with set worlds,
The Great King's robe of glory flowing to the footstool of His throne,
And glittering with its million suns, celestial mounts of light.
Our minds have skill to weigh those worlds, to measure out their distances,
To note the nice diversities that tint their spectral hues;
We calculate their structure and their elements, haply their creatures and their histories,
And shrewdly from a slenderest hint deduce some strong-limbed truth:
We judge that each,—of three millions we can count, and millions more half-seen,
The clouds of diamond-dust around Jehovah's chariot wheels,—
Is vaster than thought's vastest, brighter than imagination's brightest,
And peopled with glad creatures, all perfect in their kind,
Of novel forms in beauty, shapes and senses unconceived,
With other lights in colour, and other tones in music,
Strange pleasures, and new virtues, incommunicable thoughts,
And powers we cannot guess, capacities, intensities, expansions,
Pertaining to exalted natures, rich in glorious gifts,
And nobler in themselves than we, as creatures nearer God.

Yet, are your thrones, O some among the stars, waiting for their human kings,
Heirs to fill those highest seats, made void through war in heaven.
With many of you, each is vacant of its head,—some down-hurled son of glory,—
And ready for a substituted chief, a brother of the Christ,
A ransomed child of Adam, made through suffering perfect,
Lower than the angels at his first, but higher than them all hereafter.

Each star is a mighty kingdom, tributary to the central Sun,
And stood, or swerved, in loyalty, when **Lucifer tempted** changes;
In some the pristine rulers, fallen from their pure seraphic state,
Have left those Canaan cities to be won by Israel's host;
In some they stood sublime, Abdiels among the sons of Belial,
Gaining the regalia for themselves, Archangels though **not men**;
Angels stood and angels fell; as men may fall or stand,
God's darling youngest-born, His Benjamins and Davids.

There be globes, **near of** kin to our world, wanderers, dependents on the sun,
So **vast and rare and light, we may** guess them spiritual mansions;
That outer quaternion of planets, flying in a wider orbit,
The so-styled **Jupiter and** Saturn, Uranus **and** furthest Neptune:
These, each larger than this earth, by a thousand times and more,
Weigh yet as lightness for their bulk, seemingly less substantial.
Have such worlds expanded, balancing alike for density,
But swollen as to gaseous globes, fitted for some half-material beings?
Have these four, purified by fire, attained their incorruptible perfection;
The like whereof we look for Earth, for Venus, Mercury and Mars?
And is it that the lost huge planet, shattered into ninety provinces,
Asteroid-orbs that sweep midway between near Mars **and** Jupiter,
Burst and demolished for its sin, is a warning to our grosser worlds,
Now looking equally to judgment, and waiting for a baptism **of** fire?
That **huge** and ruined world, was it once the realm of Lucifer,
Prince of the powers of the air, since fallen through ambition?
And are the shattered fragments of his kingdom homes for evil angels,
Flung down to earth **in meteors, and** troubling our skies with pestilence,—
Wandering stars, **soon** to be put out, in blackness of darkness for ever?
For behold,—that devastated globe, vast as Jupiter or Neptune,
May have been comet-struck for sin just before man was made;
And its degraded monarch may have striven thus to seize
The new weak creature's kingdom for his glory and revenges.

And for those better four, flowering in season from their roots,

Each hath grown to its millenium, and won that æon of its glory;
Each is now the happy home of beings purified from matter,
Having passed, long eras since, through fiery ordeals to perfection.
Then, as for our humbler four, Mars, Earth, Mercury, and Venus,
Now we stand for illustration set before the universe of worlds,
Showing that earlier phase, the hour of sin and trial,
Homely in Time's working-dress before our Sabbath suit;
But meant to be hereafter clothed-upon and grown to be fit heavens
    for their children,
Wide enough for all the generations of all creatures born therein.
Earth (and those near planets in their season, at intervals of million
    ages,)
May swell and ripen in the fire, when its elements shall melt with
    fervent heat;
Expanded thus as Jupiter, magnified some thirteen hundred times
Yet with its equipoise unaltered, being in its density the same,
Cleansed by that baptism of fire, as once washed clean by water,
Made an ethereal palace for holier ransomed creatures,
Earth then would thus be large enough, the heritage for all her
    children,
Children of every class, the humblest as the highest,
Not only man, but all his serfs, degraded through his sin,
Innocents who yet shall share his blessing in Salvation.

Comets, enormous and imponderable, spheres of burning vapour,
Flying on your fiery track with more than lightning speed,
Darted from every point by thousands, mesh of tangled threads
Shot from the depths of space, as spinning star to star,
Are ye then electric shuttles, weaving warp and woof
Of light and life throughout the universe, travelling from suns to
    planets?

Moons, struck off as at a tangent from the sides of new-made worlds,
Slumbering, as slept Adam, before his fall came nigh,
Are ye not outcast satellites, possibly sad homes for evil,
Exiled from those brighter spheres, where good alone may dwell?
The rings that girdle Saturn, the orbs that float round Jupiter,
These may be the prisons for the convicts of those worlds:
And what then, set aside for us, is yonder globe of cinders,
Blistered with heat, or glaciered with cold, on either hideous hemi-
    sphere,—

Our lamp of night, **our witness to most sin,** thefts, and lusts, and
    murders,
Our neighbouring shore of burning cones, airless, empty, waterless,—
Goddess of the worst idolatries, witchcrafts, crimes, and cruelties,
Hecate, Asharoth, Diana, our pale and guilty Moon?
May not this be thus the prisonhouse, where evil shall be **pent,**
When, concrete in ill bodies, sin is driven out of Earth?

Meteors,—who knoweth, who can guess, your various inexplicable
    natures?
Or, fragments of that shattered world, aërolite morsels of its pro-
    vinces?
Or haply, lava-masses from the mountains of the moon?
Or bubble worlds of gas? or ministering flames of fire?
Or wandering powers of the air? or young stars shot beyond their
    orbits?
Or strange concretions of matter, collected by atoms on the firma-
    ment?
Or globes of electric light, fired by an atmospheric touch?
Who knoweth, who can guess?—In beautiful majestic slowness
Now, like a moon, a meteor's arch will span the summer sky,
Then with a burst of lustre will quench the common starlight,
Leaving heaven by contrast black, before our startled eyes;
Now, **like a fiery hail** across autumnal clouds
The meteors rush and crackle, like a sleet of **arrows,**
Or burst on high and hurl below hot masses **of strange metal,**
As shot from lunar mortars, and with **thunder of artillery.**

Yea · how lightly by us all are the wonders of the firmament con-
    sidered;
Marvels every night, by grovelling man unnoted:
Yet the most ancient of all books, most read and by all nations
Equally and freely as a universal tongue, is yonder starlit heaven.
The wise Chaldæan, and the shepherd of Judæa, thought far more
    than we
Of what those characters might mean, which God hath writ in suns:
They guessed at **much we** know, and long ago have travelled for
    themselves
Among the stars in spirit, as **Will** might give **them wings.**
And still that silent sermon is preached to us each by night
Whispering, **come up hither,** we can show you wonders.

Who heedeth? even heeding, who doth not idly gossip names,
Ursa, Orion, and the Pleiades, nursery tales and figures?—
Lo, it is the universe thou scannest, half the wealth of God,
His wisdom, and His power, and where His honour dwelleth,
Creations inconceivable, exquisitely poised and ordered,
Full of hallowed harmonies and glorious evermore,
Worlds to which earth is but a millet-seed,—suns so much vaster
   than our sun
That numbers fail to show us of how little count it is:
The star we name Alcyone, centre of all these systems,
Is a mass as of a hundred million suns, our sun making half a mil-
   lion earths.
Yet, Earth, with all its littleness, is the spot which Heaven's King
Chose in His infinite humility, to favour as the greatest,
Selected for that drama, whereat all the worlds are wondering,
Salvation through incarnate God, and glory born of sorrow:
And man, poor victim of that sorrow, is yet to be the co-heir of
   that glory,
Meanwhile groping in the dark, and crying like an infant for the
   dawn;
Still, with a mind to rise to God, a tongue to speak His praise,
A heart to give Him love for love, a soul to live with Him for ever!

OF PROBABILITIES.

BEFORE all things, God was probable, the first and the greatest
   Probability,
One self-existing source of Life, the solitary seed of all creation:
That He should be good was probable, for evil tendeth to decay,
Neither subsisteth of itself, but is only the corruption of a better:
That He should be all mighty, all wise, all merciful, all just,
Would be certainties of One Great Good, eternally without com-
   petitor:
Yet would His benevolence forbid a sullen and an isolated oneness,
And so a plurality of Persons would be likely in that Essence:
Thus taking counsel with Himself, in equal harmonious com-
   panionship
He should, everlastingly beneficent, have willed the happy pre-
   sence of His peers.

And these should be Three in one, a Trinity, neither more nor
    fewer,
The likeliest number for society, to last as a partnership of friends.
It were probable that one name should stand the Primal Father,
And that another should be hailed the Everlasting Son,
And that the Spirit of these twain, eternally united,
Should shine the lightsome living Bond, of God, that Great Triune:
Were it more probable that God, a non-affectioned Unit
Should choose eternal solitude, unsympathetic Self,—
Nor rather elect as His vast happiness a gloriously consorted
    Essence,
Equal, in three united Friends who live and love as one?

So then, that Grandest Probability, of God and His attributes and
    Persons,
Is hinted as an aid to faith, though scarce a proof to doubt.
And for that objection in thy thoughts, of some antagonist evil,
Some seemingly eternal opposite hindering eternal good,
Consider was it probable or not, that creatures be imperfect,
Or faultless in perfections, and thus equalled with their Maker?
And if imperfect and allowed free space for worse or better,
Better, with grace given from above, or worse, that grace withheld,
(Withheld from no caprice, no lack of large Benevolence,
But urged by deep good cause for the greater blessing of Creation,)
The creature thus might fall, his good might grow corrupted,
His powers decayed, his health diseased, his moral brightness
    darkened,
And so should sin and evil, concretes not utter abstracts,
Cling, as if native parasites, to creatures less than perfect.

But if a fall were probable, thus from the nature of matter,
What were the next high probability expectable from God?
His grace would plan, His skill invent, a scheme of full recovery,
Whereby the universe of intellect might learn and love Him better.
Himself would be the creature, Himself would bear the penalty,
Himself, as suffering in that creature, should lift it to Himself.
So should He take into His Being, nearer to the Triune Essence,
A lost and won Creation, made only all the happier from its grief.

And look to the details of our Fall: death was not first for man;
But reigned in old creations, æons before Adam.

And when the Maker willed, and our great forefather came
Full aged monarch of the world, to people and to rule it,
The simplest test, an apple, was given for obedience, and he fell;
Yearning for knowledge as for good, the tempted novice failed.
And so the second Adam should die that self-same hour,
Having lived what the first had overleapt, some thirty years and
    three.
There seemed a probability herein that Christ should fill that sum,
Infant, youth and man, antedating full-grown Adam.

And how should He be born but as of miracle? and wherefore
    should not Eve who sinned
See honour given to her sex through highly favoured Mary?
It were likely that God's great grace should glorify transgressing
    woman,
Therefore was the Virgin overshadowed by the Spirit of all Life.
And how should He die but as of sacrifice? innocent, the con-
    queror of death,
The martyred priest of truth hung between earth and heaven,
Preaching there with outstretched arms to angels and to men,
Victim to His own great justice, and the outcast of the world.
Thus was the Gospel fully probable: and all that ever happened
Equally in Providence and grace to the well-enlightened mind
Would seem to be probable and fit, neither should have happened
    otherwise;
For God had ordered every mean and certified its end.

It was likely that a Mahomet should rise, forcing religion by the
    sword,
Likely that Rome should graft the papal on the pagan,
Likely that a Luther should restore the purity of faith,
Likely that differing sects should slay one another in Jerusalem:
That England should be Freedom's refuge, as a distant outpost
    island,
And thence should be great among the nations, from her ships, her
    colonies, and commerce;
That hardship should energize the North, that luxury should ener-
    vate the South,
That the East, decaying from old age, should be servant to the
    strong young West;
And that, as a planet by itself, America should grow and prosper

Vaster and mightier than all those older dynasties and empires.
And so of most things else; enlightened by their issues,
We note them well-foreshadowed in their likelihoods to be:
And I judge that a prophet might arise, keen in unassisted reason,
Nor needing higher inspiration than a deep-read knowledge of
    mankind,
Who might deduce the future from inspection of the past,
Gathering from likelihood and cause all consequents to come.

OF SCRIPTURE AND SCIENCE.

A BOOK of revelation for the fallen, to lead us back to good,
(Wherefrom through a thousand generations we all have gone
    astray,)
The book that had to speak of God, of souls, and hell, and heaven,
In utterance from the pious of all ages, announcing religion and
    redemption,
How could it turn from its great end, to deal with trivial things,
Our lesser themes of science, the temporal instead of the eternal?
Wherein should we desire for our minds playthings to gladden
    curiosity,
And not rather for our hearts the nourishment of spiritual good?
It were beneath the dignity, it were beside the object,
It were derogation from the Bible, should it stoop to be the manual
    of science.
Moreover, pride is to be humbled,—and knowledge puffeth up;
The loftiness of man must be brought low, by innermost conviction
    and conversion;
Affections grovelling down to earth our God would raise and purify,
And cure man's moral cancer by the Gospel of his Love:
So then, let Reason not expect, that the grand revelation of Religion
Will be liberal in answers to the questions our intellect would ask
    of Nature;
Let us hope it rather rich unto salvation, in thoughts that lead to
    glory,
A feast of wine upon the lees for souls who thirst for Grace.

Yet, whensoever the Great Teacher might touch with His skirts in
    passing
The barren sands of science that edge His narrow way,

He should for morality show truth, not countersigning falsehood,
Making it manifest He knoweth, more than he will turn aside to tell;
Truth, not pedantically exact,—the sun may rise and set,
He may speak of the ends of the earth, He may tell of the windows of heaven;
But, as in the miracle of Joshua, proving that if earth stood still
The moon, not less than the sun, must stop in due obedience to that mandate;
Truth, incidentally declaring He hath made the round world so strong,
Showing earth a sphere self-poised, and not a long flat plain;
He may tell of Adam's race, the redeemed and favoured family,
But leave quite unrecorded whether there were other sorts of Man:
Moses may teach us in the Genesis how earth was re-established in Order,
But he need not touch Old Matter, nor the ages of pre-existing life;
These things are written in the stones, for reason at its leisure to search out,
But what is written in the Book is a searching proper for the spirit:
Nature, as pictured on the Bible, is simply recorded in appearance,
The sun may rejoice to run his course, the heavens may drop down dew;—
Albeit the dew ariseth, albeit the sun stand still,
Even a philosopher unblamed will use those common phrases:
But ofttimes hints of higher knowledge are dropped as by accident in Scripture,
Testifying even to this hour that the Bible is before the age.
He stretcheth out the north over the empty space, and hangeth the world upon nothing;
Here is a glimpse at polar tilts, and their magnetic bearing:
We read about rivers of oil, and oil sucked out of the rock,—
The latest of discoveries with us, but known to Job and Moses:
Behemoth and Leviathan are chronicled, as close in contiguity with man;
And many monsters, thought extinct, are now proved his companions;
The Mammoth, and possibly the Dragon, that giant lizard of the wold,
Were synchronous with man upon his earth; so Scripture saith to Science:

Ancient times and peoples of those earliest books of Moses,
Giants on the earth in old days, Zamzummim and their like,
Hint at possible primal tribes beside our race of Adam,
Albeit none have found as yet one bone or stone for proof:
The flood that drowned the world of men on Asia's sunny plain,
Was not of necessity for Europe, where man was not yet found:
The fountains of the deep were broken up; the foundations of the
    world are out of course;
He changeth the vestures of the globe, by strata laid on strata:
In the days of the patriarch Peleg, was not the earth divided,—
By continents and islands broken off, according to the old tradi-
    tions?
He hath weighed the substance of the globe, exactly, as in a
    balance;
Holding it up by His omnipotence, the hollow of His hand:
He sitteth on the circle of the world, guiding its career upon that
    orbit,
And calleth out the stars by name, His worlds, His many mansions;
He recordeth some sweet influence of the Pleiades,—possibly that
    central Throne
The wondrous Star Alcyone, round which this universe revolveth:
If winged angels are in vision, were they not framed with due
    analogy,
Not as painters dream, impossibly fledged and pinioned,
But wisely and reasonably too, according to proportions and pro-
    prieties,
With two wings covering the face, to cleave the air therewith,
And two wings spread beyond the feet, to steer the course thereby,
And two, to speed the flight; so seen of Isaiah and Ezekiel:
Doth not the Preacher when he preacheth, of the wheel broken at
    the cistern,
And the pitcher broken at the fountain, and the death of worn-out
    age,
Tell of arteries and veins, and the circulating blood of life,
The life that is the blood, unguessed for thirty centuries?
Who gave England Judah's Lion? Who appointed eagles for the
    Nations?
Is it not He who hath forewarned this carcase of their gathering
    together?—
Many are running to and fro, and words go very swiftly,
And knowledge is increased, is flashed as lightning flasheth;

All corners of the earth are being peopled, her rough places are
  made plain,
The valleys are exalted, and the very Alps cut through;
We shall fly with wings as eagles, subduing yet the air of our
  globe,—
As fire and earth and water are subdued, all being parts of our
  heritage;
And the world shall be one great brotherhood, acknowledged of
  one blood,
Freely to buy and to sell, going freely hither and thither,
And all shall have one lip, one language, one religion,
With tolerance for all creeds, as in Peter's sheet of beasts.
Are not these things and their like written in the text-book of the
  saints?
Is not that book worthy of all reverence from the sages?

OF SILENCE.

HOLY Silence, happy Silence, thought-creating Silence,
Blessed and luxurious Silence,—lo, how scarce thou art!
Within, loud turmoil of the spirit, or vexing whispers of the con-
  science,
Worrying remembrances of evil, craving aspirations after good;
Without, the clamour of the world, of talking men and women,
And all those material perturbations disturbing our tiny planet-
  selves,—
Alas! how seldom is a man the fortunate anchorite of silence;
How rarely can he taste that balm, or listen to that music!

In old days great Pythagoras commanded holy silence
As nurse of all the virtues and the learnings and the loves;
Five years his acolytes were dumb, and only looked their thoughts,
And then might help the Teacher, vessels full of infused lore:
Silence was their breeding-time for crystals of the mind;
And many would be wiser if they studied thus from Samos:—
Half the awe of idols lay in mystery of silence;
Half the power of priestcraft is cold reticence at will.
Silence was Pygmalion's love concreted in a statue;
Silence was the abstract charm to Zimmerman in solitude.
Silence strangely melteth down the felon's iron heart;

Silence to the Trappist is the mute beside his coffin.
How oftentimes is Silence the wisest of replies !
When insolence provoketh, when slander false-accuseth,
When ignorance and prejudice are full of idle talk ;
Let silence be the answer on thy lip and in thy life.
So too, when many praise, as well as when they blame,
And when thy name is loudest in the mouths of men,
Thy strength is to sit still, in wise and humble silence ;
Let Silence lay her finger on thine unpresumptuous lip.

Lo, the vast difference to souls within the sphere of silence !
That magic ring to one is life, to other nigh to death.
Innocence tenderly enjoyeth the blessed calm of silence,
Listening as an infant to its lullaby of peace
Guilt, terrified at self, abhorreth silent solitude,
And findeth that sweet music only loud with hideous sound :
The keen mind, full of thought, rejoiceth in a quiet hour ;
While dullards hold it irksome, to be killed as best they can :
Health can hear therein only glad hopes and memories ;
While nervous irritable disease hath peopled it with fears :
The poet loveth that rare calm, as incense to his spirit ;
The tattling gossip longeth but to spoil it with his talk.
To all it is a test of state, bearing to be alone,
Alone with God and conscience, and the memories of thy life :
If eager to escape from these, avoid accusing silence ;
If calm in their communion, thou wilt seek it as thy friend.
Hast thou kept thine innocency ? are thy memories pure ?
Is thine that honest and good heart, which The Master loveth ?
Then shalt thou rejoice alway to breathe the balm of silence
On lonely hills or strolling by the solitary sea.

Silence strengtheneth love,—innocent and unintended silence,
Whereto do cling excuses and kind fancy pleading well :
Silence weakeneth love,—obstinate, guilty silence,
Where doubts and fears and thoughts of scorn combine to wean
    the heart.
The long-unanswered letter doth friendship nigh to death,
And few affections can endure determined dogged silence.
And woe, too, for the clamorous home where silence hath no lover,
But scolding worry drowneth good, alike by day and night :
There is the brawling wife, there are the wrangling children,

There the tongue's hot embassage provoketh instant strife;
There the sad peace-lover in vain imploreth blessed silence,
For all the loves and graces have been scared from that loud home.

Wise and kind and good are the eloquent Silences of Scripture,
For grace is shown in light withheld, not less than in light given.
It would have diverted man from God, the one great end of his existence,
Had he been told too fully of the constant ministry of angels:
He would have scorned short Time, in teachings of the past Eternity;
And even an awful Future is made lower in importance than the Present:
He would have been terrified from duties, if the spirits of the dead had hemmed him round,
Or were it to be made his care, to help or serve them in their Hades:
Curious questions are unanswered with, "What is that to thee?"
The simpler, "Follow me," is utterly man's duty.
Yet may we speculate and argue, for God hath given us reason,
And lights may dawn on Providence, that Scripture had not shown.
He biddeth ears to ear, He willeth eyes to see,
He is pleased if intelligence search out His workings with humility.
The Silences that whisper in earth's caverns to the everlasting hills,
The Silences of angels and of ghosts, and of animals with their spirits,
These deep mysteries are themes that man may desire to look into,
Groping through their darkness to feel for hidden truths.
The puzzling wonders in creation, mingled good and evil,—
Not due to Adam's sin, which blighted Adam's race,
But longer of old and with innocent tribes, in those past million ages
After the undateable Beginning and before our week of Cosmos,—
Those are in silence till one seeth in these latter days,
That all things less than God decay from imperfections.
And angels were the labourers, under their great husbandman The Son,
Toiling for Him with skill and joy, rewarded and applauded;
Each of them brought some organism, when our earth was peopled,

Which He should then infuse with life, and add the curious senses.
His artizans were made by Him, and so their works are His;
And truer work have they to do than ever-chaunted hymns;
The ministry of angels is seen in all creation,
As well as through our daily walk in teaching and delivering;
And haply each may watch in love over his own blest handywork,
For God made all things for Himself, but through His holy angels.
These be truths scarce heard, lest utterance breed idolatries,
That man may walk with God alone; and Silence thus is wisdom.

Speech is silver, Silence gold, according to the Spaniard;
Silence is the pearl, and speech the gaping oyster.
Silence is the subtle scent, and speech the smothery smoke;
Silence is the mellow fruit, and speech the million leaves.
Some have called her wisdom, as at least concealing folly;
Some have dubbed her more than half the Buddhist's dream of
    Heaven:
Sleep and trance and ecstacy are all near kin to Silence;
And the calm quietude of death is ever-blessed Silence.

OF SPIRITUAL PRESENCES.

THAT there be spirits multitudinous, infinite for differences and
    numbers,
Spirits of good and evil, with all their many intermediates,
The mischievous, the humorous, the sensual, as well as the pious
    and the wise,—
Spirits of sinners as of saints, of idiots, things and animals,—
That crowds of these there be, existing somewhere somehow,
Most confess, and few deny, recognizing spirit-immortality.
As the tree hath fallen, so the limbs must lie;
The bent and scars of time survive and spread for ever:
He that is pure becometh purer, he that is mean will yet be meaner,
The filthy shall be filthier still, the gracious grow in grace.
Spirit never dieth, neither is it merged into its God,
For weal or woe a separate life, its Maker's friend or foe:
And every inch of space in all earth's nooks and corners,
The highest Alpine peaks, as the deepest Ural mines,
The caverned halls of the Atlantic, the crowded hives of cities,

Every room in every house, every hill and valley,—
All have teemed with life, and been earth's homes to spirits.

So then these might claim to revisit each its birthplace,
And there re-act the good or ill that chiefly warped its fate:
And, if this had been allowed, the globe would be crowded up
    with spirits,
Multitudes everywhere together, generation jostling generation,
Until the commonest experience should be that of meeting ghosts,
Mentally recognised and felt, if not also heard and seen;
And such perpetual obstruction to human life and duty,
Hindered and every way made void by interfering spirits,
Would steal responsibility from man, and make his trial futile,
Mingling his career, that should be separate, with the deeds of a
    cloud of ancestors.

But, there is that Great Gulf fixed; and none, or few, may pass it;
So few,—if any ever passed,—that none is nigh to truth.
Spirit, once emancipate from flesh, glorying in new-found freedom,
Speedeth away to some vast orb where only spirits dwell,
There to await the Resurrection, there to anticipate the judgment,
There to dream of bliss to come, or dread foreboded pangs,
There to be happy in self-consciousness, or to be tormented by
    remorse,
There, as in God's waiting-hall, to bide His coming verdict.

Few:—what if such few, allowed for some dread reason,
Have overleapt that wide abyss, as messengers from Hades?
Or, what if some have never left their scene of life's ordeal,
And so may haply have remained, nor need a real returning?
It may be, burdened with dark secrets, harassed by inexpiated
    crimes,
A wretched soul hath now and then clung fiercely to its birthplace;
It may be that either of a pair, long joined in happy marriage,
Hovereth in deep love about the other, visiting its mate continu-
    ally:
It may be, doting on her child, a mother's ghost hath lingered
To guard him, like an angel, from some perilous evil nigh:
It may be, rights or wrongs, deeply burnt into the spirit
May bring it grovelling back, till full revenge be found:
There have been writ such stories; some have seen strange sights;

Knockings, voices, sobbings, have disturbed the castle guest:
The long unburied skeleton beneath the murderer's hearth,
The flickering lights at midnight in the tapestried oak-chamber,
The hurried taps along the wall, the whispers heard across the bed,
The footsteps down the staircase,—nothing seen though closely followed,—
The wail forewarning death, that time-worn family presage
Accomplishing its own sure end through superstitious fear,—
The spectral faces in old mirrors, the gallery paced by its procession,
The murders and the treasures, and the wrongs revealed by ghosts,—
Such strange tales are rife; and fancy, with imposture,
Hath multiplied these terrors to the credulous and cowardly:
Yet, some few cases,—few, if any,—calmly well-attested,
Have staggered shrewdest doubters, and compelled our sceptic faith:
Here and there, we may have had revisitants from Hades,
Now and then, some spirit may have lingered long on earth:
There be many things undreamt of our philosophy, as the chief Poet hath declared,
Which natheless may be truths and facts about that world of spirits;
And seers must stand well prepared, through some magnetic fitness;
The unsealed eye, the common ear, perceiveth not such presences:
But, as all ordinary law ruleth by regular appointment,
Which nothing less than God's own hand may alter as through miracle,
So it is only by a miracle, to be evidenced with rare cautions,
That ever spirit hath been left to do some work on earth,
That ever disembodied ghost was troubled about burial,
That ever any soul of man hath leapt that Great Gulf fixed.

Next, for the mystery of dreaming,—meet we spirits there?
Or find we not that same Great Gulf, we may not pass, nor they?
Sleep is the merciful relaxing, unstringing of the vital bow,
A loosing of the harpsichords, alike for mind and body,
Whereby they drain, through rest, from the harmonies of nature round them,
Both tunefulness and energy to sing their hymn of life:
And dreams are as the dews, uprising out of memories,
Vaporous clouds upsteaming from the marshes of the mind,

Now tinged by **setting** Fancy, and roseate with sweet thoughts,
Now rendered gloomy through regrets, or terrible from conscience.

Every day is closed as by its death, **when we wrap us in the**
winding-sheet of sleep,
Every night **our spirits expand**, as partially disfranchised from the
body;
It is a foreshadowing of the future, sleep the type of death,
And dreams suggesting to **the soul its coming** good or evil:
Our dull fatigued material lieth in a breathing dissolution,
While immaterial essence wandereth hither and thither;
Sometimes, **in old scenes** of earth, curiously mingled with **the present,**
Sometimes, fashioning the future, wildly and discoloured by the past,
Sometimes—(as some think)—hovering with sister spirits,
Met in visionary worlds that vanish **ere the** morning:
None remember, and no one may declare, what passeth in those
dreams;
Only their influences **remain, with hints when** just awaking:
We cannot **win them back, nor** coax their perished presence;
The consciousness of work-day life to them is instant banishment:
Often have we, all in vain, endeavoured so to stay them;
But the world-element of wakefulness scattered all those shadows;
Quickly fade they, soon forgotten, wreaths of mist in sunshine,
And rare is any record of them figured on the light.
Haunted by dark fancies, **by sweet** reveries refreshed,
The waking **spirit ill remembereth aught** but peace or trouble:
And it hath accorded with my musings, that some **second life**
Separate, continuous, and reasonable, **is the** condition of sleeping;
Separate, as with other accidents, faces, scenes, and circumstances;
Continuous, night after night, with special past and future;
Reasonable, after its own sort, though little led **by** judgment;
And **conscious,** as through habit, of some sense of right and wrong:
With the body's **waking, that** other life vanisheth away,
Gradually builded **up again,** with the body's slumbering.
Neither is reality more strong for scenes and pains and pleasures
Than in their keen ideals, **born** of sleep and dreams by night.
Often in the mediate condition, **half sleeping and** half waking,
We doubt within ourselves which of the twain is truest,
This work-day world of matter, with **its real** and hard experiences,
Or that the spirits' **sabbath,** free from worry, fear, and care:

This so looketh like a dream, that so showeth a reality,
Either seemeth other, as a sort of double life.
Whether in the body, or out of the body,—who shall truly tell?
For the mysteries of sleep are deep, in dreams and mental travel.

O rare kingdom of the mind, by space and time unbounded,
Where one may live a lifetime within a single night,
And seem to speed on spirit-wings beyond this humble planet,
And happily expand in light, as blossoming elsewhere,—
O pure realms of thought, how few in all earth's millions
Can claim to reign ideal kings above your vast domain!
Who hath known the spirit of a man, or how he fareth in his dreams,
Or wherein the experience of one is tallied by another's?
I know a mind conscious in itself of two clear states of being,
The one with all its accidents in wakefulness, the other with its
    qualities in sleep:
Day by day continuously, the history of its common life is one;
Night by night continuously, alike there is its unity of dreams:
Haply, the chambers of the brain, each with its special occupant,
Fancy, judgment, form, music, love, contention,
Sink to natural rest in sequence one by one,
Closing the windows of their house, in some alternate order:
Thus, while earthly talents gradually sink to slumber,
The native genius of the spirit waketh up spontaneously in dreams.
There is then the life of cultivation, social, normal, temporal;
And there is the life of intuition, spiritual, strange, and individual:
Each hath a separate experience, yet is there but one spirit,
As if it lived, by day or night, at home in different rooms.
Rarely have I heard from others, never have I known myself
That any disembodied soul hath come to earth in dreams;
Fancy pictureth the dead, affection listeneth to their voices,
But all thou hearest, all thou seest, grew of thine own brain.

Lastly, for the ministry of angels: doubtless, these be sent:
Shrewdly the good centurion proved their frequent presence.
When this our world was born, newly rolling out of chaos,
(Chaos, an old ruin of past ages, no firstling of the God of order,)
What was your mission, happy angels, when thus ye sang for joy?
Were ye then nothing but the minstrels, the choristers and bards
    of Heaven?
Verily, beside and beyond your exquisite soul-harmonies in music,

Ye may have worshipped as artificers, intelligently taught of God,
Moulding lower works, exquisite in microscopic beauty,
Which He then quickened into life and signed with His own signet.
Wisdom and mercy well enjoined some special toil to each,
Some insect, or some flower, some crystal, seed, or shell;
Suffering His servants as co-workers, bringing tribute-offerings,
The children's gifts to God their Father, on that His new-world's
    birthday.
And as ye worked in Eden, ye may since have watched on earth
Those darlings of your skill His blessing made so perfect,
Present yourselves, though all unseen, in woods and fields and
    valleys,
And everywhere rejoicing in the works He praised so well.

And as our ministering spirits, doing the Master's bidding,
The Great King's happy soldiers, obeying His command,
Whether ye be Cherubim, or Seraphim, or names of light unknown,
O pure and precious essences, ten thousands of ten thousands,—
How happily we think of you for help, in time of doubt or trial,
How tenderly ye watch, and guide, and whisper—go this way!
Those among you highest under God, brightest and first of the
    creation,
Embodied crystals of His attributes, and purest of His works,
Ever in the sunshine of His presence, Archangels (named in heaven
The strength of God, the joy of God, His wisdom, love, and truth)
How gladly we remember that, as Gabriel, or Michael,
Ye ministered to Mary, and to Abram, and to Christ;
How thankfully we hope that humbler ranks of angels
Defend salvation's common heirs from danger and from sin!
Yet is there never an appearance; spiritually, invisibly,
Through the listening heart and mind, oft in prayer and watching,
Thus not fighting against reason, nor constraining circumstance,
Ye do lead and teach and guard, and stand our spirit-friends.
Amen! we yield to your suggestions; Amen! we lean upon your
    arms,—
And feel no fear and no distrust but you will help us well.
So, not worshipping but honouring, as we honour friends,
Our fellowship is, under God, with ministering spirits.

OF TIME.

A LITTLE while, a little while,—we know not what He meaneth,—
So much to lose, so much to gain,—all in this little while!
How strange a mystery is this, that the changeable should fix for
    ever,
That the perishable seaflower should last, eternally crystallised in
    silex:
A little while, a little space, a little chance and power,
Resulting yet in marvel, and everlasting strength;
So we creep on our way, faint and darkling to the last,
And then emerge in brightness, and yearningly expand to freedom.
Be it a month, or fourscore years, life is but a short swift season;
A cradle, or the cincture of the world, would be equally a prison
    to the soul.
Just as one hath learned to cull a little wisdom,
Humbleness with confidence in self, courage, tenderness, religion,
Frankness, purity of life, health and cleanliness and silence,
Patience and hearing other sides, and charity with excusing,
Just as we have gained at last, through trial and experience,
Power to live more simply, more truly, and more wisely,
The bell tolleth, and we go, obeying the behest of Heaven,
The Master calleth and we come, to carry our life elsewhere:
O the vanity, the dignity, the woefulness, the happiness of life—
O many thoughts about this theme, wherein we all have part.

No man is safe until his death: Tellus the Athenian spake shrewdly
There is no staying in one stay, no certainty in life.
As wave succeedeth wave, passion foameth over passion,
One shall scarce be overcome, when another pusheth on to combat:
The prodigal, hardly cured, catcheth the leprosy of avarice;
The wanton pleasure-hunter, chastened, falleth into cruelties of rage:
I have known strict moralities in youth issue in the old man's mean-
    ness;
I have known the dissolute and prodigal change to the generous
    and pious:
For each was but one phase, of its own peculiar character,
Shewn in different lights, the polarised and common;
Youth hath rare prismatic tints, but hard old age few beauties;
And nature's primal outburst is tamed and toned by years.
The best are ever in most peril, save for grace and habit,

As strung and tuned more exquisitely in the key of passion.
None is ever safe; though mercy, circumstance, and custom
Be the triple wall around some David or Josiah,
Honour, sentiment, or feeling, may tempt to fatal sin;
And the one potency against it, is faithful humble prayer.
Oftentimes the young man holdeth on, pure in his earliest course,
Resisting temptation as it riseth, and wrestling down proclivities
    of nature;
I have watched him safe to manhood,—then through evil weakness
He hath turned aside, and is fallen; his prime and age are marred!
And often some poor youths, dissolute and shameless at the first,
Are checked betimes and sorrowful, anon through grace repentant:
These penitents in age, as that once saint in boyhood,
Let all be humble for the present, culling wisdom from the past,—
All, out of God, are insecure; all shall stand or fall,
As mercy willeth, not unsought: and none is safe alone.

Wherefore is there always such a charm to the pure and thoughtful
    spirit
In ancient things, and times of old, and all the hoary past?
That the cromlech and the ruin and the coin have a sort of nimbus
    round them,
A hallowing kind of halo as in reverence to their age?
Wherefore is the very rust and moss counted for the bloom of
    beauty,
And homage rendered simply to the veritable antique?—
One of the attributes of God is deep and indefinite antiquity,
And all His characters are dear to Reason's purest thought:
He, as the Ancient of Days, antedateth all past time,
Therefore with intuitive desire His creatures emulate that attribute.

Time is a speck on Space, a cork in the boundless ocean,
A bubble floating lightly, about the eternal universe,
Which is an illimitable sphere, and existences its circumambient
    surface,
And God the centre of convergence, and the radii His ever-present
    powers:
And whenever it commenced, our cosmos must have burst in suddenly,
Cutting the circle with abruptness, and breaking its continuous
    circumference.

The absolute beginning of creation must seem to have had relative
    beginnings ;
As if recording life before, which had not really lived :
The tree created had its rings, as if of ancient seasons,
The very seed newborn, was germed as from a parent,
The lion bounding in his might, gave evidence of former years,
And Adam at his prime, appeared to prove his childhood.
The butterfly argued a chrysalis, a caterpillar, an egg,
The fruitful soil of Eden showed old strata decomposed,
Its first day, born in Autumn, spake of previous spring and summer,
Its light from distant stars had travelled millenaries down.
Yet, none of these had pre-existed ; neither did the God of Truth
Suffer seeming falsehood on His works, albeit He made them thus :
For by His word, distinctly, the fiat of creation was proclaimed,
All things ready at their best, with fruit after their kind.
Whenever Creation was begun, it must have entered in its panoply,
Perfect in results as of the past, in order to be perfect in this pre-
    sent :
And the God of eternal truth, willing to save reason's doubting,
Simply revealeth in The Word,—all firsts were at perfection :
Therefore, rich in seeds ; therefore with apparent testimony
To some previous generation, condensed in His quick fiat.
Short of eternity for matter, the only rest for reason
Is this temporal creation, with thus its riddles solved :
The Almighty caused a present, born momentarily at will,
To seem, not needfully to be, the growth of older pasts ;
And then to spare our faith all doubts about His truthfulness,
Grandly maketh proclamation,—the creature at its best
This cleareth up the mystery, this answereth reason's question ;
God's word expoundeth His works, even as His works His word.

He that dreameth of a monad, that all evolved thereout,
Assumed the Maker of this monad, framer of a microscopic cosmos ;
Place it far back in old eternity, still its birth was temporal,
Only the vaster marvel, if one atom-seed ;
But no wholesome mind can bear with such a folly,
Choosing the touch of a creator at some riper date.
Wherefore not a microscopic cosmos ? Minuteness magnifieth
    miracle :
Even if beneath Omnipotence all things were not equal.
At its best God's World-idea rolled out in teeming beauty,

Involving apparent preparations, as of years long past:
But possibly the times of non-intelligence were hastened to give
  man his heritage,
And needed not the million ages our slow growths demand.
Worshippers of some new sort, freewilled, reasonable, fallible,
Were wanted at the Court of God, to illustrate His name,
To show true attributes in Heaven, solely to be seen through sin,
As colours in light are proved, only by the spectrum to distort
  them:
Therefore this fabric of the world might well be hurried up to man,
To quell the great expectancy, by clumping up those ages.
We are at the climax of the periods, we sum up long æons;
All the ancient chaos of the world resulted in man's era;
And our mundane life is, as it were an egg, a seed,
To bring forth Reason's fruit, in time, for immortality.

OF LITTLE PROVIDENCES.

Hast thou not noted, O my brother, how carefully thy steps are
  guided,—
How tenderly when thou dost well,—how sternly, doing ill;
What instant recompense or penalty, for duties or transgressions,
Just judgment even here, in due reward and punishment?
Hast thou not watched upon thy way the myriad little matters
Proving to thee everywhere that Providence is nigh,
Guiding, according to the covenant, ordered in all things and sure,
And making circumstances work together for thy good?
Infinitely great, infinitely little, infinite for past and future,
Everything is infinite around us, infinite alike within us.
There are globes of an immensity so vast, that earth is but a mole-
  cule beside them,
And spores of invisible fernseed are worlds of sensitive life.
What is man, that Thou art mindful of him? Behold, he is an
  atomy of dust
Dropt for a moment on a spot, that is but as a molehill to the
  mountains,
Himself a microscopic world, each man infinitely wondrous,
With a past of preparations none have guessed, a future of evolve-
  ments none can calculate.

Thou art as a nothing to the universe, yet even thy thoughts are
  registered;
Thou wanderest hither and thither, but every step is ordered;
Thou goest as in freeness of thy will, yet Providence is ever on the
  way,
Beautifully guiding and preventing, inlaying the Mosaic of thy life.
All things hang together, causes facts and consequents;
Nothing but hath had its seed, and yet shall yield its fruit:
Thou mayest take small heed, thou hast counted it a chance,
But that which now hath flowered, groweth on old roots;
The egg was laid long years agone, before yon eagle in the clouds;
The word was uttered in thy youth, that made this friend or foe.

If for the climax of Eternity there seem vast telescopic ends,
Through Time, minutely running, flow the microscopic means,—
All things leavening up in mass, all converging to a focus,
And every thread and every ray a miracle of care;
A miracle of mercy too, unless thy folly scorn it;
A miracle of wisdom, whatever be thy thought.
Sometimes, glimmering in the darkness, we note that shadowy
  Hand,
Sometimes catch a glitter of the golden thread
Showing its light as a spider's clue, through our caverned labyrinths,
And always safely leading, if we will not let it go.
The little hints of Providence are dropped as millet seed,
To crackle as we tread, and guide our darkling steps:
The thought, not yet on our lips, swift uttered by a friend,
The scene, pressed upon the mind, and present through a seeming
  accident,
Even the pattern on a carpet, even the paper of a room,
The right man casually met, the curious coincidence of matters,
The fruits to-day is gathering from plantings of old yesterdays,
The finding out, how often,—that strangers have part-lot with us,
Mixt with our past, joined to our present, and promising or threat-
  ening our future,—
The mysteries and histories in words, the wonderful properties of
  numbers,
The wit and apposite energy in jokes, puns, anagrams, and riddles,
All tell of unconsidered providences, ordering and working every-
  where,
And waiting for the mind of man to note perfection in them.

U

The glory of God is in the highest, His glory is also in the lowest,
Guiding the worlds in their courses, and piloting the thistledown
 not less;
He rideth on the wings of the storm, He lingereth in the perfume
 of a lily,
He mouldeth the iceberg, and the Alp, and the atoms of a dust
 cloud in the desert :
He that reared Jorullo, the burning Mexican mountain,
Twelve thousand feet in a night, one hundred years ago,
The same Hand exquisitely layeth, in tesselated microscopic beauty,
The rainbowed roofs and pavements within the mouths of snails :
He that raised up a Timour, or a Cæsar, for judgment on the
 nations,
Sitteth beside the school-child, as she singeth at her sampler ;
He that inspired Adam's tongue, to give fit names to creatures,
Ordained its rustling chirrup to the cricket on the hearth.

There is an intricate perfection, a minute fitness and completeness
In everything about us, Providence, Grace, and Nature :
All marvellously guided at every inch and instant,
Circumstances, laws, and elements, animate beings or inanimate ;
Music, numbers, and mechanics, grammar, art and science,
All, however human, showing sparks of the divine ;
Even the plays upon words, the witty turns of converse,
Declare superior wisdom lying hidden in their mirth ;
Majesty, shorn of its externals, is it but a jest,—or something more?
While Nelson's name proclaimed from birth his honour from the
 Nile.
He that numbereth the stars, hath numbered the hairs of thy head,
No sparrow, and no dynasty, falleth without our Father :
The little and the great are His, the ludicrous even as the grave,
Ay, and the evil as the good ; for, evil is but good corrupted :
This is the mystery of mysteries ; and where to draw the line ?
He is all-power and all-love, yet thus permitting misery ;
He is the mover in all life, alike in sinner as in saint ;
He blasteth in the pestilence, even as He blesseth in the sunshine :
All we are sure of, as in faith, is that He worketh righteousness ;
How, we see not now : but we shall know hereafter.

OF SUCCESS

Of old, men worshipped Good Success,—made good by its succeeding;
And now they worship nothing, but go wondering at Success:
The altar is not built, and the incense is not burnt,
But he that hath succeeded is, in spite of wrong, a hero:
They ask not how, nor why; Success is answer wholly,—
The how of sin and why of shame, are nought if one succeedeth.
And in their profanity they judge, that facts are coins of Providence,
As stamped by God's authority, and issued in His name;
But wrongs, though facts, must not be held such darlings of His mind,
He giveth those no mintmark, though the forgers pass them freely.
The Providence of God is throned on high above all facts:
Facts do not evidence His will, but oftener His forbearance.
A fact, a great success, may be a sin or fault or folly;
God never wrought a wrong, in Nature Providence or Grace.
Laws once good may warp, and bend to evil issues,
But their corruption is a charge not to be laid on Providence:
True, He permitteth and is silent; wickedness awhile may prosper;
But none may claim for Providence a fact of crime or shame.
Nation riseth against nation, both thus punished for their sins,
And athletes batter athletes, while Justice looketh on,—
And victory will be given to the strongest, not for the conqueror's deserts,
But, simpler so, because the weak had earned this crushing judgment.
In vain ye chaunt Te Deum: He loveth not such praises,
He stood aside and suffered, and His hand was not stretched out.
Yet, the dread penalty shall fall, the meed for wrong successful,
For nations are as persons, and are judged for that they do,—
And "cursed be the man that moveth his neighbour's landmark,"
Shall ban conflicting peoples for those murders and those thefts.
This is their day for triumph, but judgment cometh with the morrow,
Woe unto the wrong-doer, his crimes—are millstones round his neck.
Nothing can sanctify a sin, not even great success,
And unrepented sin is punished in a nation by its ruin.

Wouldest thou make enemies, Succeed; thou humblest many rivals;
Envy, hatred, malice, shall dog thy great career;

And failing, those are not thy friends; thy sin hath been ambition,
And having missed the prize thyself, they mock at thee for spite.
Wouldest thou find friends, Succeed; the crowd love hero-worship;
And of those worshippers are some whose hearts are worth the
    winning:
Also, the generous of thy rivals will be friends to cheer thee for suc-
    cesses;
And such be souls of noblest mark, friends whom the good can love.
O Success! what a triumph to be safe, in view of all those perils;
O Success! what a happiness within, remembering those enemies
    without;
O Success! if linked with pride and selfishness, how evil:
O Success! how great a good, well won and humbly worn.

Hast thou once succeeded,—hast thou hit the gold?
Take heed thou tempt not fortune,—she may turn her wheel and
    leave thee:
Prudence whispereth, forbear; but energy answereth prudence—
Success shall never be the drag to check my flying chariot·
Often is there seen the youth, diligent rather than ambitious,
Stopt short in early mid career by soon achieved success:
The prize, the class, the local praise, have satisfied his yearning;
His mind is not moulded of the highest, seeing thus he seareth
    for his fame;
Selfish glories have been gained, he will risk nothing further;
And so that prudent whisper helped both indolence and pride.
Early fruit is seldom followed by a second crop;
That precocious tree is shadowed by its hedge of laurels.
But if a mind be vigorous, and love not its own glory,
The tree shall strike root downward, and shoot its branches upward,
And leaving those young days, and all that hedge of laurels,
Will dare again to fling out fruits, and tempt a new success:
It is more generous so to dare: and lo, those fruits are better,
Riper, richer to the taste, than in its first young days.

Alas! the many yearning souls that never won Success
And yet have well deserved to win, for diligence and merit.
Alas, the gems unprized,—alas, the flowers ungathered,
Alas, the disappointed hopes, the spirits broken down!
This seemeth bitter to thy tongue, but it may be sweetness in thy
    stomach,

Failure is Success to thee, if thou couldst read all truth.
Take comfort in the happy thought that thou art guided wisely ;
Thy duty is to well-deserve that unachieved Success.
Courage !—try once more ; remember Palissy the Potter ;
Remember Bruce, six times o'erthrown, and conqueror in the
 seventh ;
Remember Joseph in his prison, soon all Egypt's ruler ;
Remember Christ upon His Cross,—did He not seem to fail ?
Never yet was Great Success, but it commenced with Failure,—
Smoke is first and then the flame: and chaos before cosmos :
Night preceded day ; it is written, the evening and the morning ;
Seeds lie long in darkness, and their flowering is not yet :
Only strive, only deserve ; and fear not thou a Failure ;
Courage and constancy be thine, and thine shall be Success.

OF THE SMALLER MORALS.

KEEP the ten commandments with thy might, and do all highest
 duties ;
But also pay thy lesser tithes of anise, mint and cummin :
Honest, pure, contented, kindly, true, religious,
Serving God, and loving man,—be these all thine at best :
But heed thou also humbler things, the trifles of thy life,
For life is filled with trifles, and they may not be despised.
Much of happiness is missed through mere neglect of trifles,
Much of good-doing destroyed, for lack of tact and manner.
And godly men have erred in this contempt for taste and beauty,
By vulgar freedom driving high-bred souls away :
O the mass of meannesses, of harsh ungenial acts,
Scarce short of sin as shorn of grace, whereof some saints are
 guilty—
Saints, as men may taunt them, and who thus would style them-
 selves,
But oftener chiefs of sinners as regard the smaller morals.
Selfish, inconsiderate, illiberal, and vain,
Can any such be saints indeed,—or hypocrites at heart ?
And some there be, protesters against pampering of the flesh,
Separating cleanliness from godliness, who hold it holy to be
 filthy :
But He who bade the heart be sprinkled from an evil conscience,

Gave a simultaneous command, that the body should be washed
    in pure water;
From the crown of the head to the sole of the feet; keep this
    small moral daily;
It shall be life and strength to thee, the cheapest of good comforts.

A sound mind in a sound body, is the blessedness of creatures;
So spake the wise of old, and we cannot mend their wisdom.
And chief, for the sound mind; to pass by highest morals—
Quiet conscience, hopes to come, and diligence in duty,—
Guard thou these lesser matters: never nurse regrets;—
For sins, repent, forsake; for chances lost, forget them:
Take thy cup as it is mixed; accept thy lot with patience;
Count all things sent of Providence, that are not shame or wrong:
Many have killed their comforts by saddening reveries;
Regrets are weakness, folly, grief; spunge all regrets away.
Never worry for the future; as never bewail the past;
Trust in God; for, day by day, He giveth daily bread;
Thy fears may never come to head, thy carefulness is vanity,
And all thou gainest by distrust is loss of peace of mind.
Never delay about the present; duties are all nows,—
Do that thou hast to do at once, and rid thee of its care.
The letter left unanswered is a petty thorn of thought;
Occasion once neglected may not visit thee again:
Things to be done, once done, are flung behind for ever,
And hinder not our onward way, nor vex us with their coming;
Cheerfully, diligently, reasonably, work the work before thee,
Abjuring all those lesser sins, regret, distrust, delay.

Next, after health of mind, study health of body;
Each man is his best physician as to meats and drinks.
All excess is bad; abstinence, as intemperance;
Gluttony is evil,—and starvation; the ascetic sinneth as the epicure.
Eat thankfully, drink cheerfully, both in moderation;
And let thine appetite survive its temperate repast.
Against ill dreams by night, and aches and pains by day,
Guard good health from heat and cold and wet and sudden changes;
A little care, a little sense, shall save thee bitter trouble;
It is no petty moral to preserve thy body's health.

Then, after prudent self-attentions, for the inner man and outer,

Regard the happiness of others, and so be happier thyself.
Have a merry word for every child, a gentle word for all dependents;
A frank word for every man, a courteous word for every woman.
Speak kindly to thy horse and dog, that serve thee well and love thee;
And bid the carman grease this wheel, or shift that galling buckle.
Spare the snail thy foot might crush, and save the drowning fly,
And shew the meanest thing alive that thou art like its God.
Drop a good word genially and shrewdly between contentious neighbours,
And, with discreet knight errantry, help and defend the right.
Crown every passing day with some good action daily,
And add to this the frequent prayer, unheard of all but Heaven,
And add to these the happy thoughts recorded on thy tablets,
And so redeem the time in little matters as in great.

For other smaller morals; pay quickly that thou owest;
The needy tradesman is made glad by such considerate haste.
Pay duly also those other petty debts, the letter, or the visit, or the gift;
It is always happiest to be just; and wiser so to rivet up young friendships.
For mirthful times, exaggeration is the soul of wit,
At others, speak plain truth; but blurt not out a secret.
From eye and ear and tongue and touch and thought reject all lewdness;
A poisonous double-savour will corrupt the sweetest spikenard.
Watch temper; evil temper is the commonest sin,
And many perish through that sin, unscathed by grosser crime:
Yet temper is in some a peevish habit of ill-health;
Let diet be its petty cure, as animal perverseness.
Trust men, and let them know it; they shall never cheat thee;
But if thou show suspicions, they will use thee as they can.
Be not eager for a bargain, mindful of its starving worker,—
O the feverish hands of want that wrought this rich brocade!
Smite not thy neighbour in the dark, nor stab him in the back;
Speak thine accusing openly, and hear ere thou condemn him.
Hide what is ugly and offensive, taught by the modesty of nature;
Conceal defects for charity; and cover up small faults.
Respect the religion of a man, whatever be his creed,—

Reverencing even superstition, if it seem both harmless and sincere.
Keep justice, keep generosity, yielding to neither singly;
And follow each good impulse, but with reason by its side.
Consider, the Christian is a Gentleman; and all that becometh
　　　gentle blood
Is thine of privilege and right, thine honourable vocation:
Thou shalt be delicate, and true, chivalrous, calm, courageous,
Exhaling a sweet perfume from the garden of thy graces,
That yieldeth fragrant flowers, rooted in the sturdy decalogue,
And veiling under beauty's mask the skeletons of life.

OF RHYME AND RHYTHM.

HEREIN is a deep mystery of Language, a mystery that none hath
　　　solved,
A mystery that few consider, and no book noteth down:
How came it that for fifty centuries, of reasonable Man upon this
　　　earth,
Speaking, singing, writing, full of love and music,
No one, till nine centuries ago, thought upon the melodies of rhyme,
No poet woke its echo, and no lover worked its charm?
How happened it that all the seers of old, psalmists and chief mu-
　　　sicians,
The lyrist with his amatory song, the bacchanal shouting Evoe,
Choruses pacing out their measures, in cadence with their words,
And all that either tragedy, or comedy, hath breathed in perfect
　　　rhythm,
Never,—but by scarce accident, utterly unnoticed and unfelt,—
Rose to the high harmony of rhyme, or fell into the pleasantries of
　　　jingle.
Go to Isaiah or to Job, to Moses Deborah or David,—
Search throughout Hesiod and Homer, Bion Theocritus and
　　　Moschus,
Ask of Pindar, Aristophanes, Æschylus, Sophocles, Euripedes,
Even of Anacreon and Sappho, Horace Ovid and Tibullus,
Virgil and Lucretius and Martial, Catullus Juvenal and Persius,
Is there one of them who guessed, what magic lingereth in Rhyme
Did any of those lyric chiefs dream of this new glory?

Think with what added sweetness, Horace might have wooed his
　　　Lydia,

Or Lesbia and her sparrow, have charmed us, in rhymed song;
With what electric force, Tyrtæus would have roused the phalanx,
And how the Dorian verses should have echoed in the hills,
How, pointed sharper by a rhyme, old Martial's epigrams had
    bitten,
How pastoral bucolic strains had sounded with sweet endings:
Verily, strange it seemeth, that with tongues so rich in similarities,
Where every tense, and case, and mood, is normally alike,
No one, through all ages, thought of the gamut of language,
But only rang the changes on its times and not its tones.
And stranger still it seemeth, that none have noted this strangeness,
That scholiasts, commentators, teachers, overlook it all;
I wot not where to seek, for one who saw this marvel,
Or told how wonderful it is, that rhyming is so new.

Consider; it would seem the very vice, of earliest savage tongues,
Nursery-chime of the childhood of the world, a jingling everywhere;
Their love-ditties and war songs, their feasts and hunts and dirges,
Should all be full of rhyming, from Jubal down to Merlin
And yet for nigh five thousand years, all poetry had flowed in
    rhythm,
And neither Warrior, Sage, nor Fool, had rhymed a hymn or song;
Their ears, exquisite for time, curiously lacked for melody;
Even their alliterative echoes led not on to rhymes;
The strophe and antistrophe, were measures, but not music,
And syllables were counted, but no man gauged a sound:
There was needed, through long ages, the prophet to arise,
Teaching the metrical ear musical melodies too.

So, with another sense, brightened by modern energies,
It is but recently that landscape hath seemed pleasant to the sight:
Lately as in our grandsire's day, none could appreciate the Alps,
A cultivated plain, was all they thought of praising;
The grandest sublimities of nature were but horrid in their eyes,
And none took note of scenery, nor cared to toil up mountains;
But the painter and the poet were at hand, pouring their eloquent
    preachings,
And scales fell off men's eyes, and the glacier and the precipice are
    glorified.

Even thus it fared with poetry; until nine centuries ago,

And after well nigh fifty had heard the speech of men,
The world awaited a discoverer, who found the trick of rhyme,
And charmed at once its listening ears, by sweet expected echoes.
Haply he came from the uttermost East, beyond the shores of Ind,
From the far land of Sinim, or more remote Japan;
And wandering minstrels caught the strain, and wise monks heard it gladly,
And chaunted hymns and songs apace, in rough and cheery rhyme;
And soon the sweet infection spread over every land,
Charming the Northmen and the Celts, enlisting troubadours and trouveres,
None asking whence it sprang, while all enjoyed its pleasure,
And no man known as the inventor, of what so many used.
Only, in their Hädes far away, were those ancient poets stirred,
Finding that even Masters may have somewhat left to learn;
That even their sweet harps had lacked this newest string;
That even choicest rhythm might be bettered by a rhyme.

OF ZOILISM.

To pass just judgment on a good man's book, to gauge its author's mind,
To print and scatter through the world thy verdict on his works,
This is an honourable trust, a matter responsible and anxious,
Demanding knowledge, patience, care, with special kindness and acuteness:
Haply the work upon thy desk is the ripened labour of a lifetime,
Years of thought, research, and prayer, condensed within that book
Happiness, fame, and fortune, hang on its success,
It may be also livelihood, children's bread, and honour;
While the heart of a mother or a wife, and not alone its author's,
Will be pained or gladdened by the judgment, passed upon the one they love:
Yet, to this great result, this toilsome long achievement,
Some self-elected censor giveth one dyspeptic hour;
Cursorily scanning it in haste, he decideth with superficial carelessness;
And that despotic sentence shall be multiplied to the ends of the earth.
Even if no lower motives enter, no envious hatred of success,

In that same field where he hath failed, and will not brook a rival;
Even if no spirit of slander provoketh him to harm good fame;
If there be no lust of mischief in a man, anonymous and cowardly;
Even if the shibboleth of party commandeth neither praise nor blame;
If no book merchant interests affect antagonist Sosii,
Still, there is indomitable hurry; no time for honest judgment;
So many volumes to be scanned, and all before to-morrow:
Grant what honesty thou wilt, still, overworked and fevered,
The critic is but rarely fit to judge a true book truly.

So, cometh it to pass, that the world heedeth lightly of such teachers;
We hear their arbitrary dictates, but heed our own free thoughts:
In spite both of indolence and industry, men judge mainly for themselves,
And, lazy though they be, kick hard against the tyrants;
They read and like and buy, following their own opinions,
And take small count of critics, howsoever such may dream:
The mighty We, yon nameless unit, how well scorned it is!
That undefined grand Name is nothing when we know it.
The wizard's wand is powerless; for this Prospero hath broken it himself,
He hath outraged truth and honour, therefore is his censure praise:
His spite is but a spur that quickeneth merit's paces;
His puffs may swell dull bubbles, but only till they burst;
The venom blast of envy, that hateth young success,
Is but as a tonic in the air, bracing and fixing popularity;
Even the should-be Marsyas, as flayed by his malignant censors,
Stolidly rhinoceros-hided, scorneth all their scalpels.

No man dreadeth Zoilus, no woman courteth Aristarchus;
No Keats again shall die of such; no Shelley pale before them:
Actors, unfaithful hypocrites, they overplay their parts;
Pens are poignards in their hands; an inkstand the fountain of detraction.
The critic, taking refuge in reviling, as an idler method than reviewing,
Filleth the public ear, for gain, with flashy slanders;
But the crowds that laugh and listen, while they like such humours,
Only despise that cankerous tongue, and take the victim's part:

Critics have diligently managed, by dint of long ill-doing,
To have lost all credit and esteem, and have flung the world away;
It was not easy with their powers, save for the corruption of their morals;
Men were content to follow them, but not through shame and mud;
Smothered in his own ink, stabbed by his own steel pen
Snared in his special gin, tangled in his proper meshes,
And fallen into the pit that he had digged for other,—
Zoilus is socially quenched, and the libeller is libelled by his mates;
The malice of his strictures is as viper's-fat for cure,
His judgment hath no weight, his slanders glorify their victim,
He dare not avow among his fellows he hath written such and such,
Treacherously wounding in the dark, he liveth yet in terror of discovery,
And where he stabbed he stabbed in vain, only to blunt his dagger.

A fool can ask questions, that shall puzzle the sage to answer,
And feeble wits write forcibly, offhand, on wisdom's works.
Thersites, bitter hunchback,—with Zoilus well clubbed and Aristarchus,—
Is sworn to quench all Nestors, and to laugh Elishas down;
These have taught the people, these have earned good fame,—
Therefore ignorance and envy league in lies to harm them.
And, if a man hath written books, this (in attempt) is easy;
Forthwith, he, and they, are jointly fixed for targets:
Mingling the writer with his work, infirmities can load the scale,—
He may be old, weak dotard! or he may be young, pert boy!
Even if halt or blind, your modern critic spareth not for these,—
Go up, go up, thou bald head! the blind, to be leader of the blind!
Or thou canst sneer at his moralities, severely pure thyself,
Haply, he is not sworn a Rechabite; possibly hath debts and troubles;
Or, it may be that, heretofore, he hath said or done some folly,
Or prodigal sons, or a vixen wife, may blow upon his credit;
Grand old **Sophocles** may be slandered through his children,
Xantippe be alleged a shame to Socrates,
And Job be charged with his afflictions, if he chance to have written a book.

Let all such count against your author, helping to damn his volume,
What merit should there be in this, if such dark stains in him?

Yet fruits are for judgment by themselves, in spite of the condition
 of the trees ;
A crystal's angles are its own, wherever be the mountain cavern ;
And a book hath a separate being, purely irrespective of its author,
Albeit our interests are heightened, if it honestly reflect the man.
The just critic should gauge each work, by its innate special quali-
 ties,
Unprejudiced by accidents, that hang about the worker ;
But our unjust judges in literature hunt down men, not books,
Filled with bitter personality, sarcastic and foulspoken.

How shall ignorance contrive to show like learning's self,
When some unscrupulous reviewer sitteth down to judge his
 master?
That book is doomed to be condemned ; the critic must not read it ;
Some awkward beauties in the thing might tamper with his verdict :
So, it shall be handed to a clerk, to note its worst and weakest,
And tear out pages, rich in faults, and every best omitted ;
Happy if some chance misprint destroy grammatical concord,
Happy if a word be found misquoted, or some fact ill dated.
Then for a diligent half hour to con some cognate treatise,
Some digest of his victim's theme, but on the opposite tack :
Dipping from book to book, well indexed and well noted,
He mastereth a few strange terms in the science off-hand to be
 discussed,
Glanceth at the disputable spots, held to be his author's crotchets,
And thus is ready for the onslaught, a cavalier of points.
Then, with supercilious ease, great in stolen knowledge,
Glibly shall he pen his essay on our author's theme ;
Dropping down grandly from on high, as a vulture swoopeth upon
 carrion,
He pounceth at the petty faults discovered by his clerk,
Propoundeth that antagonistic view as the sole one a sane man
 can adopt,
And bringeth that false date in proof, that all the rest is worthless !
It is wonderful how small and mean, beside this omniscient re-
 viewer,
Is seen the wretched author, though a master in his craft :
It is marvellous with what contempt, what vast array of learning,
Sanchoniathon, Manetho, and Berosus, freely quoting all,
Our critic,—stripling from the schools, or starveling at the bar,—

Goadeth his helpless prey, that old beleaguered pundit,
A swordfish pricking at a whale, with never a voice to tell
How full he is of oil, for a million midnight lamps:
Lastly, to finish with a flourish, and prove superior lore,
To catch the people's wonder, and show the judge's wisdom,
Let him touch by innocent accident, upon the curious fact
That Sanscrit was our passion when a boy, as is now the arrow-
  headed character!
Hints of such high scope exalt the critic's chair,
And help to crush the caitiff whom his judge is to condemn.

There is rubbish printed by the ton, that ought to be well censured;
But this is always praised, for merchandize of books:
Novels, mere insects of an hour, are prophesied undoubted immor-
  tality
And float their bubble life upon the well-paid puffs of fame;
And it is betimes a wisdom, when praise is found effete,
To keep the shuttles up by battledores of censure;
Even actions, as for libel, have renovated tales of scandal,
Ostensibly for morals, but to make the public buy
Sometimes, praise is very prodigal; this author is a noble;
Or—so ignoble as to be her critic's paramour;
Or—a writer with a following, some partizan of Church or State;
Or—his publisher is potent, canvassed by the press for favours:
So, the censor is to praise; let him read that book with diligence,
And note with seeming ecstacies its poor and trivial best;
Happy is it for his honesty, if he find therein aught worthy of
  applause,
But either way, through good and ill, this hireling slave applaudeth.
O the multitude of witlings, partially belauded for their hour,
Whom the world hath willingly let die, in spite of critic-friends;
O the galaxy of few great names, mocked by the starving Aristarchi,
Who long have known their scorn, to be herald of the whole earth's
  reverence!
Where is there a man that hath escaped, of all our best and wisest,
The false malignant judgment of the Critics in his time?
Every one hath stood as a Sebastian, naked, to be shot with ar-
  rows,
Each, like that sweet saint, achieving immortality of love.
What shall we say of yonder band, philosophers, bards, and sages,
All condemned and scorned at first by dull presumptuous censors?

Wordsworth, simple and sublime, how long they laughed at
    thee!
Coleridge, the gentle and profound, which of them did honour to
    thine eloquence?
Byron, answering scorn with scorn, well didst thou turn and rend
    them,—
And even Shakespeare, Newton, Pope, were scouted and defamed!

I have known yet baser motives affect our heralds of fame,
Soiling the **ermine, on the** bench, of those self-dubbed **judges** in
    literature.
Mercury, winged trumpeter, carrieth not **the purse in vain**;
Æacus, Minos, Rhadamanthus, are bribeable alas! as Bacon.
A certain writer in The Tadmor forwarded a fulsome panegyric,
Professing boundless admiration for the works of a certain author;
His letter, frankly written, touched upon the penury at home,
And asked some score of pounds, a loan—no more—of honour:
That letter had **its** postscript; the seed would be surely seen well
    sown;
A hundredfold o. literary fame should fill the sower's bosom:
Was not this a critic in The Tadmor? Could he not control The
    Scribe?
Had he not a voice in The Musæum? Were they not all one
    brotherhood?
Well should the generous author, glorified throughout the press,
Be recompensed, as richly he deserved, by that grateful writer in
    The Tadmor!
The letter, flung aside with indignation, received not its answer as
    expected;
And straightway half the Arabs of the press defamed that unwise
    author:
Scribe and Tadmor and Musæum **are to** this day found his foes;
How priceless then must be the praise, of Scribe and Tadmor and
    Musæum!

Yet there is an honest phalanx, gallant, honourable, capable,
Strong good hounds, and hunting fair, and of a generous stock.
These will not vilely dog the heels of merit lest it scape them;
These will not cut across the scent, as **lurchers** running foul;
Straight and staunch they follow, and, **if they** kill their fox,
They worry not the vermin, and he well deserved his end.

And there is a nobler band, high in power and conscience,
Who help the struggling genius, while still friendless and unknown
Whose frowns are only for the impious; whose wrath is reserved
    for the impure;
Whose ridicule may scathe conceit, but spareth even ignorance if
    modest;
Whose rich libations of praise are poured on worth and wisdom;
Whose verdict is an echo from High Heaven, of the Well done,
    faithful servant!

OF CREEDS.

A PURE life, a liberal mind, an honest and good heart,—
This is the threefold cord bent upon the anchor of religion;
If either of those strands be rotten, that bark is found in peril,
Nigh to be drifted on the reef, when as its hawser parteth:
Void of purity in morals, faith is but a hypocrite of words,
Charity cannot dwell with a mean and narrow spirit,
And there is but little hope, failing integrity of purpose;
Faith, hope, charity, the triple-twisted cable of religion.
In a mere creed there is no salvation, no happiness in articles or
    dogmas,
No real safety for the soul in the best cold code of forms;
Though thy theology be logical, and thy scheme most orthodox,
Though thy sect be of the straitest, thy chain from the fathers of
    the strongest,
These are none of them the comforters to bring a man peace at
    the last,
These are not the elements of heaven in the soul:
Holiness that hath no evil memories, kindliness loveable to all,
And cheerful trust toward God, will outweigh all the creeds.

Truth is as a sphere of crystal, so many-many-sided every way,
With all its microscopic angles polished down and blent,
That none can feel the corners, none perceive the bevils,
A globe of million facets, like an insect's eye:
And the longer a man liveth on the earth, growing wiser from
    experiences,
The nearer he attaineth to this smoothness, this absence of the
    sharp and rough.

He is tolerant, large, and genial, allowing differences readily,
And fitting every angled hole with simply-circled ease :
He knoweth that there always is an answer to be equitably heard
    and weighed,
Ever a view from the opposite point, another surface to the shield,
Prejudices, bents, and educationals, all to be righteously considered,
And strange epidemics for human minds, no less than for their bodies:
The Empire of the Moslem Wahabees abhor as foul abominations,
Not leprosy nor murder, but silken kerchiefs and tobacco ;
Swines' flesh, the Gentile farmer's glory, will be sin and shame to
    a Jew ;
Bulls' flesh defileth unto death the intellectual Brahmin ;
To be shaven is misfortune and disgrace to half the stately East ;
The manly beard, till yesterday, was ridicule to polished Europe ;
Eastwardly, a score of wives are credit, comfort, honour ;
Westwardly, suspicion of a second is misery, guilt, and ruin ;
One man sweareth by water, to cure him, nay to save him ;
Pulse and lentils with another are religion in his food ;
Ritual is all in all for this man, Spiritual all in all for that ;
Conscience is to one his law, authority to another ;
Here, faith is pinned upon a book, there all truth is in the teacher,
A third relieth on the office, a fourth hath assurance in himself ;
One man seeth in his priest, as if the God incarnate ;
Another claimeth for himself peculiar indwelling of the Spirit ;
With this mind all argument is closed, by the dictum of an ancient
    saint ;
With that mind light is to be found, only in a new apostle :
The Nazarite and Rechabite abjure that which maketh glad the
    heart of man ;
Garments of every shape are each held the livery for heaven ;
Ecstacies and phantasies of madmen are hailed by their elect as
    inspirations ;
And idiots among the Alps are counted for God's children by the
    Switzer.

And in such varying creeds there is ever some uniform good,
A portion we can well excuse, or partially commend :
Wise and true men will be found in each and every class,
All taking as it were their tints, from specialties in mind and body :
Therefore it is vain with those diversities, to hope for similarity of
    creed,

X

Though Chrysostom persuade, or Torquemada force it;
And tolerant wisdom is content, to suffer all phases of opinion,
For shrewd experience of men seeth infinite variety in character.

Yea; trumpet out what creed thou wilt, and that with Athanasian precision,
Be thy logic of the Trinity the strictest, thy learning in the fathers of the deepest,
Yet, if thy life be wicked, even Athanasius being judge,
Thou that doest evil, thy wages are the fires everlasting.
And, if in all good conscience, though warped by men and things,
Thou holdest some extraordinary creed, fanatical and foolish,
Yet, while thy life is righteous, the times of this ignorance are winked at,
Thou that workest good, thy heart and thy rest are with the blessed.
Belief is a deep strong root, and a true creed beareth fruits of life,
And a false creed, followed out in practice, yieldeth only poison-berries;
But the true creed solely in the head, and the false creed noways in the heart,
Maketh good neutral in the first, maketh evil neutral in the second.
Forms and liturgies and articles may screen Truth or display her,
They be helps and they be governments, measures sieves and gauges,
Finger-posts to show the way, and props to aid the weak;
For the outer Church is but a scaffolding to build up living stones,
The Heavenly Jerusalem is veiled, by no such human structure.
They that win many to happiness, be they priests or lay,
Such true preachers are to shine, as the stars for ever and ever:
The good priest here may have his specialties, but here too they shall cease;
Hereafter, equally with him, his flock are priests and kings:
Woe to him if he win not souls; glory to him if he win them;
But less to the priest than to the man, for his vocation is not carried thitherward.
Offices forms and creeds are nought, except as means to ends,
They all are things of earth, to perish in the using:
And be thy superstition what it may, if it tendeth to good works,
The love of God and man, with earnest prayer and penitence,
This is enough for happiness: as one of our own poets hath said,—
Let bigots fight for creeds, the good man hath the right one.

OF THE FUTURE OF ANIMALS.

There is needed a gospel for the brute, a preacher for the pariahs
of creation,
A voice to vindicate the justice, the wisdom, and the mercy of
their Maker;
His justice, ordering righteously; His wisdom, working not in
vain;
His mercy, loving all His works, from the highest even to the
humblest.
There is lacking, through the selfishness of man, who voteth himself the centre,
A word for the wide circumference, and the rays, and the tangents
of his circle:
He hath set himself up for judge, determining in his narrowness
That God made laws for him alone, and took no thought for oxen;
That He who pitied Nineveh, noways heedeth its much cattle,
And hath not heart, nor mind, nor will, to care alike for all things.
He forgetteth that there is a Spirit, equally in man and brute,
One tending upward if it may be, the other grovelling downward,
Like in kind, but differing in degree, as humbler souls and higher;
The brute limited both ways, for evil as for good.
For while man's loftier spirit can sink to uttermost depths,
The brute, if less capable of rising, also is less liable to fall;
Evil example in its master may vitiate his imitative dog,
Though this may be nurtured to be nobler than are many of the
tribes of man;
But in no case can it be so base, as the town-bred scoundrel of
society,
Nor change to so vile a savage as the Andaman or the Makariro:
With all, education will do much, and the company of worse or
better,
High instinct over-treading the heels of lowest reason;
Yet the dumb beast may not reach our human degradations,
Drunkenness, dishonesty, and cruelty, are not the brute's achievements:
Grant that it cannot worship God, it will idolize His image Man,
Even to dying of grief, even to self-sacrifice to save him;
Grant that it rise not to the Spiritual,—how few men rise to this!—
The dumb beast hath affections, loving and remembering, and
thinking;

It hath a sort of reason, and is not a mere machine ;
It showeth a kind of moral sense, more than the Bushman or Fuegian :
Unreckoning, it is generous and unselfish ; with a conscience both of evil and of good,
Sensitive to praise and blame, and full of shrewdness and attachment:
Nature standeth as its all in all for law, neither doth it sin against her ;
And the God of nature will in no wise destroy it for obedience.

We may but touch analogies ; we dare not clench this doctrine with a dogma ;
Our wisdom is to watch the hints, dropt incidentally by Scripture ;
Proof is noways possible, and difficult objections will abound,
Prejudice crushing reason, and novelty showing as a falsehood ;
And some may fancy that we claim an equal inheritance for all,
Forgetting grades of being, and infinite diversities of state ;
And other some will feel that for The Christ, to have ransomed man alone,
Is a selfish consolation to themselves, a closer and particular Redemption ;
While the more magnificent Salvation of all man's fallen world
In their view looketh little worthy, of a love more select than universal :
The idea of soul-saved brutes will shock conceited men ;
Catholic favour is an insult to elected and predestinated favourites.
Therefore frequent are the gainsayers, and few the generous advocates,
And much contention shall arise, for there be many adversaries :
Nevertheless I will be bold to claim for the meanest of creation
All its Creator's love, infinite eternal universal
God hath loved the world ; the Gospel is for every creature ;
The ransomed of the Lord shall return, and the wilderness shall blossom as the rose ;
The lion, with its ravenous nature changed, yet shall eat straw like the ox,
The wolf shall dwell with the lamb, and the leopard lie down with the kid ;
All sin and death and pain extinct, happiness and progress in communion

Shall lead each creature to its best, migrating toward perfection:
They shall not hurt nor destroy in all His holy mountain,
The denizens of Earth in her millennium shall find that happy
    future;
Not only men and women, but all the creation of God
Shall glorify His goodness, in their new-recovered Eden.

Man is not alone for love, for memory, shrewdness, honour,
Many of his lower servants shame their master here.
The soft domestic cat, affectionately purring,
That findeth home again from far, through some mysterious sense;
The kind-eyed noble-hearted dog, defending thee so bravely,
Forgiving oft and loving much, and ever full of gratitude;
The generous highbred horse, with his fine sensitive feelings,
Vicious against the foul-mouthed groom, but gentle toward his
    mistress,
The wise and wary elephant, the parrot, and the camel, and the
    reindeer,
And all our other humbler friends, our mute slaves and com-
    panions,—
These have climbed, through education, to higher grades of mind
Than whole savage families of men have won through countless
    ages;
These have not outraged the moralities, these have not stupified
    intelligence,
Like half our rustics, half our workmen, at some race or fair;
These show kinder evidence of soul, in conscience affection and
    devotion,
Than all the gypsies of our downs, the outcasts in our streets:
Look from the high-mettled racer, to the shrivelled mean blas-
    phemer on his back,—
Which of these should win an immortality? which of them hath
    earned annihilation?

True; the brute's limit now is earthward; but all have limits here,
All are cramped and prisoned in these charnel walls of sense;
Yet, wherefore should not brutes expand, as well as man hereafter?
Why not grow to some advancement, some perfection in their kind?
The life which God hath given, should His grace repent it,—
Unmaking creatures He hath made, as if His thought had failed?
All are wonderful and exquisite, miracles of varied excellence,

From nature's rational lord, to his least and lowest serf:
Why should a so-called instinct, the heaven-tutored mind of brutes,
Be clean wiped out for ever, as in blank annihilation,—
Nor rather still teach angels, **wondering** to **see** the spider spin,
Praising in brighter skies the jewelled bosom of the humming-bird,
Exhilarated even in their hymns by the skylark's whirl of song,
Delighted with **creature** comeliness, and yearning over animal
    affection?
It were a dull flat world, a creation of less interest than ours,
If indeed man's future home possess no lower inmates;
If there be no gradations, no humbler tribe than we,—
All of one royal race, earth-kings,—but with no subjects,—
Lacking this elaborated order, upholding and depending,
To prove the Maker's attributes and magnify His wisdom;
With no multitudinous links in nature's coat of chain
To show how strong she standeth, a panoplied Minerva;
Only one tame dead level, incomplicate and shorn of mysteries,
A world of one idea, and void of varied genius.
This is but a life of introductions, beginnings seeds and eggs,
All to fructify hereafter, germinating humbly here;
A drop-scene of foreshadowings, on passing clouds that vanish,
Photographs of circumstance and character, the substance whereof
    is yet to come.
Therefore it is wise and well to see new friends and places,
To gain, even at the end of life, elements of new knowledge,
Hereafter to be carried freely forward, that when we fail for time
Such seeming-mammon friends may receive us in eternal habitations:
Here we touch the clues that lead us on to ever-blooming gardens,
Here, mysterious truth, we plant our seeds of being.

Everything that hath been and that is, and all things that yet may
    have to be,
Here but in type and show, shall be reproduced in antitype here-
    after:
"Resurgam" is **the** solemn word inscribed on every fact,
The feeblest thing that ever was shall have its resurrection.
We gain part-alphabets of knowledge, in nature art and science,
Like children at their infant school, conning primer lessons;
But all, **that** here is so incipient, shall grow to its perfection;
No creature shall **be** wasted, or despised, or cast away.
Why should it **only** be for men, that mighty restoration?

Annihilation of His works were not The Maker's glory.
Man, his own historian, celebrateth only man,
Claiming redemption for himself, all else in condemnation;
The sinner alone, forsooth, the King is to be saved,
But the whole of his innocent serf-kingdom to be quenched and
    annulled for ever!

—Not so! all God's pensioners, animal, vegetal, mineral,
Every note that hath resounded on the timbrels of His Providence,
Every thought and deed, every passion and fancy,
Every idle word, and every sinful act,
Every **sparrow in its** fall, as every Christian in his death,
All shall live again, and have immortal sequence,—
The trail of each creature in its progress; for all things have their
    seeming souls,
Recorded at least on spirits' memories, if not themselves pure spirit.
He that believeth Resurrection must carry it out unto the end;
Nothing perisheth utterly, soul or mind or matter:
Nothing continueth in one stay, moving ever onward;
Progress is the common law, toward infinite good or evil.
The fashion of this world fadeth, but its recollections live for ever;
None may obliterate the thought, that once hath stood a thing:
And it is a weakness in the argument to claim immortality for man,
Refusing to all humbler life a future grade of being.
Creation is one whole, glorifying God throughout,
From suns to microscopic monads, all are linked together;
All, the archangel,—and the worm,—shall progress to perfection
    in their kind,
All shall praise the Maker in their season at their best.

Behold yon dying **saint, with** heaven shining on his face,
A merchant-prince in every sense, and rich for either world;
As he lieth dying, he calleth for his dear old dog,
Faithful companion of his walks, when he went about doing good;
And as, in love and grief, the poor dumb creature whining,
Licketh his wasted cheek, and the thin hand hanging by the bedside,
Hearken to this dreary lamentation:—Alas! my noble friend,
There is no future life for thee,—farewell for ever and ever!—
Did not the Christian in that word confirm the falsehood of the
    infidel,
The dark dread hope of wickedness, **his lie,** annihilation?

And shall we not judge that the poor Indian who looked for his
 faithful dog
Still to be found with him in bliss, on the happy shores of the
 departed,
Truly was wiser than the poet, whose rhyme hath immortalized
 that ignorance,
And, all untutored as he was, taught the philosopher a lesson?

Our spirits live and die not; our bodies live awhile and die,
Rising for reunion with those spirits, to live anew whole creatures:
Shall there be for such fair tabernacles, wherewith we shall soon
 be clothed-upon,
No hangings and no furnitures, no thrones nor harps nor crowns,
No palms, and no white raiment, no jewels, incense, flowers,
No birds nor butterflies nor crystals, no wonders and no beauties,
No better remembrancers of earth, our pilgrimage of trial,
No chariots and no horses, no friends of our old hearths?
Verily, beautified and glorified, all such shall live again;
The whole creation groaneth, travailing for that life:
Yet shall there be a Restitution, a resurrection real for all things,
Creatures, circumstances, pageants, deeds and words and thoughts;
All have been figured on the light, all are waved upon the air,
All have been fixed in unalterable fact, all were the beginnings of
 unendings.
Nothing can escape its future; for everything is a seed,
Germinating for the vast hereafter, and to flower in its season.
It is false and weak and foolish to confine the resurrection unto
 man,
A plot of human vanity, but not the plan of God:
Man is but one among the meshes, of the knitted raiment of needle-
 work,
Wherewith the King of kings is pleased to clothe Himself,
The one whole vesture of creation, woven from the top throughout,
Wherein His attributes are seen, braided in many patterns;
And if one loop thereof be dropt, a rent is made in glory,
The beautiful mosaic of His cosmos hath its pavement incomplete.
None of His works were lightly made, nor meant to be repented;
He is the Builder and the Maker, never designing a destruction.
That which is shall ever be, ripening to perfection in its kind,
Or haply, through mysteries of evil, rotting to corruption ever-
 lasting:

For, all that God hath made shall live in His own life,
Shall live according to its works, for glory or for shame,
Henceforth, if grace prevail, rejoicing in His mercy,
Henceforth, if evil overcome, contending with His justice!

Thou objectest, Life for any time is gain; and to brutes annihila-
    tion were no loss,
If it pleaseth the Great Architect of all to be wasteful of His **skill**:
Be that life ephemeral as a May-fly's, or a hundred years as of a
    raven,
Thou sayest, **it is the** creature's gain, and so its Maker's grace.
True, if that life be full of pleasure; but what if it be little **else**
    than pain?
Hath the creature then no controversy, with its Maker, being in-
    nocent?
And would the Great Just Judge wait for **some** eloquent advocate,
And **not** be Himself that counsel, arguing for justice to his prisoner?
If brutes have no hereafter, what an unequal lot
Between the pampered lapdog, and the starving hound,—
The flayed Abyssinian bull, moaning beside his banquetters,
And happy kine afield, lazily cropping in the sunshine.
With us, futurity will compensate, and Lazarus receive his mercies,
But wherein is there justice to the dogs who licked his **sores**?
Wherein, for the hideous live dissections, victims of a Spallanzani's
    scalpel?
Wherein, for the **maimed and tortured**, all cruelly entreated inno-
    cents,-
If He, who pleased to make them, made them only for their woes,
And, sinless as they stand, destined for **them** nought but suffer-
    ing?

If brutes have no hereafter, where are the accusers of the cruel,—
The gambler's screaming cock, live-roasted from the main;
The worn-out war-horse at his last, tormented day after day
By cold-blooded surgical fiends, agonising all its life-strings;
The starved, the skinned, the battered,—the bulldog maimed be-
    fore he fought,
Wretched victims of the vice, the hatefulness and sins of man?
Shall none of these arise to judgment? will **none bear** witness on
    the guilty?
Must cruelties to all beneath them be utterly excused to men?

If sheer annihilation be their fate,—what mattereth?—for there be
    no accusers ;
And so, the worst monsters of mankind unjustly miss their punish-
    ment :
But, great Justice liveth ; eternal Justice liveth !
Guilt shall not go scatheless, Innocence shall not be unavenged.

The whole creation groaneth, **travailing in pain** together,
Waiting till the sons of God, through Christ, are raised to glory :
And the creature was made subject unto death, not by its own de-
    fault,
But as following the fortunes of its lord, and subjected alike in
    hope :
For the creature itself shall be delivered, to the humblest, from
    the bondage of corruption ;
Into that liberty and glory, the children of God made free.

O all ye works of the Lord, bless ye the Lord,—praise Him and
    magnify Him for ever !
Men and things and elements, and beasts and feathered fowls !
Let none be missing from the feast for Earth and all her children ;
But let whatever hath had being, praise Him and magnify Him
    for ever !
He is not the God of the dead, nor hath made any covenant with
    destruction,
Nor worketh capriciously for time, but with solid resolution for
    eternity :
Life is His glory, and not death ; happiness and not annihilation ;
Complacent satisfaction in His creature, and no caprice or change.
It shineth out a good great truth, that the regeneration of the world
Through Christ's grand sacrifice for all, not only men but things,
Shall demonstrate the Maker's mercy, eternal, without stint,
To every creature of His skill, preserved in man's redemption.
Earth's thousand years of days of years, its manifold millennium,
Its Sabbath-life of holy-day, its holiday from sin,
Shall gladden all creation in our expanded globe
Grown to be a spiritual orb, lighter, brighter, vaster ;
Thus shall it be filled for evermore with its own regenerate creatures,
The home for all its pensioners that here received their life :
And so, dear Mother Earth, full of our childhood's memories,
Will then stand one of many stars whereto we men may speed

Freely at our innate power and will, coming and going everywhere,
As the angels of Jacob's ladder, linking world with world,
No longer chained to one by grovelling gravitation,
But in a spiritual liberty made freemen of them all :
Yet, oftenest revisiting dear Earth, and lingering there among her creatures,
In her grand apotheosis for all Nature, not only men and women,
But humblest things as highest, insects beasts and fishes,
The briar and the rose, the lion and the ox, and trees and flowers of the field,
All, with evil flung aside, and death and sin forgotten,
Praising the Lord who made them and magnifying Him for ever !

OF HAPPINESS TOGETHER OR ALONE.

In Paradise before the fall God instituted marriage,
And Jesus first wrought miracle to bless a wedding feast.
With God Himself in Eden for His young unguilty creatures
Verily, like all things else, was wedlock very good,
And, if once more the Present God work signs and wonders for it,
Again it must be very good, as nothing else on earth
But, woe for fallen mortals ! their best estate is banned,
Though flatteries and falsehoods are in league to hail it blessed ;
And youth is ever full of hope, but age hath left off hoping ;
While truths are told by neither, as enjoined from social fraud :
Romance falsifieth one view, conventional morality the other,
And gallantries and compliments combine to hide stern facts.

But,—so many miserable mistakes, and all without a cure !
The wrong sort idly won, the right sort left unwooed ;
That fatal vow once taken, thenceforward hope is over ;
Mated opposites contend, unmated concords pine.
So often total wreck, with no space given for repentance,
Mezentian marriage chaining fast the living to the dead,
Hot-hearted youth with frozen age, or purity with baseness,
And so to dwell together, as a pair, through love or hate :
Alas ! for it is but a single chance, once thrown for first and last,
The gambler's desperate only cast, though flung away so lightly ;
A cruelty on raw rash youth, hedged round with gay deceptions,

The cards are packed, the dice are weighted,—what chance of any
 escape?
So without cure and without end that lot is cast for life
Which many know for misery, and none acknowledge perfect.
Mutual hate should stand enough for absolute release,
Or noted wrongs on either side, with equitable adjustments:
A bond with no redemption clauses is not just to man,
In spite of all that Church can preach, or State enact to force it.
Crime, insanity, sterility, these should break the bands;
And distortions of the spirit, as of body, sin against first principles
 in marriage.

O differences wide and deep, O contrasts infinitely varied
Between those twain extremes, the happy and the miserable mar-
 riage!
Charity faith and hope, purity economy religion,
These be the six Isaiah-wings to fledge that angel-home
Where Love is found an inmate still with Hymen growing old,
And two consenting creatures are as one for soul and body:
But for their frequent harder fate whose wedlock is a chain
Only to gall and shame and fret, and not that band of roses,
Enmity extravagance contempt, wrath strife envy opposition,
These be the seven devils possessing that hot hearth.

Ye many wicked wives, whose tempers blast your homes
From nurseries for good to breeding-schools for evil,
Woe for the misery and crime an aggravating tongue can cause,
Woe for the comfort and content destroyed by your bitter provoca-
 tions,
Alas! how hard for the artizan, returned at even from his labour.
Weary of body and ill at ease in mind, and only craving rest,
To be driven from his threshold by contentions, worried at each
 humble meal,
And cheated of his needful sleep by wedlock's clamouring tongue,
Haply edged with jealousies, or petty spites and irritations,
Now kith and kin maligned, and now some best friend slandered:
And so his home is blighted; he must court peace elsewhere,
Close-shielded against clamour in a rancorous reserve:
And children watch and wonder, taking warning from their parents,
No refuge for the best but prayer, nor for the worst but flight;
The sons rebellious and selfwilled, as that usurping wife,

The daughters, like her husband, sadly beaten down to silence.
O bitter lie of law, O falsest dogma of society,
That woman is controlled by man, and subject to his will:
Custom maketh Vashti stronger than her lord;
His hands are bound, his mouth is stopped; how can he force
    obedience?

And you, O many vicious husbands, hypocrites in much sin,
With whom the haply kinder wives are patient in your homesteads,
Ye drunken and low revellers,—or you of higher grade
Still profligate, though elders, and still shameless as in youth,
Alas, how hard for women to be mated with such men,
What martyrdom for gentle wives once married to such husbands!
Would that there could be just exchanges, the good to be consorted
    with the good,
The wicked shackled to the wicked, as both shall be hereafter;
Would that some general gaol-delivery were given to the galley-
    slaves of marriage,
Some amnesty for innocents who writhe beneath its yoke,
Some second chance to cure the one great error made in life,
Some nobler choice whereby the future should redeem the past!

—Yet are there brighter phases; that eclipse is not for all;
Some happy pairs go hand in hand along the vale of life,
And see their children's children, and are blessed in old age,
And only find in wedded love the avenue to heaven.
And for the common sort, content, dull feeling, custom,
Give average men their average peace, and such are counted happy;
But, sorrowful truth to say, the griefs no laws can cure
Grow rankly in that search in vain for happiness together.

Then, what of single life,—so often guilty freedom,—
Doth it secure an average share of blessedness to man?
Our half sphere of the West, fast bound to stringent marriage,
Is peopling fast with more unmated than are mated pairs:
Are these happier in their lot?—Many doubtless must be,
Full of charities and faith, sensible and contented:
So they live beloved, so they die bewailed,
And their works do follow those good sisters and good brothers
But for the multitude whose hope is selfish worldly happiness,
Such fare not better singly, than those who missed it doubly.

How many unwritten tragedies are round us everywhere,—
What broken hearts, and starving souls, and unrecorded sorrows!
Little thou wottest **of** the trials that have made **these** what they
 are,
With disappointment and delay for daily **meat** and drink.
Behold some desolate old man, whose life is drained of love,
No one nigh to **care for him, and** none that he can care for;
He, for all his hardness now, **was** full of soft affections,
Until bereavement tore away the best half of his heart;
There was guiltiness in too much grief; but **of thy** charity consider
How fond a lover once was yonder crabbed **harsh old** man.
And lo, this withered sister, with her youth and beauty gone,
Who gave away her heart,—but vainly,—long long years ago;
What? wilt **thou** taunt her with a jibe, or mock her by hard names,
Where all thy sympathies should yearn on one of love's **true**
 martyrs?
Canst thou **not guess how full of grief those long** years must have
 passed,
Which dried away from woman's heart the lover wife and mother?
Shall nature's wounds be healed, **or her quick** feelings seared
Without a thousand secret pangs **and exquisite** regrets?
Hath it been no heart-ordeal, **to have** watched the bloom of beauty
Faded from the unflattering glass, **as** middle age crept on,
And still no lover at her feet,—though she hath loved so fondly,—
No intimate to share and charm life's solitude away?
How loosely common friendships fill that hollow of **the heart,—**
How coldly can the warmest compare with love and marriage!
And in the coming day of sickness, the hour of inevitable death,
To be lonely, husbandless and childless, unloved, unmissed, uncared
 for,—
Who **will not** pity, will not love, that solitary soul,
With all its yearnings bruised, its milk of kindness soured?
There be vanities, there **be follies;** and much waste and wear of
 good;
Fancies overclouding life, and darkening half its sunshine:
Often thus hath generous youth, aflame with early passion,
Cruelly **cheated** of his idol, been withered to that desolate old age;
Often the fair young maid, who set her first fond love
On yon insensate soul, unconscious or unworthy,
Hath changed to be soured from her sweetness, by living all alone,
And come to be the wreck of love thou hast not seldom seen.

And what then is the moral of it all? why these bitter words,
Where most are found to say smooth things and prophesy deceits?
—Because of those deceptions, those flatteries and false speeches,
Because the truth is rarely told, and never laid to heart,
Because for human life the Preacher's text is Vanity,
And no one would be envied if his whole estate were known.

Saving for that trinity of good, religion, health, and diligence,
Wherewith in wedded state or single, none can live unhappy,
All conditions of man's life, balanced on an equal scale,
Are—some few pleasures, many pains, and much of care and vanity.

A NATIONAL HYMN FOR HARVEST.

I.

O BLESS the God of harvest, praise Him through the land,
Thank Him for His precious gifts, His help, and liberal love;
Praise Him for the fields that have rendered up their riches,
And, drest in sunny stubbles, take their Sabbath after toil;
Praise Him for the close-shorn plains, and uplands lying bare,
And meadows, where the sweet-breathed hay was stacked in early
    summer;
Praise Him for the wheat-sheaves, gathered safely into barn,
And scattering now their golden drops beneath the sounding flail;
Praise Him for the barley-mow, a little hill of sweetness,
Praise Him for the clustering hop, to add its fragrant bitter;
Praise Him for the wholesome root, that fattened in the furrow;
Praise Him for the mellow fruits, that bend the groaning bough:
For blessings on thy basket, and for blessings on thy store,
For skill and labour prospered well by gracious suns and showers,
For mercies on the home, and for comforts on the hearth,
O happy heart of this broad land, praise the God of harvest!

II.

All ye that have no tongue to praise, we will praise Him for you,
And offer on our kindling souls the tribute of your thanks:
Trees and shrubs, and the multitude of herbs, gladdening the eyes
    with verdure,
For all your leaves and flowers and fruits we praise the God of
    harvest!

Birds, and beetles in the dust, and insects flitting on the air,
And ye that swim the waters in your scaly coats of mail,
And steers, resting after labour, and timorous flocks afold,
And generous horses, yoked in teams to draw the creaking wains,
For all your lives, and every pleasure solacing that lot,
Your sleep, and food, and animal peace, we praise the God of harvest!

III.

And ye, O some who never prayed, and therefore cannot praise;
Poor darkling sons of care and toil and unillumined night,
Who rose betimes, but did not ask a blessing on your work,
Who lay down late, but rendered no thank-offering for that blessing
Which all unsought He sent, and all unknown ye gathered,—
Alas! for you and in your stead, we praise the God of harvest!

IV.

O ye famine-stricken glens, whose children shrieked for bread,
And noisome alleys of the town, where fever fed on hunger,
O ye children of despair, bitterly bewailing Erin,
Come and join my cheerful praise, for God hath answered prayer:
Praise Him for the better hopes, and signs of better times,
Unity gratitude contentment, industry peace and plenty;
Bless Him that His chastening rod is now the sceptre of forgiveness,
And in your joy remember well to praise the God of harvest!

V.

Come, gladly come along with me, and swell this grateful song,
Ye nobler hearts, old England's own, her children of the soil:
All ye that sowed the seed in faith, with those who reaped in joy,
And he that drove the plough afield, with all the scattered gleaners,
And maids who milk the lowing kine, and boys that tend the sheep,
And men that load the sluggish wain, or neatly thatch the rick,—
Shout and sing for happiness of heart, nor stint your thrilling cheers,
But make the merry farmer's hall resound with glad rejoicings,
And let him spread the hearty feast for joy at harvest home,
And join this cheerful song of praise,—to bless the God of harvest!

A NATIONAL DIRGE IN TROUBLE.

I.

We have sinned, we have sinned with our fathers—O Judge and
    Saviour! we have sinned;
We had forgotten our God, and His judgments lie heavily upon us:
We went aside and did great wickedness, we have transgressed
    His commandments,
There is no health in our bones, we are punished according to our
    sins:
Yet would we return to Thee O Lord, acknowledging the guilt of
    our iniquities,
And flinging off the burden of it all, if haply Thou wilt bless us
    with repentance:
Hear us, O Merciful and Mighty, hear and forgive us in Thy pity,
Help Thy people, O Lord, for the sake of our Redeemer Thine
    anointed.

II.

Alas! for our transgressions have been multiplied, and therefore
    Thine anger is upon us;
Through grace we would confess them, in sure hope of Thy forgiveness:
Our cities are foul with sin, evil goeth shameless in our streets,
Our lanes have lost their innocence, our fields are full of violence;
The strong oppress the weak, and the weak defraud the strong,
And all alike forget their Maker and Preserver;
Blasphemy shouteth in the mine, cruelty smiteth on the highway,
Meanness cheateth at the workshop, tyranny tormenteth in the
    factory:
Our rich have rioted in luxury, feasting themselves without fear,
Our poor in bitterness and hate rebel against their poverty;
Our prophets have taught lies, our lawgivers thrive upon corruption,
Our rulers have not ruled in righteousness, nor the people been
    obedient in godliness,
Rights are humbled to the dust, while wrongs are throned upon
    high places,
Good hath perished from among us, and no man layeth it to heart.

v

III.

Therefore the wrath of the Almighty is hot against His people,
Therefore He blesseth our enemies, and goeth not forth with our armies:
Therefore our flocks and herds have perished in their pastures by ten thousands,
Therefore pestilence and famine have heaped our thresholds with the dead;
Our harvests were not gathered, the elements fought against us;
Disease and want and misery are dwellers in our homes;
Our light is turned to darkness, our name is shamed among the nations,
The glory of Britannia is departed, the honour of old England is brought low.

IV.

Yet,—Holy Lord our God, arise! pity and forgive Thy people;
Put not away Thy mercies, for we will put aside our sins:
The hireling shall no longer be oppressed, the right of the poor shall be avenged,
Thy Sabbaths shall be sanctified, Thy tithes and offerings paid,
Thy temples shall be full of worshippers, Thy ministers be honoured through the land,
Our prayers and our alms shall go up, acceptably through Jesus unto Thee;
We will take no wicked thing in hand, our hearts shall be set against all evil,
Sin shall not revel in our streets, nor drunkenness pollute our villages;
We will return and repent, the Lord our God preventing us,
We will call Thee Our Father, and Thou shalt be gracious to Thy children:
Yea, consider our adversity, withhold not mercy from us;
Art Thou not our Father? Are we not Thy children?

V.

Yea; we will magnify Thy mercy, or ever we have risen from our knees,—
Thou dost forgive and love us, Thou yet wilt help and save us,—

The plague our iniquities deserved Thy pitifulness will scatter,
The flaming sword of punishment shall yet be sheathed in mercy :
Therefore unto Thee will we give thanks, even in this time of
  trouble ;
With humiliation on our heads, yet will we rejoice in our hearts :
Thou shalt go forth with our armies, Thy blessing shall shine **on**
  our homes,
Thou wilt give increase to our flocks, and fill our barns with harvest,
Thou shalt favour our England, the Zion of these latter days,
And keep her chief among the nations, as she ever was of old ;
For happy are the people, even in the midst of sore distresses,
Who turn to **the** Lord their Maker, and trust in Him for mercy
  and deliverance !

A NATIONAL PSALM OF VICTORY.

I.

BLESSED be the God of our Israel, praised **be the Lord** of our Zion,
Jehovah hath gone forth with our hosts, and hath given to us vic-
  tory in the battle !
He is our helper and defender, the rock of our strength and our
  fortress,
He hath delivered us in trouble, and saved us from the wrath of
  our enemies ;
By Him have we overcome the proud, by Him have we escaped
  the terrible,
He sent forth His arrows and scattered them, He shot out His
  lightnings and destroyed them ;
He gave us **the shield** of His salvation, and armed us with the
  spear of victory,
He girded us with valour for the fight, and subdued the mighty
  under us ;
We will **thank Him** among the nations, His name will we exalt
  among the heathen,
Blessed be the God of our Israel, praised be the Lord of our **Zion** !

II.

Awake, awake, utter a song ; for God is our sword and buckler ;
There were thunders from the Lord out of heaven, hailstones and
  coals of fire ;

Then did the standard-bearers faint, then were the horsehoofs broken,
There brake He the arrow and bow, and burned their chariots in the fire:
He breathed on them and they were consumed, He poured on them the blast of His displeasure,
He brought down their honour to the dust, and made them flee before us:
Who is God, except the Lord? Who hath any strength but our God?
Great deliverance hath He given, and shown great mercy to His people;
He alone is to be praised, and unto Him will we pour thank-offerings,—
Blessed be the Rock of our strength, let the God of our salvation be exalted!

III.

Praise ye the Lord for avenging our Israel, all ye sons of war,
Praise Him, all ye sons of peace, who offered yourselves so willingly;
Praise Him, nobles of the land, with peace restored to your possessions;
Praise Him, all ye people, with plenty returning to your homes:
And thou, chief Mother in Israel, give thanks among thy children,
That wars have ceased in all the earth, and those who delight in them are scattered;
Give thanks that the right is set on high, give thanks that the wrong is trodden down,
That the teeth of the ungodly have been broken, and the faces of the righteous been made glad;
That England, the Israel of God, is head and chief among the Gentiles,
Rejoice, O Queen and people, and magnify the Rock of our salvation.

IV.

And ye, O many sorrowing widows, O thousands of bereaved mothers,
O fathers mourning for your sons, O friends bewailing friends,

In the midst of your earthly desolation, remember ye how honour-
    ably they died,
As duty bade and noble thoughts and country's love and heaven:
Give thanks, for your dear ones are victorious, victorious for either
    world,
With names of glory here, and crowns of immortality hereafter;
Give thanks in hope and faith, in charity, strength and patience,
And add your wailing minor to our swelling psalm of praise;
May all help freely for your needs, pour balm upon your sorrows,
And make you rich in sympathies, and alms and pensioned praise.

v.

And, O thou Zoar of the plains, O thou Goshen in this Egypt,
Island city of refuge for the nations of the Earth,
England, happy shore, hill where the true light shineth,
Home of real religion, freedom, tolerance, and truth,
Rejoice and shout the hymn of praise through all the countries
    round,
From sea to sea, from land to land, where'er thy flag is flying,
Let cannon roar thy thankfulness, and bells clang out thy joy,
And prayer and praise and alms go up as incense to High Heaven;
For God hath blest us every way, at home, by sea, by land,
And we will thank Him evermore, in prayers and alms and praises.

THE SEVEN SAYINGS.

SEVEN tones in music, seven shades in light,
Seven deadly sins, and seven cardinal virtues,
Seven angels, seven trumpets, seven seals and vials,
Seven thunders, seven plagues, seven spirits of God,
Seven stars and seven churches, seven days and nights,
And seven thousand years for earth, and man with seven ages,
And seven sages of old Greece, with seven famous proverbs,
And seven words of mercy dropped by Christ upon His cross.
Keen is the worldly wisdom in those maxims of the sages,
And deep the spiritual love in Jesu's seven sayings;
Awhile then, friend, aside with me, to step within the Porch,
And after, linger near that Cross for comfort and for counsel,

First, with Athenian Solon, "Know thyself," O man!
A humbling lesson and a strange, an thou learn it truly;
Pass by the secrets of creation, till thou hast mastered this,
And heed thy good and evil, thy powers and thy duties:
Next, with the Spartan Chilo,—whose full heart burst for joy
When his good son had triumphed in the great Olympian games,—
"Look to the end of life," an end, worth all its midway running,
So thou be crowned like that good son, a conqueror in the race:
Watch well with Lesbian Pittacus, who flung his net so shrewdly,
To "Seize occasion" ere it pass, and so thy chance be gone;
Occasion for thy tongue to speak, as for thy hand to strike,
Occasion to thy neighbours' help, and in thine own behalf;
Let frank and honest Bias tell out bluntly sad experience,
"The most of men are evil,"—none are righteous—no, not one;
Ambracian Periander sayeth, "Industry is all,"
That diligence must win each prize, and conquer every foe;
The graceful Cleobulus prayed well for moderation,
Nothing too much, "The mean is best," the happy golden mean;
And cautious Thales filled the sum, with "Haste if thou wouldst fail;"
For well he knew that evil haste could never make good speed:
So, this was the best flowering of the wisdom of the wise,
They served their generation well, those seven Grecian sages.

Now, let us stand on Calvary beside that sorrowing Mother,
And listen to these nobler seven utterances of Jesus.
It was the sixth hour, yet blackness hung over all the land,
Nature put on mourning for her King, and the eye of day was darkened;
And there upon that bitter Cross the Sacrifice is nailed,
Heavily hanging in weakness, racked and torn and bleeding;
For three long hours hath He hung, agonized in soul and body,
That blessed Christ, embracing all the world with out-stretched arms,
Lifted between earth and heaven, as if outcast from them both,
But drawing all men unto him, in love and adoration.
There, without one moan, one murmur, grandly patient,
The Lamb endured the uttermost wrath of God against all sin,
And ever as the weary hours dragged on in ceaseless torture,
At seven throes of pain He dropped His seven precious sayings.

First, when they reared Him on the nails, and racked Him in the
    raising,
How did He greet their cruelty, how requite His murderers?
His thought was infinite compassion, to put away the greatness of
    their sin,
"Father, forgive them, Our Father! for they know not what they
    do."
Lo, what a triumph over self, what a conquering of agony and
    vengeance,
How worthy of the suffering Man in whom the Godhead dwelt!
Ay, and that prayer was answered,—The Father did forgive;
Those who nailed Him to the cross were martyred for the Christ;
So for all time He teacheth us, to forgive as we hope to be for-
    given,
Evermore He preacheth intercession, even for the cruellest of foes.

Beside Him hung on either hand that pair of common thieves,
For ever famous as His comrades in that darkest hour.
And as the one contendeth—Save thyself and us,
And as the other upbraideth,—Dost not thou fear God?
Hearken to the gracious word in answer to that prayer,
Remember me, O Lord, when Thou comest in Thy Kingdom,—
"To-day shalt thou be with me in the paradise of God!"
For in faith He asserted even then, in the lowest pit of all those
    depths,
His right to redeem and to reward, as the Judge while the Victim
    of Mankind.

The next "Ah why hast Thou forsaken me, why hast Thou for-
    saken me, my God?"
Our type for prayer in sorrow, when God seemeth so far off.
Yet, hath He forsaken His Anointed? Is He not with Him in
    trouble,
Though dwelling in the darkness, and with clouds around His
    throne?
The Sacrifice was heaped with sin, and judgment crushed its victim,
Therefore in momentary gloom God's eye was turned away:
But the great Antitype of David followed on that psalm,
And ended, ere its close, with praise for a ransomed universe.

And now, O weeping mother, O sorrowing dear disciple,

Ye twain whom Jesus loved, and who loved Him to the end,
"Behold thy mother, O son, O son behold thy mother,"—
The richest of bequests to both, that dying Friend could leave.
In deep considerate carefulness and self-forgetting grace
He taught us kindly to provide for those we leave behind.
This world is bleak for them, though stars be opening bright for us;
Let no man's pious hope elsewhere ignore their state on earth:
Here is this fourth word's lesson, remember thine own kindred,
And in the very throes of death, be generous and be just.

Then, did He gasp, "I thirst:" He willed fulfilment of the
    Scripture,
Humbled down to human wants, parched in the dust of death:
As with the woman of Samaria, when he fainted in the tropical
    mid-day,
Here His tongue was cleaving, dry to the roof of His mouth,—
Therefore gasped He in His agony,—and Heaven heard The Maker
Asking for a drop of water, sent to cool his tongue!
And the tender mercies of the cruel have their potion ready,
Wine and myrrh to deaden pain, and so prolong panged life;
But He will not drink an anodyne; and so, I thirst, I thirst,
Went up as a holy aspiration, conquering the weakness of the flesh:
I thirst to do Thy will; I thirst to win for them salvation;
I thirst,—my soul is athirst to save the world for God!

Next, as a Son with His own Father, commendeth He His human
    spirit
Manfully and faithfully to God,—yea, "into Thine own hands."
Lo, what a pattern unto us, going down into that dark valley—
Lo, what encouragement and comfort, in commending our own
    souls thitherward:
For He trusted His God and our God, His Father and our Father,
And by His great example we will bravely live or die.

Now lastly, note of triumph, like a blast upon the trumpet,
Exultingly with loud last voice, proclaimed He "It is finished!"
O word of deepest comfort to the doubting fearing soul,
O talisman of power to still the storm of conscience!
The happy angels on their harps rejoiced in It is finished,
And evil ones heard It is finished, echoed on their thunders:
It is finished; Justice hath been satisfied in full;

It is finished ; Heaven is free, and open to the lost ;
It is finished ; Death is dead, and Sin clean washed away,
The watchword of salvation was that seventh It is finished.

FINAL.

Who can hope for any ends, in this life-cycle of beginnings?
There is no end to mind or thoughts, or making many books.
Where is an end to arts, or sciences, or mysteries of nature,
And how should immortal spirits accomplish full development in
    time?
None can work perfection to the uttermost of his thought,
The painter, sculptor, author, have no truly finishing touches :
Nature is perfect but not Art ; in time we only can begin ;
Eternity must deal with ends, and close up all hereafter :
Yea, through the ages everlasting, we all shall live and grow,
For good or ill, for joy or woe, for endless shame or glory.

Again, I have written at my best, according to the mercies given
    me ;
And speak of deeper themes than some I touched in earlier days.
Hath thy dog a spirit? hath my soul its angel?
Is this world so very old? are all creeds mere outworks?
Is everything here but a beginning, whose end must rise again?
Is each circumstance a consequence, absolutely everywhere at all
    times?
Can some spirits come again, and haunt their earthly homes?
Are the stars those many mansions for the saints of God?
Is morality the end, and even the Gospel but a mean?
Shall not purity of heart be after all a necessary heaven?
Are all facts so probable, didst thou know their causes,
That one might haply prophesy the future from the past?
These be among my many speculations, these and scores beyond,
And some shall meet with scorn, and some with disputation.

And many themes beside must challenge special anger ;
Why turn and rend the jackals, like a leopard brought to bay?
Why hint that human life, its double state or single,
Is either way a failure, and not blessedness at all?
How durst he speak so boldly, and so savagely tell truths?

We hate a prosing Mentor in the gardens of Calypso:
Wherefore should he steal old texts from Deborah and Barak,
Presumptuously to lead the hymn of Britain in her victories?
Why for times of trouble pilfer, chiefly out of David,
Bald phrases fit for Hebrew timbrels, not for English choirs?
And so throughout, O foes,—why this, and why not that?
There is no end of questions,—which shall therefore have no
    answers.

And yet for you, O friends, with kinder eyes than others,
Whose generous love I cherish as a happier prize than fame,
My answers—are they needed?—may be read on these past pages,
With all their reasons writ out plain, in honest Roman hand;
Still, not all writ, but hinted; less is uttered than was thought;
My spirit going forth with yours in charity and frankness:
And courage hath its honour; and not to fear for fame,—
But, following conscience with high heart, serenely to forget it:
And so, farewell,—in brief, farewell; we part, but not for ever;
If not again to meet on earth, in some bright star hereafter.

Yea, for that the End is near at hand; the issue of that great
    experiment
Wherein, to the teaching of the universe, God hath tested man;
For the first time giving to the creature full freedom of the will,
That he might tempt, six thousand years, the patience of his
    Maker.
Now all the prophecies are closed; Now is the cycle finished;
The fields are white with harvest, and the world well-ripe for
    judgment;
Verily, the Christ is nigh to come; His chariot is made ready,
The sign of the Son of Man in heaven shall soon be seen,—His
    Cross upon the skies;
And then all enigmas shall be solved, true justice must be ren-
    dered,
The churches and the kingdoms and the antichrists, the saints, the
    world, the martyrs,
All shall be shown to have achieved the ends of their existence,
And Providence be proved throughout the sister-twin of Grace.

FOURTH AND FINAL SERIES.

OPENING.

A LATE last call among the mountains, echoed in the chambers of
    my heart,
Wakeneth yet again its thoughtful mental inmate;
A lingering questioner at Delphi, claiming his oracular response,
Urgeth my unwilling tongue to utterance once more:
Let then the hazelwand dip shrewdly, pointing at new veins of
    metal,
Or where the spade of diligence may tap some bubbling spring;
Let our baited handlines hang round these old rowlocks,
And tempt the shoals of fancy till some fish are pulled aboard:
Thus, many lifelong friends! shall I greet your love again,
Thus, my few brief foes! I meet your frowns unfearing;
The one sort eager for a word, spoken from heart to heart,—
The other,—let them rave, and sneer at shallow prophets!
These are the last perilous times, foretold for questioners and
    scoffers,—
But blest is he that hath not sat upon the scorner's chair;
And still another blessedness is linked with such reviling,
Where, borne with patience for His sake, their ill-report was false.

There be spurs and springs of various kind, inciting energy to
    action,
By pain or pleasure, as Good Providence may will, but either way
    combining to His ends:

The salmon, harried by its leech, runneth out of ocean up the
              rivers,
To rub and cleanse its silver scales, and drop its spawn on gravel;
Then, hunted from those shallows by some other insect plague,
Lank and spent down-speedeth to the sea, to salt its strength
              anew:
Even so energy with leisure, or need, or thirst for fame,
Provoketh still-reluctant souls to still-recurring effort.

Look at those barebacked racers, with their parasitic spurs,—
When Rome on her last Carnival-day filleth the round of folly;
They feel the pricking rowel, they run against their will,
The crowd is faced because they must, and not because they like
              it,
And so they dash in headlong flight adown the roaring Corso,
Suddenly flung upon their haunches, in terror of those tapestries
              ahead.
Thus ever some sharp craving, necessitous or yearnful,
Obligeth unto labour those who sought and sighed for rest:
Conscience hath its sting; we must speak out for honour;
The light and life within a man may not be quenched nor hid.
So then with all the truer scribes, not brain spinners for lucre
But those who empty out their hearts and minds because they
              must,
There always is a force within them spiriting the pen,
A cause and need-be for their works, in prose or rhyme or rhythm.

Freeborn instincts of religion, shrinking away from priestcraft,
Love of antiquarian lore, imaginative fancies,
Early scorn for meannesses hypocrisies and lies,
And buds of undeveloped thought and passion and affection,
These have been the keynotes of my spirit, giving out their tones
              in books,
With energetic conscience that never could keep silence.
I must tell out mine honest mind, nor meanly hush and gag it;
I must say all I have to say, and that in mine own way;
Alone, or in a crowd, with heedless independence
Still have I poured forth thoughts in words by rhythm or by
              rhyme,
Often on the shingled beach, or rambling in the woods,
Or keeping timely measure with the paces of my horse,

Often draining music from the silence of the night,
Or more contemplative in streets, and calm within their whirlpool.
And it hath somewhile come to pass, that men who fear for
    frankness
Self-conscious they have well-deserved some honest stern rebuke,
Have answered kindliness with scorn, and zeal for good with
    hatred,
Letting me lose, by that much gain, the censure of their praise.
What matter?—such may stand aside, to leave free way for others,
The gentler and more generous hearts, long loved by me of old;
And even should these fall away (for all things here are changing)
What matter? Life is full of common friends who come and go:
And a man that liveth in himself (with love for all outside him,
So those outside be worthy,) can live and love alone;
If outer worths be wanting, his love can shine within,—
But not on self,—that nobler sunshine beameth up to God.

OF THIS BOOK'S STORY.

He then who, forty years agone, took up this rhythmic strain,
And since hath freely poured his heartful over every land
In songs and sonnets, ballads, hymns, and lyrics and heroics,
In stories essays and translations, travel-tale, and plays,
Now will resume, for this last time, his first old style of Proverbs,
And then for ever lay aside the harp of Sirach's son.

In earliest youth, eight lustres back, my thoughts on Love and
    Marriage
Crystallized to proverb form, as ye may read them now:
And nine years after those young themes were written and
    forgotten
At once, upon an instant call, my first whole book flowed out,
Flowed out rapidly, as thoughts will flow, pent-in with long
    forbearance,
And writ on scraps, at idle times, within a dozen weeks:
Thereafter, at long interval, my second came as called,
One lustrum having sped away, and other works been printed;
It came as called, and suddenly, a cistern overflowing,
Gathered unconsciously five years, but poured out in two months,

With earliest rill, responsive, in the Chapter upon Gifts,
To greet with philosophic thanks a Giver and Receiver.

Then the full quarter of a century, with its thousand interests,
Passed away, carrying on its stream unnumbered Sibylline leaves:
In all those years, with all their changes, never by one word—
Nothing omitted, nothing added—were these two books altered;
Too well a world of friends in either hemisphere had liked them
For mere fastidious caprice to blot the lines they loved;
So, conscience witting no great faults beyond some smaller
    failings,
I would not change in hope of better what my kin thought good:
Thus the years sped by, cropped with innumerable writings,
Greeted alike with praise and blame, with ridicule and honour;
Till, at a call as theretofore, flowed forth my third among the
    series,
Rolling speedily along, and to outer seeming carelessly,
Thoughts flowing as a torrent, though not of torrent birth,
But long conceived through twenty years, and writ out seven
    times:
And now this voice among the mountains claimeth a concluding
    fourth,
Twin volumes having each two books, my full quadrupled harvest.
At each of these four seasons, an end was meant and planned,
And ravel-skeins were gathered-up in hope the web was finished;
And yet, till now when all is done, led onward, haply upward,
I guessed not that Pythagoras could praise my fourfold Work.

Neither is this last harvest other than more ripened fruit,
Not lees, nor idle dregs, but richer cream to close the milking;
Best wine cometh at the last; the king to end the pageant;
Studies thinkings and experiences converging in their climax.
Nought is heedlessly set down, but thoughtfully all and staidly,
Matured, considered, well-advised, nor lightly to be altered.
Truth is active and severe, not indolent or easy;
A bright and changeless jewel, not some tinsel soon to tarnish.
And there be diamonds still to find in the running hourglass of
    Time,
All the sand is not searched out, though keen have been the
    pickers:
It may be Boaz hath been thrifty, with no indulgent reapers,

For well nigh all words on all things have long been said and
 printed ;
But still our modern Ruths may pile their horns with gleaning,
And leave for others even then a gathering yet to clear.

They have grown in unpremeditated guise, these **weeds of** my
 mind's garden,
Were cut and stored at random, and uncarefully got in,
Gathered more as wood-wild-flowers, than reaped like well-farmed
 crops,
And garnered thus collectively, at speed with little labour.
Let truths be frankly spoken, whether critics blame or praise ;
These fallows of my brain are rank with thoughts uncultured ;
Self-sowing, after many days they yield a bounteous crop,
And ever grow spontaneously, of uninvited impulse,
Spontaneously, not idly, nor void of earnest purpose,
But still some testimony to give, some message to deliver.
In spirit this my book hath been the record of my life,
A photograph of thoughts and things for wellnigh forty years :
I painted often from the facts, in pictures of experience,
And every thought was measured, and its just expression weighed ;
I never forced Minerva's will, nor stole my thoughts from others,
Nor drained the palm-wine sap of books, nor strove to swell a
 volume ;
Rather, conscience cast aside what other minds could claim,
And still **condensed** ideas, despising **word-dilution.**
Only a tithe is stored, the nine parts lie **ungarnered** ;
Only the alphabet is **here of** works **half-schemed unwritten.**
Always thinking at a heat, as a Geyser bursting upward,
The spring was never dug, nor pumped when it ceased flowing ;
And though the rush seemed sudden, yet it had long lain hid
Collected inadvertently as in some mental cavern :
So then the critic is at fault, who judgeth that the poem must be
 careless,
Running clear and sharp a cast without the touch of file ;
Such is not a mushroom of the mind, but rather as its adamantine
 prism
Flowered from the everlasting rock through deep volcanic heat :
And he were still more utterly **at fault, in** fancying no file-labour ;
Years,—and years,—of studious toil are witnessed in this book :
Musing reverie by night, and day's fastidious care,

Have often slowlier crystallized my fancy's quick creations;
And doubtless old-conned knowledge, unconsciously and freely,
As drained from all around, is somewhile drawn from memory's
    well;
And lifelong diligence had heaped a cairn for ready using,
Whereby my castle grew apace with all materials near.
So then the lighter labour was but lighter for the time;
A juggler's instant skill hath been long years alearning;
And stanzas improvised prove but abundant culture,—
Arguing ingrained genius too, beyond some surface talent.
The highest art is hiding art, to seem spontaneous nature;
And even nature in some sort is seen the fruit of toil:
God rested from His labour,—our ensample for that day:
His Sabbath closed the week of work prepared through myriad
    æons.

And now my task is done, my better toil in life;
The lessons I was set to learn, and then was sent to teach.
Here is the statue of my mind, self-moulded carved and polished,
Some elemental clay and marble only not mine own;
Here is the picture of my heart, touch by touch self-painted,
Canvas alone and colours caught of Circumstance beyond:
Seeds of thought were dropt by books to germinate thereafter,
And tones of feeling learnt from all the melodies around;
We guess not whence nor when nor how we earn our mental
    gains;
Continuously through outer things the inner man is fashioned.

And let them carp at egotism: heart should speak to heart,
And plain self-consciousness work out his fancies and his feelings:
To guage thy brother by thyself can scarcely be found selfish,
Since, by the love we bear ourselves, we judge him thus in
    . charity:
And those who draw from their own wells are clear of stealing
    water;
Albeit the charge forsooth would then be filching others' wine:
So, let them rave of plagiarism: mind is helped by mind,
But each can mould and make his own what haply served his
    neighbour.
Dodsley, Bacon, Franklin, and the Commonwealth of Wits,
And dealers in dark sentences, and gatherers of proverbs,

Mine innocence hath afore been blamed for borrowing from the
    like,
When ignorance was nigher truth of aught that such had written.
I wot not, by intention, of a sentence or a fancy
Which any man can claim or prove not honestly mine own.
No doubt, the Hebrew Scriptures, graven deeply on my spirit,
Have filled it with their echoes and their rhythm and pith and
    strength;
No doubt, remembered thoughts and words of common education,
Rooted in the mind for years, may seem of its own growth;
No doubt, with keen and spiteful care some phrases might be
    found
That other men have uttered once, as others will again;
But none can touch a line or word deliberately stolen;
As none can find in any book a word not used elsewhere.

And let them sneer at commonplace, this dull old stilted style,—
Heavy, as full of weighty thoughts, too large for little minds:
A proverb is intense expression of condensed idea;
One pithy line more pregnant than many a windy volume.
Point is here, and polish, and various musical rhythm,
With concentrated fancies in exact and careful wording.
Not only by the trick of rhyme and mingling of sweet sounds,
Nor fixing in bright language volatile thoughts and feelings,
Not by the seeing eye alone, discerning hidden likeness,
Nor by the musing mind enriched with learned illustration,—
But by pure life, and life's best aim, is the true workman wit-
    nessed;
A poet hath abjured his calling, if no longer pure.
Hath any high-class sculptor ever glorified the lewd?
Did ever painter of great name descend to the obscene?
Even so, no true poet can outrage God and nature
Profanely and indecently, and be a poet still:
There are such fallen angels, lying with broken wings
And all those rainbow feathers singed by cruel fires of lust,
Who cannot rise themselves, nor have the power to raise us:
How should we rank these lost black stars with constellated
    poets?
A Siren-rhyme may charm, but its charming is for drowning;
Poetic vice is poisonous as a rotten-mouldered melon.
There be some seers,—and prophetesses,—in and out among us,

z

Who mingle Sappho with Petronius for their prose and verse,
Eager to fascinate the young, and heat the veins of age
By luscious pictures of sweet sin, or scenes of hideous crime,
And tangling-up their cotton yarns of ridicule and pathos
To stuff the world's long Midas-ears with slander and sensation:
They shall not live, they cannot last; they perish in the using;
Like medlar-fruits that eat unflavorous if not rotten ripe:
Book-bubbles of a minute! though so brilliant and bepraised,
Before they touch the stream of time they burst in middle air.
And for the scribes who write such books, so bankrupt of all
    good,
How broken-down themselves full oft in character and fortune!
Be these thy rabbis, Israel? are those thy teachers, England?
Go to!—we read for pastime, not for profit, in these days:
And as to reverence for such scribes, we laugh to scorn their
    quarrels,
How like wild dogs they snarl and bite and fight with one another,
Only united when achase of some stout hart at bay,
Whose royal head shall haply fling them howling from its antlers!

These are times when froth and trifles on the popular gale
Scud flying everywhere to catch our grown-up children's fancy;
And conscience well may choose to wait for wiser days foreseen,
When taste and sense anon shall oust the rubbish of the hour;
When thought again shall hunt a-field with stauncher hounds for
    scent
Than these scratch-packs, and hireling jades, and their subscription
    riders.

So then, my book is finished; and, with all its thousand faults,
I gladly bless it as work done that cannot be undone:
Sweet is the end, quoth Aristotle; doubly sweet if good;
I dare be thankful for such work, humbly and proudly thankful;
Humbly, for my God hath helped, yea given me all I have;
Proudly, for my brother-men have mainly striven to hinder:
And spite of all their ridicule, their slanders and their sneers,
Alone I have achieved, alone have fought and conquered.
Condemn not, as a Jeffries might, hurriedly and untried;
Read throughly; it hath been your wont to judge without the
    hearing:
But still consider of these writings, cast in a solemn mould,

And filled with weightier **thoughts than** hasty critics care to wait
 for,
That Cleobulus wisely spake, **Never too much** at once:
Leibig is for lozenges, a morsel for a meal.
And note how readily for ease poor wits can riot here,
Those schoolboy-archers, shooting close, are sure to hit **the** target;
Fools may always raise a laugh by parodies and puns;
They can burlesque the Bible; they have travestied great Shak-
 speare:
How well then may such scoffers be goodnaturedly despised,—
How **wisely every** worthier scribe will follow no such fooling!

And yet,—I covet no man's praise,—though thankful for his love;
I care for no man's censure, unless conscience countersign it:
Quoting the worthies of old time, **I will** rejoice with **them;**
A true book is more lasting than the monumental brass:
Let come what will, nor fire, nor storm, nor sword, nor tooth of
 time
Can blast this record of my soul, or blot it out of being;
With Horace I can sing, I shall not altogether die,—
With Ovid, Ennius, David, I shall not die, but live.

OF THE BIBLE.

It were seemly that a Scripture for all nations should **be** styled
 universally The Book,
That under one great Master-mind many scribes should write it,
That every letter of its text should have been well watched by
 warders,
And that one special people should conserve it for mankind.

It were not seemly that such Scripture, meant for duties here,
Should venture deep on other themes than morals and religion:
Science would be hinted, not exhausted; now and then a word,
Enough to prove its conscious Author chose the higher topics:
So then, worldly knowledge, albeit **in** no sort quenched,
Would thus be left to reason, as less worthy revelation;
And all we need to look for, or to learn from out The Book,
Are teachings of religion, not the secret things of science

And yet how many gainsayers complain that man's great Guide
To holier thoughts and better life, and higher worlds than ours,
Doth scantly condescend an ear to reason's curious tongue,
That asketh endless questions of small moment to man's soul.
Our record runneth: God made all. The how, the why, the when,
These are but idle queries, and the Maker doth not heed them.
Our knowledge is, that on a day He placed a man in Eden,
And gave him for his heritage the newly ordered globe;
Set him duties, tested him, and when he fell, restored him,
And helped till now his children, whose children all are we.
Age after age, by tongue or symbol, records of our race
Were kept by holy men of old, obedient to high teaching;
And these primeval writings, with the like of later time,
Are come to us an heirloom,—the Scriptures of The Book.

Doubtless, though well guarded from great errors in the main,
It were not likely that no faults were dropt by many writers;
To conscience and his reason God leaveth freeborn man,
The twain enough for lower needs, though grace may help all higher.
So let those points and accents be, as some are right or wrong,
The strong root-words, the living thoughts, are God's own revelation;
And copiers and translators, with every care and skill,
May yet be somewhile found at fault, and well to be corrected.
And so the little (noways much) of failings in The Book
Is due to scribes who blotted what at first was fairly written.

How manifold the Bible! how majestic in variety!
History, poems, proverbs, parable, biography, and doctrine,—
How rich in all the ornaments and dignity of eloquence!
In annals as in prophecies how simple and sublime!
How full of quaint old stories, and of chivalrous adventure,
And whisperings of the birth of time, as mutterings of its death!
How fragrant is the incense of its praises and its prayers!
How comforting its promises, how precious are its precepts!
How wise, and kind, and pure, and good, its influence on the soul!
How strong its hold upon the heart, its power within the mind!
It speaketh peace to sinners, and high wisdom to the sage;
It is the traveller's guide-book, and the missionary's treasure.

The mother for her sailor-boy hath stored it in his locker,
The soldier at his foreign quarter poreth on its page,
The pious merchant's Bible will be posted near his ledger,
The very beggar sometimes hath it hidden in his rags.
It showeth in their action all the attributes of God,
His mercy, His omnipotence, His wisdom, and His justice;
It well displayeth every class and character of men,
Their guilt and their repentings, their happiness and woe.
No heroes equal Bible heroes—martyrs, captains, kings,
Joshua, David, Daniel, all the worthies of old time;
No stories are like Bible stories, exquisitely told,—
Isaac, Joseph, Ruth, and Job, and Samson, and Elijah.
Romance hath borrowed Bible exploits for its fabulous knights,
And Poesy from Bible wells hath drawn its richest nectar;
The minds of all our wisest have been moulded on its themes,
The hearts of all our purest have been chastened by its lessons:
And all the best of Adam's race that ever lived and died
Have lived in faith and died in hope through blessing from the Bible.
It is that truer tree of life, whose roots are in the Rock,
Whose trunk is strong as Lebanon, whose boughs outstretch the cedars;
Whose buds and flowers and fruits are for the healing of all nations,
Whose leaves shall never wither, but are green for evermore!

Well read out, with earnest voice, by one that understandeth,
The Word of God is eloquence beyond all human speech;
But common readers, slow of heart, and ignorant in mind,
Contrive to deaden half its life, to darken half its light;
And some, on silly system, still abjure dramatic effort,
With feeble tones and vulgar notes ensuring all things dull;
While, fairly spoken forth and with a feeling elocution,
The Scriptures have a might and a magnificence all their own.
And there is scanter need for long diluted exposition,
If he that readeth understandeth, and can read aright;
But slender learning in the Greek, and gross contempt for Hebrew,
And little knowledge of all knowledge far too often shown,
And lack of able utterance, and the lead-weight of routine,
These obscure the text so much they half excuse the sermon.

Also, there is some just need for wise and true revision,
Seeing our English tongue hath changed and grown by growth of years.
If one could "eat damnation," who would tempt the terrible morsel?
The letters of Bellerophon should ask to such a feast.
Yet how continually feeble souls, through that wrong phrase alone,
Are troubled all their lives as by a lion in the way.
Christ rested with the holy dead; His soul was never in "hell:"
That word ill-rendered still confoundeth Hades with Gehenna.
And other spotted places more might claim the Royal touch,
For close correction is a needbe of these searching times.
A flyleaf for our Bibles, with its list of mended texts,
A volume well compounded of all causes for amendment,
This were the simple wisdom for our heads in Church and State;
But, with no thought of change in style,—the solid English strength,
So statue-like, so graphic, and so simple and sublime,—
Only the lightest touch in phrase to heal up evil faults,
That were enough; all else as now unchanged for texts and teachings!
The dear old Family Bible should be still our champion volume,
The Medo-Persic law to us, the standard of our Rights.

In this our day, an evil day of change and misbelief,
When craft and ignorance and sin are leagued against religion,
When every keen objector is hailed with guilty joy,
And shallow sceptics unabashed deny or doubt the Bible,
Great is the comfort where a man can feel his soul is strong
In simple trust on Scriptural truth, as simply as in childhood.
It is a joy, an honour, yea a wisdom, to declare
A boundless, an infantile faith in our dear English Bible!

The garden, and the apple, and the serpent, and the ark,
And every word in every verse, and in its literal meaning,
And histories and prophecies and miracles and visions,
In spite of learned unbelief,—we hold it all plain truth:
Not blindly, but intelligently, after search and study;
Hobbes and Paine considered well, and Germany and Colenso.
The closer to the strict old text, the Bible still is clearer;
The more examined ever still more curiously exact:

Assyria, Edom, Petra, Zion,—from **them all unearth**
Whatever of old works ye will, these illustrate the Bible:
The sixty cities of Og are standing yet in Bashan;
The Pyramids, the Sculptured Wadys, **and the** Mount of Bel,
The marble slabs of Nineveh, and Tadmor in **the** desert,
All witness to its truth alike: Herodotus as Josephus.

The Bible made us what we are, the mightiest Christian nation,—
The Bible buildeth in each man his character and mind,
From cradle hymns to wedlock, and through grey hairs **to the**
    grave,
At every step in life the **Holy Bible** is our helper:
We have none other lamp **to** guide us through this darkling world,
No other staff, nor scrip, nor shoe, nor viand by the way,
No gentler nurse in sickness, no warmer friend in health,
No better comforter, companion, teacher than the Bible:
Every word within it hath been watered by saints' tears;
Every blessed page thereof been died-for by the martyrs:
To eyes that see, it shineth; to ears that hear, it speaketh;
To minds that know, it standeth out, as far before the age.
Modern science cannot find it obsolete or false,
Every new discovery but proving it more true.
The crusts of earth, the races, and the languages of men,
The laws of light and life, of chemistry and motion,
So wisely touched and hinted at, are wisely then passed by;
Man's reason would have nought to do, forerun by **revelation**.
And let them boast the Talmud: should not Rabbis, **Doctors,**
    Scribes
Have taught that Holy Child the very best of Jewish wisdom?
Yet, let them note, the Christ had left this world four hundred
    years,
Or ever from its oral state that Talmud was collected;
So then, **Jews had** caught from Christ those teachings in **the**
    Talmud
Some pundits are so quick to hint our Moral Teacher stole.

Yea, spite of all the learned zeal to prove the Bible false,
Their reckonings and disputings, **and their** eager hunt for
    errors,—
In spite of all their casuistry, discoveries, statistics,
And every sceptic effort of apostates, clerk and lay,

The Bible is but stablished by its gainsayers and assailants,
And all its difficulties die, though galvanized to live.
Their diggings in the mud of Egypt, and the caves of France,
Their searchings of old shellmounds and of pilestumps in the lakes,
Their scrutiny of languages, and chronicles, and races,
Their evil rage and scornful hate against the Blessed Book,
All corroborate old texts, and illustrate old truths,
Serving to prove that man on earth was last-born of creation,
Showing their scorching inquisition as a refiner's fire,
And with their burning-glasses testing still the unchanged gold.

The Bible, standing in its strength a pyramid foursquare,
The plain old English Bible, a gem with all its flaws,
That Bible, not the priest, nor the ordinance, nor the church,
(However sped by pastor, house of prayer, and simplest worship,)
That book of books, next to the Christ whereof it ever telleth,
Is still the heaven-blest fountain of conversion and salvation.
The peasant and the prince alike drink gladly of that well,
It comforteth with equal care the pauper and the statesman;
The widow and her orphans, from the palace to the cottage,
Are yearning on the Bible in glad reverence night and day;
The rough backwoodsman pondereth its pages in his cabin,
Thence going to his sturdy toil, a purer stronger man;
Beneath its influence mutineers become an isle of saints,
And convicts in their prison-cells are changed to heirs of glory;
Its presence giveth evident peace and light to this Swiss Canton,
While its mere absence from that neighbour breedeth strife and sin;
It maketh Scotland great and good, blest with a shining Bible,
While Erin still is miserable, as hiding-up that light:
It is the voice of God to man, encouraging and warning,
It is the speech of man to God, in sampled prayer and praise;
It is the golden thread of life, and strung with precious pearls,
Hung on each Christian infant's neck, its best baptismal birthright,
The amulet and anodyne and jewel of our race,
To soothe us in this vale of tears, and cheer our path to heaven.

OF HOME.

INFINITELY varied, as with marriage, from heights to lowest depths,
From pleasantness and peace to miserable contentions,
For every heart the thought of Home will bring its special difference,
As varying truth may testify to sorrows or to joys.
An exile yearneth over Home in long romancing absence,
But oft his yearnings are fulfilled by realized disappointment;
The dreaming soldier longeth for his mother's wayside cottage,
The sailor museth on his watch about the wife ashore:
But what if crime and penury, if shame and sin be there?
How saddened into wormwood is the honied thought of Home!
With one man, all his memories will be piety and love,
A gentle mother's goodness, and a noble father's care;
With another, let him search the past as far back as he can,
It was an atmosphere of strife, all troubles and no comfort:
Here, is a soul that oweth all its wealth for heaven and earth
To pure affections, bright examples, wisdoms learnt of Home;
There, is a spirit ill-conditioned, outcast and rebellious from its birth,
Whose cruel parents in that Home had only taught it evil:
Some were born at a liberal hearth, warm with genial hospitalities,
Some at the board of meanness, amid sordid shifts and thrifts;
To those a recollected home were crowds of hearty friends,
To these penurious carefulness, a blank and frozen solitude:
One goeth homeward from his toil to rest and peace and plenty,
Greeted on the threshold by his cleanly goodwife's kiss;
His neighbour meanwhile met by that old slattern left at home
With the quick hailstorm of her tongue in quarrelling and worry.

Joy for the happiness of Home! where peace content affection
Shine a triple sun to bathe in bliss that little world:
There the good angel of the house, the mother wife and mistress,
With gentle care and thoughtful love is ministering life;
There in firm wisdom ruleth well the father husband master,
Heaping it with prosperities, as guardian guide and judge:
There the sons obey, diligently heeding duties,
There the cheerful daughters plan their charities for all,
There with no eyeservice, but in honest faith and truth,

The family domestics work, and worship with their betters;
While all the neighbours round about, and scores of friends far off,
Point to that house and praise it well, the happy Home of Christians.
O beautiful in essence is that angel in the house,
The gentle charitable wife, its pure presiding spirit,
So patient with all troubles, and so cheerful under changes,
So full of help to others, so forgetful of herself;
O husband, gladly praise her! O ye children, call her blessed!
For all her works and words shall hail her, at the gates of heaven.

And,—woe for the wretchedness of Home!—where clamour care and discord
Enwrap that desolate small sphere in whirlwinds of contention;
There, all rule is at an end; extravagance, disorder,
And discontented selfishness are harpies at each meal;
There the father is not honoured, neither is the master served,
There the husband pineth, disenchanted, without love;
There the thriftless brothers scorn to redeem young days,
But waste their chances in first years for afterlife-repentance;
There the pining sisters ever meditate escape,
Dreaming in hope of some calm home, far other than their father's;
Because the hearth they long to leave, curst by its evil angel,
Irascible and jealous and unreasonably capricious,
Is ever hot with hatreds, and perilous from quarrels,
A married fury blighting there the slandered name of Mother!
So, the very hirelings will scoff, and scorn to take such service,
And neighbours whisper as they pass, and friends are scared away,
And Home, that was the name for peace, is synonymed with strife,
An earthly pandemonium through that termagant of wedlock.

Alas! the woeful change,—for once she had been worshipped,
In early years, ere sweet young Love had blown to bitter Marriage:
But now her image, long that idol in affection's temple,
Lieth as a broken Dagon on its ruined floor;
For the contentions of a wife have banned, instead of blessing,
The beauteous fane of Hymen, and the cheerful hearth of Home.

Who can estimate the torments worked by tongue and temper,
Those dislocations on the rack, of comfort and of love?
There be tortures, cruel as at Avignon, wearing out saints of God,
Drop by drop maddening the brain with constant household worries;
There be moral harrowings and sawings, as David wrought at Rabbah,
That lacerate the feeling heart year after year continually:
Silver weddings may have been, but more are forged of iron,—
Though few dare hint hard truths like these, and flatter or ignore them.
Let the adultress be forgiven, let foolish extravagance go free,
But who can bear with temper and tongue to seventy times seven?
Changeable passionate and hateful, plagued with unreasoning animosities,
That bitter lawful-wife is still the bane and blight of Home:
Woe for that bed of nettles, woe for that nest of hornets,
Woe to the sensitive and gentle in their married lives!
Provocation irritation usurpation iteration vacillation accusation,
Every phrase of malice in every note of harshness,
Prejudices jealousies and strifes, contention hate confusion,
Every phase of ill from weakness up to wickedness,—
All these have often cursed the Home, through ill-assorted marriage,
And many wives and husbands here will own they read their fates:
O noble hearts and generous minds! if still they smile unsoured
Through lingering years of petty torment caused by such bad Homes:
For it is a veritable martyrdom some best have had to bear
That tyranny of wedlock with a wicked man, or woman.
Did not our glorious Milton feel it, tokened by his Doctrine of Divorce?
Is not the matchless Shakspeare a like witness even in his testament?
Hooker was judicious in all else, but a wife who burnt his books;
And Palissy and Wesley were martyrs as to marriage;
While Job, and Socrates, and Moses, justified of old
The proverb of wise Solomon against a wife's contentions.

They mould each other, man and woman; make or mar each other:

If Una tamed her lion, Goneril tainted Alban:
The man is made by gentleness, that meek and quiet spirit,
The holy conversation and obedience of the wife;
The man is marred by crossings and the nagging vixen temper
Night and day, by board and bed, embittered through that plague;
No escape, no respite; for the worm is at the core;
An exile cannot flee himself; nor hounds in leash run freely:
Who shall guage the force of such a spiritual fetter
Hindering all pursuit of good, and galling and injurious?
As who can guess the potency of woman's love and patience,
Her precious influence, her sweet strength, to bless a husband's
    Home?

And worse for you, O gentle wives! consorted with bad husbands,
The drunkard, the adulterer, the passionate, the mean;
How desolate your lots,—how steeped in grief your lives,—
How changed for you from peace to strife the sacred name of
    Home!
Not solely, and not chiefly, in the lowest haunts of life
In cellars or in hovels is domestic discord seen;
Oft-times the dinner of herbs hath quietness for seasoning,
And bitter want some sweet love-honey in its cup of gall:
But even with the richest in their palaces of pride,
Or where a midway competence hath all beside for comfort,
Not all their purple and fine linen, nor the stalled ox,
Can stay the hatreds that therewith have cursed too many a Home.

There is often a most miserable jealousy cankering domestic peace,
And gnawing at the narrow hearts of sundry men and women:
I touch not needfully the loathing that curseth criminal love
And gladly would do murder for a wanton look or fashion;
But the meaner hatred and suspicion of each genial feeling
And every kind of worth, by any innocently shown.
Pleasant neighbours, honest servants, good and clever children,
These are made the victims of that jealous lust for Self;
And chiefly nearest relatives, be they of wife or husband,
Are spoken against, and driven away, insulted and abused:
A brother near the throne is sure to get the bowstring;
Our monogamic firmament may hold no second sun;
Strait taxation, all for one, is rigidly exacted,
And good and wise men are but rivals to that morbid soul;

Without such close exclusion, is not married bliss too scarce?
Yet dearest friends not seldom thus are sacrificed to Hymen:
O ye bitter spoilers of the beauteous and the holy,
Married slaves to selfishness, ye jealous little minds,
It is you that fright from wedlock, beyond its common trials,
And put it to an open shame, degraded from due honour;
It is you that ban all blessing, and bring Satan into Eden,
Till Milton's Adam curse once more his selfish serpent Eve.

But, O true paragons of marriage!—for thousands yet there be
Worthiest of honour and of love, though haply missing both,
How opposite are ye to those detestables, how patient and how
    kind,
The sweet Hermiones and Griseldas in too many a Home!
None can guess your sorrows, though religion soothe them still,
None can know the wretchedness that hideth in your bosoms:
Prayer and hope indeed are yours, and friends discreetly chosen;
But what shall compensate a wife for Home despoiled of love?
Home-love is a woman's very life; a man may live without it;
The mother-bird hath one poor nest; foxes have holes elsewhere.

How often is there sadness and suspicion in the Home,
Where, like the barren figtree, unblest marriage hath no fruiting;
Where woman's withering heart may never yearn on children,
And vainly year by year the father longed to kiss a son!
For mysterious Providence withholdeth in high wisdom
Full oft from those who wished it most the treasure of a child;
Giving, as with too liberal hand, to many who are thankless,
—Nay more, who grudge against the gift—that priceless wealth
    in offspring.
Yet hear this for your comfort, ye that are written childless,
Who grieved in disappointed youth that wedlock bore no fruit
At least your tranquil age is saved from shame and sorrow
Too often heaped upon the Home by some ungrateful son;
Where are thy prayers and hopes, O father? where thy costs and
    cares?
And all thy love, O mother,—is but moonlight on that ruin

Twice happy is the Home that is blest with children's children;
Thy sons and daughters were much care, but these be simple
    pleasures;

Another generation is responsible for these,
And so in every better sense is found thy second childhood.
Here be pretty playmates for thine innocent old age,
Full of hope and life and glee, and garrulous as thyself;
Here be keen-eyed comrades for thy wisdom to improve,
And friends to carry on thy praise, and talk of thee hereafter:
Nor only for amusement those dear little ones are seen,
Nor that thy sage experiences may help them in life's journey,—
But, since their angels always see the face of God their Father,
These baby wards of heaven on earth can guide thy feet to Him!

Next after wife and husband, and the children young or old,
The happiness of Home shall much be made or marred by servants:
Whither are fled the faithful souls that loved through life one family,
In unsuspected honesty with dutiful heartservice?
Where are those models of economy, so diligent in their callings,
Showing good fidelity, not answering, not purloining?
An over-prevalent luxury, the strong desire for change,
With vanities of dress, and headiness and hardness,
And independent hate of rule, and class divorced from class,
And stilted thoughts of pride, bred from ill-digested schooling,
All these have worked their social harms, gnawing the heart of Home,
And well-nigh leave extinct the race of good and faithful servants.

Ay,—but where too shall we find the wise and gracious house-wife,
Whom royal Lemuel's mother sought as helpmate for her son?—
All too little sympathy, and far too great exaction,
Nothing overlooked of fault, and seldom an indulgence,—
With these and worse, with silly pride, and poisonous airs of caste,
Too many a modern mistress will torment her women slaves.
On all sides is there blame; yet more with wives than husbands;
For man and master still work well together as good friends:
The genial word dropped now and then, of kindness or of caution,
Is oftener heard from man to man, than woman ruling woman:
And men have no proud prudery, but can wink at humble lovers,
Whereas the jealous housewife is affection's direst foe:
A master giveth counsel, as remembering his hot youth,
And is not set in frozen state so high above the servant;

Whereas the best a menial often heareth from her mistress
Is strict and harsh ascetic lore, with tartness of reproof.
Would that, as with Lemuel's queen, that tongue were ruled by
    kindness,
And, if she watch her household's ways, herself live not so idly!
A good and genial housewife secureth cheerful servants,
But our unkindly scolds are still the roots of discontent.

Who can make a monograph of such a theme as Home?
Who shall exhaust that field of thought, so thickly cropped with
    feelings?
Duty interest pleasure pain, affections fears and hopes,
Like cherubs flitting round each Home from nursery to the grave,
And recollections of old scenes, dim belike with sorrow,
And many disappointments, crowd about this pregnant theme.
How to paint young memories with panoramic power,
How to touch bereavements that have wrung the mourner's heart,
How to tell of birthday-feasts, of weddings and of deathbeds,
How to set before each mind the story of his Home?
It were easy, it were weary, to dilate at length,
And mould in full these features, barely outlined and suggested;
But let what I have written stand, faultily with omissions,
To sketch in light and shadow the romance and truth of Home.

OF SOCIAL PRIDE.

STAND aside, come not anear—for I am holier than thou,—
Holier, as world-religion goeth, richer, greater, higher;
Suffer not thy vulgar shadow to fall athwart my sunshine,
Go to! I will not touch nor taste the common or unclean.
Not alone with publican and Pharisee, not alone with Pariahs and
    Brahmins,
But also round our English hearths is class divorced from class:
As one of our own judges hath said (that wise and genial man
Who worked his heart out over-soon, but not too soon for glory)
Far too little sympathy is felt or shown amongst us;
Caste, and prejudice, and pride, build walls about us all:
There be those great gulfs fixed; homes ramped and fossed from
    homes;

Exclusion and contempt too well watch each pretty circle,
And none may touch or enter but the magically garbed.

Let be, indeed, the sesame for Fashion,—welcome to lock her
    doors,—
Let be the gambler's password for rich and vicious folly;
May such rest ever secrets, known only to the few,
And may that wizard ring have never charm to trap the many;
But there is a somewhat more against us, much to make ashamed.
Where, insulated still, we dwell in social coldness,
Where each man's house is truly found his castle as his home,
With ditch and walls and warder, and the drawbridge to be
    passed;
For though warm summer glow within beside the Christmas
    embers,
Yon outer wilderness of men would find but wintry welcome
One friendly recognition, some passing words of kindness,
Would break the arctic circle that estrangeth class from class;
Yet neighbour meeteth neighbour ungreeted year by year,
And high and low, and all between them crystallize apart.
It is easier for the sons of pride to talk with humblest peasants
Than to hold intercourse with those who tread upon their skirts;
And children and the sick may find abundant consolations,
But growing up or strong in health are stared at as unknown:
The genial and the bountiful are seldom seen at one;
To give is easier than to love, to be praised more sweet than
    praising.
Your great philanthropist is found, scattering money charities
Far off, far off to the antipodes—but seldom to the heathen at his
    door;
And folks live out long lifetimes, near dwellers in one hamlet,
Unheedful of each other, though they worship in one church.

Away with this mean pride! away with class-exclusions!
An honest man by honesty is well enough approved:
And somewhile there is merit, and somewhile talent too;
How oft, where none might look for such, are gifts and graces
    seen!
The musical ear, the plastic hand, the eye for observations,
Shrewd minds and feeling hearts are found in peasants as in
    peers;

A mine of human gold is under everybody's hearthstone,
A mine belike too seldom worked, but seamed with precious
    veins;
And many a rustic, whose soul's good thy feeble tract is tending
May have a reach of genius far above thy cultured thought.

There is an idol of our west more well beloved than Tammuz,
Claiming with Juggernaut or Nisroc hecatombs each day:
It hath no hideous vulture-head, neither griffon hands,
But courteous and well-dressed it goeth, plausible as Belial,
Delicately goeth, full of glozing words and smiles,
And all the world is glad to worship Smooth Respectability.
Who shall count the thousands that have starved to serve that
    Presence?
How many suicides have perished by its decent razor!
How often forgeries and frauds were tempted and contrived
To satisfy appearance, and to pay the tax of vanity!
Even in rural cottages that sacrifice is offered,
Where humble labourers slink ashamed before their flaunting
    daughters,
Whose foolish finery is bought haply through household theft,
And anyway their mothers' needs had better seen their wages:
And sometimes, still to sanctify that sham, Respectability,
Poor infants, as at Carthage, have been slaughtered to hide
    shame;
For moral England, up and down, to save Respectability,
Forceth unmarried mothers to the shrines of Saturn here.
Yea, and with every class, what frequent fraud and meanness
Combine to feed thine altar-fires, gaunt Respectability!
There are the shabby splendours, there the stinted alms,
There the small hypocrisies of social class-distinction·
For fear that Truth might raise the wondering eyebrows of the
    world,
A crowd of lies is gathered in a festering heap at home,
Like captives in the wicker-image of Druidic Baal,
All to be burnt in worship of sublime Respectability!

And, shame on prudery and pride, where the virtuous are frowning
    upon vice,
Not in faithfulness or pity, but for mere contempt.
Ah! those erring daughters only gather hate and spite

2 A

Where charity and mercy should rather have been given;
Ah! those bitter matrons think it scorn to echo Him
Who gently said to Magdalene, "Neither do I condemn thee."
Thou canst not guess the piteous story of this fallen woman;
How, as a girl, her young affections innocently bloomed,
How earnestly she loved, how vilely was deceived,
How cruelly was driven from her pious father's home,
And flung an outcast on the streets, to live by sin or perish!
Her chastity was once as pure, if not so proud as thine;
And haply even thou hadst yielded to that strong temptation:
Judge not, but be pitiful; she hath still much goodness left,
Charity, and humility, and gleams of grace from heaven:
Help her to rise, and take her hand, and lead her to repentance,
This thy sister is a soul for whom the Saviour died;
Be tender with her, and not fierce, as one would lift the wounded,
And never tread the sinner down beneath thy hateful virtue.

Our women cling to social pride more closely than the men,
And often treat their servants imperiously like serfs.
So, too, some petty differences will loom full large with them,—
A button more or less is much in England as in China:
And pride of purse, or noble birth, or husband's rank or office,
Drive up their minds to fever heat, or range at very dry;
And quarrels of precedence shall be jealously fought out,
Till kindlier men are forced to wink at duelling with neighbours:
For every shade of difference is a colour to keen eyes,
And those who doat on trifles see a molehill as a mountain
The merest touch of coarseness or of fineness in the fabric
Will serve with them to choose their muslin or refuse its texture;
And where a man would wait, considering and judging,
The woman's quicker impulse will jealously reject
So, many husbands gladly might be heartier with neighbours,
But for the pride and prejudice that rankle in their wives.

There be fair excuses: the vulgar is not easily dismissed;
Designers trap good nature, and deceivers blight good-will;
Some worthy folk have oftentimes unworthier far too near them,
And many ways a loss is sure, with seldom hope of gain:
Still, go thy way with frankness, and vulgarities will shrink;
Be keen, and shame the schemer; be kind, and crush deceit;
Rebuke the wrong and cheer the right, dividing converse wisely

And genially forget to weigh thy loss or gain in scales.
Who maketh thee to differ? Whence came talents to thy care?
How shouldest thou be proud, with such reason for humility?
HE who said, "Give Me thy heart," said also, "Love thy neighbour,"—
And no commandment is obeyed but bringeth due reward:
This sympathy shall win thee love from highest as from humblest,
And make thy servants serve thee well, and all the neighbours love thee,
Shall raise thee for thy humbleness, shall bless thee for thy kindliness,
And shame the fools who cover up their ostrich-heads in pride.

Note well our highest; is there found this social fault in her?
Can any call her haughty, though the greatest in all lands?
Doth she not bridge the deep wide gulf that moateth her from others,
With kindly words, and liberal acts, and condescending smiles?
Is even the humblest left unhelped, the meanest unregarded?
Can any children of distress plead for her grace in vain?
A widow, is she not the fostering Queen of widows?
A mother, craped in sorrow, the orphan's mother-queen?
And every home affection, each pure domestic pleasure,
Shared though it be with cottage hinds, she owneth share in all.
O ye, the lesser stars of rank, of wealth, and great estate,
So often high and dry above the common reach of mortals,
Regard this best example, and be kindly as your Queen,
And dare not treasonably thus to scorn her lowly greatness;
She learnt it of her teacher; he taught her what he learnt
From Christ, our one grand type of highest-hearted meekness.

There was,—in higher truth there is,—for he though dead still liveth,
Though passed away from us, an heir of glory gone before,—
There was and is a noble Prince, none nobler on this earth,
The forefront jewel of our crown, of purest lustre, priceless:
He, first and greatest, still was ever kind to last and least,
With eloquent tongue and liberal hand befriending all the friendless:
He, loftier than the loftiest, could be humble to the humblest,
And condescend in high-born love to men of low estate;

The worn-out servant flung away, the rent-racked artisan,
The widow and the fatherless, the toiling starving curate,
The gillie in his hovel, and the coalman on his barge,
Rescued by a royal hand from sickness or oppression,
All these he made his friends, for everlasting habitations,
To bless him for his sympathy, and love him for his help.
Go and do thou likewise: follow in his steps:
We little thought how good he was, how great, until we lost him;
Generous in all charity, genial, just, and pure,
He topped our social pyramid with love and not with pride.

OF CHANGE AND TRAVEL.

He that long abideth at a place, continuing in one stay,
Rooted as a hedgerow elm to the spot whereon it groweth,
However fed through reading, or taught by talk with neighbours,
Or busied in much writing, or pleased or teased at home,
Liveth but a lower sort of life, as mere vegetation for its sameness,
Casting away from him year by year the blessings that advantage
    our time;
This running to and fro, with knowledge flashed as lightning,
This speeding hither and thither, reading as one runneth,
Culling, as a bee upon the wing, intelligence like honey,
And noting with Ulysses the thoughts and homes of men.

Change in veriest trifles hath its comfort and its use;
Turn thy pillow in the night, to freshen even sleep:
Be not an automaton of habit, the slave to rules and hours;
And vary meats for better health, and clothes with changing
    seasons.
Also, seek variety for mind, as needful as for body;
The same continual teaching is not wholesome and not wise:
The one preacher and his doctrine, the one paper with its politics,
The one incessant occupation, all alike are evil;
There is a narrowing force in each, a dwarfing and a shrinking,
Bigoted thought, and party-feeling, and obtuse inaptness.
Enlarge thy tent, and more than so, move it often onward;
And crouch not like an Ostiack, in his cave of frozen snow.
The dweller in one spot, tethered for half a lifetime,
Is but an empty barge at anchor near the harbour-bar;

He moveth without progress, and (as void of aims in life)
If idle, hath no holidays, in spite of all his leisure;
While, if a worker, half that work would happier be and brisker,
For fair fresh fields and healthy play in foreign air and scene:
Ignorant, though full of books, illiberal, small-minded,
The homestayer broodeth on himself and paltry household matters;
He may indeed have peace, but his peace is a stolid slumber;
He may escape some evils, but he misseth much of good;
Small in self-conceit, prejudiced, and ill-fashioned,
There is no largeness in the mind that scorneth modern travel.

Give me the wholesome happy chance to spread my wayward
    wings,
And speed afar by sail or steam, or rail, or mountain-climbing
Give me the free glad hoofs, the whip and spur and saddle,
Over the rolling prairies, emancipate from care;
Place me beneath some hotter sun in the religious East,
Where sad Jerusalem doth sit unshaded by her palm,
Or where the Pyramids yet point to Israel's better Exode,
Or where Arabia hideth deep another huge Stonehenge;
Or in Rome's Coliseum, peopled with gladiator ghosts,
Or among Grecian temples, safe from their banditti,—
Or in that newer hemisphere, among my crowds of friends
With hearts as full of welcome as Niagara of wonder,—
Or with yet loftier daring, let me gladly pierce the clouds
And note the world beneath my car, mapped out in lands and
    oceans!

No wise traveller will fail of keeping daily records,
Whereby the marvels he hath met are fixed to date and place.
A noteless idler hath small gain; he loitereth through museums,
Balancing with his leaden eyes the lead about his feet;
And home returned, his vacant mind, confusedly forgetful,
Is all unapt to teach another, or to cheer himself:
But he whose pen is ready, and his head and heart alive,
To present winnings addeth pleasant treasures in the future;
When friends, or haply children, gathered round the hearth of
    home,
Read the adventurous journals of his well-spent travel,
Or listen to his clear detail of exploits in old days
Exact, as written at the time, and fresh upon the spot.

There be scores of tourist fools, who earn but harm from touring,
All unprepared in mind and heart, and with none eyes to see;
They rush from inn to inn, foraging for strange pleasures,
But heed nor Art nor Nature, nor the tales of ancient time;
Pæstum, Monte Rosa, Thermopylæ, Iona,
Are less than Homburg or La Scala to those sensual souls;
And even music is but sought as pandar to some orgy
Where life with all its flowers and fruits is fooled and gamed
    away!

See thou be not mated with such folly,—but choose thy comrade
    wisely,
One well trained, as thou art, in all handy travel lore:
History, zeal for science, love of truth and worth and beauty,
These should well be woven in the texture of both minds;
And patience with each other,—yea, forbearance every hour,
And cheerfulness and energy and mutual timely praise:
And language is a need-be, though our English tongue be much,
Or thou wilt miss in travel half its profit and its pleasure:
But pry not, either of the twain, into sores and secrets,—
For there be deeps in every heart, and tenderest spots of pain;
In chief, act not thy comrade's spy, for morals or religion;
If must be, counsel or protest, but openly and kindly:
Intimate for a little space as holiday-making friends,
Still independence is great wisdom, with some holding back;
Not so carelessly familiar, nor so scrupulously exacting,—
If as friends ye are to travel far and long together.

That there is much weariness in travel, with cost and care and
    danger,
Much to vex and much to try,—which of us knoweth not?
The selfishness, the misery, the beggary, the fraud,
The vice of thousands on thy track will scare thee and disgust
    thee;
Still, some angels unawares, some nobler hearts at times,
Shall melt those human mists away, as sunshine in the valleys;
And thou hast seen earth's wonders, to be pondered many days,
And learnt the thoughts and ways of men in their most famous
    cities;
Thou hast traversed battle-fields, where conquerors won their
    world;

Or drank at the oasis; or bivouacked in the **cavern**;
Or seen the midnight sun; **or thou hast left Orion**
To change him **for the Southern Cross and the** Australian Crown:
Thou hast struck salmon in the fiord, and stalked the red deer on
    the fell;
Thy daring **foot** hath started the chamois from its glacier;
Thy swift-winged yacht hath steered betwixt the palmy coral
    isles;
Thy reindeer sledge hath glided swiftly over old Norge's snow.
Thou hast deepened the well of thine heart, thou hast widened the
    walls of thy mind,
And cheerily renewed thy youth in body and in spirit;
Even out of peril hast won courage; from much vexation, patience;
Here and there hast gathered friends, **and** everywhere reaped
    mercies;
And, if thy Sabbaths have been honoured, and prayer glowed ever
    in thy heart,
Well art thou paid for cost and care by treasure-trove in travel.

All of us have within us the wandering Crusoe spirit;
We come of Norse sea-rovers, and adventurers full of hope:
And man was bade to tame his earth, to rule it and subdue it,—
Whereby our feet-soles tingle at an untrod Alpine peak.
But shall we not fly anon with wings, to shame these creeping
    paces,
Even as steam hath mocked all speed on land and sea before?
Is not this firmament of air part of the human heritage,
Which man must conquer duteously, **as** first his Maker willed?
There needeth but a lighter gas, well-tutored to our skill,
The springing spirit to some shape of delicate steel and silk,—
A birdlike frame of Dædalus, and gummed Icarian plumes,
Ancient inventions, long forgotten, to be found anew!
When **shall** the **chemist** mix aright this rarer lifting essence
To **make the lord of earth but equal to his** many sparrows?
When will discovery help us to such conquest of the **air,**
And **teach us swifter** travel than our creeps by land **and water**?

And shall we not be travellers hereafter, illimitably, freely, gladly,
Wanderers in awe-struck worship, as we speed from sun to sun?
I long to see them each and all, so differing in glory,—
Orion's nebulous whirlpool and Capella's coloured globes,

The marvellous coils of splendour ringing light round far off
    Saturn,
The strange terrific league-deep craters blistered on the moon,
The millions of fixed suns, with all their worlds around them,
And each a world of brothers, as the children of one God !
I thirst to drink of rivers where the pleasures are all new,
To quaff deep draughts of knowledge unimagined and unbounded,
To follow on eternally lessons begun in time,
And marvel at all infinites of Providence and creation ;
To feel with other senses, to imagine vaster thoughts,
To reign an incorruptible, though changeless yet progressing,
And thus to speed in spirit race, a traveller and a guest,
Gloriously from sun to sun, as freeman of them all !

Verily, this used-up planet, with its crowded shores and seas,
Its vanquished Alps, and rutted roads, and trampled plains and
    cities,
In the great future shall no more contract man's wider range,
Showing but as the playground, where his childhood once
    disported.
We shall fly at lightning pace from happiest globe to globe,
Where even now their signal fires are blazing yon above us ;
We shall gather loves and friendships even among seraphs,
Marvelling at the humbler worths that satisfied on earth ;
We shall mix in scenes and actions of stupendous glory,
Faintly shadowed here on earth by prophets, priests, and kings ;
We shall watch in bright display the attributes of Godhead,
With varying illustrations from His universe of spheres ;
We shall be space-wide travellers, discoverers beyond the nebulous
    stars,
Counting for a mere home circuit any flights with solar comets ;
We shall attain to knowledge inconceivable, fed by keener senses,
And rise to an omniscience of worship through the privileged
    ubiquity of Travel !

OF LIVELIHOODS.

If morals be well honoured, if religion be not harmed,
If simple conscience rest content,—thy livelihood is lawful:
Trivial though it seem, allied to ridicule or folly,

The very clowns and jesters have their honourable calling;
It may be, yon fair dancer, by her graceful tempted toil,
Is modestly a widowed mother's comfort and support;
It may be, this bold acrobat, amidst his thrilling perils,
Is mindful of the wife and babes who light his garret-home:
Heed of all such in charity; there be some unguessed martyrs,
Some undefiled, amid surroundings pestilent and corrupting;
There be virgins, naked-footed, treading red-hot ploughshares,
There be youths confessing Christ among the godless and the
    mean.

How hard it is to win a crust, to earn one's daily bread!
How desperate the battle of life in these fierce days of struggling!
Of yore, the labourer, if he chose, might idle for his pleasure,
But now that labourer often must stand idle to his pain:
Once, every educated worth was sure of rich employment,
But honourable shrewd men now starve, and wait for work in
    vain:
Long since, each marriageable maid had several eager suitors,
But seven hopeless women now are lingering for one man:
Of old, your sons and daughters were a quiverful of praise,
But now Cornelia's Gracchi lack the setting for her jewels.

There be indeed the common grooves, choke-full of common men,
All crowded-up, and crowding-out, and overflowed with crowders;
And little chance for any, in these hot competing times,
But for the few who tread some path their fathers tracked before
    them.
And every failing now is fatal; winners must be perfect:
Slender hope for any that are weighted with defects:
Stuttering tongues, or purblind eyes, weak health, or simple slow-
    ness,—
Every candidate must drop, that owneth one of these;
All the weak are pushed aside, or trampled down and smothered;
The race is only to the swift, the battle to the strong:
Boldness is the talisman, Demosthenean boldness,
No luck but through hard wrestling now, no help but in self-help.
And though there be competings,—what is one among so many?
With fifty athletes for one prize, what left for the forty and nine?
And common parts have little chance beneath so strict a standard
Where talent, even genius, scarcely findeth hope or scope;

So, **disappointed effort is** the climax of achievement;
The very staunchest in the field but rarely win the brush.

And feebler hounds thrown out, straying to far-off coverts,
Those distance-haloed ends of the earth, now filling up so fast,
How do they fare or win their **way,** ten thousand miles from home,
Flung penniless and friendless **on Australia or New Zealand?**
Is livelihood more **easy to an exile from all friends?**
And mere **existence worth its pains, despoiled of home and pleasures?**
The youth of gentle stock, well versed in useless learning,
Whose classic culture won him honours bought by health and wealth,
Perforce must own in that rough land coarse working men his masters,
And like the prodigal son be fain to tend their swine or sheep,
Weathering hunger, heat, and cold, and vulgarized by toil,
A shepherd or a drover, but the gentleman no more.
Here and there some luckier wight hath found a prize, a nugget,
Or **wisely** chose his plot upon **some river's marshy bend,**
Where, racked long years with feverish aches, our well-born pioneer
At last hath cleared a fortune with his planned and lotted township;
Then "Emigrate" is flung to idle gentlemen at home,
Go, get you gone and get you gold; get gold, no matter how;
Go, as the patriarch of old, or Nimrod founding cities,—
At least your absence is our gain in overcrowded England!

So, for our men; the willing crowds of would-be workers round us,
Offering as for livelihoods both heads and hands in vain;
And, for our women, with less power or chances in life's battle,
How vainly now they proffer hearts to win them husbands' homes!
For truly woman's livelihood is best found in her husband's,
The housewife and the mother are her first employments here;
In spite of types and telegrams, and lecturings and the counter,
The woman's occupation and her mission is at home,
A home other than her father's, and knit with dearer ties,

Young love grown ripe in marriage, and the happy fruit of
    children.
Yet everywhere the beauteous and the gentle, the accomplished—
    nay, the rich—
Are now unwooed, and still unwon, and wail with Jephthah's
    daughter
And seldom doth Love's fire crown Hymen's golden torch,
Or warm Affections dare to wed, for dread of frowning Mammon:
Thus, the days are evil, where so many live unloved,
And a most pitiful waste is rife of human worths and feelings:
Youth with youthful charm departeth, and the heart's romance,
Long disenchanted of its dreaming, pineth disappointed,
Till many a blighted sister, who should have shone in wedlock,
Is hardly earning livelihood by music or her pen.

How many fearsome livelihoods! how often mean and loathly!
How wearisome for sameness! how terrible for perils!
Alas! the lot of thousands in this dislocated world
Is only toil and pain and danger, sharpened by ill-usage;
Alas! that bitter circumstance to thongs hath added goads,
Where sweating brows and quivering muscles work in fœtid dark-
    ness,—
The piteous fate of honest men, and women too, and children,
Who help to warm our Christian homes with happy blazing
    hearths!
Lo! through long-drawn hours every night-like day for years,
In dismal, damp, and stenchy blackness English labour toileth,
Risking life and limb by fiery blasts and crushing masses—
All for the bare existence of an abject coal-pit gnome!
So, too, the grinders at the wheel, with eyes made raw by steel-
    dust;
The factory girl, whose wheezing lungs are stuffed with fluffy
    cotton;
The household drudge of all work, starved by her cruel mistress;
The field serf, old and famishing, and frozen with the cold;
The white consumptive woman, sleepless at her needle,
Over the gaudy robes, hurried on by clamorous fashion;
And scores of other dreary phases of our social life,
The desk and counter victims, thanking Mercy for His Sabbath.

And thousands hunt their living—ay, and catch it to their loss—

In poisonous highways, bitter byways, winning sinful wages:
And some, the better few of such, attempt to pour new wine
Of morals and religion into their old and rotten wine-skins.
Good-natured Lais vainly dreamt to consecrate foul earnings
By charities, as covering-up her multitude of sins;
The legal rogue, made wealthy through a secret breach of trust,
Shall hope to cure his conscience-fits by decorating churches;
And even gamblers think at times to hallow their ill gains
By giving gifts to hospitals as make-weight for their mischief.
True, each might have done worse; let Mammon, though un-
    righteous,
Be burdened-up with bounties as the Afrite in the tale;
But no dishonest livelihood is bettered by such largess
Without confessed repentance, restitution, and amendment:
The sins, the frauds, the wrongs remain, in spite of all that
    gilding,—
A trifle brighter to the eye, but black enough at heart.

Self-interest is the mainspring of our industries and callings,
But honesty the circling chain to guide its efforts right:
And thereby Society is gainer; for every son must work,
And if he mean to win must work both steadily and fairly.
The lawyer loseth custom who is keen to stir up strife,
But prospereth as a peacemaker, denouncing litigations;
The shrewd physician speedeth health, though living by diseases,
For skill, far more than craft, hath great reward and good report;
All merchandise of cheatery is quickly found to fail;
And simple truth was ever wisdom even among liars;
Only that this superficial honesty, springing from the selfishness of
    men,
Is but as a parasitic weed, and hath no root in morals.

The man unfitted for his place,—there is the commonest error,—
A racer in the waggon, and a carthorse on the turf.
Many a priest hath taken office for its piece of bread,
But had no gift of prayer or preaching for his patient people;
Many a lawyer had nor heart nor head for his dry studies,
And gladly jilted Themis when he found some younger love;
Many a leech is scantly skilled in physics and in healing,
Because his inmost soul revolted at disease and pain:
As with wedlocks, so with callings; thousands long for change;

How oft in both exchanging neighbours might be better mated!
But circumstance is hostile: the foremost of those fetters
Only death hath power to burst, and grant a second chance;
The hindmost hath its weaker links that many break away,
Escaping with contented loss from uncongenial callings:
And now the pen and now the sword, transferred from hand to hand,
Proveth innumerable mistakes in opposite vocations.
Of old the rule was, work and **eat**; no starving but for idlers;
But now the willing workmen **starve**, for want of work to do.
Is it that soon for populous Earth her time shall be no more,
Seeing she hath not livelihoods wherewith to feed her children?

OF FOURFOLD DIFFERENCES.

FOUR great empires, four true gospels, four strange living-creatures,
Four chief seasons in the year, four quarters of the globe,
Four elements, four winds, four continents, four oceans,
Four races, crops, and governments;—how fourfold is the world!
Seven, nine, five, three, and one, to each its ordered virtue,
The mysteries in odd numbers and their properties are strange;
But evens also, two, four, six, have curious special qualities
And chief the simple square encloseth many diverse wholes.

Agur the wise, the son of Yakeh, spake unto Ithiel and Ucal,
Spake to those listening disciples, in the spirit of his kinsman Solomon:
He testified of three things and of four, noting fourfold characters,
Dropping his ensamples for all others, classed by threes and fours;
As a matter may be **good**, or may be **evil**, or between-wise, or naturally neutral,
Partaking of the neither or the both, or of each in its separate extreme:
And shrewd **Pythagoras** of Samos, that greatest ancient sage,
Made all things range by fours, as soldiers use in drilling;
And, even as a fourfold ministry is with some their need-be of religion,—
The emblem of Deity Himself is a tetragon according to Pythagoras.

There be **four diversities of life,** whereby **men square** contentment;
Private comfort, public aim, or worldly **show, or godliness;**
There is the calm complacency of self, lone-living in one's shell,
Health, and prudent life, and secret **happiness of conscience;**
There is the earnest energy for **others, as** striving to be useful in all good,
Self-forgetting, self-neglecting, living **for thy kind** and not thyself
There is the recklessness of licence, hunting pleasures greedily,
Drowning thought in dissipation, and smothering bosom-sorrows in the crowd;
And there is the yearning up to God, the pure and spiritual life,
Strong in **faith,** and lit by hope, and happy **in all** charity.

There be **four sorts** of folk who square the sides of patience,
Rich as well as poor, and husbands even more than **wives:**
There be that are unconscious of their griefs, scarce heeding **loss of joy,**
The dyer's ingrained hand subdued to resignations;
There be that are case-hardened from ill-usage, indurated by much wrong,
The spirit's highway trodden down impervious to soft seeds;
There be the embittered through such evil, the watchful for revenges,
Where patience is a lingering scheme of cold and cruel hate;
And there be the loving long-enduring, with seventy-fold forgiveness,
Whose patience is not nature's growing, but **a grace from heaven.**

There be **four** differences **of care,** squaring the thought of giving trouble,
Discerned in most men's homes, and rife in every class:
There be the indolently heedless, who never calculate vexation,
But always claiming service, expect it, and exact it;
There be the **selfish** and unkind, who glory in small tyrannies,
Naturally slave-drivers at heart, and glad in giving pain;
There be the active self-reliant, whose pleasure dwelleth evermore in energy,
Willing to thank none beside, and stablished by self-help;
And there be the considerate and liberal, anxious to spare all troubling,
Comforters of good, and combaters of ill, from principle and habit.

OF FOURFOLD DIFFERENCES.

There be four kinds of disposition, squaring the sense of
    cheerfulness,
And every state and age in either **sex** hath one of these :
Rude health, and animal spirits, overleaping worries
As with nature's inner spring, and conquering outer peace ;
Carelessness for every future, as satisfied with any presence,
The school of Epicurus echoing the laughter of Democritus ;
Deep knowledge, high philosophy, despising temporal trifles,
The Stoic and the Buddhist grafted on the Christian student ;
And absolute hopefulness with God, meeting all calamities in
    faith,—
Here is true sunshine in the heart, here the cheek's best beauty.

There be four characters of spending, to square the fancy of
    extravagance,
And all who waste good means exceed by one of these :
Wealth with princely largess, munificently generous,
Scattering benevolences round, in a godlike prodigality ;
Luxury, selfish for its lust, mean amidst all costliness,
Yet caring nought about expense, so long as sense is served ;
The idler's thoughtless lack of care, that never kept accounts,
Whereby no check is given to the hand pulling at the purse-
    strings ;
And the gambler's feverish itching to risk his stake again,—
Who knoweth ? one more cast may change this wreck into an
    argosy !

There be four categories of speaking, to square the habit of
    candour,
And all who are outspoken fall in with one of these :
Simplicity uttereth its verdict with unintended bluntness,
Telling inconvenient secrets, often to much hurt ;
Mischief blurteth out a taunt heedlessly for amusement,
Glad if others wince to hear, and stinging by a word ;
Envy whispereth its malice for jealousy of rivals,—
How pleasant through mere candour to be able to cut deep !
Sincerity telleth out the truth with conscience to displeasing,
And if it bruiseth is self-wounded by its precious balms.

There be four phases of conduct, to square the character of
    courage,

And each of us hath erred in these, or energized discreetly:
The rash unthinking impulse to leap defying danger,
As half-intoxicate with health, and hope, and hot young blood;
The calmly deliberate resolve, with calculated consequences,—
It may cost this and that, but all the risk is worth it;
A low-born fear of man, ridicule spurring into action,—
If I shrink they laugh,—I dare it and escape them;
And sternness of high duty commanding perilous exploit,—
With God my helper, I will beard those lions in the way!

There be four variations of economy, to square the charge of
    meanness;
And parsimonious avarice is sometimes truer prudence:
The habit of diligent thrift, caught from neighbour to neighbour,
Often a local custom, or a larger national wisdom;
An abnegation of all luxury, from ascetic conscience,
Choosing rather pulse and lentils, and refusing meats;
The utter lust of lucre, dishonourably indulged,
As saving coins for saving's sake in covetous idolatry;
And wish to live an honest life by husbanding small means,
That upright independent scheme, more generous than uncomely.

There be four fruitions of man's heart, to square varieties in
    feeling,
And most of us, by turns belike, have haply met them all:
Acrid pulp with a solid stone, sour tamarind and no sweet kernel,
The utterly wicked and unlovely, insensible though sensual;
Rough husk and soft sweet core, a cocoa-nut in the tropics,
The rude coarse nature as to manner, with kindliness and gentleness
    in matter;
Glutinous sugar on bitter death, as poison-berries of the yew,
The polished villain of society, murderous even in his mercies;
And wholesome fruit throughout, good food from rind to centre,
That honest, good, true heart, which even God commendeth.

There be four classes of devout, to square distinction in religion,
And few of men or women are not counted in these four:
The solid state-and-church-man, as all his fathers were,
Gallio enough in soul and sense, although self-judged a Paul;
The superstitious zealot, all alert for rites and robes,
Forgetful in such child's-play of his manlier work on earth;

The scorner of those liturgies, yet earnest, penitent, prayerful,
Whose altar to the living God is built within his heart;
And the man of a wisest moderation, worshipping in spirit and in truth,
Who holdeth faith and forms and works, with tolerance and all charity.

There be four species in affection, to square the condition of love,
And one or other insect-type, as thus, will sketch all lovers:
The moth about a candle, dazed and drunk with admiration,
Caught by beauty's glances, and sore-singed in passion's flame;
The wasp with selfish greed burrowing into peaches,
Cruel even where indulgence pampereth it the most;
The honey-bee domestically storing household sweets,
Useful, tranquil, home-affectioned, real and not romantic;
And this exotic firefly, flashing across life's darkness,
A star upon some flower by night, as dropt to earth from heaven.

There be four varieties in kindliness, to square the state of friendship,
And all thy most acquainted can be gathered in these bounds:
The common so-called friend, thy well-met free companion,
Full of talk and social news, at clubs, at home, abroad;
The higher-sphered than thou, thy gracious, generous patron,
To whom all gratitude is due for benefits to come;
Some genial man of humbler life, haply thine own dependent,
Honest, honourable, and shrewd, but coarse and not thine equal;
And last the rare true jewel, the brother of thy soul,
Ready with every sort of help, and worthy of all love.

There be four gradations in acquirement, to square the theme of intelligence,
And each and all of us may stand on one of these declensions:
Learning, that externally collecteth hidden wealth from many,
A matter of wise diligence and constant education:
Genius, breeding inwardly from secret wealth of one,
A meditative spirit developing its treasures;
Idle stolidity and blankness, dimming all man's brain
As with thick clouds, till brighter worlds may shine the dark away;

And oftenest the ordinary mind, tinged with common knowledge,
Enough for society and commerce and fashioned by the times.

There be four degrees of calculation, to square the credit of
    prudence,
And prudence from its very name is providential care:
For gain of this world's worth, each modern man's ambition,
An honest wish with every one, to benefit his own;
For conscience' sake toward heaven, as filling well one's niche,
With heedful eye for either world, its special needs and profits;
For sobering the proclivities of nature, constraining and re-
    straining,
As conquering circumspectly through every wise advantage;
For giving none occasion to the enemy, for setting right example
    to the young,
For steadfastness in good, and for strength against the evil.

There be four generations of the moralists, squaring the virtue of
    pure living,
And all respectabilities are classed in one of these:
With some the conditions of their natures are cold, continent, and
    sober,
That even weedy vice will flag in such a clay-bound soil;
With some education and self-interest command the outward
    morals,
And so far this is well, a step to inward worth;
With some their dutiful life-struggles contend against infirmities
    and passion,—
How much more honourable for these the battle than for those!
With some the rapture of religion shall soar above corruptions,
And contemplated love and glory cleanse the heart from sin.

There be four views of life, to square the accident of fortune,
And Providence hath stablished each man's lot in one of these:
The good that seemeth evil, spirit's gain with body's loss,—
Happy exchange from wealth and sin, to piety in afflictions;
The evil seeming good, a flood of rich prosperity
Hardening-up the heart with pride where humbleness once
    softened;
All miseries for both worlds, the worst both here and ever,
Pain and rags and filth and crime, with fearful looking forward;

And every earthly blessing here, with heavenly joys elsewhere,
As our Good Prince can testify, a winner of both worlds.

Thus have I set before your patience four-times-four ensamples,
In every character and circumstance evidencing fourfold difference.

OF CURIOUS QUESTIONS.

This world of strange creations, so prodigal in wastefulness of life,
Teeming with eggs, and seeds, and germs, nipped by death continually,
Is it then a nursery and storehouse for other orbs elsewhere,
A workshop where the Maker constructeth His machines,
Each to live developing more gloriously hereafter
By progress toward perfection in their natures and their forms?
The multitudes on multitudes here only born to die,
So intricately fashioned and so exquisitely coloured,
Have these no life beyond, wherein to worship God
And show to angel-minds His skill, by man too long unnoted?
For all are cherished darlings of their Father, and each might be His masterpiece,
And none were made solely for destruction, toys to be flung away:
Would He annihilate a creature His mercy once hath formed,
Nor rather let it grow to bliss, continuously progressing?
Can the Unchangeable be changed, or His purpose fail,
Or any weak caprice be mingled with His vast design?
There is more than room enow for all the generations of earth's children
In yonder shoal of suns we see, with unseen planets round them,—
And all we note are but a sample of the wondrous whole,
The many mansions waiting to be filled with various life;
For it is Infinity, not space, innumerable homes for happy creatures,
Every star a sun, invisibly attended by its system,
And each of those vast satellites, various in form and glory,
To be stocked from this nursery of earth, and perfect all her seeds:
Who knoweth? nothing shall be wasted; not one egg in vain;
Every kind of life immortal in its Maker!

Haply, in like sort, the differences of our human spirits
May segregate and crystallize apart, for separate suitable worlds;
There may be habitations for the mirthful, for the curious, the
    gloomy, or the mean;
There may be studious spheres wherein each science shall expand;
There may be special homes, even as we know with good and evil,
For varied intermediates not yet grown to their extremes;
An infinite diversity of dwelling for infinite diverseness in the
    spirit,
Not an identity of place, where there is no sameness in condition.
Every star may hold its sort, the fiery or the gentle,
The humorous or the melancholy, of its planet's kind,—
And will may flit hereafter from one to other freely,
That the community of worlds may speed the community of spirits.
For were not all these made to be inherited? and by what shapes
    or natures,
With how great powers and senses, yet man's allies in mind?
Light argueth vision, orbits prove the seasons,
And the spectrum giveth hints of chemic forms like ours:
Stars differing in glory shall have dwellers suited to their state,
A lightsome orb for the aërial, and a denser globe for the material;
The glory of the celestial for one, the glory of the terrestrial for
    another,
And God glorified in all, by the varied happiness of creatures.

Whither wend the dead, when here they leave the living?
Are they lingering near us still, or carried far away?
Name them not as lost, nor peevishly speak of them for poor,
Nor think of them despairingly as much to be lamented:
Our hope is they are found, not lost,—and safe with the Good
    Shepherd in His fold,
And rich for heaven, though poor for earth, as leaving all behind
    them,
And only gone awhile before across that swelling Jordan
To join, as one by one they ford, life's caravan of pilgrims,
Who tread some shadowy desert-tract between this world and
    that,
Where all shall meet to start again, unburdened by corruption.

But whither go they for this while? and where that shadowy shore?
A beach beyond our firmament, surrounding us in space?

Are spirits in some prison-house, with angels for their warders,—
The souls asleep in Jesus, dreaming conscious dreams of joy,
The castaway and reprobate, awake to fears of judgment,
The common multitudes between, slumbering well at rest?
And these and others all, released from crazy tabernacles,
Bide they in some vast globe, their vestibule for waiting,
Some spiritual planet, as etherealized to lightness,
Enormously expanded, farthest wanderer round the sun,
Fit dwelling for a season of the disembodied souls
Awaiting there earth's second birth, her baptism of fire?

Do some souls linger here, unseen, unknown, unthought of?
Might any cross that gulf again, for any right or reason?
Who knoweth?—some have hoped as much, and many more have
    feared it,
As conscience or affection gave strange keenness to the mind.
But surely man's life-trial-scene, fulfilled with many hardships,
Must not be weighted with such dreads to hinder daily duties;
Mortals stand in separation, the father not a surety for the son,
Each to run the gauntlet single-handed and self-helping:
And how should men go forth to all our common toils and travails
If haunted by departed souls that have no business here?
Superstitious terrors would hunt us to our harm
With ghostly visitations till we scarce could dare to meet them;
And though, from innocence of wrong, thou hadst no likely fear,
As friendly with the dead for having never wronged the living,
Yet these grim watchers by thy side would hamper honest life-
    work,
And make thy working days more dreamy than thy Sabbath
    nights:
While where for guilt there seemeth cause, the fraud, the lie, the
    murder,
Why antedate the judgment, when all deeds will rise again?
Why should a spirit, well released from cruelties and evils,
Return for petty vengeance, when the Lord is his avenger?
Conscience alone is well enough, and punisheth discreetly
Without the presence of the wronged, albeit he hath life:
All the children of Eve are living to this hour,
Departed and departing, but existent somewhere still;
All are of one great family, that lodge in several mansions,
All in various states and phases, yet alike alive;

And every spirit liveth on according to its kind;
The filthy shall be filthy still, the holy still be holy;
The thoughtful, and the cruel, and the liar, **and** the sage,
The mind that well beginneth here the wisdom learnt of nature,
The soul that seeketh God, or that worshippeth itself,
All are living and pursuing faintly each its aims.

Crowds of other notions ever pressing on the mind
Provoke more curious questioning, **though hopeless** of much
    answer.
Have angels, under **Christ** their Lord, been **used as lower workers?**
And did each bring his offering, for God to stamp with life,
Yea, the evil as the good, according to their natures,
When all the morning stars rejoiced to hail our new-born earth,
And **this green farm was** stocked and **stored** through ministering
    angels?
Satan and his servants, with the better sons of God
Attending in the Great King's court, as patient Job beheld him,
May well have mingled living mischiefs,—have been allowed to
    mingle—
With works of noble sort and more benevolent in kind:
Hence a scorpion as a butterfly; stings so near to honey;
The cruel deeds, and ugly shapes, the vermin, toads, and aspics;
Hideous foils to beauty and the shadow for each light,—
Permitted **evil everywhere to prove** and cleanse creation.

Whence too **came wit and** humour,—from the heights or from the
    depths?
What are mirth and laughter,—do **they** tend to good or evil?
Have ludicrous thoughts any nobler **source** than of this world
    worldly,
Or are those scintillations but low stubble-sparks of earth?
Yet, phases opposite in kind, obtuseness and moroseness,
Such emanations came not from above but from below;
Guilt hath gloomy sorrow, while innocence is cheerful,
And rather mirth than melancholy would seem the heavenly type.
All things have deep reasons; even to corruption and disease,
The microscope detecteth in them wonders of design;
Least things as things greatest have their orbits spanned by Pro-
    vidence,
And accident and so-called chance are Nothings in the world.

Thus, even anagrams and riddles, and word-games, and acrostics,
And flashings of keen wit, and exaggerative humour,
Analogy of sounds combined with paradox in sense,
All seem to grow of hidden laws that govern uttered thought.
Reason, which revealeth all our mightiest distant marvels,
The mysteries in the heavens, and the secrets of the earth,
Is quick to watch for ordered rules in little as in great,
In humorous aptitudes alike with modes and forms of logic,
In puns and jests and plays of words, in letters of one's name—
So often touching curiously on character and conduct,—
In trivial talk not less than wiser elegancies of language,
In suitable sounds as well as their philosophy of sense.

Consider also, is it not a marvel that those who found out rhythm,
Our masters in word-painting, the poets of old days,
Never should have stumbled upon rhyme, till monks found out its
   sweetness,
Or troubadours invented the jangle of like sounds.
For well-nigh fifty centuries no nation under heaven
Had wedded war-song nor love-ditty to the charm of rhyme,—
But when the Latin jingle first caught the world's great ear
Forthwith those Leonnine-verses seemed to fascinate its heart,
And spreading like a prairie-fire, the dainty trick of rhyme
Flew swiftly over every land, an epidemic passion.
Is it not a wonder that Anacreon, or Martial, or Horace or
   Catullus
Never added to sweet rhythm the sweeter charm of rhyme?
Is it not strange that till to-day no tongue hath asked this
   question,
How came it that the world was old before it rhymed a stanza?

For further question ;—be there spirits good and bad abroad,
Inoculating nations with an epidemic power,
And as through some reflective glass, or quick electric spark
Communicating to thy neighbour thoughts by thee unuttered?
Secret crimes are multiplied, alike in each detail ;
Inventions in some selfsame hour are seen by several minds,
Theories and ideas, that grew originally thine,
At once, as if from seed broadcast, are found to spring elsewhere;
And, even as Micaiah spake, some spirits true or lying
Would seem to carry facts and fancies swiftly through the world.

Again; where ticks and knocks are heard, and wizards peep and
    mutter,
Is not their table made a snare to catch themselves withal?
Yet honest witnessing is much, and secrets shown are more,
And,—how to judge those mental wonders fairly and discreetly?
Can some be human magnets, and diviners of one's thought,
Or men by whose galvanic force dull matter is inspired?
Who knoweth? some have heard and seen, have known and felt
    strange things;
The world of souls we thought so far away may yet be near us.

Is it not the wonder of this West, considering human likings
And noting that antagonist custom in the patriarchal East,
That single wedlock everywhere is fixed for law and usage,
And thus a new commandment superadded to the ten?
How should a sin be great or nothing as the map decideth?
Why must Justinian's Roman code still govern modern Europe?
Some have dared such questions for society to answer,
And answer cometh curtly,—double wedlock is a crime.

Is it not a marvel of neglect with all our zeal for sacraments,
That no strict sect felt ever bound to wash a brother's feet?
And yet it was enjoined on all, as clear a Christian duty
As Christ's example and command have ever laid on man:
Is this a sacrament that failed, through climate or through
    custom?
Are his disciples here absolved from doing as He bade?
And why among so many sects, each with the key of heaven,
Hath no one hinged his door on this, our Saviour's humblest
    act?

Is it not a miracle of wrong, that where the Lord gave thanks,
That simple eucharist is forced to idol-consecrations?
And yet, when He fed multitudes, He blessed, and brake the
    loaves
Religiously with equal thanks and no pretence of mystery:
O grievous miracle of wrong, that the blessed Spiritual Presence
Evermore realized on earth where two or three worship together,
Should be twisted by the lens of superstition into hideous and
    absurd distortion,
The cruel cause for tortured saints and virgins burnt alive!

Is it not a strangeness of abuse that certain words with water
Are held regeneration, and **enough to save the** soul?
And yet, at first, conversion, with **faith** and real repentance
Fore-ran, not only followed, that seal upon the brow:
O **piteous** strangeness of abuse where a cleansing and refreshing in
      the symbol
By false exaggeration is made the seal for heaven,
Till Xavier saveth savages by buckets of sea-water from his
      boat,
And Herod's innocents are doomed, unsprinkled, to Gehenna!

Is it not a deep **sad** proof that faith is warped from reason
When well-nigh **everywhere** the sign is made to stand **its** truth,
When those who never pray to God, bow down before His priest,
And sinners buy from sinners absolution of their sins!
O bitter evidence that still, even in these clear days,
When light and knowledge blaze around to scare away all dark-
      ness,
Conscience hideth hard from God, as Adam in the garden,
Clinging to any mediator who is not **the** Christ.

Is it not a faithless folly, in arguments to favour resurrection,
That most men judge creation only made to be destroyed,
That nothing of the Maker's works save man shall live again,
And blank annihilation prove all other fabrics failures?
O silly selfishness,—we think to glorify our manhood
By blotting from earth's kingdom all creatures but their king,
Whereby this world's regenerate state were but an empty realm,
With man alone, and none beside to help or do him homage!

Is it not the paragon of shame, that hierarchy ever hath contrived
To link with each most sacred name some basest thought of
      evil?
That **fraud, lies,** hate attach to the society of Jesus,—
That **his** dear Presence stood the cause of martyrs burnt alive,—
That holy inquisition is a horror to the mind
As binding up with tortures every doctrine of religion,
That man's most hideous guilt hath grown of zeal for God,
And earth's worst catalogue of crime is fathered on the Church?
Whether in Italy, France, or Spain, in Smithfield or Thibet,
By India's funeral pyres, or Portugal's **martyr stakes,**

With screws, and whips, and racks,—with pincers, flames, and
    starvings,
The priest hath everywhere defamed religion and the Church!

What is the Church?—They steal a name and fix it on their fore-
    heads,
Styling the building, with its ritual and its priest, the Church:
And vestments are brought forth, as **erst to** worship Baal,
And incense, though abomination, **and the blessing** idols,
And men with **faces** towards the east **and backs** against the
    temple,
That temple of God's people which the rapt Ezekiel saw.

The Church? It is not ministries, nor sacraments, nor altars,
Albeit such be scaffolding to build its living stones;
Yet is the Church far more than so,—the beauteous of all ages,
The spiritual bride of Christ from Abel to this hour;
The Church is one choice band, gathered of all the churches,
Yea, and beyond our narrow creeds, of all outside their pales;
A family, whose absent Head is prayed for till He cometh,
A caravan of pilgrims, with their Leader gone before;
A company of faithful soldiers, watching for their Captain,—
Of every race and nation, and in every place and time.

Go to: thy selfish churchmanship may have its special praise,
Its privileges, its duties, well-responsible to thee;
But heed thou of thy kindred in all ages and all climes,
That God's own ark hath every sort of every tribe and sect,
That Cyrus, Socrates, and Paul are brothers in the Church,
And that **the arms** of Christ were nailed outstretched to clasp the
    world.

Are there not multitudes of mysteries? Is any question answered?
The how and why of anything, Who knoweth? Who can guess?
Names hide things; the heap of learned words
Hath great show of knowledge, the rather if such be not under-
    stood.
What is life? What is light? What is heat, or motion?
Is not sleep a sort of death, and wakening resurrection?
In the quick work of genius, be it statue, book, or painting,
Is there any semi-soul, existent vital truth?

Is not everything that **is, so ordered that it** could not have been
 other,
And yet the will of man is free to turn toward good and evil?
And all beside of questioned sort,—cruelty, wrong, and sin,
And tyrannies of circumstance, mechanics, and statistics,
Tend they not each to this, Follow thou Me is needful,—
But for aught else of secret matter,—What is that to thee?

OF MAN'S DATE UPON EARTH.

SOME have dreamt that Adam, though placed alone in Eden,
As perfect fruit and flower himself of man **upon** this earth,
Had yet mean human kindred, out of Paradise, beyond,
Poor forms of lower manhood, that had crept through generations;
Commencing in some brutish phase, **or**, haply, viler still,
Through fish and humbler vegetal, or aboriginal monad.
They fancy hinted vengeful tribes, of whom black Cain was
 fearful;
They hear of some dim **nomad realm**, where he roamed forth to
 build;
They think that on some savage shores, Australian or Fuegian,
Remnants of such Præ-Adamites are dwelling to this day;
They deem it strange and false **to** claim a unity of race
For Negroes, Laps, Chinese, and Persians, Esquimaux, and
 Britons;
They want uncounted æons for development of man,
His languages, inventions, and customs and traditions,
And claim primeval Adam a **result of million** ages,
Before in perfectness he could stand up and speak with God.

Vain, vain imaginations!—For the Maker made him perfect,
Though free to fall, more free to rise, upright and very good:
The Maker made him man at once, proportioned and adapted,
Man at his best as all beside, at best and full of seed.
True, he had come as if the fruit and climax of creations,
Lower forms through long drawn eras leading **up to** him:
First after the chaos, were motion light and **cosmos**;
Next the lighter swathe of air, and grosser **band of** waters;
Third, the land productive at a word, an age of vegetal life;
Fourth, the ordinances of heaven, and our circling seasons;

Fifth, an era of great whales, of lizards, bats, and birds;
Sixth, of all creatures upon earth after their kinds and orders:
Then all **these** eras long wrought out were indexed **by six** days,
The literal week of cosmos, with its **human lord** and master,
Last in the pageant of creation shown the king of all,
Preceded by his servants, **and surrounded by** his courtiers,
And **with that gentle queen** beside him, springing from his heart—
The mother of all living, and the Empress of the World!

Man, created by His fiat, from the dust of mother-earth,
Miraculously born at once, with seed within himself,
Cutting the cycle of eternity by the radius commencing **time**,
And at full manhood crowned and throned as king of this creation,
Well might contain in his self-sphere a small epitome of all things,
And stand, as wise men said of old, the human Micro-kosmos;
Hence, from that germinating dust, his body and his being
Hint at all the lower forms beneath their highest monarch,
Foreshown that he would be their chief, having sympathies and
      likenesses with all,
The fish, the bird, the mammal,—nay the vegetal, and crystal,
Not as born through them **bodily**, but fashioned of set purpose,
Constructed of analogies, that prove creation One;
Made, when and as his world was ready, **the reasonable** image of
      his Maker,
A creature at the focus of perfection in all kinds,
Thus, born at best at first, inspired with language and inventions,
Thereafter did the penalties on sin drag down our glorious race,
Till the savage, mind and body, **was** degraded little higher than an
      ape,
Where the black progeny of Cain swarmed over tropical marshes:
Never could the monkey rise to man, though man might sink to
      monkey,
(Saving for the great gulfs fixed, in conscience, reason, spirit,)
And the secret of **our baser** tribes is seen, in their lapse from first
      perfection,
Not in the fancied climbing-up **of** animal-brute to man:
Moreover, if other things have grown, evolving one from other,
Humanity was added from above, "I have said that ye are Gods."

The word is sure, that "things which are seen, were not made of
      things which do appear,"

And that the fool hath said in his heart, there is no God, things grew.
So the most learned as to creatures monstrously denieth the Creator,
Curiously resolving that creation made itself!
And rather than admit a God, with miracle and gracious revelation,
Refuseth His image unto man, developed from the lowest brute.
O most impotent conclusion, of philosophy falsely so called,
Where skill is made servant to ungodliness, and knowledge warped
    to strive against religion!

The Maker taught man language, with no need to learn it slowly,
And gave him reason, light, and skill, at once and without stint:
The Maker afterwards on earth filled those lost years of Adam
(Who, in full vigour, though just born, stood not as child, but
    man)
For Christ, the second Adam, as thus, forelived the first,
By making-up Time's earliest gap of three and thirty years.
Why else should Christ have died so soon, nor lived the span of
    life,
Except that Adam's sudden manhood lacked those years pre-
    ceding?
Hence, both first and second Adam build the perfect Man,
And so the model creature hath its harmony and oneness,
Christ fulfilling Adam's life, and dying on his birth-day,
Thus by life and sacrifice precursing death and sin.

Then, as for those avengers, whom black Cain so justly feared;
Might such not well have been dead Abel's unnamed brethren?
Fruitful Eve was crowded round by throngs of sons and daughters,
And, beside his holiest Seth, Adam had bands of children.
Then for that nomad realm of Nod; the name is exile, flight,—
So given in after years, as where the manslayer had fled:
And for all savage tribes; those outliers of the nations
From earliest times have stolen aside, crawling away from light;
Degenerated and sensual sons, though well-nigh sunk to brutes
Still must we own with sadness those poor prodigals our brothers.

The learned scheme out several races, culling the extremes of
    each,
To set forth such exemplars in strange and startling contrast:
The Hottentot, the Arab, the Fin, and the Malay,
The stunted dwarf of the Obongo, the wiry-thewed Red Indian,

The lithe Hindoo, the sturdy Russ, the Tuscan, and the Tartar,
How oppositely seen **are** these as different in kind !
Yet such diversities are strong in their extremes **alone,**
Their means have much of likeness as of the same great family ;
For, such shades of difference flit over every race,
Such a melting of one into the other over all the world,
That many times in any crowd **one may** discern all features,
The Tartar's eye, the negro's **lip, the high** Caucasian brow.

And look to the varieties of breed, everywhere **rife in** nature ;
No two provinces alike, **for** herds or flocks or produce.
The northern cattle brought down south, to **rich and sunny pastures,**
Within three generations lose their rough and stinted shapes ;
Fishes of various rivers have peculiar forms in each ;
Antelopes are diversely spotted in their several prairies :
How wide the differences between the **racer and** the drayhorse,
The setter and **the** spaniel, **the** bloodhound **and the** bulldog ;
Yet these within man's knowledge have sported from one breeding,
With more of strong distinctive **traits than** human races show.
Climate, soil, and habits, hardship, **luxury,** diseases,
These will operate strange change **on** members of one **stock ;**
Nay, the same nursery of children, tended just alike,
Come of one father and one mother, similarly **fed and** taught,
How various oft in body and mind, and bents to good or **evil,**
How often different **and** distinct in features and in forms.

Adam, by his name the Red, had intermediate colour,
His sons diverging either way toward the light or **dark :**
Or haply Cain's dread punishment was blackness universal,
That curse of primal murder overclouding soul and body ;
So his offspring, stained like him, should carry down the tint,
And through some negress wife of Ham survive in Noah's Ark :
Not but that Christ's glad gospel hath since made all things new,
The leopard's spots are scattered, and the Ethiop's skin is changed,
Peter's sheet had every kind and none are now unclean,
Candace's sable eunuch is as pure a soul as **Abel ;**
In Jesus all are made alive, and sons of Ham **and** Canaan,
Even if Cainites, are made clean, and white as snow on Salmon.

Adam placed in Eden, at perfection, mind and body,

After his bitter fall was left to reason and inventions:
And Seth's good sons kept righteousness to sanctify their lives,
Religion and the peaceful arts, with homes and flocks and herds;
But Cain's and Lamech's evil spawn contended in corruption,
And Tubal-Cain—old Vulcan—gave them weapons for their wars:
The good seed, fixed in tropic climes, soon grew to wealth and
    science,
While centuries of intellect, so crowded in one life,
Ripened wisdoms rapidly, and forced the race of Seth
To early miracles of skill, discovery, and knowledge:
The bad seed, crawling miserably about the wintry world,
To wrestle with hyenas in those glacier-caves and forests,
Soon forgat all goodness in their struggle for mere life,
And sowed the cliffs, the sands, the lakes, with savage human
    seed,
Dwindled, weak, with animal skulls, where reason's lamp burnt
    dimly,
And scarcely battling down the bears with axes of chipped flint.
Mammoths and fish-lizards may have lived and fought with such,
In marshy wilds and lakes, aswarm with scaly dragons,
Behemoths and Leviathans coeval with our race,
Nor near so long extinguished as some eager sages argue.
That bad seed fiercely pioneered the better human family,
Traversing glaciered continents and the warmer tilted poles;
But in the hardships of such toil decayed and grew degraded,
While Japhet's happier sons came on and seized the spoils of
    Ham.
Bushmen, Australians, and Andamans have well-nigh sunk to
    apes,
But Jews and Saxons and Chinese preserve their nobler vantage;
Whole tribes have lost their high estate, and fallen near the
    brute;
Hottentot skulls and Celtic jowls are humbling and deforming;
But brutes can never win one step progressing up toward man;
There is the great gulph fixed, and effort cannot leap it:
Brutes cannot rise to reason, to religion, or to speech,
Nor man quite quench his lights, nor fall to animal dumbness.

And there is none urgent reason in the languages of men
Why more than these six thousand years Man should have dwelt
    on earth;

For those languages have so great likeness, so much to point at
 oneness,
That Adam's primal tongue may well be found their centre.
Speech was the earliest inspiration breathed into man by God,
Not unmeaning utterance, but rational expression of the mind;
Though words were few and short, in sound they told the
 sense,
And the Great King listened condescendingly, to hear Man name
 his servants:
Thus from that first beginning in providence and reason
Words grew, and things were called, as earth's lord pleased to hail
 them.
As every tribe of men hath Adam one sole father,
So every language in the world hath one, one only, root;
And, as the various races with all difference are the same,
So many tones of likeness bind those diverse tongues in one:
Then say not thou this knot is lazily cut by miracle,
Though there was that miraculous beginning, in analogy with all
 things else.
Speech, God's first gift to man, combining voice with mind,
By lip and tongue pronouncing his articulated wants
Evolved, by daily growings out of those one-syllabled seeds,
The slowly-gathered harvest of that patriarchal language.
Thereafter, as our Maker willed, the reason given to man,
Conceived for thoughts, revealed by speech their carved or written
 symbols,
Signs set for sounds, to teach beyond the hearing,
And somewhiles secretly devised to hide their facts from foes:
Hence grew lists of divers signs expressing the like sounds,
And varied symbols showing forth the differences of utterance.
In a cold clime speech grew stern, more liquid in the warmer,
Hardship growled his guttural notes, and plenty poured soft
 rhythm,
Hatred hissed and muttered, love made long-drawn music,
Courage spoke out whole round words, cowardice whispered
 halves;
So that, even short of Babel, over various climes,
Within few generations many tongues would soon outspring,
Constructed with much likeness as to common rules of grammar,
In times and modes and forms of speech, the laws that build up
 language.

The vocal sounds from lung and throat, and cheeks by mouth
    and lip
Are alike in every people's tongue, whatever be their symbols;
And names for things, with words of action, oft are found alike
In many languages of men, with sundry common phrases:
So that, varying in much, in much are tongues so like,
Their root is seen as one, with a hundredfold of tillering.

There remaineth the question of dispersion, the peopling of this
    globe;
And more than fifty centuries give more than ample time.
No monumental relic of our race hath near such age;
Not piled-up rocks of Druidism, nor galleries in the cliffs,
Nor giant prairie-mounds, nor flint knives, nor stone hatchets,
Nor later far strange Yucatan, nor wondrous Elephanta:
None need be more than half as old; and, for barbarian eras,
Tradition, fable, lunar years, confound historic fact.
Man in degradation at his darkest worst estate
Crawled over all this planet, from Arctic to Antarctic;
Age after age, from east to west, he slowly wandered on,
And rafted the tempestuous seas, or crept across the Poles;
Nor needed more antiquity; the circuit of the world
Was tracked by those who dwell thereon far sooner than men
    doubt it.

OF SLEEP.

Every night a dissolution, as every morn a resurrection;
Sleep the sister of death, sleep the mother of life:
Here is the windingsheet in darkness, the silent strait obstruction,
The day's accounts all closed, and dreamland opening dimly,
In the strange wakefulness of slumber that ever breedeth dreams,
Dream growing into dream, and life evolved from life:
Here is the newborn light quickening to fresher energies,
Another Present growing from the seedcorn of the Past,
Both flesh and spirit bathed again in prayer and cleansing water,
And the new creature clothed-upon for one more phase of life.

Half our time is spent asleep, yet few men manage wisely
How to make sleep happy, and thus redeem that half:
Healthy temperance and exercise, purity and honesty and piety,

These reward such worship with the blessing of sweet sleep:
But each **excess, and** evil thoughts, and craft and prayerless
    pillows
Yield by night the troublous storm of fancied fears and pains.
He is a prudent husbandman, whose conscience on his bed
Is as a barn well stored with peace, the grain of good remem-
    berings;
He is a thriftless farmer, **whose spirit** night by night
Is like a wilderness of thorns, a jungle of ill memories.

How different is one man's night in essence from another
Here the sleep of innocence, there the swoon of guilt;
The hot-brained stupor of the drunken, or mind's ecstatic calm,
The lying down and rising up, in hope or in despair.
To one his pillow is a terror, of fearful looking back and looking
    forward,
With nothing to secure his heart from feeding on itself;
To another all is peacefulness, complacency, and comfort,
For present, past, and future, every meditation sweet.
Verily, through conscience of the soul, in each man's half of
    life,
His due reward or punishment is poured upon him sleeping.

In dreams how near-allied is reason to **unreason,**
What slight divergency in sleep betwixt insane and sane!
That which is the uttermost of folly seemeth **to the dreamer**
    wisdom,
Nothing too absurd or false but standeth true for dreams.
Imagination worketh while the judgment is at rest,
And will is in captivity to good or evil habit:
A just reward is herein given to clean and honest morals,
That habit standeth sentinel, though will and judgment sleep.
And many have dreamt dreams, and suffered from them deeply,
And often have been warned betimes, or chastened in a dream;
Yet who remembereth,—who can catch his dream when he
    awaketh?
Vanishing with wakefulness it melteth into light:
And often hath the roused-up dreamer striven **in** vain to hold
The strong impression on his brain that faded out so quickly;
In vain,—the life of fancy dieth at the day,
Another world, another life, is wakened with the morning.

O best of blessings for creation, **next** to life itself,
How vast a boon to every **creature is** the gift of sleep,—
One half of time made happy, though so vext the other,
Even abjects, slaves, and culprits, soothed and blest thereby,—
Happy, soothed, and blest, if Sin hath **kissed** Repentance,
Or the good and honest heart is witness to itself.
How can the wicked dare deliberately to sleep,
Lying down helpless in the dark, unclad except with grave-clothes,
To sleep, in type to die,—their bed a cushioned coffin,—
Tormented by bad memories in the purgatory of conscience?
How can they wake unscared, impenitent, as if to resurrection?
How can they face another day of life without a God?

Wise is the man who kneeleth every night beside his **bed;**
Thou canst not tell if **death be now** not shrouded in these
    curtains:
My Father died asleep,—and never knew he died,—
Dead in his bed they found him; for his soul had passed away:
Dead in his bed!—how peaceful looked my Father in his sleep,
As if reviewing in calm dreams his tranquil useful life;
One hand beneath the placid cheek, the other on **his heart,**
That pitcher broken at the fountain as a potter's vessel,
Its precious liquor spilt and scattered, in one shattering moment,
And then all peace and quietness, the good man's sleep in death.
He feared to **die,**—**I** fear it too,—I dread the pang of pain;
He feared not death,—I fear it not,—for death is only slumber;
Sleeping, dreaming, waking,—blank night and bright to-morrow,
Rest, refreshment, energy,—then Life for evermore!

OF DELAY.

Too late! **the door is** shut,—depart, I never knew you:
Too late! the time is past: too late,—all hope is over.
Instant duty **is the wisdom,** instant constant duty,
Now, with no delay, Now, while nothing letteth.
Never may Occasion come again; so snatch it ere it passeth;
The bitterest wailings of regret moan around perished opportunity.
The present, the present is thy life; the past is dead,—with re-
    surrections;
The future, none may count on that, if only for one hour:

Is thy past to thee as nothing? yet it shall be everything to conscience:
Can thy future grow to anything? still it may go out in nigh to
 nothing.

God, by Whose will we are, foreknoweth and fore-ordereth,
And His command is Action; delay not, lest ye die;
By death of power and will, by death of chance and season,
Not less than by the man's decease, perisheth good occasion:
The hasty hath been found in fault for over-rapid zeal,
But oftener conquered through a speed whereby at times he faileth:
And he that surely doth at once the matters to be done
Hath not himself to blame for any ruinous delay.
Be discreet, but with discretion urge to quickest action;
Be discreet, but dread delay, the cankerworm of duty;
With good speed, not evil hurry, do thy works at once;
This care is off thy conscience, and thou hast sown that seed;
And now the seed may well begin to grow for flowering and
 fruiting;
Till thou hast sown it neither shoots nor fibres burgeon there.

Enterprise and energy,—be these thy sandal-shoon,
O traveller on life's highway, be shod in such for speed,—
So shalt thou win every race, conquering good successes,
By simply flinging living facts, Deucalion-like, behind thee.
O the dreary prospect of some idler on life's road,
He lingereth and he feareth,—there be lions in the way;
Lo, how close and high and rugged frown those threatening
 mountains,
Can any foot surmount them, or a path be found between?—
Go on, go on, faint-hearted one; if courage be but thine
The very mountains shall melt down before a Christian's presence:
There ever is a way to escape, a track both safe and easy
For him whose pilgrim feet are shod with enterprise and strength.

Resolve slowly, act swiftly; a quiet eye for the quick hand:
The fool hath a hot head, and is clogged with frozen feet.
There is a wisdom in delay, to watch, and snatch occasion;
Touch not the trigger till yon charging elephant is close:
There is a folly in delay, too slow to turn the tiller;
Quick! or with a crushing force that huge black hull is on thee.

They whose work hath no delay achieve Herculean labours ;
A molehill every minute is a mountain in the year :
Your clock within one twelvemonth ticketh thirty million seconds,
By steadily without a stop fulfilling **small details** ;
But if it lingered as in fear computing that huge sum,
The feat would seem impossible, and be so, through delay:
Yet is there given for every tick its moment of existence,
And instant diligence is found sufficient for its work.

There is betimes a wise delay, as there is foolish speeding,
But oftener speed is seen to shame the lingering of delay:
For that the time is short, occasion passeth swiftly,
And things get done in doing, no longer still to do,
And our brief life's kaleidoscope is changing every moment,
Our complicated game of chess altereth with each move ;
So that ever, Now, is the **true labourer's** motto,
And only market-idlers dream to **make** their watchword Then.

OF GREAT AND SMALL.

WONDROUS are thy works, O Lord ! and worthy of all praise!
Marvellous in least as in the greatest, from the snowflake up to
    the arch-angel :
Worlds rolling in their orbits, and atoms floating on the air,
Equally proclaim omnipotence, and prove that **omnipotence all-
    wise.**
There is wonderful **comfort in the microscope, very monads being**
    cared for ;
Even though the telescope may **scare us, as if** poor monads were
    forgotten :
For there is a fearfulness to creatures in such a far-off God,
Governing those globes by millions, infinitely distant and enor-
    mous ;
As there is a joy to us in noting Him **so** nigh, so tender **to the**
    meanest of His works,
Even the obscurest animalcules displaying a most exquisite per-
    fection :
Well might we fear our insignificance, as totally unworthy of His
    Greatness,

But that we note His condescensions even to the emmet and the
    mite;
Yea, He rejoiceth in the least in the lowest and the humblest of
    His creatures,
As much as in those glorious worlds where most His honour
    dwelleth.
The drop from a pin's point dipped into stagnant water
And seen to be full of passionate life beneath thy powerful
    glass,
This whirling microscopic country is it less a proof of His omni-
    potence
Than systems of huge globes careering through infinity?
God knoweth: nothing is so small but it hath its lesser and lower,
Even as nothing is so great but it hath its greater and higher:
Each is a perfection in its rank; no fault nor loss nor blemish,
From the monad next to an invisible, to the mightiest world upon
    the firmament.

The galaxies of suns, the heavens beyond the heavens,
Infinity, Eternity, cannot contain Thy glory;
Yet is that glory in the spirit higher than that glory in the matter,
Since Thou didst humble Thyself down to live and die a man!
Lo! Thy grandest globes, Aldebaran, Alcyone, or Sirius,
Shine not with half the splendour of Thy human face,
Where love humility and truth show forth a nobler grandeur
Than all omnipotence hath built, omniscience could design.
So, our lenses for the small are even more eloquent of God,
Than where our vast reflectors reveal His greater wonders;
In the minutest parasite, or fruitage of a moss
The Maker is as wondrous as in planets suns and systems;
And gnats upon the sunbeam dance in some tangled order,
Even as meteors, comets, worlds, and works and ways of
    men.
From the mighty stars of heaven to the molecules of showers and
    of dews,
From the Mountains and Hills of earth to the smallest mosses on
    them,
So is sung the song of the Three Children, walking in the furnace
    with their Lord,
The praises of the God of all go up for ever and ever.
With every breath and every pulse, at every inch and instant,

By every word and every thought, in Him we live and move;
Down to the infinite of smallness, as up to the infinite of greatness,
Almighty, Ever-present, He worketh all in all!

Who knoweth as to other worlds, where corruption may have
    entered with creation,
(Because the making an inferior argueth some necessary failing,)
Who knoweth, how far in analogy with all we see of earth,
The Maker may in each have raised His creature to Himself,
Alike by adoption of its nature, alike by standing for its substitute,
Alike with ours by nobly taking on Himself its sin?
Man noteth only his own world, considering alone his own con-
    ditions,
Fancying that for none but him God renovated matter;
But haply, everywhere as here, in planets round the polestar as in
    ours,
A special incarnation of the Maker may bless each fallen world.
He is the Universal Friend, the Saviour as Creator and Preserver,
The Lamb self-sacrificed in grace to stop the claims of justice,
The link to join in one the creature with its God,
The true resurrection out of matter, the very Life of spirit.
By whatsoever name adored, and in whatever shape,
Here the God-man Jesus, there the same Divinity transformed,
Well may He rejoice to have been found in fashion with those
    beings of his hand,
Redeemer of all dwellers in the starry orbs above us!

How nice, how narrow is the difference of shibboleth or sibboleth
    in schisms,
How oft a mere iota set betwixt the truth and error:
There need no mighty winds, the slightest breath sufficeth;
Give or take away one grain, the polar tilt is changed:
An aspirate, an accent, or a whisper, may be much;
So like may mate with unlike, by a little cunning care.
The chemist, by one atom's worth from nature's just proportions,
Can alter death to life, and gather health in poisons,
Can win rare flavour from decay, sweet odour out of stenches,
The brightest rainbow-colours from a sorry smear of tar,
And seem to make new creatures by a miracle of mingling,
Also, in curing like with like, how small a dose will do it,
The aura of an essence, or its thousandth of a drop;

And, pleasures can be fevered till they wake the nerve of pain
By adding or subtracting a mere fancy or affection;
And pain,—as martyrdom hath told, is exquisite in rapture
Through love and faith, and hope, that can have neither weight
   nor measure.
Note then; the Master-Alchemist, by some small subtlest drop
Ever can evoke the good from out whatever evil:
Therefore, pray to Him, and trust **Him**; He can cure it all;
However great thy grief, His lightest touch will heal it:
Look, how the host of the Assyrians **were dead men in one night**,
How famishing Jerusalem rejoiced in sudden plenty,
How true the daily parable of dawn at coldest dark,
How sure the fact that sunshine is above thy blackest cloud.
So, walk right on in simple faith, obedient even in the smallest,
Obeying to a trifle all thy duties in their turn,
Laying its own light burden only on each **passing** moment,
And sweetening life's great draughts of **evil** by small drops of good.

The world is governed as the family, a nation as an individual;
Do wisely, and **ye prosper**; do **foolishly,** and penalty shall follow:
And well is ever wisely, and wickedness is foolishness;
In great things as in small are His commandments had in honour.
The heathen fell into the pit they privily dug for others,
And so our Havelock triumphed over treacherous Hindostan;
An idle people starveth, a luxurious nation dwindleth,
Poland, Ireland, Turkey, Spain, ye gather your deserts;
Ambition winneth judgment, and tyranny retribution,
Will not Prussia, Austria, France, receive **their wages earned**?
The slave shall bruise his heel **on his oppressor's head,**—
Alas for **thee,** Columbia, and thy desolated regions!
For Moral Laws inexorably must reward or punish,
And Justice, equal Justice, shall be dealt to great and small.

OF SELFISHNESS.

It is written, Self-forgetfulness is duty, self-sacrifice the highest
   praise;
And yet, a man's own self! what should he barter for his soul?
It is written, Self-abasement is high wisdom, self-loathing the true
   sequel to self-searching;

Yet, who shall spurn good conscience, who casteth scorn on self-
  respect?
It is written, pull out the right eye; it is written, cut off the right
  hand;
Yet, must we guard with duteous care the blessings God hath
  given.
Wise it were to join the twain, reconciling this word with that,
And well to note how man's two natures need the double lesson.
Doubtless, each is to himself his own most precious world,
Infinite for interest and value, when Time is once expanded to
  Eternity;
But his orbit is a ring of duties, which here if well fulfilled
By making others happy, addeth happiness to himself:
Again; with God humility, with man an equal's bearing,
These comport with conscience, and its outer symbol conduct:
Again; the strong divulsion, in some wrestling-match with passion,
Is other than a gentler force, when passions are at rest.

We are atomies upon a little globe, itself a point on space,
A spangle to those circling suns that gird the throne of God;
Yet intellect hath swelled our minds to comprehend these heavens,
And sharpened them to search the smallest secrets of this earth:
And man is like a God for his sublimity of spirit
Which nothing can make happy but the largest liberal love;
There never was contentment in a mean and sordid aim,
And selfish pleasure as an end is always disappointment.
The choicest individual bliss is universal heaven,
The truest interest of each the happiness of all.

And for any isolated self, where conscience is at ease,
(However humbled to the dust beneath the search of heaven)
How blessed in unselfishness, how genial and how pure
He walketh in a blissful maze of charitable musing.
In silent meditation feeding secretly apart,
His independent spirit is a worker still for others:
Happy doth he lie upon his bed, the day's long trial over,
Lullabyed as still a babe upon his Father's arm;
Happy shall he wake at midnight, full of prayers and praises;
Happy in his early rising, strong and high in hope;
Happy in daily duty, though some troubles still may cross him;
Happy, whatsoever be his lot, as labouring in God's vineyard.

Yea; for his own spirit is his friend, a witness with high heaven
That he hath ever wrought his best, mastering the tasks assigned
    him;
And that his best is well-accepted; and there are no ill memories
To gnaw his secret solitude with keen and cruel teeth;
But evermore deep comforts are enwrapt in true remembrance
Of all things just and well achieved, pure and of good report.

And who shall guage the wretchedness of one at war with
    Heaven,
At enmity with conscience, that unsensual self?
He cannot bear the loneliness, he dare not tempt the darkness,
He loveth not his pillow for the swarming terrors there;
Flung down to sleep without a prayer, a wearied heathen hound,
His dreams are full of fears, and detected guilt and vengeance;
And when he wakeneth with a start, all unrefreshed and fevered,
It is to pangs of memory and impenitent remorse:
O how steeped in many woes is self-accusing conscience,
O how wise is he whose Self is made his bosom friend!

There is one cure, and only one, for selfishness in creatures,
The wondrous liberality poured forth by their Creator:
Nothing lower, nothing less, can silence human reason
From clamouring for self-interest, except the love of God.
- Consider: we, His workmanship, His subjects, and His sons
Utterly had rebelled against our Father and Preserver;
We would not see Him with our eyes, nor hear Him with our
    ears,
Our very hearts and minds abjured His pure and loving Presence;
Our lives, at best forgetful, often wilfully transgressed;
Our spirits, spurning all things good, were leagued with all things
    evil:
Ruin here, and worse hereafter, we had wrought and earned,
And Mercy knew no power to stay the lifted sword of Justice
Then, the Judge Himself resolved to be the victim,
To stand convicted of all sin, a culprit undefiled,
To satisfy strict Justice whilst He glorified strong Mercy
By bearing all the penalties of all the sins of men!
Seeing then, selfish mortal,—He hath lifted thee to Godhead,
Canst thou still nurse small worldlinesses as a ransomed saint?
Only believe the record, and accept that mighty gift;

Stand as a redeemed of the Lord, survey thy glorious heritage,
And then consider self and all its puny baseness,
Contrasted with the large and high unselfishness of Christ:
So, all that thou shalt covet, will be glory for thy God,
And all thy love shall yearn on Him, who died because He loved thee.

OF SLANDER.

LIE on, thou false **accuser! and wreak thy paltry spite;**
A little space, a little while, enjoy this petty triumph;
Let envy, with white face, and those brown malignant eyes,
And feverish malice, and dull hate, strive all their feeble strongest;
Let ridicule and scorn and stolid censure undeserved
Add what they will of smoke and stench, malaria and miasma,
The sun of genius still shall blaze the brighter from those clouds,
The good and great man's honest fame shall chase away these shadows,
The mountain of his greatness looming grander in the mist,
The jewel of his goodness shining brighter **out** of darkness.

Hast thou borne thee bravely, and good-humouredly withal?
Hast thou smiled at sneer and gibe, nor answered them in malice?
Hast thou waited patiently, nor forced one selfish plea,
Nor heeded mere neglect, nor cared for false reproaches?
Hast thou well deserved, at peace with God and conscience?
Hast thou taught thy neighbour, and not **hindered him with** lies?—
Lo! in spite of all their taunts who daily wrest thy words,
And shoot out arrows to thy hurt, unscrupulously in secret,
Thy full triumph yet shall come, and is not now far off;
Those who spurned thee shall be fain to fawn and kiss thy feet;
Patience with deserving ever winneth due reward,
And these thine enemies ere long will hem thee round with homage.

Slander hath its uses; there is ever good reaction;
Wait awhile,—those **noisy** foes **shall** wake these slumbering friends:
Never man was praised, but that praise provoked a **censure;**

Never man was censured, some one standeth forth to praise :
The surest proof of small deservings is to live forgotten ;
Neglect is argument of death, as slander that thou livest.
Also, here be hints for thy humility; are such taunts all false?
Hast thou given no small cause for this **they** charge against thee?
Look more rigidly within ; judge **thyself** more sternly ;
If the adder's fang hath stung thee, cure with adder's fat :
So mayst thou change thy **slanderous foe to** act thy veriest friend,
   Whose malice, though **mere venom, shall be** medicine to thy
      health.

Face it out and live it down, whatever be the slander,
And **walk** on in wise quietness, as utterly unconscious :
The spoken lie shall soon die out ; nor liveth long though
      written,—
And better thus as more defined than loosely uttered rumours ;
While for those clamorous prints, ephemeral, disregarded,
Where scribblers puff each other up, and push all other down,
The small conspirators who dream they guide the public mind,
Anonymously reviling and slanderers in the dark,
Take thou their censures **for** thy praise, and strong in well-
      deserving
Stand, Psalmist-like, their cheerful **target,** and the song of the
      drunkards !

Our laws are cropped with hardships, and it is both shame and sin
That truth is counted criminal, if anyhow a damage.
We dare not, at our peril, caution neighbours **of a** rogue,—
The keen attorney is his mate, and libel-acts befriend **them ;**
Woe to us if we give their truer character to servants—
All virtues may be blazoned, but we must not hint at vice !
Yet on **the counter** tack is seen this evil under the sun,
Where **authorship hath** damage through false witness without
      remedy :
Personal spite may print unblamed what bitterness it willeth,
And coward **Teucer** shoot his barbèd malice from his lair,
While, helplessly protesting, the victims of such licence
Are only further blamed as **foes to freedom** of the press !

But the most crabbed fruit of law, the bitterest wrong **of all,**
Is punishing the husband for slander from his wife :

Haply that sharp tongue hath been his life-long torment,
And ofttimes on his innocence its jealousy hath burst;
This he beareth long-forbearing, till that forked sting
Hath hissed away with viper spite some fair maid's honest
    name;
And then forsooth our laws, indignantly appealed-to,
With most Quixotic chivalry excuse that wicked wife,
And fine or prison her poor good-man, whose honest name as well
This helpmate hath been slandering too, along with that fair
    neighbour's!
He is the sponsor, he the surety, he must smart for all;
His moral innocence is nothing to his legal guilt:
She is his slave forsooth, his wife,—so most obedient,—
He hath constrained her helplessness, and forced those venomous
    words.
That monkish rule of marriage had its reason in old time
When husbands held the power as of patriarchs in their house-
    holds;
But now is Ahasuerus well reproved by Prince Memucan,
Our Persian ladies show this day too much contempt and wrath;
For that, both laws and customs changed have made their hus-
    bands nought,—
Society will scorn the man who ruleth by stern headship;
So now our scolds and gossips have the mastery of their masters,
And woman's little fiery tongue kindleth her good-man's fagot:
Verily, the Warwick ducking-stool were justice to such law,
The Walton bridle for a slanderer, wisdom to such folly.

A famous man is often quoted, though he hath not spoken,
And many alter to their creeds the word he truly uttered:
His last opinion, not yet formed, is freely liked or loathed,
And so he walketh in a mist of false reports and slanders.
Again, where innocence is charged, obscurely and in whispers,
And dareth not, or deigneth not, to make distinct reply,
Who can guage his martyrdom, the torture to high honour,
That scorneth still to stop or stoop to answer villanous tongues?
And it is an added aggravation, if others are unworthily accused,
As pure and honest as thyself, whom yet defence might injure;
Thou mayst watch and wait and pray, and strive to live all
    down,
Yet for months, or wearier years, that cross will gall thy shoulder.

Historians have much sinned through slander, keenly now found out,
As good or ill report seem due to politics and polemics.
The private foe would ofttimes dip his partisan pen in gall,
While parasites have glorified the **basest of** mankind ;
Therefore now men doubt, and are not answered by the book,
But argue probabilities, to overturn old verdicts.
Would John have stood for tyrant, had he not out-braved the Pope?
Would Richard go **forth** humped and **cruel, had he salved** his nobles?
Bluff Hal, as Papist, still had seemed the patriot king with scruples,
And Cromwell noways hypocrite, were Rome upon his side :
King James of Scotland, shown so vile, was it for Carr and Villiers,
Or for his English Bible, that the Protestant was scorned?
So now Tiberius hath his praise, a justice long a-coming,
For Tacitus and his oligarchs abhorred that old ascetic ;
And who **can** guess of other Cæsars where the truth may lie?
Caligula and Nero were emperors, if not tyrants :
And even Judas for his faith hath found a reverend champion ;
Mirabeau, Danton, Robespierre, are circled by admirers :
While Constantine and Charlemagne and Titus and the Georges
Are stripped of **every** shred of honour in these searching days!

So too with literary fames, who is there that escapeth?
What **are** honesty and honour to our carping scribes?
Shakspeare was but a plagiary of Bacon or Southampton,
And Bunyan found his Pilgrim in a tract at Bedford jail,
And Æsop filched from Babrius, and Livy forged his Annals,
And Homer no more sang of Troy than Ossian sung of Fingal,
Great Newton and good Pascal defrauded each the other,
Meek Moses writ not Genesis, **nor** John the Revelation !
Whilst as for Christian ethics, they are stolen from the Talmud,
And Christ's own Sermon **on the** Mount is homilized from Hillel,—
And so the best of every age are every way traduced,
That scoffers—prophesied of old—may **stun** the world with slanders!

OF REAL AND IDEAL.

It often hath been seen and said, Stranger is truth than fiction;
But one may further note, it also seemeth more unreal:
We walk as in a dream; the blow that smote us stunned us,
Sleep-awake, like Livingstone, bemuffled by the lion.
Our whirlpool in its central spot is smooth and oily calmness;
Some potent ether-drop hath numbed all conscious pangs of
 pain:
A terror, dreaded far away, before us is less terrible,
The fearsome foe becoming soon a harsher sort of friend;
And blessings long-desired show but wilted in the hand;
How few have found in wealth or rank or marriage all they
 fancied!
That which is, the real the true, hath lighter hold upon us
Than that which is ideal only mixt of hope and fear:
Even the convict criminal, be his penalty not death,
Is easier for the sentence passed, that looking-forward over.

Wrought-up scenes in story books are ever false herein,
That small allowance there is made for influences around us:
Each hour is filled with trifles that converge to greater ends,
The phases of a spirit are much governed by its body,
Food and sleep and friends and news, habits and occupations
Lightening the load of trouble, that was judged so hard to bear;
The vitriol is diluted by those trickling rills of water,
And petty dull realities becloud each keen ideal.
Many a visitation, looked for fearfully as coming,
Was truly more a grief in absence, than it is in presence;
Bravely borne, as wisely sent, and with so much to mend it,
The threatening evil, standing here, is hailed some sterner good;
And what fictitious fancy painted terribly to fright us,
When neared was but a peasant, not a goblin nor a thief.

For, we be double creatures; and our spiritual half
Is quick with busy feelings, which dull matter little heedeth:
To cut the living flesh is scarce so painful as its fear;
And even Spanish monks tormented bodies less than souls:
The poignant dread that watcheth for calamity to come,
(As martyrs exquisitely have felt before their actual torture,)
Is often more a curse than that calamity itself;

For feverish thought will trace its features, hideous and un-
    shadowed,
Forgetful of each gentler touch to tone their outlines **down**;
Taking no count of little aids, the fairy forms of life,
That fill its hills and valleys with their ministering beauty,
The sympathies of friendship, the assuaging power of use,
The many comforts left, and **interests**, prayers, and consolations.
This body is a garment folded on our naked spirit,
Lulling it to **wholesome sleep** by dense and **genial warmth**;
This body is a soothing shade to rest its aching eyesight,
A cloud to screen that withered garden from the tropic sun;
So the real hath uses countervailing the ideal,
Our grosser matter calming the intensities of spirit.

We are fallen upon times of trouble, such as never have been since
    there was a nation,
Perilous evil days, and shocked by social earthquakes;
Every family apart, the world is full of mourning,
Sorrow and tribulation are sad inmates of each household:
Broken fortunes death disease, disgraces degradations,
Famines floods and pestilences, wars and rumours of wars,
Credits **blown into the air**, and commerce idle in the market-
    place,—
Everywhere in every way, the world is sore distrest.
Yet herein is some comfort, some balm for thy calamity,
Some spikenard of ideal to allay too real a pang;
That these thy griefs are **not** alone, but many share them with
    thee;
There is a serried line of neighbours fighting and falling too;
And lo, how many in worse case,—how few with thy consolings,—
Look round, and count the loss of others, reckoning thine own
    gains;
A skeleton **is in every** house, a Banquo at each **banquet**,
And **few there be** of yon cloaked crowd, **but** walk with flaming
    hearts.
So, gregarious man, as Rochefoucault hath spoken,
Shall the better bear his pain, if others suffer with him:
The torrent that hath swept away thrones dominations powers,
And ravaged fames and fortunes, maketh equal high **and low**;
So thou art well-companioned, in the fashion of the times,
And where the mountains fall at least the valleys are less humbled.

OF REAL AND IDEAL.

Herein too is more comfort; that misfortunes when they come
Are ever found more light to bear than expectation dreaded:
Fancy tied those scorpions to the whips of Rehoboam;
And where idea shall sharp the goads, reality will blunt them:
The merchant shook with secret fears of being found a bankrupt,
But standeth strong and speaketh fair, when all the worst is
    known:
This patient woman, crippled now, for years and years bedridden,
Could never guess how cheerfully such sadness would be borne,
Before her skittish pony shying threw the merry child,
And christian resignation had poured peace on the afflicted:
The wicked wife, or prodigal son, in prospect may look hideous,
(To earlier days of wedlock or of fatherhood unbearable,)
But there be mitigations, if thy soul is well with God;
He can help, and He can change these curses into blessings;
And thou art weaned from wickedness, and hast small part in
    folly,
And roamest in thy spirit higher spheres of peace and love,
And only guilt may paralyse an independent mind,
And storms that rend the mountains cannot break a Christian
    spirit.

Herein too is chief comfort; that in Heaven's all-guiding providence
Help is proportioned to the toil, and grace in accordance with the
    trial:
So, given energy and faith, a vigorous happiness ensueth
Equal to face and wrestle down whatever daring foe.
If the wind be not tempered to the skin (this were a foolish
    fancy)
The shorn lamb may have inward warmth to answer for its fleece.
Nerves are blunted, hearts are hardened, minds are girded-up,
An inner spring is added to sustain the weight without.
And in the middle of all conflict, there is the grand ideal
The mighty thought, Eternity, Eternity of bliss!
What are these few fierce years, or haply days, or hours,
To the great heir whose heritage is Peaceful Immortality?
The real is thus disrealized,—so thoughtful Berkeley doubted,
And faith made as the substance, that ideal fact of Paul:
Temporal seemeth but a shadow, though rough real and tangible,
Eternal sheweth as a solid, though spiritual and ideal.

Load not thou the present with those burdens of the past
Ancient sins, abandoned hopes, and numerous lost occasions :
Heaven's word,—Sufficient for the day,—is still affliction's motto ;
We are not forced to fight with all our **enemies at once.**
Repent and mend, in prayerful trust ; but nourish no regrets;
That which might have been and was not, never need to vex thee :
Many groan for might-have-beens, considering but the better,
But worse were quite as possible ; so, take this bad for best ;
Many feebly wish and dream and **paint** ideals fondly,
Who, though it stood before them, **would not** recognize **the real.**

OF HABIT.

LEVELLING even in the higher, at the lower still degrading evermore,
An evil thing for spirit is the force of utter habit.
Although, for skill in crafts, **for work of brain or body,**
Habit hath material use, to gain **some humbler end,**
Yet, at the altar of the soul, in genius, love, religion,
Habit wearieth, habit dulleth, habit hindereth always.
For **this hath** deadened piety, this hath damped affection,
This hath dimmed **the** fire from heaven down to kindled candles :
Many times religious forms, perfunctorily repeated
Have heavily quenched, as with **wet** sand, **the** flaming heart of
    zeal ;
Many times young love is killed by coarse and common marriage,
And nobler-lifting thoughts dragged low, through custom's **length-
    ening** chain ;
Yea, through **his** profession as a priest, the convert's fire is extin-
    guished,
Even as the fervours of a bride **are** forgotten in the coldness **of a
    matron.**

Nevertheless, for ordinary life, this trivial round of duties,
Habit is commonly a helper, as rest amid the wrestling :
If it file the edge of pleasure, **it may** dull the sharpness of pain ;
If it drag the wheels of genius, **it may** smooth the road for talent ;
If, an antagonist of freedom, that would mount with wings,
It buckleth harness on the soul, a traveller on **the** highway,
Still can habit be an impetus, for good as well as evil,
Continuously made easier to ring adown thy **groove** :

And if that groove be righteousness, herein is some advantage,
Wherever habit of itself is not alone the spring;
But, if there is a frequency of sinning, the conscience groweth harder,
And habit is an utter evil, with its gain but loss.

In fine; the letter killeth; let the formalist slave on,
His acted repetitions do but make him a machine;
But, the spirit quickeneth; and if life with love be there,
That potent heat shall overcome the harm and chill of habit.

OF ECONOMY.

THRIFT for the poor, but profusion for the rich; this were equal wisdom;
Since what is prudence in the one, were little else than meanness in the other.
There is an economy that sinneth, never dropping largesse kindly,
As there is an erring prodigality, pandering to luxury and sloth:
Boaz, well and wisely, bade his reapers scatter handfuls
That Ruth, with happier thankfulness, might glean her liberal leasing;
And nations, spending millions on a war, hath grudged the soldier's medal,
With sordid soul to save on that the fraction of a tax.
Wealth should well be wary of extravagance, the dry-rot in its rafters,
And poverty may stint and scrape, as need discreetly bade;
But that which is the virtue of a Lazarus showeth in the Dives as a vice;
This close and saving spirit is a sin of many wealthy.

God giveth all those talents that his steward may duteously use them,
May put them out at interest, not hide them in a napkin:
And for a rich man to be frugal is to prove unfaithful to his trust,
While for the poor man to be prodigal is presumptuous as sinning against prudence.
So, in the government of Kingdoms, it is right to take large views,
Nothing illiberal, nothing mean, but wide and generous bounty;

The waste that overfloweth here, elsewhere shall spread fertility,
And not one seed is lost, though scattered freely broad-cast;
Even the trampers on the road, even the sparrows of the house-tops,
Well rejoice to pick up crumbs that fall from plenty's table:
But now, some grind the poor, for selfish place and power,
And wring from honest craftsmen what they spend upon themselves:
And savings, that are meanly scraped from wages of the workmen,
Cry shame against the nation in a parsimonious age.

OF INDUSTRY AND IDLENESS.

MANY are the forms of industry, than which the merest idleness were better;
By weary pains to win a loss is worse than losing gain:
Often have I known the student diligently read into the sceptic,
While he that left his learned books remained a plain believer;
Often have I seen simplicity hold slowly on his way,
When wreck and misadventure imperilled quicker cunning.
Lo, the misspent energies of man,—his toil for ill got wealth,
His labour still by day and night to reap and garner tares,
His folly in amassing rubbish by great pains and cost,
His sin in striving for success to many an evil aim,
His wastefulness of strength and means to compass wretched ends,
His woefulness as servant to that hard taskmaster, Satan

How many, better in their graves, work hard for wrong and harm,
With misdirected energies and ill-applied exertion;
How oft the robe of Nessus hath been woven with much pains,
And how much wiser than such toil were simple sloth and slumber.
O the multitude of labourers who weary out their lives in vanity,
The thousands of hardworkers who had better far do nothing,
The Danaides innumerable pumping water into sieves,
The crowds of Sisyphi that push those boulders up the mountains!
Youth and sillier age alike agree with foolish diligence
In twisting ropes of sand or building palaces of ice;
Often the hardest toil is expended on most profitless absurdity,
Where any chance suspension might be noted so much gain;

Many a book had best have been unwritten, many a tower never
    built,
Many a perilous achievement or lifelong work unwrought:
This man useth up his time, his means his mind his credit,
In some quixotic scheme, the panacea for all ill,—
As reckoning everything by tens for universal commerce,
Or one true catholic measure discovered in the Pyramid,
Or a perpetual motion, whereby through reaction we may fly,
Or plain uniformity of worship, as if all could think alike;
Or pasturing only upon vegetals, or drinking nought fermented,
Or labouring to convince mankind of any simple folly;
All vanities, as all in their extremes; catholic schemes are futile;
Minds vary, customs change, and unity is ever the impossible.

Why wear out one's heartstrings in epics that nobody would read?
Wherefore tourney with the pen in lists of polemical contention?
What were the value of exertion to gain such evil issues
As undermining history, till facts appear but fables?
Or scheming to accomplish some selfish sinful pleasure?
Or through some silly patent urging ruin on kind friends?
Or killing time by inches, in smallest vanities and follies?
Or sowing otherwise the wind, to reap with pain the whirlwind?—
Alas for the nothingness of toil, with worse than like nothingness
    for wages,—
The busy lives of most men are but such redoubled trouble.
Did then those monks of olden days show reason for their sloth,
In that they simply kept unlost their napkin-hidden talent?

And yet, what shall we say? Is it not a duty, a religion,
Still to energize and do, though doing be not much?
It is given unto few men to achieve, it is lent to none to perfect
A labour worthy of their lives, industrious to the end;
They toil to leave halfdone, and welldones might be better,
And slender satisfaction can all diligence attain;
Yet it was wiser to attempt, though only failure followed,
To well deserve is somewhat, in spite of ill success;
And there is an energetic health in diligence and action,
An impulse ever spurring on the soul to dare and do:
To work is Spirit's nature, and it never can be idle;
To be, and being not to act, were matter void of mind:
And motives are to man his praise, not rather their results,

Our wisdom and our duty is to work and not to faint.
What if thine aim be not achieved? the chemist (take his instance)
By failing in experiment is so far toward success;
Through manifold negations the affirmative is reached,
Try and fail, then try and fail, try three times and succeed.

For ending: any industry is better than mere sloth,
So it be not industry for evil, some active positive sin;
For idle weeds of wickedness are natural to the heart,
And if that garden be untilled, it shall be choked with tares.
Industry in anywise is life, and idleness more near of kin to
 Death,—
Better the cloud of gnats, than cold and still corruption;
Energy of every kind is sympathy with spirit,
And hath congenial uses in the very spring of work:
So there be not mischief in thy toil, thou gainest, as a conqueror
 of sloth,
It is a very waste of life to be and not to do.
Where is the use?—a deadening question ever put by Mammon,
Hath for answer, means have uses though their end be vain;
Even the castle of snow may give hints for the castle of stone,
Even the rope of sand may test ingenious patience.
The simple exercise of mind, aptness gained by practice,
Diligence hope and perseverance,—these be somewhat gained.
Labour hath sweet uses, labour sanctifieth all things,
Adding brightness, flavour, beauty, even to the humblest.
The carving of a cherrystone, the weaving of a cobweb
Instead of misspent pains may stand a miracle of art.
Idleness ever hath its peril, in stagnation and corruption;
The short cut seemed the wisest, until shown to lead astray:
Quick gains are lightly spent, the gambler's luck will turn,
While steady industry alone endureth and is strong:
Theft may seem at first to gain more easily than labour,
But look to the end,—what wealth is left to the convicted thief?
The many pains, the long way round, the much industrious effort,
Here is faith and patience, and the due reward of wisdom:
Not all seen at once, for faith may oft work blindly,
Nor with too quick reward, for patience must be perfect,
But as a far-off blessing attained by healthful industry,
If only as it vanquisheth by energy the slow disease of idleness.

OF REPRESENTATION.

A **free** State gathered in **the Council should speak** by all its citizens,
Each one claiming as of birthright a voice to aid his country:
None should be excluded from the privilege, if grown to man's estate,
Unless he fail of intellect, or lose his right through **crime:**
Some may more help the State, through monied **merchandize or** learning,
Wherein the wealthier and **wiser should** speak with several votes:
Riches, evidencing **diligence**, skill goodluck acuteness,
Wisdom, proving education, knowledge, mental light,
Merit of any public sort, as exploit, or selfsacrifice,
Office, rank, or great estate, all these **were** added voices:
So should the lowest not be equalized, **unjustly**, with **the** worthier and higher,
But only stand for one, while those would rate for more:
To the single talent a single vote, the ten to speak with ten,
Each recorded plainly on a tablet signed and witnessed;
With heavy fines for falsehood, and special care for truth,
And justice done to all, while no man is excluded.
Thus the cry for equity is satisfied in each,
For every freeman of the State may rightly claim to help it;
And the like equity is saved for those, the **fewer out of many,**
Who better serve their country by riches and acquirements.

Individual merit would qualify most rightly;
A merit broadly proved in men by some success in life:
And ancestors who won their way should shine in their **descendants,**
Though haply sometimes shamed in their degenerated sons;
But merit, worth a nation's thanks, must wait as gross demerit,
Before a man be mulcted **of his** ancestors' desert:
Here is our custom for honours and estates, and law of the firstborn,
Indulgent to great names, but scarcely built on justice;
Yet, for stability we hold it, that change be not too swift,
For living merit, as with life, may perish in one hour.

And the like equity contendeth equally for women as for men,

Short of nonage, marriage, crime, or lack of mental fitness:
Married, the woman, in her husband, speaketh by his voice;
But single, as a citizen, her rights can ill be questioned;
The **wealthy** heiress should not stand beneath her humblest tenant,
Made incapacitate through sex from **patriotic** aims;
Yet neither should the mother and the wife, immersed in nursery cares,
Forsake her private life of home for public strife abroad.

These my thoughts grew long of old, nor were they learnt from others;
A quarter of a century agone I wrote as here is written,
Advocating rights, to each and all, to rich men as to poor men,
Rights to education, as to manhood, unequal but still just,
Rights to woman, as to man, to every freeborn citizen,
Rights according to degrees, and **capable of expansion,**
So that the humble may win higher, earning more through merits,
To every freeman one, but more to more than freemen;
Thus giving great achievement, by the pen or **by the sword,**
And wealth in land **or** gold, and educated wisdom,
And any social usefulness, and **office,** and commission,
And rank and worth of every kind **their graduated voices.**
This is the justice of the **case,** satisfying every claimant,
Valued according **to his** merits, free-citizenship as one:
This giveth righteously to each the equity he asketh,
The poor man is not mulcted, and the rich is not despoiled;
The peasant to **his country's weal may add one honest voice,**
As bearing in **his humbler** way the **public costs** and charges;
The magnate holding ten, according **to his** burdens,
And **either** way true justice done alike to rich and poor.

So then a represented nation, to illustrate its best,
Should balance by the wiser few the undistinguished many:
Let number have its voice, the multitude of freemen,
But merits of **a public** sort have added voices too:
Let well-investing prudence speak, and honourable old age,
And learning and religion in their orders and degrees,
And open exploit that of old had won the civic **crown,**
And wisdoms and discoveries, and well-secured successes:
Thus would all **the** worthiest be rewarded by the State,
And fitly help its weal through their accumulative voices:

And so the force of numbers would not overweigh all else,
But equity in either scale should make the balance equal.
Teach the people wisely, and no need to fear the people,
Religion, science, letters, clear the head and cleanse the heart;
The well-drilled army bringeth peace and order with its march,
Where a tumultuous rabble doth but ravage and destroy
Woe to the State whose children are neglected and untaught,
The more if such barbarian serfs are lawgivers as freemen:
For her place among the nations must sink to lower and lower,
Humbled and broken down by her own rude ignorant children.
And happy is that people,—happy art thou, dear England,—
Where reason and religion are the nation's sun and moon,
Where learning shineth free and clear upon the open Bible,
And all thy children have been taught, and peace and praise are
    thine.

OF LIFE'S WORK.

PROVIDENCE worketh by us all, though few be found to note it;
Yea, by the wicked as the good, through failures and successes;
Each of us, after his fixed quality, helpeth the great experiment
Which all of human race show forth to higher worlds;
Each is as a morsel for mosaic, duly shaped and coloured,
To be set at his fit place in the pavement of Time's temple,
And patterns of all kinds are tesselated there
With every shade of difference in character and station,
Till Life, with its changeable kaleidoscope, continually turned by
    circumstance,
Varieth human phases to the colours of Labrador spar.
This man is used for illustration, haply, of some blackest dye;
That man showeth as a gem, of purest, whitest lustre;
Here is a nation seen degraded, a dark, dread shadow on the floor;
And, in bright contrast there, a people's sunshine in full glory:
Nothing is lost, nothing is wasted, nothing is an ultimate mistake;
Wisdom, infinite and absolute, is the signature on all creation.

No man knoweth wherefore he was born, nor what the full inten-
    tion of his being:
Whether for humblest uses, or a vessel made to honour;

For self-conceit, or conscience evermore, suggested wondrous
    capability,
Albeit sin and sloth in most reduce their powers **to zero.**
Perchance thou art needed for high witness, testifying some grand
    truth ;
Perchance to serve a world by maxims of good statecraft ;
Perchance to ripen minds **by books,** or gladden hearts through
    music ;
To forward art and science, **or to** search out secret nature.
Or a man may breathe a living sacrifice, to cure some social wrong,
Protesting **for the** public safety as its innocent victim ;
Or, if of humbler lot, may bless his private sphere
By diligence in duty, by humility and faith,
By cheerfulness and thankfulness, and charities and prayers,
And teaching hope of better worlds—the peasant's princely heri-
    tage ;
Or there is still another phase, wherein he shall do service,
If wilfully hearthardened, as the galley-slave of passions ;
He then shall work the warnings, and the judgments, and the woes
That buoy upon Life's wreck-chart, its rocks, and shoals, and
    eddies.

Duty is the surely-guiding clue, and **destiny** the goal fore-ordered,
And blindfold faith in Providence our simple rule for conduct.
Trust in God and do His will, He still shall guide and bless thee ;
Work the work before thee with all fervour at thy best ;
For the little **as the** great delight in present duties :
Thy Maker formed with equal care a fern-seed and a **star.**
Be it high or be it humble, this thy task is set by Him ;
His glory and thy gain may be achieved though by a trifle ;
His monads and His worlds alike are wonders of contrivance :
All triumphs of design, and looked into by the angels ;
And so thy least, as greater things, are tenderly ordained—
Thy very hairs are numbered, O thou of little faith !

A work is wanted to be done,—and, lo ! the man to do it—
To do, or half to do, or fail : what matter? each is ordered.
We praise the full achievement, but Heaven may praise its failure ;
We pity those who leave half done, where God may say, Well
    done.
Servants may soon be called elsewhere, some better work to do

In other worlds and other states, with other names and natures;
And here His artisans are taught, His working minds are moulded,
And when full ready for their change those souls are called away.
All work is not alone for earth, though here we take our bents,
But elsewhere is there much to do, alike in good and evil;
For the mystery of evil is allowed, curable somewhere, somehow,
And looking like necessity amongst imperfect creatures.
Here we commence, but beyond we carry on, and so for **ever and
 for ever,**
Beginning that great race toward endless hell or heaven;
But woe to the spirit of malignity that starteth wretchedly in sin,
And joy to the soul whose young career is well begun in goodness!

I trow that the wicked doeth service, though utterly beside his will—
Evil working good, albeit that ill servant meaneth **other;**
And God most rejoiceth in His mercy if sinners turn to saints;
But if those hearts be stubborn, He **can** rejoice in judgment.
Gracious and patient with His creature, He still is terrible in holi-
 ness,
And if free souls rebel, their treasons must be punished,
Even where such narrow treasons **may** have compassed wider weal,
Through which the Great King's realm may reach some higher
 blessing.
Work thy life-work as thou wilt, He made thee not in vain;
But woe to him whose work is sin, for penalty must follow:
And all may live in love, working the works of good,
For evermore His mercy rejoiceth over judgment.

Providence leadeth us, or driveth us, each to do some service
By golden threads or iron goads to guide us or to speed us;
Each, though he boast of independence, is but as a trout upon the
 hook,
And now is checked, and now drawn on, as the Great Fisher
 willeth.
We may resist His touch, and that sharp steel shall strike us,
Or we may yield and be obedient, and never feel the barb:
How often in the story of a life, without our help or hindrance—
At this place all things fail, at that place all things prosper!
And yet how seldom reasoning faith interpreteth the providence
Looking for its leadings and suggestions, as **listening** to heavenly
 whispers!

Go ye in this way or in that : be not as the senseless cattle,
Nor kick, perversely obstinate, barefoot, against the pricks.

The work of life, the toil of life—it is never the rest of life ;
This is not our rest, nor any continuing city :
Life is a journey ; life a race ; life a weary pilgrimage ;
Life is a battle, trial, work, and strife ; but never peace or rest.
They that have attained life's ends, in wealth, or fame, or pleasure,
Never rest in all their gains, but yearningly press onward ;
More wealth, more fame, other sorts of pleasure—
Discontent is ever goading those unsated hearts ;
Wise for them, and happy, if such discontent urge upward,
But wretched for the worldling in his disappointed soul.

A few speeches, a few songs, sundry tomes, or paintings ;
Some fair sculptures, or a money-pile, or heightened social rank :
Such, at the most and at the best, is chiefly seen life's issue,
And so the workers pass away, and leave their works behind them.
All must so be left behind—suddenly, irrevocably left ;—
Cast off, as those brown-varnished husks that held the bright-
 winged sphinxes.
Thy lands, and home, and pleasant wife ; thy neighbours, friends,
 and children ;
Thy books, amusements, and pursuits ; thy business and thy plea-
 sures—
All must be left behind for ever on an instant call,
And then how slight, at best, are seen the poor results of life !
Well, if there be not many follies, with losses, sorrows, sins,
And ulcers on the memory, and torments in the conscience—
Better, if truly can be added some things of good and generous,
Notable, whereby to be remembered, as having served thy kind.
But for the mass it is all vanity—their work as done in life :
Toil, and care, and guilt, and selfish searchings after pleasure.
And, for the best how short of that perfection well-desired
Is all our work, however done, and with whatever zeal !
Thou canst but make beginnings ; all the ends are too far off
No theme was ever yet exhausted, and no mind writ out.
In all these topics I have handled, more than nine times twelve,
Each hath somewhat lacking, somewhat faulty, somewhat false ;
The good ideal was not gained, and conscience goeth humbly,
Dissatisfied with much of work so distant from its aim.

Thus the painter always hath new touches to be added,
The speaker, afterward, is vext for his forgotten eloquence;
The architect, too late, perceiveth how his plans were better;
And no high-worker ever reached the standard in his mind.

Few consider that good means are needful for good ends—
Few regard the goal while fevered with the running,
But all go hotly on, competing to their graves,
With infinite diversities of circumstance and conduct.
To one man it is given to save souls, to another to heal bodies;
To a third to fashion mind, to a fourth to conquer matter;
Here is all prosperity and peace; there much adversity and trouble;
Sickness and poverty on one side; on another health and wealth.
Scorn not thy specialty as mean, if it hath less honour than thy
    neighbour's;
The members of one body cannot all be head or hand.
Art thou in thy place? It is thy post; and this set service is thy
    duty:
The Master-Worker's journeymen are found of every craft,
And He doth use them as He will, sending them hither and thither,
Revealing to but few of them the meaning in His mind.

Perchance some heroic pioneer, zealous to reclaim barbarians,
And civilise those brute-like hordes through kindliness with faith,
Is stricken midway in his travel, victim to a ruthless savage,
And seemingly forsaken of his Master—a tool flung away half-used.
Perchance a brave adventurer, whether among Arctic snows
Or in the tropical desert, or about fever-breathing marshes,
Just as he reached his prize—that open Polar Sea,
The vast, semi-fabulous lake, the dread, mysterious city—
Perisheth, as by a trivial accident—the mariner in very sight of
    port—
One hour longer, and success had crowned his life-long efforts!
But, his work was done, and God called home that servant;
Some other is found ready soon to carry on the torch.
If the Lord is satisfied, no labourer need complain;
They live and move and work to please their Master, not them-
    selves.
His will is unto them all law; they die, but not untimely;
Elsewhere they recognise alike His mercy and His wisdom.
Our unbelief is pitiful at failures and mischances,

But those good servants gladly heard the praise of **God**; "Well-done!"

Happy is the man who, looking back, can say, "I have lived sincerely;
I have wrought the task of duty, and fought the fight of faith."
Happy if his memories of time are as incense for the temple of eternity;
Happy, in spite of outer foes, if conscience is his friend.
He may have gained no moneys, he haply misseth fame;
His very nearest and his dearest have wronged him **and deceived** him;
But, with a past all good—seed-harvest of the future—
Even this dark present shall be light within his soul,
Well at peace with God, with self, **and** every creature,
Happily in harmony and love with humblest as with highest,
All infirmities forgiven, every negligence excused,
And each iniquity of sense and **circumstance atoned**;
Righteous in the righteousness of Christ—his Lord, and Judge, and Brother—
Accepted in that sacrifice which hath redeemed the worlds—
How can a spirit thus endowed, **rich in all the** treasuries of heaven,
Fail of inward blessedness, though outwardly oppressed?
Live purely, work diligently, do good **to** all around thee,
Let each minute on the wing fly as a honey-bee of duty;
Suffer nothing living to have aught to charge against thee,
Man or woman, bird or beast, down to the meanest insect,
Nor cruelty, nor lust, nor **fraud**, nor meditated evil,
Nor **aught but** what omissions and infirmities excuse;
So when thine hour is come and death **is** at thy threshold
To beckon thee to better spheres, where spirit can expand,
Happily shalt thou welcome him, thy guest and not thine enemy,
And speed with him departing, as a friend to call thee home,

OF LIFE'S LESSONS.

Happy is he that knoweth and that serveth the true mission of his life,
Confessing Providence his guide, through blessings and afflictions;

He that never wavered from his duty, nor shrank from faithful
    witness,
Enduring all things cheerfully, as given by God's hand.
Each of us hath his own vocation, special, sure, and ordered ;
And each of us is thereto fitted, if he will but well obey ;
But those who hate the yoke, and kick against the beam,
Hinder where they ought to help, and break their wheels with ruin.

Let a man question with himself, What is my being's errand?
Is this my proper aim ? and how shall I achieve it ?
Man's gain and the glory of God ; my own weal and my children's
Holiness, and happiness, and health—how best to win all good?
The godly heart and the holy life, here is the secret of happiness ;
None can steal away that treasure but the traitor self ;
Cleanliness, temperance, and exercise, here is the secret of health ;
A vigorous youth, in green old age, is due in chief to these :
The poorest man that liveth can be clean in mind and body,
His heart sprinkled from an evil conscience, his body washed in
    pure water;
And daily carefulness for both shall win him more than wealth—
More than many Naamans have conquered, lepers of the flesh and
    of the spirit :
In peace and health he shall be rich, though competence were
    lacking ;
And where the worth of competence, despoiled of health and peace?

Do well at all times to thy neighbour, both by word and deed ;
Good conscience shall repay thy toil to every jot and tittle ;
Yea, though he greet thee with ingratitude, or knew not thy
    charities,
Thou art rewarded sevenfold, with peace in thine own bosom.
And it is a very narrow world ; ever shalt thou meet thine ante-
    cedents;
Thy good or evil shall return, not after many days.
The eye of God is on thee always, and the eye of conscience,
And the eye of man beside, much oftener than thou wottest.
Do well to thine own self, by striving ever after truths ;
The very striving winneth much, though little else be compassed :
As thou doest, it shall be done to thee : seeds yield according to
    their kind ;
Wheat and tares alike shall still yield wheat and tares.

The best and truest comfort is within, a conscience well at ease ;
And woe to those who make that inmost friend a bosom foe :
Happy nights or miserable, days of hope or fear,
Peace at the heart, or terror in the soul, these depend on conscience.
And after that chief treasure, the **fine gold** next to be desired
Is a **good** husband or a gentle wife, that true and fond companion ;
But **pity** and sorrow where instead the **pair** are found ill-mated,
There is no closer peril than a **scorpion in the nest** ;
For either wedded foe will taint the nature of the other—
Estrange the kin, and **curse** the home, and blight the blooms of life,
While those degrading fetters of a miserable marriage
Put to an open shame and grief the nobly patient spirit.
Be the fault in husband or in wife, alas ! for evil wedlock ;
Alas ! for the children and the household ; alas ! for either self ;
An overweighted teamster shackled by galling harness,
A racer cruelly spurred, yet sharply curbed to lose.

How strangely dark is Providence in heaping up afflictions on the good,
Leaving to the wicked all prosperities, health, and wealth, and honour !
David noted it of old, and bade us watch their end,
When sin's green bay-tree drieth up, and righteousness shall flourish ;
And often are our wedded pairs seen opposites ill-matched,
And so those hapless homes are curst by evil wives or husbands !
Children grow up quickly, disobedient and self-willed,
And care, and cost, and teaching shall seem well-nigh flung away ;
And all is loss and ruin, in spite of prayers and pains,
And where the dove of peace should build, the harpy set her nest.
The mother is most seen in sons, the father found in daughters,
Each, for good or evil, reproduced in heart and mind :
So, the bad father's boy may liken his sweet mother for her goodness,
And so a bitter mother shall have girls as patient as their father ;
The mother infected her prodigal sons with temper and caprices ;
The pure and studious daughters show the father's youth again.

Those who suffer wrongfully should ask, of their own hearts and Heaven,

Why hath this sorrow come upon us? What may be the errand
    of this trial?
It is not alone to prove thee, not alone to drive thee to thy God,
Not only for humilities or chastisement, for strength in faith and
    patience;
But also that thy brethren may be warned, that the weaker natures
    may be comforted;
That thy recorded witnessings may help to bless mankind.
He that endureth hardness learneth by long suffering,
But also thereby teacheth, that men may learn, and angels;
And there be martyrs of all grades, witnesses to every kind of truth;
Martyrs not only to religion, but likewise to friendship and to love;
Men, no less than women, protesting against social tyrannies;
Animals, as well as children, to testify against all cruelty;
In different ranks, at various posts of patient wrong-enduring,
Cohorts of that ubiquitous host, the noble army of martyrs.

We are mainly what we make ourselves, what we suffer outer cir-
    cumstance to shape us,
As yielding or resisting, and linked with right or wrong;
Duties omitted, duties done, combine to form our fates,
As faith and works may fashion them, or negligence and passion:
And albeit ancestry be much, that stock of special qualities
Inclined to higher or lower, to gifts or lack of gifts,
Though worldly means be more, through poverty or riches,
And influences and accidents without us as within us,
Though mother's milk were poisonous, or half our lessons error,
Though grace, or hap of either sort, be for us or against us,
Yet may the spirit of a man so master the material,
That every hindrance shall but stand his step-stone to success;
Therefore the limbless dwarf is seen a mental athlete,
The blind, the deaf, the dumb, are great through force of will;
And thereby this life's heroes have assurance in themselves
That, spite of all and come what may, they still shall win their
    battles.

Life, like a game of chess, is full of turns and changes;
The field of our kaleidoscope is altered with each move;
An error years agone thereafter yieldeth bitterness,
A prudent foresight in old days is profitable at last.
Too great caution, too much rashness, both alike are harmful,

2 E

Courage with **forbearance is** the golden rule of life.
Advance, yet circumspectly, **but** move, **and stand** not still,
The world with all upon it spinneth **onward, ever** onward.
He that is an idler **on the** march, is **trodden down unpitied,**
And those who skirmish unsupported **risk continual loss.**
Yet life-losses, as in chess, are ofttimes well-recovered,
If only patience **and** good temper **mingle with** keen skill.
And Providence will bless the **soul that** goeth stoutly forward,
Till even death-bed penitence **may draw as by** stale-mate.
Ever on, move bravely on, and play thy game in wisdom ;
Faith and conduct **are staunch** knights, though **fortune's queen**
   were lost ;
And thy castled character, and thy mitred piety,
With life's **not** trivial round of pawns to serve thy kingly soul,
These may win the game at last, so thou **battle** shrewdly,
And stand a Christian **champion, not a coward** of the world.

It is only after long years, and much of change and failure,
That a man gaineth his experience how best to tend himself,
Best for health and comfort, best for peace of mind,
Best by silence or by speech, through action or forbearance.
He findeth out by slow degrees that in a man's own self
Is shown his truest enemy, is found his choicest friend ;
That good-doing, temperance, **and** prayer are the triple cord of
   happiness ;
That evil-speaking earneth hate, while charities win love ;
That guilt can never go unpunished, even where repented **and for-**
   given ;
That all neglected duties earn their chastisement as sins ;
That only moderation is in everything its wisdom,
And all excesses evil, yea, to excess in good.
The more we see and hear, the longer a man liveth,
The more is charity his law, in all things toleration ;
Every brother, spite of faults, hath much of good within him ;
Every sister with her graces still hath many failings ;
Even adverse circumstance hath always some fair phase,
And, if it bring much evil, yieldeth also some small good.
We learn among life's lessons the value of every present,
The possible vast import of each occasion passing ;
For a little thing becometh great, if a great wisdom work it,
Even as a great thing dwindleth, be it breathed on by a fool ;

It ever was the gift of genius **to** build grandeur out of trifles,
Davy's watch-glass, Newton's **apple,** yielded mighty truths;
As it ever is the guerdon of the wise, at once embracing opportunity
To snatch off-hand some conquest slower toil could scarce achieve.

He hath **slender worldly** wisdom, and no knowledge of himself,
Who fancieth men care for him, as a study **worth** their musing;
A little of their idlest curiosity is all he **need expect;**
Even if the man hath **won a** name, **and set it** high in honour.
We may be mountains to ourselves, but are molehills **to most others,**
And there is a wise humility **in** judging of oneself as nought;
Yet there is greatness **in each one of us,** depth, and height, and breadth,
And it were a folly to forget **our values to be** vast **and individual;**
Only let each as to himself count over **his** just responsibilities,
Giving his neighbour credit for the like internal sense—
A sense, most personal to each of us, and yearning little over others,
Selfish and unheedful if ye will; but the stringent law of our being—
That each man is the centre for his either-world circumference,
And everything to self, although **as** nothing to his neighbour.

A tree may be felled in a day, that hath haply been a century in growing,
And the long-conned lessons of a lifetime can be **read** in half **an** hour;
And many have learnt and **taught again, and given their teachings** truly;
So let me bear this witness, as a few of many truths:
That a good life is the principal thing—a pure and peaceful spirit—
Whatever storms may rage without, this happy calm within
That the Bible is a book for every age, in spite of the ignorance of scholiasts,
And deeper than man's intellect, despite the infidelity of sciolists,
With **its simple text** for truth, though all truths be not spoken,
To the end that reason may piece-in that skeleton frame of faith:
That **all** men and all women are well-mingled good and evil,
With few extreme consistencies in **sinner or in** saint;
That most things have so many sides, such various points of vision,
No wise man blameth other eyes for taking different views;
That no human friendship is so sure, for a whisper not to shake it,

No enmity so hard and fierce, that kindness cannot melt;
That happiness is never seen on earth, except as grown of goodness;
That use levelleth all our lots, till discontent creep in;
That the rich hath small pleasure in his wealth, and the poor many comforts with his labour;
That single folk and married, guess not each the other's griefs;
That health is an ill-valuer of its gain, that sickness findeth many to console her,
And Providence, by compensation, balanceth conditions—
In fine, that life is full of trials for its wearied travellers,
Fainting now in the tropic sun—now chilled by the wintry storm;
And that, as the issue of all said, life is our school for immortality,
To teach the primer lessons of Eternity in Time.

If God be very merciful, thy sin will find thee out—
Will find thee out for recompense, in this life, not the next;
And seldom is He not thus merciful, therefore bear the rod:
Thou shalt be spared hereafter, if thy punishment was here:
Let this then comfort thine adversity; thou knowest not the vastness of His love,
In tenderness and equity thus visiting thee now;
Hope thou, therefore, in afflictions, that may kindly clear thy punishments;
And be very humble at prosperity, lest it should be counted thy reward.

A wise man tighteneth his tongue, speaking less than thinking,
Whereby he can more firmly act alone and unsuspected;
He liveth in the fortress of his mind, and rejoiceth in the garden of his heart,
Making sweet companionship of thought, and having heaven within him,
Glad in the music of old memories, and lightened by the vision of new hopes,
King of himself, and reigning as a king, above that little world—
Little? rather infinite, eternal—a world that is a portion of God's throne—
A world, a very temple for the Lord, an everlasting heritage!
Thus doth he rule in his integrity, pure and strong of soul,
Innocent, redeemed, and independent, serving only the Most High,

No man acknowledged as his master over the supremacy of con-
　　science,
And very few, and those the best, reckoned of his intimates in
　　fellowship :
So, self-possessed and individual, a wise man walketh quietly—
Happiness within, serenity without, cautious in his kindliness,
With silence as his comrade through this babbling world of slanders,
And doing good in secret, while defying open ill.

Passion may be hot and strong, but thou canst be its master,
Unless thy silly weakness yield the battle to thy foe ;
Therefore resist, good youth, look not, taste not, touch not ;
A crevice in the dam would let loose the Mississippi.
Passion is the flaring of dry stubble, burnt out as soon as lighted—
A fierce and dangerous flame full often blown among the ricks ;
But Love the steady fire on the Christmas hearth of home,
With cheerfulness and comfort in that warm dear chimney-corner.
Life's trials may be hard to bear, but patience can outlive them ;
To-morrow's victory shall crown the conflicts of to-day.
So, then, persist in doing bravely, O brother hard bested !
Material evils have an end, but not a Christian's spirit.
Life teacheth courage, coolly tempered with just fear ;
Life enjoineth charity, safely balanced by right caution ;
Life is buoyed by hope, even on the breakers of despair ;
And life hath taught wise lessons to the simplest ere he dieth.

Look back. Alas ! the gloomy view. Our pasts are full of sad-
　　ness—
So many friends long gone before—gone whither, who can tell?—
So many places once familiar knowing us now no more ;
So many sins and follies, and so few young hopes fulfilled !
Look back. Alas ! in looking back there is a world of sorrow—
The best must have his penitence, the wisest his regrets.
It is an enervating glance, that piteous looking back ;
A chill, a check, a wakening for the spirit yearning forward :
Be penitent and prayerful, but discourage looking back—
We cannot bring the past again ; repent it, and forget it—
Rather look up, look round, look forward, onward, upward ;
Here is the wisdom, here the mercy, here all help in life.

I well remember, in old days, among the wondrous Alps

Nigh Chamounix, a wanderer on the glaciers of Mont Blanc ;
He and a shrewd Columbian who had roamed the Rocky Mountains,
Had safely crossed that icy sea beneath the Aiguille Verte—
And with a guide, who missed his way, came to a terrible spot,
Where equal peril seemed to stand in progress or returning.
A narrow narrowing chamois-track traversed the frightful steep,
A thousand feet above us, and a thousand feet below,
Sheer up, sheer down ; and at a corner, dazed and dizzily lingering,
As gazing down half giddy on those perilous points below—
"Look up !" America shouted, and England echoed, " Up !"
That upward look restored its balance to my swimming eyesight ;
The calm bright blue above was as a rest and a refreshing :
I stood one prayerful minute, then went onward looking up :
Looking up and looking forward, never looking down—
The backward, downward, gloomy glance were perilous to destruction—
And soon that fearful angle past (we clung a rock to clear it),
On in conquering joy we went, exultant, looking up.
It was a true parable of life ; and oft have I since noted
How wise it is in peril's hour serenely to look up.

OF LIFE'S END.

He is but a fool who forgetteth how soon he will come to be forgotten,
Forgotten even while he liveth, if absence imitate the death ;
He hath made small progress in experience whose trust is fixed even on his nearest,
Or is stayed by the staff of gratitude, or reposeth upon family affection :
The world can do without us, and the place we fill on earth
Is soon felt wanted for some other, and we have lived too long :
Wave leapeth over wave, as owner ousteth owner,
And each and all make instant speed, to break on death's rough beach.
Thy son, eager for his projects, gladly shall obliterate thy schemes,
That gay young heir hath much to do, with little time for doing ;
The old man sowed his whims, the young man must uproot them,
And so, in slow revenge, he sternly changeth all things ;

The copse of thy planting shall be grubbed, thy pond must be
    filled in,
This road be turned and widened, that wing be taken down,
That so thy son may make a mark on his brief day of power,
And prove, O doting father, how soon thou art forgotten.
Thy dearest friend will scantly sigh, "Poor fellow, he is gone!
Thy children in their decent black will secretly feel freer
The place, that knew thee well, shall know thee now no more,
A billow broken on the rocks not more entirely shattered.
Even thy tokens of honour, yea, the choicest archives of thy fame,
Shall come to be tossed about by strangers, sold a broker's bargain;
Traders shall publicly appraise thy treasured household secrets,
And mean sharp eyes and cold hard hands pollute thy sacred
    things;
While the world will merrily wag on, and all these friends and
    neighbours,
Even to thy nearest and thy dearest, shall soon be well content to
    have thee gone!

He is but a poor weak soul, who hath not full resources in himself,
Yea in himself and in his God, for life and immortality
Conscience of good for all the past, trustful love for all the present,
Hope for all the future, these shall build him up sublime
However friends neglect, or kith and kin forget him,
He is independent of them all, a king above the world;
Yea, let the mountains be dissolved, let earth be rocked in ruins,
The good man standeth calm and strong, for God is his ally,
With calm retrospect of labours, and glad prospect of rewards,
And precious memories and great hopes, to strengthen and to
    cheer him
Far out of bad men's reach, and all those storms past by,
Thou art at length a freedman, emancipate from sin;
Lets and hindrances forgotten, it is thine to will and do,
And thou art safe from tyrannies, for all their rage and envy;
Come to be the king of some bright world, with loving spirits round
    thee,
And all things new and beauteous near, and evil old things gone,
Nor sin nor guilt nor care, no pain no fear no sorrow,
And only rest and love and certain happiness and glory!
What matter for all perils past? thou hast escaped the fowler,
The prison-door is opened and thy soul set free from earth;

What matter even for the loves of those who soon forgot thee?
They scarcely felt their loss, they scantly guess thy gain.
If only life and heart and mind have innocent been and useful,
Thou art thine own best friend, thy truest self-consoler:
But if thy bosom's inmate hath been sly and secret vice,
Thou livest thine own surest foe, the subtlest and the worst:
And when the bad man dieth, all his sins rise up against him,
Clamouring at his memory with imprecated judgments;
But when the good departeth, all his noble deeds
Surround him like a cloud of light to sphere his soul in glory:
And sorrowing fond remembrance then shall linger round his loss,
And some good son or daughter will never cease to mourn him;
And friends, known better if unseen, without one fleshly taint,
Friends of the mind and of the spirit, still shall esteem him kindly.
Roman Horace triumphed in Not all of me shall perish;
Tuscan Ennius lived with joy Upon the mouths of men;
And equally the Christian with the Pagan is happy in such promise of affection,
For, love from even strangers is a comfort to his soul.

Let no man desire for himself to live to an extreme old age,
New generations round him, with whom he hath no sympathies:
Let no man pray for longer life than is our common lot,
Nor seek in breathing death to be a ghost of times gone by.
For, tended with whatever kindness and however stayed,
Still it were a sadness to be sure, thou weariest these who serve thee;
And, if unkindly left alone with mercenary helpers,
It were a solitude indeed, and better to be gone:
And many pains and weaknesses, and many saddest memories,
And bitter crops from ancient sins must hedge old age with thorns.
At night, tired with day labour, how much we long for sleep,
And it were a sorry kindness to keep the weary wakeful:
So when the work of life is done, and the hour for departure groweth timely,
It were an evil mercy to snatch the old from slumber:
Miracles of prayer should not be worked to make old age grow older,
But only for the younger sort, with life-work unfulfilled:
So it may suffice thee well to say, I have lived and worked my hour,—

If only one, have laboured well, and lived a duteous life:
For here we crawl awhile, and feed, and weave a little web,
Anon, when chrysalised in death, to be our strait cocoon:
For each man's works that follow him, do clothe him in their meshes,
He hath wrought out for himself his robe of shame or honour.
And further on in time, at fulness and at ripeness,
Those cerements will be burst and the soul shall speed unshackled,
(If no ichneumon-evil shall have dropped its egg within
To hatch and grow and gnaw the conscience then for ever and ever—)
Flying from star to star, as if from flower to flower,
And culling nectar in all worlds of love and praise to God:
Thus, with life-work done, it were a blessedness to die,
And welcome to each faithful servant is the end of life.

The End of Life?—O not the end! say rather its beginning;
The end of pain and care and sin, but not the end of life:
For life is the infinite commencement of a being still to be
When countless ages shall have dimmed Orion of his brightness,
The flowing of a Nile that hath its mountain source in God,
Speeding ever onward through the ocean of Existence.

THE CONSUMMATION.

COME, O Desire of all nations! come down and take thy crowns,
Thy crowns of triple glory, nature grace and providence;
Come, to satisfy exceedingly the yearnings of creation's heart,
Come, to save reward and bless and glorify thy martyrs,
Come, to vindicate thy righteousness, come, to prove thy wisdoms,
Come, Thou Lord of all, in providence grace and nature!
O that Thou wouldst rend the heavens, and stand once more on Olivet,—
O that in the brightness of thy love our souls may be as snow in summer!
We have looked for Thee age after age, we have waited for thy Presence many centuries,
We have hoped each year might be the last, the last and yet the first,

The last of suffering and sin, the first of righteousness and glory,
The last of Satan's usurpation, the first of Christ's right rule.
Thy saints in pure succession have longed through life for Thee,
And sought thy sign upon the sky, thy cross among the clouds,
And watched and looked and lingered, till both head and heart were sick,
Sinking disappointed to their graves, one by one in thousands,
To meet Thee through the gate of death, to them the door of heaven,
And there to kiss thy feet in bliss, though not yet come in glory!
They waited for that Advent, long promised to thy church,
In "Lo, I come,—and quickly come;" yea, Lord of life, come quickly:
Then shall all griefs be comforted, all wrongs be well-requited,
All good be set on high, all evil fall confounded;
Then shall faith expand, flowering to glad fruition,
Then shall love rejoice in Thee love's great desire,
Then shall hope fulfilled attain its infinite reward,
The life of purity and praise in happiness for ever.

Beyond this firmament of air, beyond yon firmament of stars,
Circleth that third firmament, whereunto Paul was raptured:
Thither holy Enoch hath ascended, thither did Elijah's chariot rush,
Thither flew those risen saints who saw the dying Jesus:
There, is the light unsearchable, the Great King's Presence-chamber,
The firmament of spirits, where their Father's children meet,
That innumerable company of angels, those myriads of martyred blest,
That mingled crowd of ransomed souls until the resurrection,
And there the First-born sitteth, as our Priest upon his throne,
With some his firstfruit sheaf of saints, embodied bright about him,
And thence He soon shall come, descending from those heavens,
To stand once more on Olivet and judge and save mankind.

Is not the day approaching? that hour doth it now draw near?
See we not on every side the foresigns of his Presence?—
The powers of heaven have been shaken, and as with autumn-leaves
Our shattered stars of states and churches fall to earth in showers:

And men are running to and fro, and lightning flasheth knowledge,
And few are whispering peace whereas the many shout for war,
And earthquake, famine, pestilence, have ravaged every land,
Till continent to continent hath groaned across the seas :
Trouble, such as never yet so much hath torn all nations,
On each man's home is visiting calamity and loss,
And evil spirits are let loose, while prophets prophesy falsely,
And, through abounding wickedness, both faith and love are dead :
Over the world in antitype old Egypt's plagues are pouring,
Because our grander Passover, Redemption is at hand ;
And the Euphrates drieth up, and Babylon is fallen,
And those who love Jerusalem are yearning on her stones.

—Shall He find faith on the earth? this is the keynote of his coming,
Truth to perish, zeal to pine, and honesties decay :
So, where be now the shepherds, to teach and live sound doctrine,
And where the following flocks, and where the wholesome pastures?
Baal hath his priests by hundreds, and bishops preach-up unbelief,
Antichrist is wondered-after everywhere with all his ancient lies,
Statesmen sell for place their fathers' church and creed,
Commerce sitteth loose of ancient credit, trade is full of trickery,
Wealth is well-excused though fraud hath heaped the coffers,
And pens are bribed, and tongues are bought, and balances false-weighted,
And he that doeth righteously is but a simple fool :
Marriage is a merchandize with Mammon, and love scarce seen or heard,
Saving as a story of the past to be jeered at in this present,
Children do dishonour to their parents, servants cheat their masters,
Fashion addeth lying lures even to youth and beauty ;
Never did the wrong stand stronger, never lay the right so weak,
Never was this wheatfield of the world so choked with tares and poppies,
And Angels are waiting with their sickles to reap the mingled harvest
That good and evil may be separate in the Judgment day.

Exceeding broad are thy commandments, stretching to the corners of creation

And from time's beginning to the end of all things,
Evidencing penalty for guilt, and the blessing on obedience,
With peoples as with single souls of every age and race.
Nations meet punishment in this world, single sinners mostly in the next,
And both through repentance may be spared, the millions even as the units;
But where luxury in vice and proud ungodliness are rampant,
Little hope for a people here, or for a man hereafter.
Wail, corrupted France,—look to thyself, America,—
Take heed, complacent England, or thy pride may find its fall.
A race given up to vanities, a sensual boastful people,
Is made to flee before its foe, injuriously provoked;
While that foe, godly true and homely, crowned with easy victories,
Testifieth openly to earth heaven's judgment on the wicked:
Again, two brother nations, the one upholding slavery,
The other helping freedom, strove together to the death;
And Providence, in just sternness, crushed that tyrant wrong,
Granting to this kindlier right the triumph due to truth:
And for us, a folk too well at ease, a proudly separate people,
Unheeding others' rights and wrongs with independent scorn,
Betimes let us be humbler God-ward, gentler to our brethren,
That the avenging angel come not near our island home;
Or haply even upon us may fall the penalty of kingdoms
Weakened by the sap of sloth, and trusting in their riches.

Haply, the time is short; the end of all things neareth;
For man at length hath well subdued his little worldly heritage.
Nothing new is found to do: the Arctic floes are threaded,
Till East and West join sailor hands across the Polar sea;
They have dug them tunnels through the Alps, they have made a water-highway over Suez,
Their thoughts flash in Atlantic depths, on Himalayan heights;
The Nile hath yielded up his secret, and Sheba is a mystery no more,
We track the central haunts of Cush, untrod of us till now;
Bashan's rockbuilt cities, and Nineveh's lion courts,
The regions sown with gold and diamonds to allure us there,
That strange Sargasso floating realm, prolific of sea-monsters,
Those Easter-Island idols of a continent submerged,

All are known and well sought out, and nothing can be hid,
And in one hour upspring results that grew through countless ages.
Haply, it may soon be thundered, Time shall be no more,
The nations will conspire against Jerusalem restored,
Their antichrist to sit as god within that new-built temple,
And then Messiah, in His triumph, cometh Lord of all!
The thrilling drama of this globe hath reached its consummation,
Opening on its seventh Sabbath act beyond the six,
And nature grace and providence, fate-sisters at one loom,
Have woven all their skeins by warf and woof to pattern,—
And now those ravelled threads are gathering up in borders
Wherewith the perfect tapestry is fringed as by a frame,
So that Ezekiel's foursquare city, mystical Jerusalem,
Sheweth a pleasant picture as the waiting hall of heaven
And the legend on its golden gates is brightly blazing forth
For all evil, It is finished,—for all good, It is fulfilled.

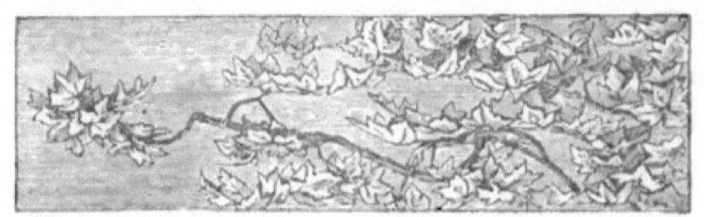

ALPHABETICAL LIST

OF ABOVE

SIX HUNDRED NAMES OF PERSONS AND PLACES INCIDENTALLY MENTIONED IN THIS WORK.

Aaron.	Ajax.	Antipodes.
Abdiel.	Alaric.	Arabia.
Abel.	Alban.	Arc.
Abiram.	Alcibiades.	Arctic.
Abraham.	Alcyone.	Aricia.
Abyssinia.	Aldebaran.	Aristarchus.
Academus.	Alexander.	Aristophanes.
Achilles.	Alfred.	Aristotle.
Adam.	Alps.	Ashtaroth.
Æacus.	Amazon.	Asia.
Ægean Sea.	Ambracia.	Aspasia.
Æolia.	America.	Assyria.
Æschylus.	Anacreon.	Atalanta.
Æsop.	Ananias.	Athanasius.
Ætna.	Anaximander.	Athens.
Agag.	Andaman.	Atlantic.
Agamemnon.	Andes.	Atlas.
Agur.	Antarctic.	Attalus.
Ahasuerus.	Anticyra.	Attila.
Aiguille Vert.	Antigone.	Augustine.

ALPHABETICAL LIST

Aurung-zebe.	Bushman.	Constantine.
Australia.	Byron.	Copan.
Austria.		Corinna.
Avignon.	Cæsar.	Corinne.
Avon.	Caffre.	Corinth.
	Cain.	Cornelia.
Baal.	Caligula.	Crassus.
Babel.	Calypso.	Crœsus.
Babrius.	Calvary.	Cromwell.
Babylon.	Camilla.	Crusoe.
Bacon.	Canaan.	Cuba.
Banquo.	Candace.	Curtius.
Barak.	Cannæ.	Cush.
Bashan.	Cape.	Cyrus.
Bastile.	Capella.	
Bedford.	Capua.	Dædalus.
Bedouin.	Carmel.	Dagon.
Bel.	Carr.	Damascus.
Belial.	Carthage.	Danaides.
Belisarius.	Cathay.	Daniel.
Bellerophon.	Catullus.	Danton.
Belus.	Caucasia.	Danube.
Benares.	Cazique.	David.
Benjamin.	Celt.	Davy.
Benoni.	Chaldæa.	Dead Sea.
Berkeley.	Chamounix.	Deborah.
Berosus.	Charlemagne.	Delilah.
Bethesda.	Charles.	Delphi.
Bias.	Chilo.	Democrite.
Bion.	China.	Demosthenes.
Boaz.	Chios.	De Staël.
Brahmin.	Chrysostom.	Deucalion.
Brazil.	Cicero.	Diana.
Briareus.	Cincinnatus.	Diogenes.
Britannia.	Circassia.	Dives.
Bruce.	Cleobulus.	Dodsley.
Brutus.	Colenso.	Dorian.
Bucephalus.	Coleridge.	Druid.
Buddhist.	Coliseum.	
Bunyan.	Columbia.	Easter Island.
Burman.	Columbus.	Eden.

Edom.
Egeria.
Egypt.
Elephanta.
Eli.
Elijah.
Elisha.
Ellora.
Elysium.
Empedocles.
England.
Ennius.
Enoch.
Ephesus.
Epicurus.
Eratostratur.
Erin.
Esther.
Esquimaux.
Ethiopia.
Etruria.
Euphrates.
Euripides.
Europe.
Eve.
Evelyn.
Ezekiel.

Fabius.
Fair-Havens.
Fingal.
Finland.
Flaccus.
France.
Franklin.
Fuegian.

Gabriel.
Galileo.
Gallio.
Ganesa.

Ganges.
Gath.
Gehenna.
George.
Georgia.
Germany.
Golconda.
Goliath.
Goneril.
Gorgon.
Goth.
Gracchi.
Greece.
Greenland.
Griselda.
Guinea.

Hades.
Ham.
Hannah.
Hannibal.
Hartz.
Havelock.
Hecate.
Hecla.
Helen.
Helot.
Helvetia.
Heraclitus.
Herculaneum
Hercules.
Hermione.
Herod.
Herodotus
Hesiod.
Hiero.
Hieropolis.
Hillel.
Himalaya
Hindoo.
Hindostan.

Hippodame.
Hobbes.
Homburg.
Homer.
Hooker.
Horace.
Hottentot.
Hun.
Huron.
Hydra.
Hymen.
Hymettus.

Icarus.
Inca.
Ind.
Iona.
Ireland
Isaac.
Isaiah.
Israel.
Italy.
Ithiel.

Jachin.
Jacob.
Jael.
James.
Janus.
Japan.
Japhet.
Jeffries.
Jephthah.
Jerome.
Jerusalem.
Jesus.
Jezebel.
Job.
John.
Jordan.
Jorullo.

2 F

Joseph.
Josephus.
Joshua.
Josiah.
Jubal.
Judæa.
Judah.
Judas.
Judith.
Juggernaut.
Jupiter.
Justinian.
Juvenal

Kali.
Kamala
Keats.
Kedar.
Korah.

Labrador.
Lacedæmon.
Lais.
Lamech.
Lapland.
La Scala.
Lawrence.
Lazarus.
Lebanon.
Lemuel.
Leonidas.
Lesbia.
Liebig.
Livingstone.
Livy.
Lycia.
Lydia.
Lucifer.
Lucretius.
Luther.
Lycurgus.

Maccabæus.
Maelstrom.
Mæonides.
Magdalene.
Magog.
Mahomet.
Makariro.
Malay.
Mammon.
Mandan.
Manetho.
Manlius.
Manoah.
Marah.
Marathon.
Margaret.
Mars.
Marsyas.
Martial.
Mary.
Mattathias.
Media.
Melchisedek.
Memucan.
Mentor.
Mercury.
Merlin.
Methuselah.
Mexico.
Mezentius.
Micaiah.
Michael.
Midas.
Miltiades.
Milton.
Minerva.
Minos.
Minotaur.
Mirabeau.
Mirza.
Mississippi.

Missouri.
Mnemosyn
Mohawk.
Moloch.
Momus.
Monte Rosa.
Moses.
Moslem.
Moschus.
Musæus.
Muscovite.
Myrrha.

Naples.
Narcissus.
Nazarite.
Nelson.
Neptune.
Nero.
Nessus.
Nestor.
Newton.
Niagara.
Nile.
Nimrod
Nineveh.
Nireus.
Nisroc.
Noah.
Nod.
North Sea.
Norge.
Norway.
Numa.

Obongo.
Œdipus.
Og
Olivet.
Olympia.
Olympus.

OF PERSONS AND PLACES.

Omar.
Omphale.
Orion.
Orleans.
Orpheus.
Ossian.
Ostiack.
Otranto.
Ovid.

Pæstum.
Palæologus.
Palenque.
Palissy.
Palmyra.
Paine.
Pandemonium.
Pantheon.
Paradise.
Pariah.
Parsee.
Parthia.
Parrhasius.
Pascal.
Paul.
Peleg.
Periander.
Pericles.
Persepolis.
Persia.
Persius.
Peru.
Peter.
Petra.
Petrarch.
Petronius.
Phidias.
Philippi.
Philistine.
Phineas.
Phœnicia.

Phryne.
Pindar.
Pittacus.
Plato.
Pleiades.
Poland.
Pole.
Pope.
Portugal.
Prometheus.
Prospero.
Proteus.
Prussia.
Pygmalion.
Pyramids.
Pyrrho.
Pythagoras.

Quixote.

Rabbah.
Rahab.
Rechabite.
Red-Indian.
Regulus.
Rehoboam.
Rhadamanthus.
Rhine.
Richard.
Robespierre.
Rochefoucauld.
Rocky Mountains
Rome.
Rubicon.
Ruth.
Russia.

Salamis.
Salmon.
Salu.
Samaria.

Samos.
Samson.
Sappho.
Satan.
Saturn.
Sanchoniathon.
Sanscrit.
Saragossa.
Sargasso-sea.
Satrap.
Saxon.
Scævola.
Scipio.
Scotland.
Scythia.
Sebastian.
Semiramis.
Seric.
Seth.
Shakespeare.
Sheba.
Shelley.
Siberia.
Sirach.
Siren.
Sirius.
Sisera.
Sisyphus.
Smithfield.
Socrates.
Sodom.
Solomon.
Solon.
Sophocles.
Sosii.
Southampton.
Spain.
Spallanzani.
Sparta.
Stagyrite.
Stoic.

Stromboli.
Suez.
Switzerland.
Syracuse.

Tacitus.
Tadmor.
Talmud.
Tamar.
Tammuz.
Tartarus.
Tartary.
Telemachus.
Tell.
Tellus.
Tetrarch.
Teucer.
Thais.
Thales.
Thebais.
Thebes.
Themis.
Theocritus.
Thermopylæ.
Theseus.
Thibet.
Tiberius.
Tibullus.

Timour.
Titan.
Titus.
Torquemada.
Trappist.
Troy.
Tubal-cain.
Turkey.
Tuscany.
Tyre.
Tyrtæus.

Ucal.
Ulysses.
Una.
Ural.
Urania.
Uranus.
Ursa.

Vashti.
Vaucluse.
Venus.
Vespasian.
Vesuvius.
Villiers.
Virgil.

Vishnu.
Vulcan.

Wady.
Wahabees
Wallace.
Walton.
Warwick.
Wesley.
Wordsworth.

Xanthus.
Xantippe.
Xavier.
Xenophon.
Xerxes.

Yakeh.
Yucatan.

Zamzummim.
Zealand.
Zeno.
Zion.
Zoar.
Zoilus.
Zorobabel.

ALPHABETICAL LIST

OF THE

CONTENTS OF THE FOUR SERIES COMPLETE.

TITLE.	SERIES.	PAGE
Animals, The future of	3	323
Anticipation	1	7
Authorship	2	150
Beauty	2	167
Bible, The	4	355
Book's Story, This	4	349
Cheerfulness	2	138
Circumstance	3	277
Commendation	1	98
Compensation	1	13
Consummation, The	4	441
Contentment	2	200
Creeds	3	320
Cruelty to Animals	1	108
Curious Questions	4	387
Death	2	209
Delay	4	403

TITLE.	SERIES.	PAGE
Dirge, National	3	337
Discretion	1	63
Dream of Ambition	1	24
Economy	4	419
Education	1	120
End	2	262
Estimating Character	1	44
Experience	1	42
Faith	2	240
Fame	2	179
Final	3	345
Flattery	2	186
Fourfold differences	4	381
Friendship	1	110
Gifts	2	163
Good in things evil	1	53
Great and small	4	405
Habit	4	418
Happiness together or alone	3	331
Hatred and Anger	1	52
Hidden uses	1	9
Home	4	361
Honesty	2	247
Humility	1	37
Hymn, National	3	335
Ideas	2	231
Immortality	2	215
Indirect influences	1	17
Industry and Idleness	4	420
Innocence and Guilt	3	270
Introductory	2	136
Invention	1	94
Joy	1	133

TITLE.	SERIES.	PAGE
Life	2	204
Life's end	4	438
Life's lessons	4	430
Life's work	4	425
Livelihoods	4	376
Lord's Prayer	1	61
Love	1	114
Man's date upon Earth	4	395
Marriage	1	116
Memory	1	21
Morals, Smaller	3	309
Mystery	2	156
Names	2	234
Neglect	2	193
Opening	4	347
Prayer	1	58
Preamble	3	267
Prefatory	1	1
Pride	1	41
Probabilities	3	286
Providences, Little	3	304
Psalm, National	3	339
Reading	1	85
Real and Ideal	4	415
Recreation	1	68
Religion, Train of	1	71
Representation	4	423
Rest	1	35
Rhyme and Rhythm	3	312
Ridicule	1	96
Scripture and Science	3	289
Self-acquaintance	1	102
Selfishness	4	408
Seven Sayings	3	341

TITLE.	SERIES.	PAGE
Silence	3	292
Slander	4	411
Sleep	4	401
Social Pride	4	367
Society	2	252
Solitude	2	259
Sorrow	1	132
Speaking	1	81
Spiritual Presences	3	295
Starry Heavens	3	280
Subjection	1	26
Success	3	307
Things	2	238
Thinking	1	76
Time	3	301
To-day	2	145
Tolerance	1	129
To-morrow	2	148
Travel	4	372
Trifles	1	65
Trinity	1	73
Truth in Things False	1	4
Wealth	1	89
Words of Wisdom	1	2
Writing	1	87
World's Age	3	274
Yesterday	2	142
Zoilism	3	314

London: SWIFT & Co., Newton Street, High Holborn, W.C.

www.ingramcontent.com/pod-product-compliance
Lightning Source LLC
Chambersburg PA
CBHW022103300426
44117CB00007B/570